3/11/79

HAPPY 9TH BIRTHDAY ERIK !!!!
    ENJOY THIS BOOK AND ALL BOOKS ——
THEY ARE TREASURES, LIKE YOU.
        LOVE
            MOM AND DAD

THE BOOK OF
SHARKS

THE BOOK OF
SHARKS
WRITTEN AND ILLUSTRATED BY
RICHARD ELLIS

GROSSET & DUNLAP
A FILMWAYS COMPANY
Publishers • New York

Plate 1. **Portrait of a mako** (*Isurus oxyrinchus*)

We need another and a wiser and perhaps a more mystical concept of animals. Remote from universal nature, and living by complicated artifice, man in civilization surveys the creature through the glass of his knowledge and sees thereby a feather magnified and the whole image in distortion. We patronize them for their incompleteness, for their tragic fate of having taken form so far below ourselves. And therein we err, and greatly err. For the animal shall not be measured by man. In a world older and more complete than ours they move more finished and complete, gifted with extensions of senses we have lost or never attained, living by voices we shall never hear. They are not brethren, they are not underlings; they are other nations, caught with ourselves in the net of life and time, fellow prisoners of the splendour and travail of the earth.

Henry Beston
The Outermost House, 1928

Grateful acknowledgment is made for permission to reprint the following:

Portion of material excerpted from "Big Game Fishing in the New Zealand Seas" by Zane Grey, *Natural History* Magazine, January-February 1928, by permission of The American Museum of Natural History.   Portion of material reprinted, by permission, from *Evolution of the Vertebrates,* by Edwin H. Colbert. Copyright © 1969 John Wiley & Sons, Inc.   Portion of material excerpted from "The Great Mako" by Zane Grey, *Natural History* Magazine, May-June 1934, by permission of The American Museum of Natural History.   Portion of *Jaws,* copyright © 1974 by Peter Benchley. Reprinted by permission of Doubleday & Co., Inc. Portion of material reprinted by permission of Charles Scribner's Sons from *Islands in the Stream* by Ernest Hemingway. Copyright © 1970 Mary Hemingway.   Portion of *Kon-Tiki* by Thor Heyerdahl. Copyright 1950 by Thor Heyerdahl. Published in the United States by Rand McNally & Co., and in England by George Allen & Unwin Ltd. Portion of material reprinted by permission of Charles Scribner's Sons from *The Old Man and the Sea* by Ernest Hemingway. Copyright 1952 Ernest Hemingway.   Portion of *The Outermost House* by Henry Beston. Copyright 1928, 1949, © 1956 by Henry Beston. Reprinted by permission of Holt, Rinehart and Winston, Publishers.   Portion of material reprinted, by permission of the publisher, from Perry W. Gilbert: *Sharks and Survival* (Lexington, Mass.: D. C. Heath and Company, 1963). Portion of material reprinted, by permission of the publisher, from Gilbert, Perry, Mathewson, Robert F., and Rall, David P., Eds., *Sharks, Skates, and Rays.* Copyright © 1967 The Johns Hopkins University Press.   Portion of "The Shark That Hibernates," which first appeared in *New Scientist,* London, the weekly review of science and technology. Portion of "Size of the Great White Shark (Carcharodon)," Randall, J. E., *Science,* Vol. 181, pp. 169–170, 13 July 1973. Copyright 1973 by the American Association for the Advancement of Science.   Portion of *Sportfishing for Sharks* by Captain Frank Mundus and Bill Wisner. Copyright © 1971 by William Wisner. Reprinted by permission of Macmillan Publishing Company, Inc.

CONTENTS

LIST OF COLOR PLATES

Note: Where the designation "(RE)" follows the caption of a black and white picture, it indicates that the illustration is a photograph of a painting by the author.

ACKNOWLEDGMENTS

A book such as this is the work of many hands, some of them involuntary, all of them important. For my initial exposure to the world of fishes I am indebted to the members of the Department of Ichthyology at the American Museum of Natural History, especially James W. Atz and C. Lavett Smith. When the book became a real possibility, I shamelessly imposed myself on dozens of people, asking questions, visiting them, and taking up their time in my quest for information. During the last two summers, I was an all-purpose nuisance at the Narragansett Laboratory of the National Marine Fisheries Service, where Jack Casey, Wes Pratt, and Chuck Stillwell opened their files to me, providing me with much-needed assistance and experience. Likewise, Perry Gilbert, David Baldridge, and Stewart Springer of the Mote Marine Laboratory in Sarasota, gave freely of their time and expertise. I am grateful for my association with all the "shark people," most of whom are discussed in greater detail in that section of the book, but I must pay special homage to Stewart Springer, who, despite his own workload, took the time to read and comment on many portions of the manuscript. Needless to say, despite all this professional advice and assistance, I take full responsibility for any errors of fact or interpretation that have managed to survive the attempts of all the experts to correct them. My research took me all over the world, mostly via the mails and the telephone, from South Africa and Australia to California and Cambridge, Massachusetts. The personnel at the Oceanographic Research Institute at Durban were especially helpful, in providing valuable books, pictures, and information. Myvanwy Dick at the Museum of Comparative Zoology at Harvard was extremely generous; she provided me with rare scientific papers, photographs, and advice. Valerie Taylor and I have established what I consider a wonderful correspondence, and she and her husband, Ron, have shown me more kindness than I could ever have expected, in granting me permission to use photographs that they normally (and rightfully) reserve for their own use. All the photographs of my paintings, in black and white and in color, were taken by Vincent Miraglia. I must also thank Henry Bigelow and William Schroeder, who wrote the one book that I consider essential to the writing of this one, and Francesca La Monte, who gave me her own copy of this invaluable book. At Grosset & Dunlap, Lucy Kanson and Bob Markel were especially helpful. I am also indebted to Linda Reiman, Diane Deitchman Tong, and Art Weithas, who helped to create order out of the chaos I presented. I am most grateful to my wife, TA, and to my children, Timothy and Elizabeth, for their patient understanding during the long gestation period of this book; it must have been hell for them to live with a man obsessed.

THE PREDATORS

The two islands that make up New Zealand are situated on a flat plain in the south Pacific Ocean. It is the equivalent of a continental shelf, although it is too small to be so designated. Also on this plateau are groups of much smaller islands called the Aucklands, the Bountys, and the Chathams. To the east of the main islands of New Zealand is the 5,000-foot-deep Kiwa Canyon, extending partially into the Cook Strait that separates North and South Islands. An extension of the Kiwa Canyon stretching northeast toward the Hawaiian chain is the Kermadec-Tonga Trench, the deepest part of all the oceans, some six miles deep at its greatest depth.

At fifty fathoms, the waters of the Southern Ocean are dark blue. Little sunlight reaches this depth, and the small portion of light that does filter down is virtually drained of all its colors. There are no reds or yellows here, no greens. If something is not blue, it is black. The water is enriched by a boundless supply of microscopic plants and animals that make up the broad base of the food pyramid. Waters rich in oxygen because of thermal upwellings support the richest congregation of plankton in the world. This plankton, in turn, supports the small fish which are the food of the larger fish, and so on to the larger carnivores and piscivores, the predators that ride the apex of the biologist's food pyramid. Only the great baleen whales, or rorquals, have sideslipped the multitudinous links in this chain—they feed on the plankton and the small crustaceans; some of the largest animals in the world feed directly on some of the smallest.

Where the Southern Ocean meets the Pacific off the eastern coast of New Zealand, the continental shelf drops off sharply, and the cool deep waters mix with the warmer green waters of the shoals. The drop-off is the habitat of the pelagic hunters of the seas and their prey—the open-ocean predators that patrol these rich waters for their food. In these waters can be found some of the fastest fish that swim; here the business of life is eat or be eaten. Every fish is chased by another fish, just a little bit larger, or a bit faster. In the sea there is no demarcation between the hunter and the hunted, as there is on the African plains. There are no "antelopes" which are always the prey or "lions" that are always the hunters. Given the opportunity, a fish normally classified as a baitfish will eat a small hunter.

There is one kind of fish that is hard for other fish to eat, and this is the billfish. Nature has given a small group of fishes a hard, pointed snout, which is thought to be primarily an instrument for obtaining food, but it can also be a powerful offensive or defensive weapon. Collectively, the billfishes are among the most sought-after game fishes because of their grace and power,

(Overleaf) Plate 2. **Longfin mako** *(Isurus paucus) and* **broadbill swordfish** *(Xiphias gladias)*

RICHARD ELLIS-1975

in and out of the water. Some of them leap spectacularly when hooked, while others fight the angler for hours without showing above the surface. The marlins, sailfishes, and the swordfish are the best known of the billfishes.

The broadbill swordfish is often seen "sunning" or "finning," with its dorsal fin and the upper lobe of the tail fin out of the water. But it is really a deep-water dweller. One look at the dark, lustrous eye, hugely out of proportion to the rest of the fish, confirms this. The swordfish is rightly named, for unlike its relatives the marlins, who have a rounded and fairly short bill, the "sword" of *Xiphias gladias* is long, flattened, sharp-edged, and pointed. A big swordfish will have a sword roughly one-third of its overall length. A big swordfish can be fourteen feet long.

Because of the intimate relationship that exists between a fish and the medium in which it lives, it can sense movement, change, action, and other creatures in the water without seeing, hearing, or smelling. Fish have a series of sensory organs on the outside of their bodies, usually in a line that runs their entire length. This sensitive system, usually called the "lateral line," is highly visible in some species. On the swordfish, the line begins just behind the great gill covers, and extends the length of the fish to the broad caudal keels, which protrude horizontally at the base of the tail, like meaty stabilizers.

Everything about a big swordfish is massive. It is a heavily built fish, especially in the "shoulders," which taper off to a narrow caudal peduncle before the crescent-shaped tail flares vertically, bisecting the plane of the lateral keels. The fins are heavy and fleshy, not thin and bony-ribbed as they are in many other fishes. Like most other fishes, a swordfish is able to regulate its density to the ambient water pressure by the use of a swim bladder, a gas-filled organ that the fish can inflate or deflate autonomically, and bring its overall density close to that of the surrounding water. This means that a fish that is stationary in the water is weightless; it displaces exactly its own weight in water, and since it is submerged, it is integrated completely in its medium.

The broadbill swam slowly at fifty fathoms, sculling in the dark water with measured, steady sweeps of its crescent tail. It presented a majestic, solitary aspect, purposeful but unhurried. The great fish braked gently by imperceptibly increasing the angle of its pectoral fins. Its own momentum carried it forward for another ten yards before it glided to a stop. It hung suspended in the darkness, sensing movement from far above. With the limited light reaching this level, even its large eyes were of little use.

The swordfish again altered the angle of its pectorals, dropping the trailing edge, and thereby giving it a gradual angle of lift. With a twitch of its tail, it began to swim toward the surface, sensing with all its faculties the movement that was taking place above it, close to the surface. As it rose, its swim bladder increased in size with the corresponding decrease in pressure. The swim bladder is also a resonating or "hearing" organ, and the surface movement was being transmitted to the fish's brain by the conductivity of the gas in the bladder, and through the water itself, to the lateral line.

Now at a depth of twenty fathoms and rising, the swordfish saw the shadow of an immense school of mullet, silhouetted against the surface sunlight, as they wheeled and turned in a tight, flowing formation. As the swordfish got closer, the mullet school collectively became aware of its presence, and tightened ranks, a common practice among schooling fishes or herding animals; in the face of danger, they crowd even closer together. This may be because the predator cannot concentrate on any single individual in a milling, tightly packed throng, and will be unable to attack accurately. For a predator that would bite its prey as a means of capture, the closing of the ranks might work. For the swordfish, the packed school presented a perfect target.

Now the swordfish closed with the school, driving directly at the moving center of the mass of seething, twisting fishes. In the sparkling water of the ocean's surface, the moving mullet shone; a giant, multifaceted entity, glinting now silvery green, now iridescent blue as the angle of the school shifted in the sunlight. As its sword broke the perimeter of the school, the swordfish began to throw its head violently from side to side. The tightly packed fish were slashed and smashed, cut in half, decapitated. There was no escape for the mullet that chance had selected as the swordfish's victims, for even with death in their very midst, they still resorted to the only defense a schooling fish has: the mass of the school.

Pieces of mullet began to sink, and the hungry swordfish gulped them down. The feeding was as easy and casual as the killing had been violent, and many of the mutilated fish were missed as they floated down through the bright waters, eventually to come to rest on the bottom, one thousand feet below. There was now blood in the water, in addition to the broken and dying fish.

The combination of the blood and the dying, thrashing fish did not go unnoticed. Some 500 yards from the scene of the slaughter, another predator reacted to the signals of the fluttering of dying mullet. This predator could smell blood in the water from great distances, and it began to seek out the source of the disturbance. Banking sharply, it turned in the direction of the swordfish. Here too were strong, curved pectoral fins, but they were wider than those of the swordfish, giving this animal more maneuverability. This hunter had the same flattened caudal keels, and a tail of almost the same shape: crescent-shaped and equally lobed. Despite their similarities, these two predators were very different. Smooth skin and a bony skeleton, an absence of teeth, and but a single weapon, its sword, characterized the swordfish. The approaching animal, while sharing the fusiform body shape and the horizontal keels, was a very different creature indeed. No smooth skin, but rough, pointed scales covered its body, and in place of the swordfish's lateral line, it was covered with a network of sensory organs, making it perhaps the most sensitive and responsive animal in the world. It could sense and smell disturbances or potential prey at great distances and, contrary to popular belief, it could also see quite well. It had a large, sensitive eye, and would rely on vision to a great extent in its impending confrontation with the broadbill.

Still, the feeding swordfish was too far away to see, and even the best vision cannot penetrate four hundred yards of water. Crossing and recrossing the line of stimuli like a quartering hunting dog, the approaching fish received the messages with greater and greater clarity, and soon it was marking a straight course toward the swordfish. Its pace quickened as it neared the source of the disturbance, and the powerful strokes of its tail propelled it through the water with increasing speed. Within one hundred yards of the swordfish the animal approached steadily, its gaping, snaggletoothed mouth open, its lidless black eyes seeking the blood-smell and the flapping fish. Its sharply pointed snout, recurved teeth, and deep blue color identified it immediately: it was a mako shark, perhaps the most beautifully proportioned of all the sharks, and one of the fastest and most dangerous animals that swim.

It closed quickly, mindlessly picking up and swallowing the pieces of broken and torn mullet that had been carried by the same current that brought it the smell. This thousand-pound mako needed more than a few morsels of mullet to satisfy its hunger, and soon the swordfish was in visual range. The two great fish were about equal in weight, but the shark was more agile, and far more deadly at close quarters. Its appetite whetted by the mullet, the shark instantly launched its attack—no passes, no bumping, no preliminaries. Its upper teeth, already bared, were further protruded by the jaw mechanism that enables a shark to bite deeply despite the underslung position of its mouth. The pointed snout was forced upward by the emergence of the knifelike teeth, and the shark raked the flank of the swordfish as it flicked its sickle-shaped tail and drove downward in an attempt to escape. Parallel scars appeared on the side of the swordfish, and blood welled out of the rips in its sensitive skin. As the swordfish dove, the blood turned brown and then black, for red is the color with the shortest wavelength, and therefore the first color to go as the water cuts off the spectrum. The shark followed quickly, close on the tail of the diving swordfish.

The battle between these two giant fishes contained blind spots for both hunter and hunted. As long as the mouth of the shark was directly behind the vertical, flexing tail of the swordfish, the shark could get no purchase. For it to turn on its side would have meant to lose speed. The swordfish could not dive deeply enough to escape. At about one hundred fathoms, the shelf loomed ahead, forcing the swordfish to bank sharply. Surprised by this sudden maneuver, the shark checked by dropping its broad pectoral fins, and the swordfish sprinted along the drop-off wall, a black plume of blood trailing from its wounds. Suddenly a volcanic outcropping loomed ahead of the swordfish, and it was forced to change its course again. This time, it had to turn almost ninety degrees and, as it threw itself over, it presented its wide, vulnerable flank to its pursuer. Remaining broadside to the charging mako would have meant certain disaster for the swordfish, so it made an even tighter turn, to bring its only weapon into play. The shark tried to brake, but succeeded only in coming obliquely upon the four-foot sword. Slashing as it came about, the swordfish defended itself against the driving mako. The two terrible weapons, the mouth of the shark and the sword of the billfish, met in a silent clash. As the sword entered the mako's mouth, the shark closed its powerful jaws on it. Although strong enough to crush the sword, they did not do so before the point had pierced the soft inner skin of the shark's mouth. The two fish were attached now, the mako impaled on the sword, its teeth and jaws grinding as it writhed furiously in an attempt to pull away. Flexing its supple body into a full horseshoe curve, the mako somersaulted backward in the water. The swordfish, its only weapon splintered and useless, turned and headed for the surface.

Recovering, the mako saw the bulky shape of the swordfish as it shot toward the light. The open ocean gave no escape, no place to hide. In order for this battle to end, one of these fish would die. They were both wounded now—the swordfish raked by the teeth of the shark and its sword broken, the shark with a gaping, bleeding wound below its black, expressionless eye.

With astonishing speed, the two fish rose in tandem from the depths, through the greenish blue of the shallower waters and up into the clear green water of the surface. The distance between them remained the same as the swordfish burst out of the water, shimmering purple-bronze in the hot sunlight. Throwing off a spray of white water and bright red blood, the swordfish arched and twisted as if it were trying to leave the ocean forever—

before it hit the water again. The forces of nature and gravity conspired to draw the fish back to the water with a gigantic splash, but the tail of the fish had not disappeared below the roiled surface, when the mako appeared in airborne pursuit. Iridescent ultramarine above and snowy white below, sharp contrast to the vivid trail of blood that flowed from its injured mouth, the flying shark presented an awesome spectacle, clearing the water by at least twenty feet before it reentered in a crashing shower of spray. Diving again, the swordfish twisted, trying to shake its dogged pursuer. As the swordfish circled, the mako cut across the diameter of the circle, again coming broadside upon the fish's vulnerable flank. With a great thrust of the powerful muscles that move its tail, the swordfish lunged forward. The shark's reaction was instinctive and immediate: it did the same thing, and this brought its gaping mouth within inches of the flattened base of the broadbill's tail. In a second, they both lunged again, but this time the flick of the swordfish's tail smashed into the open mouth of the shark. The teeth of a shark are not fixed in the gums or in the cartilage of the jaw itself, but attached to a membrane inside the jaw. Some of the two-inch teeth were knocked out by this desperate swipe of the swordfish's tail, but the tail stock was driven deep into the shark's mouth. Reflex action closed the mouth of the mako, and both fish began to squirm and twist—the swordfish to escape the terrible tearing jaws, the shark to exert maximum pressure on its victim.

The water churned red with blood and froth, and with one frantic lunge, the swordfish wrenched free. The mako had triumphed, however, for it had bitten through the flesh and bone of the caudal peduncle of the swordfish, and severed its tail. Streaming blood, the once-mighty fish tried again to escape, but without its tail it had no power of propulsion. It fluttered its pectoral fins weakly and rolled its great black eye, trying to keep the shark in view as it came up beneath the broadbill's belly. Stretching its mouth open to a remarkable degree, the mako bit deeply into the soft flesh of the swordfish. Again the shark convulsed its entire body and the hard muscles rippled as it tore a great mouthful of meat from the body of the swordfish. The shark swallowed this twenty-pound gobbet whole, circled again, and hit the fish from the other side. Blood spread through the water as the mako fed on the torn, living carcass of the swordfish.

Drawn by the blood in the water and the sounds of the battle, other sharks arrived—oceanic whitetips, accompanied by their attendant pilot fish. These sharks, smaller and lighter than the mako, and a dirty ocher color, with white-tipped dorsal, pectoral, and tail fins, are numerous and ever present at the scene of a disaster in the sea. They too tore great bites out of the ragged body of the swordfish, while the pilot fish picked up the shreds. The head with the splintered sword sank to the sand at the base of the drop-off, there to be picked clean by crabs and other scavengers.

CONFESSIONS OF A SHARK PAINTER

I have always had a normal, subliminal fear of sharks, although I didn't think much about it. Like most people, I assumed that a person falling in the water where there were sharks would get eaten. My professional interest and abnormal fascination began in 1972, when I was asked by the editors of the *Encyclopaedia Britannica* to provide the illustrations for some of the animals they wanted for the 1974 revised edition. I worked at a frenzied rate, and turned out forty-odd paintings in less than a month. (They were not all sharks; I also did the whales and a few assorted rare mammals and fishes.) This brief period had to include all the necessary research and preliminary sketches, and there was little time to locate the detailed material required for unimpeachable accuracy. I had to depend on easily available material for reference, since there wasn't time to visit out-of-town institutions, or even to write for information or photographs. (However, I do have a fairly extensive reference library, and I agreed only to illustrate those species of which I had good pictorial references, or with which I was otherwise familiar.)

When the paintings were completed and sent off to Chicago, I retained a strange feeling of unfulfillment. I had painted pictures of some of the better-known sharks, but the paintings were quite small: the largest was seven inches long, including the background. I felt that the subject required more than these little renderings, and, besides, I knew I hadn't done the sharks as well as I might have—I just didn't know enough about them. The image of the shark stayed with me, like some disturbing, primordial memory. I didn't know it, but I was becoming a shark painter.

Painting animals involves at least as much research as skill, and probably more. One has to know the characteristics of one's subjects, their attitudes, biology, size, shape, habitat—in short, their natural history. Most animals are visible in one way or another, either in zoos, aquariums, or in the wild. The artist can observe the animal in its natural habitat or in captivity, or he can rely on photographs, taken by himself or others. Most "wildlife painters," therefore, choose as their subjects creatures they can see. This is not what one would call an abnormally restrictive criterion.

One can see sharks . . . In every public aquarium there are probably sand tigers, dogfish, nurse sharks, and even an occasional sandbar or tiger shark. Other species have been maintained in aquariums or oceanariums, but the frequency with which this occurs and the survival rate of the sharks are low. Besides, seeing a shark in an aquarium tank is not the same as seeing a shark in the wild, in its natural, pelagic habitat. There are those who would argue that to see a shark in the wild is to court disaster, but, as we shall see, this is not necessarily so.

As I became more and more interested in sharks, I began to examine virtually every kind of publication in which sharks were mentioned, from highly technical treatises to popular books. The problems involved in this diversified research are manifold, and not the least of them is the scientific expertise required to even *read* some of the papers. Here is a quotation from Dr. Bobb Schaeffer's essay "Elasmobranch Evolution" published in *Sharks, Skates, and Rays*" in 1967:

> The cladodont palatoquadrate has a greatly expanded postorbital ramus with a prominent otic process and a narrow suborbital ramus that extends anteriorly to the rostrum. The suborbital ramus had at least a ligamentous attachment to the anterior part of the suborbital shelf, which is expanded into a palatobasal process in the "Cladodus" neurocranium. The long, narrow, gently curved mandible articulates with the palatoquadrate well behind the occipital condyle by means of the articular process on the palatoquadrate and by a mandibular knob that fits into a socket on the median surface of the palatoquadrate.[202]

Admittedly, these sentences are completely out of context, but it is easy to see that the entire paper, which is a very important one on the subject of the evolution of sharks, would be almost incomprehensible to the layperson. Here now is a quotation from a "popular" work, entitled *Shark! Unpredictable Killer of the Sea*, written by Thomas Helm (by no small coincidence, the subject is the same fossil shark):

> At least one shark, the Cladoselache, was in full command of the early oceans three hundred million years ago, and he must indeed have been a fearsome creature. The Cladoselache was better than a hundred feet in length, and the smallest of his teeth

was the size of a man's hand. He was lurking offshore when the great dinosaurs trembled the young earth with heavy footfalls in the Triassic period, and he was on hand to welcome man when he made his appearance a million years ago.[129]

Cladoselache was, in fact, no more than six feet long, and became extinct at least 180 million years ago, a little too early to lurk offshore to "welcome man." Which is better? The "occipital condyle" or a 94-foot, 179-million-year error? Obviously, accuracy is more important than exaggeration, but the first example is unreadable by the casual reader, and the second serves its purpose badly, if indeed it serves any purpose at all. It is not the usual intention of popular writers to mislead; one would assume that their purpose would be to simplify the complex and make it easily accessible to the public. With sharks, however, creatures whose imagery lends itself so generously to hyperbole, it is sometimes difficult to resist the temptation. There are well written, responsible works on sharks, and I have made ample use of many of them in the preparation of this book.

The number of papers, books, notes, letters, and articles on sharks is enormous. This is not surprising when one considers the fascination that these creatures have held for people since first they became aware of them. We will never know this first event, of course, but we can assume that the earliest seafarers, in their dhows, dugouts, or rafts, saw the sinuous shapes that swam near the surface following their vessels, and they were quick to learn that the shapes could prove dangerous. The first reference to the shark is lost in antiquity; there is an aboriginal drawing in Australia that shows a sharklike creature in the act of eating a man. Pliny and Herodotus wrote of sharks, and by the middle of the sixteenth century, the word "shark" had entered the English language. (Prior to that, in England, sharks were called *tiburon*, from the Spanish.) The *Oxford English Dictionary*, after declaring the word to be "of obscure origin," says that

> *the word seems to have been introduced by the sailors of Captain (later Sir John) Hawkins' expedition, who brought home a specimen which was exhibited in London in 1569. The source from which they obtained the word has not been ascertained.*

In 1828, in the first American dictionary, Noah Webster told us that the word comes from the Latin *carcharias*; from the Greek *carcharios*, from *carcharos*, sharp, and the Cornish *skarkias*. There are other theories as well; the most prevalent is that the word shark derives from the German word for villain, *Schurke*. The problem is still unresolved.

The more research I did, the more I realized that there was a great chasm between the technical and the popular works. Even more important in my case, illustrative material was almost totally lacking. The technical books and scientific papers often have anatomically accurate drawings, usually profiles of a given species, with a tooth or a dermal denticle alongside for more detailed identification. The more specialized papers have dissection drawings as well as graphs and charts—fine for the scientist, but of little use to the artist. Popular works rely heavily on photographs of dead sharks. These are shown most frequently in one of two positions: either hanging upside down with a proud fisherman beside it, or stretched out flat with someone bending back the shark's snout so that the teeth will show to better advantage. One common overlap of the popular and the scientific is the regular appearance of the same drawings, usually from the classic work on sharks, Bigelow and Schroeder's *Fishes of the Western North Atlantic, Part I, Sharks*.[30]

My introduction to sharks was representational: I was primarily concerned with their shape and form. When I began painting them regularly, I realized that I had to "put them in the water," since that is the way they can best be understood—as creatures that are part of the undersea world, not as fishermen's trophies or as man-eaters with lots of teeth. I have not meant to imply that there are no good photographs of free-swimming sharks. Of course there are. Among the photographer-divers who have produced some excellent shots of sharks in the water are Peter Gimbel, Ron and Valerie Taylor, Hans Hass, Jerry Greenberg, David Doubilet, and the Cousteaus. However, like the written information about various species, these pictures are not to be found in any one volume. A book that is rich in biological information is often short on illustrations; one with lots of pictures is usually accompanied by a proportional amount of misinformation.

An example of this dichotomy is the reconstructed jaw of *Carcharodon megalodon*, which is on exhibit at the American Museum of

Natural History. A photograph of this huge jaw, shown sometimes with six men sitting in it and sometimes with only one, appears in almost every book about sharks. However, even though the museum label says, "It is estimated that this giant shark reached a length of approximately forty-five feet," anyone using *megalodon* in his book adds ten, twenty, or even fifty feet to this given length. So it is that many writers who have seen the jaw, *and read the label*, conjure up giant sharks over a hundred feet long. Most popular books discuss *megalodon*, and since it is almost impossible to prove it was *not* a hundred feet long, or (and this is even more sensational) *that it does not exist today*, this remains the *ne plus ultra* of shark fantasies: a hundred-foot version of the great white shark, with teeth as big as your hand, large enough to swallow an ox! I have brought up *megalodon* here to point out the discrepancy between the scientific and the popular approach to sharks. In a recent article in *Science*, Dr. John Randall, an ichthyologist with a special interest in sharks, says this about the *megalodon* jaws:

> *A reconstruction of the jaws of* Carcharodon megalodon *at the American Museum of Natural History has provided a concept of the enormous size of these extinct leviathans. This reconstruction, however, has been shown to be at least one-third too large, because all the teeth were regarded as nearly the same size as the large ones medially in the jaw.*[196]

Here we see the conflict between popularization and science. The genre writers want to believe —or at least they want their readers to believe— in a hundred-foot man-eater. (We can very easily disregard Mr. Helm's reference to a hundred-foot *Cladoselache*, lurking offshore "to welcome man," as an error of transposition. He knew there was supposed to be a hundred-foot-long monster; he just forgot which one it was.) Scientists give no credence to the stories of gigantic man-eaters, but still the fables persist, written and rewritten into the literature. It is hard to eradicate the deep-rooted fears that people have developed over the years, and even harder when there are those who would profit from them.

I was originally fascinated by the complexity of the elements that comprised the silhouette of the shark. Each fin is a study in itself—a complex and graceful design, made up of curves and recurves that add up to a spare, efficient animal, powerful and primitive, yet part of our life today. The tail, or caudal fin, is an example of this superb design, since it is the sole source of the propulsive power of the shark. Some species have a long upper lobe ("heterocercal" tail fin), while others have upper and lower lobes that are almost the same size ("homocercal" tail fin). In one species, the thresher, the upper lobe of the tail is as long as the rest of the shark, and has been described as one of the toughest flexible structures developed in the animal kingdom. The fins are also powerful graphic images, the most abused of which, in a literary sense, is the dorsal fin. It always seems to be "slicing" or "knifing" through the water, presaging doom to the hapless swimmer, seal, or other creature. But the other fins, the curving pectorals, the flaring pelvics, the anal fins, and the second dorsals— all these are demonstrations of intersecting curves that I believe are unequaled elsewhere in the animal kingdom.

So far I have dealt only with the gross morphology of the shark, its exterior form. No mention of skin like sandpaper, razor-sharp teeth, voracious appetite, 300-million-year evolution, man-eating. My introduction to the shark was a figurative one, essentially devoid of clichés; I was biologically uninformed, yet full of admiration. I liked the way sharks looked. They seemed frighteningly efficient, and they reminded me of the fighter planes of World War II. I grew up in the era of the P-38, P-40, and P-41; as a boy in the early 1940s, I had an almost total preoccupation with the Mustang, Spitfire, ME-109, and the Zero. Eventually I grew out of this phase, but it was replaced by a more interesting group of streamlined, efficient "machines," the sharks.

When I write of "curving pectorals" and "flaring pelvics," I am trying to discuss sharks in general. But this turns out to be almost impossible. Most sharks have the requisite number of fins, but they do not all curve gracefully. Many species are lithe and graceful, but some are not, and others are downright funny-looking. Almost nothing can be said about sharks that is categorically applicable to all species. After many attempts and blind alleys, the best I can come up with is this: Sharks are vertebrate animals that have multiple gill slits, cartilaginous skeletons, placoid scales, numerous teeth, and they live in the water. All other generally accepted concepts, while not necessarily false, have to be modified, qualified, or disclaimed to such a degree that they become useless.

Take for example the question of what a shark *is*. It is not exactly a fish, since many of the criteria used to define fishes do not apply to sharks. For instance, all fishes have bony skeletons; no sharks do. It is this particular characteristic that is used to separate the fishes from the sharks (and from the skates, rays, and chimaeras). *Osteichthyes* is the name applied to the class of bony fishes; *Chondrichthyes* is the name used for all the cartilaginous fishes. There are, of course, many similarities between sharks and fishes: they both live chiefly in a watery habitat, and both use gill structures to extract oxygen from the water. (Some fishes actually breathe air, but not many.) However, similarities of habitat and method of oxygen intake are hardly sufficient to warrant the common classification of two types of creatures. If they were, people and rattlesnakes would be in the same class.

Bony fishes and cartilaginous fishes are different in a number of ways. (Even though we are discussing the question of whether or not sharks are fishes, I shall continue to call them cartilaginous fishes. That is the literal translation of the word *Chondrichthyes*, and "cartilaginous animals" sounds peculiar. Besides, calling something a fish does not necessarily make it a fish.) In fact, the differences are so numerous that there are even those who would argue that a shark is more closely related to a *mammal* than it is to a bony fish. Bony fishes have only one gill aperture, while sharks have from five to seven, depending on the species. (Most species of sharks have five.) Many species of sharks have a placental relationship with their young, a condition lacking in all bony fishes. The skin of a shark is comprised of placoid scales (also called "dermal denticles"), which are toothlike in character, and usually microscopic in size; the scales of the bony fishes are completely different in structure, shape, and function.

So, a shark is not exactly a fish. Neither is it a man-eating, voracious, omnivorous killer, attacking boats, swimmers, whales, and anything else foolish or edible enough to enter its domain. A shark is a vertebrate animal, usually found in an oceanic habitat, with five to seven gill slits and a cartilaginous skeleton. The rhapsodic veneration of intersecting curves presented earlier is reserved for the larger pelagic species, such as the mako, the white, the thresher, and the whitetip. It is creatures like these that first come to mind when the word "shark" is mentioned. They, and many other large sharks, are all you ever thought a shark was supposed to be: they are large, fast, and dangerous, and one therefore thinks of them in that special way reserved for the large predators. It is fear, mixed with admiration and envy—they do their job so well. Any predator large enough to attack a human being, with the added ability to eat him, conjures up this morbid fascination. (Even a mosquito is big enough to attack a human being, and in the process "eats" a minute amount of human blood, but no one seems to think to call a mosquito a man-eater.) Sharks have the ability (although, as we shall see, not the inclination) to eat a person alive, and this is surely one of the most horrible deaths imaginable.

Man-eating lions, tigers, and crocodiles have been extensively treated in historical and fictional literature, and elaborate attempts have been made to halt their anthropophagous habits. This is not to say that all lions, tigers, and crocodiles are man-eaters; in fact, very few of them have been known to engage in this grisly pastime. It is only when humans interfere with these creatures, or when they become too old or sick to pursue their usual prey, that the notorious conflicts occur. Trespass is most clearly seen in the case of the shark, since it can be argued that a human's place is on the land, whether it be African savannah or Indian jungle, and, therefore, conflict with the land-based predators is inevitable. (On land, we have resolved the problem rather neatly by eliminating most of the lions and tigers, or relegating them to reserves where contact with people is controlled and minimal. For obvious reasons, we cannot treat the shark in the same way.) The shark's domain is not the human's. The human is a land animal, not an aquatic one, and he is therefore a trespasser in the water. He can swim in the ocean, he can fish in the ocean, and he can sail on the ocean, but he does not belong in the ocean. Only through the use of complicated technologies can the human even enter the world of the fish, and then he is merely a land animal, temporarily transposed, fated to look at the watery world through a face mask or a window. The human is so poorly designed for aquatic adventures that he cannot even see in the water without artificial aids. If we had been meant to be in the water, we would have been given better eyes for the job, at least.

Of course, humans have the intelligence to enable them to devise the means to enter almost any habitat, from the airless surface of the moon to the abyssal depths of the deepest oceans, but in these extremes, they are but observers, isolated by their own technology from that which they would join.

The shark, on the other hand, is the master of this marine world. It is the "top predator," the apex of the food chain—it is as if every action in the sea is taking place to feed the shark, from the plankton to the small fishes, from the small fishes to the larger ones, from the larger ones to the secondary predators, and, finally, to the shark, which probably has no enemies—except other sharks.

While working on the shark paintings, I began to truly appreciate the sharks. The more I learned about them, the more I wanted to know. Predators have always fascinated me, and the more effective the predator, the greater the degree of my fascination. I am aware that this obsession with hunters indicates something particularly revealing in my psychological profile, but this neurosis notwithstanding, I have been painting big cats, birds of prey, bears, and wolves for years. Now I have discovered perhaps the most intriguing hunters of all, the sharks, spellbinding masters of the seas.

In my paintings, I have tried to show the sharks in settings that suggest their pelagic *modus vivendi*. This means that the background is often featureless, with only a suggestion of the surface or the bottom. Without any reference points, the subject of scale comes up: How can I demonstrate the size of these creatures? I tried everything, but the only object that everyone knows the size of is a human being. Coral, boats, other fishes—all these are variables, and there is no way of guaranteeing that the viewer will know their size. In a couple of instances, I did put a human being in the painting, because I felt it was absolutely imperative to show the size of a particular species. In the rest of the paintings, I can just hope that the big sharks *look* big, and that the small sharks look small.

For years now, I have been almost totally preoccupied with sharks. I have painted them, written about them, dived with them, fished for them, eaten them, sculpted them, dissected them, and photographed them. I have been at shark conferences, shark tournaments, marine laboratories, and oceanariums. I fell into a shark tank in Florida. I have talked to or corresponded with practically everyone who has any sort of a professional interest in sharks.

A normal fear of sharks has become a consuming passion. I still retain some active fear, but it is far outweighed by the respect I have developed for the creatures I have learned about. Yet no matter how much I learn about them, I believe a subconscious fear will always lurk behind the façade of my knowledge. For all the sharks I have seen, for all the books and papers I have read, for all the people I have spoken to, I have only come to know *about* the shark, not to actually *know* the shark. It is perhaps this inaccessibility that sustains my fascination: as much as we in our arrogance feel we "know" an animal, the animal still remains outside our world; we may capture it in nets or by hooks, but the ancient shark-spirit remains free.

A NOTE ON THE USE OF SCIENTIFIC NOMENCLATURE

In a book that is supposed to be written for a popular audience, you will discover what might be a distressing number of italicized and difficult-looking words, indicating that the scientific name is being employed in the discussion of one species or another. For the sake of easy reading, I would gladly eliminate such jaw-breakers as *Chlamydoselache*, *Scapanorhynchus*, and *Cephaloscyllium*. In the interest of accuracy, however, these names and many others like them must be retained. In the tenth edition of his *Systema naturae* (1758), the Swedish botanist Carl von Linné (Linnaeus) presented the currently accepted binomial system for naming plants and animals. Prior to that date, there were Latin names, but there was no universal codification, and therefore the name of a species used in one place would not apply in another. Scientists—and anyone else for that matter—could never be sure they were talking about the same plant, or animal. The system of binomial zoological nomenclature does not make things easy to pronounce (*Chlamydoselache* is the frilled shark, which is a lot simpler), but it does satisfy the absolutely vital requirement that scientists be able to communicate with each other, whether they speak Japanese, Flemish, or Zulu. No matter what language a scientific paper is written in, the scientific name appears just as you see it here: *Chlamydoselache anguineus*. To everyone interested in this species, this unequivocally identifies it, no matter what the fisherman who caught it thought it was, or what its vernacular name is in Portuguese.

With few exceptions, I have not included authors' names in this book, since that tradition is, I think, best reserved for scientific papers, and would not clarify or simplify anything in the present volume. It is difficult enough to read *Chiloscyllium caerulopunctatum* without having to read *Chiloscyllium caerulopunctatum* Pellegrin 1914. The author, whose name accompanies the scientific name—in fact, it is an integral part of it—is the person who first described the animal to science, and the date indicates when the name was first used. Authors are forever trying to change the names of things, in an attempt to clarify or simplify. In many scientific works, usually of the complexity of a monograph, such as Stewart Springer's "Natural History of the Sandbar Shark, *Eulamia milberti*,"[219] there is a section on nomenclature, in which the history of the name changes and revisions is reviewed. In 1810,

Constantine Rafinesque, a French naturalist with "a passion for establishing new genera and species," described the shark that we now know as the mako, and called it *Isurus oxyrinchus*. In the intervening years, over thirty name changes were made. This shark was called everything from *Oxyrhina spallanzanii* to *Carcharias tigris*, and each person who changed the name thought he had cleared up the confusion. When all these would-be revisionists had finished naming it and renaming it, it was realized that the specimen named by Rafinesque was indeed the species we know as *Isurus oxyrinchus*, and its name (until someone revises it again) is *Isurus oxyrinchus* Rafinesque 1810. (In 1966, a new species of mako was described by Cuban ichthyologist Dario Guitart Manday, and it is known as *Isurus paucus* Guitart Manday 1966.[121])

The first part of the binomial is the genus, or generic name. In the large genus *Etmopterus*, every member of the genus is called *Etmopterus* something-or-other. Next comes the species name, to differentiate the members of the same genus. Thus we have *Etmopterus hillianus*, *E. virens*, *E. lucifer*, *E. schultzi*, and so on. Sometimes the names mean something, but often the the meaning dies with the person who named the species. For example, the specific name of the oceanic whitetip, *Carcharhinus longimanus*, means "long hands," and refers nicely to the particularly long pectoral fins of this species. Sometimes species are named for people, such as *Carcharhinus springeri* for Stewart Springer. Sometimes the names are hard to translate, or when translated cause more confusion. For example, *Cetorhinus* translates more or less as "whale shark," from *cetos* meaning "whale," and *rhiny*, which has been variously translated as "rasp" or "shark." Therefore, *Cetorhinus maximus* ought to be the whale shark, but it isn't. It is the basking shark. (Basking sharks are huge, and can get as large as small whales, but this does not clear up the confusion.)

A final reason for the inclusion of scientific names is that many species do not have any common names at all. Of all the species of *Etmopterus*, only one, *E. virens*, has a common name, green dogfish, and since it is neither green nor a dogfish (although it has properties of greenish bioluminescence, and is *related* to the dogfishes), it is easy to see how one can become accustomed to the use of scientific names. You too will get used to it after a while.

SHARKS

eat white shark

Painting in the collection of Stanton Waterman (RE)

THE EVOLUTION OF SHARKS

In spite of competition from the bony fishes, from aquatic reptiles such as the ichthyosaurs, and from aquatic mammals such as the whales, the sharks have carried on in a most successful way. The sharks have succeeded because, with the exception of some of the bottom-living skates, they have been very aggressive fishes, quite capable of taking care of themselves in spite of earth changes, changes in food supply, and competitors. It looks as if sharks will continue to inhabit the seas for a long time.

Edwin H. Colbert
Evolution of the Vertebrates[55]

Perhaps no area of shark study is so replete with clichés and exaggerations as the subject of shark evolution. How many times have we heard that "sharks have remained unchanged for 300 million years," or that they "reached an evolutionary level of perfection so long ago that no change has been required"?

The history of the elasmobranchs does begin some 300 million years ago, and continues to the present day. This means that there have been sharks and sharklike creatures on earth for a very, very long time, but it does *not* mean that sharks have existed in their present form since the Devonian Period, which ended about 275 million years ago. Sharks have changed since their early beginnings, and like any other large group of animals, they continue to change. The confusion lies in the *success* of the elasmobranchs, rather than in their evolutionary consistency.

Sharks may not even be as old as the bony fishes; the vertebrate paleontologist A. S. Romer says that they are "the last of the major fish groups to appear in the fossil record."[199] The cartilaginous skeleton of the shark is not an inferior development, or a degradation of a higher and more noble form. From much of the popular literature, one is given the impression that sharks started out with proper bones, and over the eons, perhaps as a result of some primordial sin, they were punished and their bones were reduced to cartilage. What probably happened is a lot simpler, and teleologically more sensible. In the Silurian Period, some 400 million years ago, two divergent lines of evolution began and continued in varying degrees of magnitude until the present. Sharks are not bony fishes that took a wrong turn on the evolutionary road;

they are a unique and distinct line that shows as noble a history as their teleost cousins.

The oceans of course have not been only the domain of the fishes—bony or cartilaginous. Even today there are fully aquatic mammals (whales and porpoises), aquatic reptiles (sea snakes and sea turtles), and other vertebrates (such as pinnipeds and the marine iguana) that spend a great proportion of their lives in the world's oceans. When the dinosaurs were the dominant form of vertebrate life on earth, they inhabited the land, the sea, and the air. In the Jurassic Period, there were primitive bony fishes and primitive sharks, but the waters were dominated by dinosaurs. There were huge, crocodilelike animals called mosasaurs, and porpoiselike creatures known as ichthyosaurs. The latter were so named because they were fishlike in their habits, but they bore a remarkable resemblance to modern porpoises, differing in that they had two pairs of flippers or paddles, corresponding to the fore and hind legs, while the porpoises have only one pair. When the ichthyosaurs flourished, there were also sharks, smaller than many modern species, but displaying all the anatomical characteristics that define a shark today. The gradual extinction of the dinosaurs took millions of years, and coincided with the increase in the size and number of the sharks.

We are fortunate that the first known shark was fairly well preserved. In the "Cleveland shales" of the south shore of Lake Erie, a fossil of a small (four to six feet long), sharklike creature was discovered. Through a fortunate geological accident, more was preserved of this shark than of almost any fossil elasmobranch since that time. In addition to the teeth and fin spines, muscle fibers and even kidney tubules remained. The animal was *Cladoselache*, a torpedo-shaped shark with broad-based, apparently inflexible pectoral fins, two low dorsal fins, and a completely heterocercal tail. At the base of the tail there were two lateral fins, probably the precursors of the caudal keels of the mackerel sharks, or suggestive of the same steadying function. The eyes were large and set forward in the head, and the teeth consisted of a high central spire flanked by a smaller cusp on each side. Although this small protoselachean differed in some respects from the modern sharks (the mouth was terminal, not underslung; there were no claspers, and the thick base of the pectoral fins must have rendered *Cladoselache* less mobile than its descendants), there is no question that this is the ur-shark, or at least the earliest shark of which there is any known record.

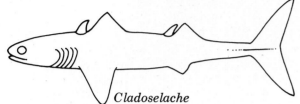
Cladoselache

To set the stage for the introduction of the sharks, let us look at the earth as it was some 300 million years ago. The Devonian seas in which *Cladoselache* swam supported other fishes—the Devonian Period is known as the "Age of Fishes." The appearance of ferns marked the limited landscape. The dinosaurs were not scheduled to appear for another 100 million years, and the earliest mammal was another 50 million years away from that. Those parts of the earth that were not covered by water were in totally different locations, according to current theories of continental drift and plate tectonics. Two hundred million years ago, only one continent ("Pangaea") existed, so that which we are calling "Cleveland" was not where it is now—in fact, 200 million years ago nothing was where it is now. The North American Plate, with Cleveland included, was probably located far to the southwest of its present location, and it was attached to what are now the European and South American plates.

Cladoselache arose, flourished, and became extinct *before* the continents began their inexorable journey around the globe. Both the sharks and the bony fishes, therefore, have been around for a very long time indeed, and they were, together, the first jawed vertebrates. Even earlier than the first sharks and the first fishes were the Ostracoderms, jawless creatures that were the first vertebrate animals. They are now represented by the *Agnatha*, the lampreys and hagfishes, parasitic, eel-like creatures that attach themselves to larger animals and suck out the bodily fluids from within, usually until the host dies. In the lampreys, we see the shadow of the earliest vertebrates on earth.

Cladoselache persisted when other early fishes disappeared. The Arthrodires, armored fishes that sometimes reached great size, and the Acanthodians, also armored but with smaller armor plates, reached the end of what appears to have been an experiment that failed. In the later Devonian Period, the elasmobranchs be-

gan to populate the seas in greater and greater numbers, and by the Cretaceous Period, 150 million years ago, most of the modern genera had become established.

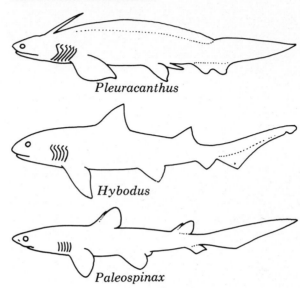
Pleuracanthus

Hybodus

Paleospinax

The first "modern" shark, that is, a species that resembled the existing species, was *Paleospinax*, a small, slim animal that bears a close morphological similarity to the spiny dogfish, *Squalus acanthias*, and displays an early example of a trait that was to predominate in the recent sharks, an undershot lower jaw. There were also a number of species of shark that could be described as "experimental"—sharks that developed certain physical characteristics that are not visible in the living groups today. These included the Pleurocanthids, one of which, named *Xenacanthus*, had a long and unexplained spine on the back of its skull; *Ctenacanthus* and *Goodrichthys*, two of the Hybodont sharks that had an elaborate cartilaginous structure in the lower lobe of the caudal fin; and *Hybodus*, a very sharky-looking creature whose fossil remains show evidence of a rib cage. *Paleospinax*, according to Schaeffer, was a "genus that can be regarded as the first known representative of a lineage that successfully entered the modern level."[202] Its jaws were protrusible, a characteristic that enabled it to bite more effectively, and that was passed along to many of the modern species.

By the Cretaceous Period, when the first flowering plants appeared, dinosaurs were on their way to extinction, and the first small mammals were peeking furtively from behind rocks, the shark tribe had reached almost its full complement. The fossil records for this period (from

(Overleaf) Plate 3. **Grey nurse** *(Odontaspis arenarius)*

100 million to 70 million years ago) show remains of almost all the known genera. These include *Odontaspis*, the sand sharks; *Oxyrhina*, *Carcharodon*, and *Lamna*, the mackerel sharks; *Cetorhinus*, the basking sharks; *Ginglymostoma*, the nurse sharks; *Squalus*, the dogfishes; *Galeocerdo*, the tiger sharks; *Squatina*, the angel sharks; *Scyliorhinus*, the catsharks; and *Carcharhinus*, the gray sharks. As far as we can tell, these genera, and some that will be discussed later, have displayed variations in size and tooth configuration, but have otherwise persisted essentially unchanged to the present time.

Somewhere between the Cretaceous and the Eocene (about 50 million years ago), there developed what is perhaps the most fearsome carnivore the earth has ever known, *Carcharodon megalodon*. Deposits from the Miocene Period suggest that this creature existed as recently as 15 million years ago. A little more than 12 million years, then, a speck of sand in the geological hourglass, separates *Homo sapiens* from this leviathan, a monster closely related to *Carcharodon carcharias*, the great white shark, but with serrated teeth six inches long and a mouth big enough to engulf a horse.

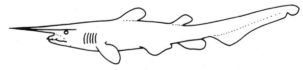

Mitsukurina owstoni

In 1889 a male shark of bizarre characteristics was delivered to Alan Owston, a naturalist living in Japan. The shark was about four feet long and resembled nothing that Owston—or anyone else—had ever seen. It had a protruding, snaggle-toothed mouth, overhung by a paddlelike appendage that was narrow in profile, but wide and tapering in plan (i.e., viewed from the top).

The shark was named *Mitsukurina owstoni*, after Owston and a professor of zoology at the University of Tokyo, but shortly thereafter came the discovery that was to surprise the zoologists and the paleontologists as well. The teeth of this most peculiar shark were almost identical to those of a species called *Scapanorhynchus*, which was supposed to have been extinct for 100 millon years! Since the fossil shark had been named first, the name *Scapanorhynchus* invalidated *Mitsukurina*, but now, for some reason best known to the taxonomists and the International Code of Zoological Nomenclature, *Mitsukurina* is again the name of

the shark, which is known by the vernacular names of goblin shark and elfin shark. Its notoriety does not lie in its nomenclature, but in the look it gives us into the shadowy history of the sharks.

Other species of shark have persisted almost unchanged, and some have retained the characteristics of the earlier or more primitive sharks. These "living fossils" include *Chlamydoselache*, also discovered in Japanese waters in the late nineteenth century. It looks more like an eel than a shark; it has six gill slits instead of five, and the gill slits are covered with frill-like appendages, hence its common name, frilled shark. There are also seven-gill sharks (*Heptranchias*), and six-gill sharks (*Hexanchus*). Both of these genera are considered primitive in that their direct lineage can be traced for over 100-million years. Both genera have only one dorsal fin, and this too separates them from their more "modern" relatives, which arose in the Cretaceous Period. Most of these primitive sharks are represented only by occasional specimens, so it is not known if they are prospering or if they are, as Lineaweaver and Backus have written, "the exotic remnants of ancient and perhaps slowly dying stocks."[154]

The Heterodontidae ("different teeth") are among the oldest of all the sharks, and among the most curious. The characteristic for which they were named is reminiscent of some of the older extinct species, in which two different kinds of teeth are present in the mouth: pavementlike teeth for grinding, and pointed teeth for grasping more mobile prey. Some of the earliest known shark fossils show this multi-purpose dental arrangement. There are two species of heterodontids—the Port Jackson shark, *H. portusjacksoni*, from Australian waters, and the horn shark, *H. francisci*, from the eastern Pacific. They have a large spine anterior to each of the two dorsal fins, which may account for the name horn shark.

According to Dr. Bobb Schaeffer, a leading authority on elasmobranch evolution, "The three groups of living sharks that cannot properly be included in the modern level . . . heterodontids, chlamydoselachids, and the hexanchids" have contributed "more clearly than the known fossil evidence" to our knowledge of modern sharks, since they have been "frozen in transition for roughly 150 million years."[202] It is extremely useful to have "living fossils," especially where sharks are concerned, since the only elements that have become fossilized are the teeth, spines, and occasionally the vertebral centra. (The preservation of the muscle fibers and kidney tubules of *Cladoselache* was a one in a million chance.) A shark's skeleton consists of cartilage, with no bone at all. Moreover, the skeleton is a limited structure, consisting of a skull (with the jaws unattached), gill arches, some cartilaginous fin supports, and the backbone. A shark is mostly muscle and internal organs, and therefore, even if we are lucky enough to find a complete skeleton, there is not much to work with. Sharks are a different and highly specialized subject for the vertebrate paleontologist, who is used to working with leg bones, hip bones, skulls, or metatarsals.

For fossil collectors as well as paleontologists, sharks' teeth are very special treasures. They are not permanently attached to the jaws, and therefore they can be lost when the shark is feeding. In addition, shark's teeth are constantly being replaced, so there are far more teeth per individual shark than we would expect of any other creature. As in modern species, the use of fossil teeth is a precise method of determining the species, but only by experts. A number of pamphlets have been written, usually by amateur collectors, on the subject of sharks'

teeth, and they seem to do more to cloud the issues than to clarify them. The focal point of almost every collection of sharks' teeth is a huge *megalodon* tooth (I must confess that in my small collection, this startling object occupies a place of honor), while the rest of the teeth are treated in a somewhat less than comprehensive fashion. With some exceptions where the teeth are so distinctive as to be definitely of a particular species, the identification of fossil teeth on the amateur level is in total disarray. While museum paleontologists have their collections properly identified and well ordered, a lay person has almost no chance of identifying a tooth found on the beach. In some parts of Florida, California, North and South Carolina, and Maryland, sharks' teeth can be picked up in fair quantities. (They are sold from bins for a nickel apiece at roadside stands in Venice, Florida.)

For our study of shark evolution, the sharks have left us far more than the fossil evidence. In many instances, they have given us themselves; the living, breathing historical record of the enduring elasmobranch. The most recent sharks—the hammerheads—have been around for 25 million years. Humans, by the latest estimate, have been around for 3½ million years.

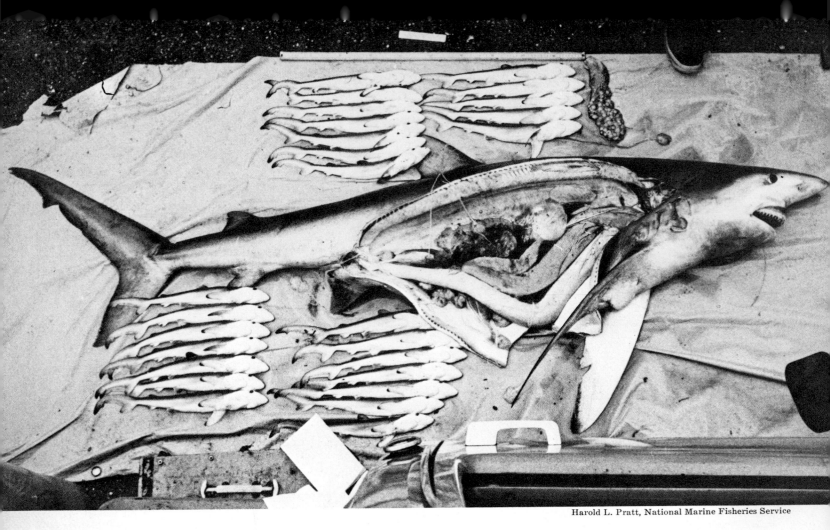

Blue shark, Prionace glauca, *caught off Bayshore, Long Island, in June 1974. The 26 embryos were almost ready to be born.*

THE BIOLOGY OF SHARKS

Canst thou draw out leviathan with an hook? or his tongue with a cord which thou lettest down?

Who can open the doors of his face? his teeth are terrible round about.

Job 41:1, 14

No other animals are surrounded by as many misconceptions as the sharks. The more we learn about these animals, the more aware we become of the great gulf between what we thought was true and what really is true. It is probably safe to say that the "conventional wisdom" about sharks is almost totally incorrect—that is, everything you thought you knew about sharks is wrong, unless you're an ichthyologist, and even then you're not in such great shape. Today's "facts" have a way of becoming tomorrow's discarded theories. I do not propose to present myself as the arbiter of truth; the best I can do is to identify some of the predominant misconceptions and offer explanations or refutations.

There is no such thing as "the shark," except in the broadest of taxonomic terms. In the animal kingdom, the phylum Chordata consists of fishes, reptiles, amphibians, birds, and mammals. The class of fishes known as Elasmobranchii ("strap-gills") is made up of sharks, rays, and chimaeras. All the recent sharks and rays belong to the subclass Selachii, and this is further subdivided into various orders, suborders, families, genera, and, finally, species. All of these categories are provisional; in the study of systematics, suborders, genera, and species are shifted around with disturbing regularity, according to the most recent revisions. A shark that has been considered a member of a given family for years is suddenly switched, or two different species are synonymized into one. No one knows just how many species of sharks there are.

The sharks are a tremendously varied lot, and almost no statement except the broadest of generalizations can apply to all of them. They are vertebrate animals with cartilaginous skeletons, five to seven gill openings, and placoid scales, and they live in water. This definition can include their close relatives the skates and rays, so to differentiate them, we shall add the less-than-categorical statement that their gill slits are located on the side, rather than the bottom, of the head. This eliminates *most* of the skates and rays, but some of the sharks seem to be transitional in this respect, with gill slits that are almost ventral, that is, on the bottom of the head.

The skeleton of a shark (when generalizing, I will try to refer to "a shark" rather than "the shark") is made entirely of cartilage. This is the salient characteristic that separates the Chondrichthyes (cartilaginous fishes) from the Osteichthyes (bony fishes). There is an ongoing debate as to whether the shark's uncalcified skeleton represents a degeneration from the bony fishes or a line of parallel evolution. Both sides have made convincing arguments, and I can only say that the concept of a shark as a poor imitation of the bony fishes' "advanced" development is widely off the mark. Sharks and bony fishes developed more or less simultaneously, as far as we can tell (we are dealing in terms of tens of millions of years), and they both seem to have been quite successful. In *Evolution of the Vertebrates*, Edwin H. Colbert wrote:

> Sharks are generally considered to be "primitive" fishes, but it is doubtful whether they are more truly primitive than the bony fishes. Certainly they appear in the fossil record at a stage somewhat later than that at which the bony fishes appear. Perhaps the allocation of sharks to a primitive position in the sequence of vertebrate life has grown out of the view that the cartilaginous skeleton, so typical of the sharks, is more primitive than the bony skeleton found in other fishes. Yet it is quite reasonable to think that the opposite is true—that the cartilaginous skeleton of the sharks is a secondary development and that the bone seen in the skeletons of the ostracoderms, placoderms and the first bony fishes is truly primitive.[55]

In terms of evolutionary change, the bony fishes are probably more "advanced," but only in that more changes have taken place more recently. There seem to have been more types of bony fishes in the past (just as there are now), so the question of what defines success has to be raised. The Osteichthyes occupy virtually every available bio-niche where there is water, from the ocean's greatest depths to shallow desert ponds, and in terms of absolute numbers, they certainly outnumber the sharks. But the sharks have achieved the most advantageous position in the ocean—they are the apex predators, and have

been so for millions of years. This is surely one definition of success, although empirically it does not guarantee survival—think of the great carnivorous dinosaurs.

While there are bony fishes that eat just about everything edible in the water (insects, plants, plankton, other fishes, invertebrates of all sorts, coral, carrion, etc.), sharks on the whole are carnivores and eat comparatively large prey. Here I have to insert the first of what will prove to be a long series of disclaimers. I have to qualify the foregoing statement with "on the whole," because at least two species of sharks, the whale shark, *Rhincodon*, and the basking shark, *Cetorhinus*, exist primarily on microorganisms and small crustaceans which they strain from the water. Most other sharks, however, eat large living prey, which they catch themselves. This is not to say that sharks will not eat carrion; in fact, there are some species that seem to specialize in it. One thing that sharks do not seem especially fond of is decomposing shark meat, an observation that was used in the development of the Navy's "Shark Chaser," the first mass-produced shark repellent. (In the development of this material, it was originally assumed that certain elements in the flesh of a decomposing shark would inhibit another shark from feeding, but it was later discovered that the presence of rotting shark simply encouraged the preying sharks to seek elsewhere for their food.) Decomposing shark is quite different from just plain shark, alive or recently dead, and a number of species, particularly the tiger and bull sharks, seem to show a marked affinity for shark meat. These species, along with the hammerheads, are often the scourge of the commercial fishermen's longlines, for as they range the sets, they tear apart or even swallow whole (an action that results in their own capture) smaller sharks that cannot escape or defend themselves. Sharks are attracted by the struggles of a hooked fish, and many an angler has seen his catch destroyed by a shark that has beaten the man to the gaff. The spiny dogfish, *Squalus acanthias*, a small shark that hunts in large schools, has been known to destroy entire nets in its efforts to feed on catches before they are hauled in. Even though a small shark may occasionally be eaten by a larger fish, for the most part the only enemy a shark has is another shark. "As a group," Stewart Springer wrote in 1967, "the sharks occupy in the sea somewhat the same position that man occupies on land: neither is particularly endangered except by others of its kind."[226]

Speaking of humans and sharks, there seems to be no question that the most prevalent fallacy is the one of anthropophagy, or man-eating. More has been written about this aspect of the sharks' behavior than any other, and, again, most of what has been written is wrong. As discussed in the chapter "Shark Attack," it now appears that the idea of a shark as a man-eater is far from accurate. (I am defining man-eater as an animal that actively seeks out human prey. That is the way the term was applied to lions and tigers that terrorized villages in the past, and I see no reason to modify the definition here.) Certainly sharks bite people, but, then, so do dogs (a lot more often, I might add), and dogs are not generally referred to as "man-eaters." Almost any large carnivore will eat human remains that it encounters in its own environment, and many of the reports of man-eating sharks are based on the discovery of human remains in the stomachs of captured sharks. But there are few shark attacks on humans in which feeding was the motivating force. Dr. H. David Baldridge, who analyzed over 1,000 cases of shark attack for the Shark Research Panel, wrote: "This mounting evidence further suggests that hunger or the feeding drive may not be as important in shark attack as heretofore believed." [17]

The Shark Attack File itself is a mute testimonial to the sharks' not infrequent contact with people. And if the shark was not trying to eat the person, what was it doing? We don't know. Some theories suggest protecting its territory, threatening the person, mistaking the person for a more acceptable food item, or "testing" the person to find out just what it is—up close, the shark has limited tactile senses, but, as we shall see, its distance-sensing equipment is nothing short of phenomenal. Usually, the best way for a shark to decide if something is edible is to eat it. Often objects found to be distasteful are spit out, but sometimes sharks swallow indigestible items anyway. This may account for the inedible junk *sometimes* found in the stomachs of sharks. I emphasize "sometimes," because most sharks eat normal shark-food, whatever it happens to be for a particular species. Of the thousands of sharks of various species examined by John G. ("Jack") Casey of the National Marine Fisheries Service Laboratory (NMFS) at Narragansett, Rhode Island, not one has been found with anything more exotic than a crumpled soft-drink can or a plastic sandwich bag in its stomach.[46] However, when something out of the ordinary *is* found in the stomach of a shark, it receives publicity

out of all proportion to its numerical occurrence, and the exception is interpreted as the rule by the public. Tiger sharks seem to be more indiscriminate than most other sharks in their choice of ingestibles; examination of their stomach contents has revealed all sorts of curious refuse, from tarpaper to raincoats. (A professional Australian shark-fisherman named Ted Nelson once found a large straw beach hat inside a tiger shark, and wore it constantly.) But even in the case of tiger sharks, they eat mostly fish, other sharks, invertebrates, and sea turtles.

Depending on their size and range, sharks eat almost everything that swims. Some species, such as the spiny dogfish or the little *Etmopterus* species, are schooling predators, and with their fellows will attack large individual prey, or schools of smaller fishes. Other species are known to be "loners," and are not often seen in the company of other sharks, either of the same or of different species. One situation in which various species of sharks are seen together is the "feeding frenzy." As popularly understood, this means that sharks, having been stimulated by the smell of blood, go mad, and ravenously tear apart anything in range: boats, people, each other, themselves. As with many of the fallacies, this one has a foundation in fact, but the popular interpretation is highly exaggerated and overworked. Feeding frenzies, or "mob feedings," do occur, but they do not take place frequently, and there is a question as to whether they ever happen in nature, or if they are completely man-inspired, and therefore atypical, behavior. Most often, the frenzy is observed when refuse or fish offal is thrown overboard in large quantities. Stewart Springer writes: "Shark feeding appears to be an automatic process that always starts slowly and gathers momentum if a series of feeding stimuli occur." [218] The sharks in an actual frenzy have probably been driven to this heightened form of feeding behavior by the large amounts of food in the water, and the large number of competitors. The idea of "one molecule of blood," or any limited stimulant, driving sharks into a frenzy is almost inherently contradictory, but still one reads about the frenzied feeding of two or three sharks, or even one shark, driven mad by its own attack. (Numerous cases in the Shark Attack File disprove this; often a shark will attack, and leave a victim bleeding profusely.) When a single shark is feeding, even in the presence of blood or other body fluids, it tends to move fairly slowly, sometimes "bumping" or otherwise testing the object. Only when more sharks appear, and the "competitive" factor increases, does a marked increase in the feeding activity occur. During the filming of *Blue Water, White Death*, when there were over a hundred large sharks feeding on the carcass of a sperm whale, Stan Waterman said, "There never was a real feeding frenzy, only normal vigorous feeding, with two or three sharks at a time working on the whale carcass."

One of the few areas where the macabre facts may outdo even the wildest fantasy is the feeding frenzy of sharks on shipwreck victims. In this situation, we have the unhappy combination of all those elements known to be inherently dangerous: numerous sharks (attracted by the initial explosion or other cataclysm) and many injured people in the water, splashing, flapping, bleeding, and doing almost everything known to attract and stimulate sharks to feed. In these circumstances, sharks do eat people; in these circumstances, sharks eat anything. Accounts by the survivors of such incidents are gory in the extreme, but it must be borne in mind that such occasions are rare, and do not necessarily define sharks' normal behavior.

"Age cannot wither her, nor custom stale her infinite variety." Thus does Shakespeare's Enobarbus describe the queen of Egypt in *Antony and Cleopatra*. Were it not for the one-sided intrusion of the feminine gender, the phrase is wonderfully applicable to the sharks. Age has not withered them; indeed, it seems to have enhanced them, although we can be sure that Shakespeare was not thinking of age in terms of millions of years, and "infinite variety" is most applicable to this large and diverse family. All sharks have a few things in common, as mentioned earlier: multiple gill slits, cartilaginous skeletons, and placoid scales, otherwise known as dermal denticles. In our examination of the physical structure of a shark, let us begin on the outside and work inward.

The dermal denticles are unique to the sharks, skates, and rays. In some species, these scales are too small to see with the naked eye, in others they are barely visible, and in still others, for example *Oxynotus*, the prickly dogfish, and *Echinorhinus*, the bramble shark, they are visible and prominent enough to be the characteristics that give the species their vernacular names. The denticles are different enough in shape to be a good species determinant, but special caution is required in doing this, since the denticles themselves differ on different parts of the shark. Under low-power magnification, it can be seen that the denticles of different

species are varied in size and shape, but they are usually comprised of one or more pointed elements, with various ridges, cusps, and furrows. In most species, the pointed part faces the tail, so that running one's hand in that direction produces a slick, smooth surface, while the opposite produces an effect like rough sandpaper. (An exception to this rule is the basking shark, *Cetorhinus maximus*, in which the thornlike denticles seem to be set in at random, and the skin is rough no matter which way you feel it.) One fear of anglers who fish for sharks is that the shark will roll in the line before it is brought to the gaff; this can result in even the strongest line being abraded as if it had been cut with a knife. For this reason, shark fishermen use an especially long wire leader. In some species, the skin is so rough that it has been used as sandpaper (it was called "shagreen"), and it was also used to cover the sword-handles of Samurai warriors, to prevent their hands from slipping in the blood and gore. In order to make leather out of sharkskin, the denticles have to be removed. The process for doing this was patented and closely guarded for many years by the Ocean Leather Corporation of Newark, New Jersey, the only commercial tannery in the country that made leather from the skin of sharks. (See "Louis Moresi: The Shark Leather Man.")

"Placoid" means platelike, and is an obvious reference to the armorlike quality of the scales of a shark. It is in the definition of a dermal denticle that things begin to get a little complicated. "Skin-teeth" is a good translation, and this is exactly what they are. They have the same basic construction as the teeth of the shark, in that they are covered with dentine and they have a central pulp canal. The denticles are not the skin of the shark, but are embedded in it. They have a wide base, a narrow "neck," and then the platelike outer surface. In some species the denticles are closely spaced and overlapping, while in others they are spaced more widely apart. Even the distance between them can serve as a species determinant; Jack Casey's NMFS flyer "Identification of the Sandbar (Brown) Shark, *Carcharhinus milberti*," emphasizes that "on the sandbar shark the scales . . . do not overlap." (This is to enable sport fishermen to distinguish it from the dusky shark, *Carcharhinus obscurus*, in which the denticles *do* overlap.) Examination of the denticles is particularly useful in separating other species where the gross morphological differences are slight; in the genus *Etmopterus*, for example, a large group of small sharks which look very much alike, some of the species are differentiated by their dermal denticles.

It is true that the rough hide of a large shark brushing by a swimmer can tear the swimmer's skin, and there have been instances recorded where quite serious damage was done simply from epidermal contact. The damage is also a function of the speed and mass of the shark in the water; a 500-pound animal that crashes into you is going to bruise you even if its skin is as smooth as silk. It is not true that a shark can "taste" with its skin, so the bumping behavior is probably aimed at testing the resiliency rather than the edibility of an object. Even if it can't taste with its dermal denticles, a shark still has an impressive selection of sensory organs. To begin with, sharks have what we consider the "regular" sense organs: eyes, ears, and nose. Because we depend so much on our visual sense as a primary source of information, it is difficult to accept the idea of an animal that depends much more on smelling or hearing. After all, most of the animals with which we come in contact live in the same medium as we do, and sight plays a fairly important role on land. Vision in water is a different problem altogether, since one of the notable properties of water is its density. Light does not pass through water nearly as readily as it passes through air, and in order to function efficiently, an animal that lives in the water must rely on other senses in addition to sight. Sharks' eyes are well designed for the function they have to perform, that is, finding prey after their longer-range senses have enabled them to locate it from beyond the range of their vision. Dr. Perry Gilbert, who has studied the visual apparatus of sharks for forty years, said: "At distances greater than 50 feet, olfaction seems to be more important than vision in guiding sharks to prey. At distances of 50 feet or less, depending on the strength and direction of the current, the clarity of the water, and the amount of light, vision increases in importance, and at very close range (10 feet or less), vision is probably the principal sense involved in directing lemon sharks to food."[99] Most sharks are nocturnal hunters, and in total darkness, vision is of no use whatsoever. However, since sharks do not sleep, vision must play an important part in their behavior about half the time.

The eyes of sharks differ in size and shape, presumably in response to their different requirements. As a general rule, where two species are similar except for eye size, the one with the larger eye inhabits deeper waters. Among the genera in which this phenomenon is apparent are the threshers (Alopiidae), the sand tigers (Odontaspidae), and the seven-gills (Hexanchidae). In each case, there is a species with a larger eye found at greater depths, where, presumably, it needs more light. The bigeye thresher, *Alopias superciliosus*, is quite similar to the common thresher, *Alopias vulpinus*, but its eye is about twice as large; there is also a bigeye ragged-tooth, *Odontaspis kamoharai* (a South African relative of the sand tiger *Odontaspis taurus*), and a bigeye six-gill, *Hexanchus vitulus*.

Many of the smaller sharks have proportionally large eyes, indicating that vision does play a fairly important role in predation, but as usual with sharks, the generalizations rarely hold. There are some small sharks with small eyes; *Brachaelurus*, an Australian carpet shark, has such small eyes that it is known locally as the blind shark. There is no real correlation between the size of the shark, the size of its eye, and its habitat. Some of the largest surface-dwelling species have small eyes, such as the whale shark and the basking shark; other pelagic sharks have relatively large eyes (the white shark and the mako, for example), while the carcharhinids, the largest family of sharks, have eyes that are more or less in proportion to the shark itself, although some species have larger eyes in relation to their body size than others. Most species that inhabit great depths have relatively large eyes, but there are some that have very small eyes. Some sharks have black eyes with no visible pupil (Peter Matthiessen, writing of the great white, said its eye was "impenetrable and empty as the eye of God"[164]). Many species have an eye that is more or less the same color as the shark itself, and a number of species have eyes that are bright emerald green. Eye color is not a constant, since it probably changes in death, but the following species have been described as having a bright green eye: the sharpnose seven-gill, *Heptranchias perlo*; the green dogfish, *Etmopterus virens*; the night shark, *Hypoprion signatus*; the bigeye thresher, *Alopias superciliosus*; and the chain dogfish, *Scyliorhinus retifer*. Of these species, I have seen only one alive, the chain dogfish, and I painted it for this book, bright green eye and all. (See Plate 11.)

Some sharks have a modification of the eye that exists in other animals, which makes their eyes seem to glow in the dark (we notice this most frequently in cats). This is the tapetum lucidum, a mirrorlike reflecting layer that lies under the retina, and reflects incoming light back through the retina, thus increasing the amount of light the eye uses. In many species, the tapetum lucidum is occlusible, which means it can be closed or contracted in bright light, when it is not required.

There are sharks with round pupils, sharks with slitlike pupils, and some with pupils that expand and contract with the amount of light available. As unimpressive as this might sound to people who are used to having their pupils dilate and contract regularly, realize that *no bony fish* has this modification of the eye.

No discussion of the eyes of sharks would be complete without a brief mention of the eyes of the hammerheads, Sphyrnidae. If there was ever a classic example of recurrent conjecture concerning sharks, the heads of these strange sharks must exemplify it. It has been said that their eyes are located at the ends of the flattened lobes of the head to assist in binocular vision; that the shape of their head helps the sharks to turn faster or dive deeper; even that this grotesque modification is a device to frighten other sharks. I can offer no ready solution to this mystery, although it has been suggested that the wide, flattened lobes, which contain the electrosensitive ampullae of Lorenzini (of which more later), help the shark to locate prey buried in the sand.

Sharks have upper and lower eyelids, although they are immovable, and cannot close the eye. Their function is to protect the eyeball itself, which can be rotated within the optic opening. In addition to the upper and lower immovable eyelids, some sharks have a third eyelid, called the nictitans, or nictitating membrane. This opaque and sturdy membrane is present in the carcharhinids, the hammerheads, some species of catsharks (*Scyliorhinus*), and some of the smooth dogfish (*Mustelus*). Its function was long unknown, but now it is believed that it is a protective device, brought into use when the eye of the shark might be physically endangered. (As recently as 1949, Brian Curtis, writing on the nictitans, said, "Just what the shark does with it is something no one seems to know.")[63] The membrane is present in the tiger shark, the largest of the carcharhinids, and in at least two attacks where the shark was large enough to be a white, the presence of the nictitating membrane identified it as a tiger. Stan Waterman told me that when he was filming a feeding tiger shark off the Great Barrier Reef, every time the shark took a bite of the proffered

stingray, the membrane was raised. It protects the eyes of the carcharhinids and the hammerheads, but what the other sharks do with, or without, it, no one seems to know.

We know that sharks can see fairly well. Perry Gilbert wrote that their eyes have "low visual acuity . . . but high sensitivity, and can readily detect an object against a contrasting background, even in the dimmest light. The importance of such an eye to a fish that usually feeds at night is obvious." [99]

We know *how* a shark sees, but we don't know *what* a shark sees. Dr. Eugenie Clark, working with lemon sharks, showed that a shark could distinguish a red target from a white one, but not a circular one from a square one. Sharks have no trouble locating bait, but identifying it may present more of a problem (after all, how many human legs has the shark seen?). Further studies on the vision of sharks may go a long way toward explaining bites on moving objects, such as swimmers, surfboards, and even small boats. We know that a shark's olfactory sense is extremely acute, but what if the object does not emit a recognizable odor? The possibility exists that a shark will bite a moving object in the water because the shark doesn't know the object is not a fish (or a seal, or whatever it expects), and when the object turns out to be a human leg or arm, the shark, whose hundred-million-year conditioning did not include much on *Homo sapiens*, rejects the food, and in so doing, perpetrates an "attack." I see this as in complete contrast to the erroneous concept of sharks attacking out of a desire to eat a human being; in fact, it might be said that this sort of attack is the result of a shark trying *not* to eat a human.

Much has been said about the sharks' apparent preference for bright colors, but, here again, we don't know what the shark actually sees. Tests now being conducted on lemon sharks by Dr. S. H. Gruber at the University of Miami may show whether or not sharks perceive color, but as of this writing, no evidence has been produced to demonstrate that a shark can distinguish one color from another, as opposed to one level of brightness from another. (Eugenie Clark's lemon shark that differentiated between a red and a white target may have been responding to the brightness or the intensity of the color, and not to the color itself.)

A shark's sense of smell is extremely acute. One of the earliest experiments to demonstrate this was conducted by Parker and Sheldon at the Mt. Desert Laboratory, Maine, in which they closed off (with wads of cotton), the nostrils of smooth dogfish, *Mustelus canis*, and the sharks could not locate dead punctured crabs lying in full view. (Sharks with their nostrils clear picked up the crabs in less than a minute.) Examination of the brain of various species of sharks showed that approximately 70 percent of it was devoted to the olfactory function, and it was therefore concluded that smell is the sharks' dominant sense. This accounts for the statements about a shark being able to smell blood in the water from great distances, or the references to the shark as a "swimming nose."

Dr. Albert L. Tester performed a series of tests at the University of Hawaii Marine Laboratory to find out how sensitive a shark's sense of smell is, and how the sharks would respond to various substances in the water. He found that sharks are particularly responsive to certain odors (introduced into the water in liquid form), such as that of ground fish ("the extracts of all food substances could be classified as attractants," Tester said), and they reacted variously to human sweat, urine, and blood. The longer the sharks had been without food, the smaller the amount of food extract that was required to stimulate them. The test sharks (blacktips and grays), showed no reaction to urine, they avoided sweat, and they "were attracted by fresh human blood in low concentrations."

To demonstrate that sharks can locate living prey by olfactory means, Tester lowered a cage with a quiescent fish in it and watched a blindfolded shark (opaque plastic cups were fitted over its eyes) locate the prey without being able to see it. To show that the shark did not hear or otherwise sense the prey fish, Tester had a unique proof:

> *The possibility of the sharks being attracted by sounds or movements of the fish was eliminated in a . . . series of experiments. First, an undamaged living fish (grouper or eel) was placed in a bucket of salt water for about 20 minutes. After a number of control periods, in which salt water from another bucket was siphoned silently into the tank, the flow was switched to the bucket containing the fish. The blinded blacktips responded almost immediately, with a typical hunting reaction, showing that they had detected, by olfaction alone, some substance given off by the fish in the bucket.* [238]

Whether or not sharks have a sense of taste has been investigated but not proven. There have been some instances of sharks taking a visually attractive bait (a squid that had been soaked in alcohol until all its natural juices had been leached out), and then rejecting it. Given a choice of two-inch cubes of grouper or two-inch cubes of mollusk, gray sharks at Eniwetok took the grouper but spat out the mollusk. The shark's sense of taste may be responsible for its rejection of a swimmer or diver once it has taken him into its mouth. My suspicion is that sharks expect their food to taste a certain way; perhaps a swimmer slathered in suntan oil or clothed in a neoprene wet suit doesn't taste good to a shark.

One of the first books to deal with the subject of men under water was Jacques Cousteau's *The Silent World*.[60] Since its publication in 1953, it has been discovered that the sea is anything but silent. It is full of sounds made by fishes, mammals, and invertebrates, and, in fact, Dr. Donald Nelson, one of the first experimenters with underwater sounds and their effect on sharks, called it "the not-so-silent world." Sharks make no sounds, although some are said to "cough" when taken out of the water, but this can be either a muscle contraction or a misrepresentation. Though they are silent themselves, sharks are very much involved with sound, since it has now been shown to be their most effective long-range sense. However, it is not altogether clear how a shark perceives sounds, with what, or if they distinguish between sound as we know it and very low-frequency vibrations. In his doctoral thesis (1965), Don Nelson described hearing as "the perception by the animal through any mechanoreceptor organ, of propagated mechanical disturbances, whether pressure or displacement, arising from a source not touching the animal." [178]

The human ear can perceive sounds in the range of 20 to 20,000 Hz (cycles per second), although no one person can hear over this entire range. The sharks' sensitivity lies mostly in the lower ranges, from 10 to 600 Hz. One of the first "experiments" with underwater sound and sharks involved Hans Hass, an underwater pioneer.[127] Diving in the Red Sea in the early 1950s, he discovered that swimming straight at sharks ("You should on no account show fear") or shouting at them would drive them away. Subsequent experiments showed that shouting is more likely to attract sharks than to deter them; in 1963, Conrad Limbaugh wrote that splashing and other noise-making seemed to attract sharks, and "blasting with TNT seemed to bring the most immediate response. Sharks seemed to come from all directions."[153]

A shark hears with its ears (and other organs), although the only external manifestation of the ear is a small duct, not easily visible. The inner ear of a shark consists of three chambers, the utriculus, the sacculus, and the lagena, and in each one there is a calcified ear stone (otolith) that is connected to a series of hairlike sensory cells. The concept of "directional" hearing has long been a controversial one. It is known that sharks have ears (as well as other sound- or vibration-sensitive organs), but how they use them to locate prey is poorly understood. It is clear that a shark can locate a sound in the water, whether it is a thrashing fish, a recording of a thrashing fish, or even a low-frequency pulsed sound. Water conducts sound approximately five times as fast as air (5,013 feet per second in water and 1,159 feet per second in air), and it has therefore been assumed that a shark has an extremely sensitive neurobiological system for locating sounds. This assumption does not explain whether the shark can hear these sounds, but does show how the shark can get to them so rapidly. At present, the directional hearing in sharks has not been completely explained, since it has proven to be an extremely complex and difficult problem. As usual, however, the scientist's problem is not the shark's, and whether we understand it or not, sharks do a pretty good job of locating an underwater sound source.

Contributing to our problem (but no doubt simplifying matters for a shark) is the presence of another sound-receptor system, the lateral line, or lateralis, system. Most bony fishes have a lateral line system, and its function is associated with perception of disturbances in the water, which can be interpreted as hearing. The lateral line system is comprised of numerous fine canals, filled with a watery solution. These canals, located just under the skin (except in the frilled shark, *Chlamydoselache*, where they are on the surface and open to the sea), usually trace a line from the head back along the flank to the base of the tail. Because of the dermal denticles of sharks, the lateral line is not always easy to locate, but it is there nonetheless. Through the lateralis system, bony fishes and sharks are able to detect motion in the water, sound, and possibly even motionless prey. It is assumed that differences in pressure, acting on the delicate hairlike processes, activate the nerves to which they are attached, and these impulses are then transmitted to the shark's

brain. This intriguing system was the subject of an entire symposium in 1967, demonstrating both the degree of interest in it, and the limited state of our knowledge.

A shark is always "listening," because its sensory organs are always on. It is able to pick up the slightest disturbances in the water, and it is especially sensitive to the sounds made by, or reminiscent of, the movement of a wounded fish. (These are sounds that no human ear could possibly perceive, since they are below the most extreme range of human hearing, 50 Hz or lower. Sharks have been shown to be most responsive to sounds in the 25 to 50 Hz range, becoming less responsive as the frequency increases.) For the first experiments on a shark's perception of sound, a recording was made of the sounds of a speared grouper; then these sounds were played back in waters where sharks were thought to be present. Pulsed sounds worked best, while continuous tones seemed to be ineffectual. In later experiments, it was shown that "blue-water" sharks could be attracted as easily as inshore species, and that although low-frequency sounds were clearly more attractive, any signal up to 1000 Hz could be used, provided it was irregularly pulsed and not continuous. Dr. Arthur Myrberg of the University of Miami demonstrated that sharks could be drawn from one sound source to another.[177] It was also Myrberg who noticed the similarity between the low-frequency sounds used to attract sharks and the sounds emitted by the rotors of a hovering helicopter. He concluded that the helicopter, long considered an ideal rescue device, might in fact attract sharks to the scene of an accident.[177]

A shark's head is covered with a series of sensory pores called the ampullae of Lorenzini. (An ampule is a small vial, and these specialized organs are sometimes called "flask cells," and contain a transparent mucus.) They were described in detail in 1678 by Stefano Lorenzini, a student of the great seventeenth-century Danish naturalist, Niels Stensen. Although the existence of these organs has therefore been known for centuries, their function has been a subject of constant speculation. One investigator held that they were used to sense pressure; another said they could record changes in temperature; and still others thought they were mechanically receptive, that is, they were the organs used by a shark to test an object when it bumped it with its nose. Recent experimentation has added another possibility to the list, and it is now accepted that the ampullae of Lorenzini are electroreceptors. Adrianus Kal-

35

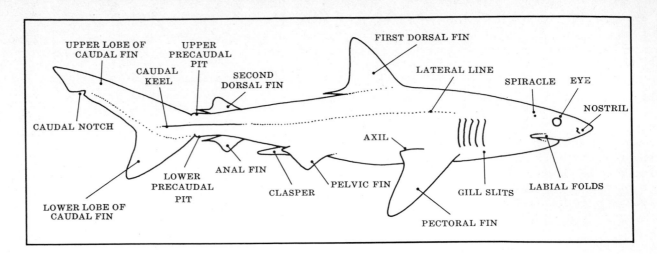

The topography of a typical shark

mijn and Sven Dijkgraaf, working together at Utrecht, showed that certain elasmobranchs (they worked with rays and catsharks) possess the greatest electrical sensitivity known in the animal kingdom. Kalmijn demonstrated that they could find prey that was buried in the sand, and could even locate a flatfish that had been placed in an agar chamber reinforced with foam plastic, "which formed an excellent optical, chemical and mechanical screen, but permitted the bioelectric fields emanating from the prey to pass through almost without any attenuation."[145] It has been suggested that the broad lobes of the heads of hammerhead sharks, amply supplied with these ampullae, are used much in the manner of a mine-sweeper; as the shark swims close to the bottom, swinging its head from side to side, it can cover a much greater area, and is therefore able to detect stingrays, its favorite prey, which often lie buried in the sand. As an electrosensitive animal, a shark can also detect large-scale electric fields, such as the magnetic fields of the earth and the changing polarity of moving water. A better understanding of these sensitivities would enable us to evaluate the navigation and orientation of the open-ocean sharks.

Sharks also have another series of sense organs, called "free neuromasts," which are found in conjunction with modified placoid scales. These are not associated with pores in the skin, they are not part of the lateralis system, and they are not ampullae of Lorenzini. These pit organs are distributed in distinct patterns, one line just below the lower jaw (the "mandibular row"), and another at the forward base of the pectoral fins (the "umbilical row"). The rest of these organs are scattered along the dorsal surface of the shark (usually not appearing below the lateral line), in differing patterns for different species. The function of this system is not yet known, but the usual suggestions have been

made—that these organs are external taste buds, monitors of water movement, salinity detectors, and so on.

Instead of a "swimming nose," a picture is beginning to develop of a shark as a sensory wonder, attuned to sights, sounds, smells, movement, electrical impulses, and even the movement of the earth. None of these sensory abilities implies any more intelligence than was previously attributed to the sharks; we can still assume that they react pretty much on the basis of instinct—but how finely tuned these instincts are! The sharks' integrated systems are as sensitive as any that exist in nature, and they are a crowning example of efficient and specialized adaptation. They have evolved, of course —stories about their not having changed for 300 million years are nonsense—but very early they developed some unique and extraordinary modifications that have enabled them to persist and flourish while other animals have failed to adapt. Certainly their sensory capabilities have contributed to their evolutionary success; even now, we have a great deal to learn about the ways in which sharks view and react to their world. We still don't know much about their reactions, and perhaps this is because we have concentrated on the disparate elements of the sharks' physiology and behavior instead of their overall integration. In *Shark Research: Present Status and Future Direction*, Bernard Zahuranec of the Office of Naval Research said:

It is our belief that in order to understand and predict shark behavior, it will first be necessary to correct the lack of emphasis which has been placed on studying the shark central nervous system. It is here where the necessary integration of various sensory inputs occurs and where the animal's motivational state and past experiences exert their influence on behavior. By having dwelled on studies of isolated phy- siological systems, shark research is at a point where we now know a fair amount about both the effective stimulus modali- ties and mechanisms of shark sensory phy- siology but almost nothing about how such sensory information gets translated into actual response patterns.[257]

A shark can be likened to a very primitive com- puter; it has the capability to rapidly process quantities of information gathered from many different programs. We know this much, but we don't know what will happen when a question is asked that is not on one of the programs. In this case, the computer is very likely to bite us.

Before dissecting a shark to see how it manages to function so effectively, let us first examine its exterior. (It is at about this time that every book on sharks presents the reader with a dia- gram of a "typical" shark, identifying all the fins, etc. This is done to avoid confusion in the discussion that follows, and it seems to me an eminently practical idea.)

All sharks have at least one dorsal fin, although it is not always "slicing ominously through the water." (Paul Budker wrote that "there is a quite distinct vocabulary used for sharks . . . shark's teeth are always 'razor-sharp,' and the tail is usually 'powerful.' In a word, the shark vocabulary is unrelievedly banal."[38] In writing this book, I have become painfully aware of my own inclination toward banality; one searches for new and different ways to describe the teeth or the tail, but "razor-sharp," no matter how overworked, is a pretty accurate term for the teeth of some sharks, and I'm certain that the "powerful tail" has appeared at least once in this book. I have, at least, avoided the "knifing dorsal fin" trap.) The primitive sharks (the hexanchids and *Chlamydoselache*) have only one dorsal fin (which is never described as even breaking the surface, since these are deep-water species); and while most species have an anal fin, an entire large family, the squaloids, is char- acterized by the lack of this fin. All sharks have paired pectoral fins; all sharks have paired pelvic fins, and all sharks have a tail, or caudal fin. The tail can be as long as the shark's body, as in the thresher; thick and lunate as in the mackerel sharks; or apparently unbalanced, with the upper lobe longer than the lower, as in the carcharhinids and many other species. In many species, the upper lobe has a notch, the function of which (if there is one) is completely

unknown. In sharks, the vertebral column ex- tends well into the tail, and this probably ac- counts for the swimming strength, since the tail is the sole source of propulsive power. Some sharks propel themselves with short, thick strokes, with the body almost rigid. This is the characteristic method of swimming of the mackerel sharks (white, mako, and porbeagle), and they also have flattened keels at the base of the tail, which presumably add stability and extra muscle to their swimming. Most other sharks that have been observed swim with more lateral body movement, flexing more than the tail, while there are some species that move more of the body with each stroke of the tail, so that the whole animal seems to undulate through the water.

The pectoral fins are used for steering, and their angle can be adjusted to produce pitch, roll, or yaw in the forward motion of a shark, while the other fins, so varied in the different species, probably serve as vertical stabilizers. (The analogy to an airplane is not inappropriate; more than one author has compared a shark to a fighter plane.)

All sharks have teeth. Teeth are the very es- sence of the shark; without them it would be just another fish in the eyes and imagination of the world. Only a very few species have the proverbial "razor-sharp" teeth for which all species seem to be notorious. The largest shark has the smallest (and most numerous) teeth. A forty-foot whale shark (a plankton feeder) can have over 4,000 minute teeth in its jaws, each less than an eighth of an inch high. Bask- ing sharks, which are also plankton feeders, have minute teeth too. But the next shark in the downward progression by size has the dentition that the cliché writers love. This, of course, is the great white shark, *Carcharodon carcharias*, whose teeth are "terrible round about"; what more could a shark's teeth be? (In order to avoid using the term "razor-sharp," I must tell the story of how I explained to a friend just how sharp the teeth are. I demonstrated by picking up a tooth and gently running my finger down the serrations. I did not know I had cut myself until I saw the blood.) The largest teeth ever measured from this species were almost three inches high. If the teeth of the white shark are the largest, then the teeth of the mako must certainly win the title of meanest-looking. They have been variously described as "fanglike," "knifelike," and even "clawlike." It is interest- ing that two sharks as closely related as the white and the mako have such different teeth. The large serrated teeth of the white shark are designed for shearing, while the pointed teeth of the mako are better suited for grasping. Some species, like the odontaspids (whose name means "snake tooth"), have awl-like teeth that seem designed only for grasping. Most of the carcharhinids have sort of normal teeth, sometimes serrated, sometimes not, but one of them, the tiger shark, has uniquely shaped teeth—backward-curving and notched, as if to hold fast anything it can grasp in its huge mouth. Other species of sharks have teeth that are comblike, thornlike, or shaped like the nibs of fountain pens. Some sharks have different teeth in their upper and their lower jaws, and some sharks have different teeth in the same jaw.

Some of the other genera, such as *Etmopterus*, have particularly sharp teeth, arranged in such a fashion so as to facilitate their peculiar biting pattern. The upper teeth are small and multicusped, while the lower teeth have only one cusp and are so directed that they form an almost continuous cutting edge. These sharks, which do not get to be more than a foot long and which usually feed on squid, grasp their prey with the pointed upper teeth, while the knifelike edge of the lower teeth carves out a bite-sized morsel. There are stories of whales being caught with little round bites taken out of them, and while there is no way to prove it, they are thought to have been made by *Etmopterus*, which the whalers call the "cookie-cutter" shark. (The larger sharks—whites, blues, tigers, and other carcharhinids—also take bites from the carcasses of whales, but no one would refer to this operation as "cookie-cutting." These bites can remove twenty-five pounds from the whale, and the sharks core them out with their sawlike teeth and with great, convulsive shudders of their bodies.)

The teeth of sharks, for all their variety, share one characteristic, and that is the way in which they are attached. They are not permanent, but are constantly being replaced, not only when one is lost, but as a constant function of growth. (One or more teeth are often lost in the act of biting something particularly tough or unyielding. The replacement tooth is larger than the one that was lost, because as the shark grows, it has correspondingly larger teeth.) The number of "functional," that is, erect, teeth varies from species to species. In many of the carcharhinids, there is only one functional row along the sides of the jaw and in front, while some other species of sharks have four or five functional rows all around. In many species there are small or minute teeth in the center of the jaw, which is known technically as the symphysis. The symphyseal teeth differ in configuration as well as size from the others. The largest teeth of a shark are in the front, and they get smaller toward the rear of the mouth. The white shark has a peculiarity that does not seem evident in any other species, nor does it seem to have any functional significance: the third upper tooth on each side of the symphysis is considerably smaller than the ones that flank it.

The opportunity to study the rate of tooth replacement has not occurred very often, but even the limited information we have obtained from infrequent observations is useful to our general understanding. Sanford Moss examined captive lemon sharks at the Lerner Marine Lab on Bimini, and discovered that the tooth replacement rate for this species is one tooth every 8.2 days. The frequency with which the teeth are replaced, said Moss, "calls for a reevaluation of estimates of ancient shark populations based on extensive deposits of fossil teeth. It appears that a single shark can produce thousands of teeth in a lifetime."[173] (In at least some species, e.g., *Isistius brasiliensis*, entire rows of teeth are replaced at one time.) The reserve teeth of a shark lie flat against the inner margin of the jaws, covered by a fold of the mucous membrane.

In almost every recent book about sharks, one is admonished not to believe the old tale about a shark having to turn on its side to bite. No doubt this tale was originally based on the physiognomy of most sharks: their snouts stick out so far over their mouths that it seems impossible for such an animal to bite something directly. However, in all the literature I have found only one instance where this tale is held to be true. In a 1916 newspaper interview, Annette Kellerman, a famous swimmer of the day, describes the ways to avoid shark attack (this was immediately after the five attacks that took place on the New Jersey coast in July of that year). She said: "If when you have watched the shark disappear you wait and then dive deep down the shark will miss you, as he has to turn on his back to get you."

With the exception of those species in which the teeth are recurved in such a way that they are always visible—the white (lower teeth only), the mako, the sand tigers—most sharks look almost toothless in life. It is when they open their mouths to bite that the teeth of sharks become visible, because most sharks have the ability to protrude their jaws, thus erecting the teeth to bring them into play. (This applies primarily to the carcharhinids and the mackerel sharks; the smaller species or those that do not feed on large prey have not developed this ability to such an advanced degree.) As the upper jaw protrudes, the snout is flexed upward to get it out of the way, and without having to roll over at all, a shark can bite a large object head-on. This approach is used in attacking and feeding on large prey, such as whales, and has been observed and photographed numerous times. If, however, a fish is at an angle other than the horizontal, the shark would probably turn to position its jaws at something other than a right angle to its prey. Sharks bite whales head-on, but they would probably roll to some degree to bite an arm or leg that was vertical in the water.

Myths about the strength of a shark's bite abound. In 1916, after the New Jersey attacks, Dr. F. A. Lucas, director of the American Museum of Natural History, and "the foremost authority on sharks in America," maintained (in the *New York American*) that no shark "in these waters" could bite a man's leg off:

> One of the commonest statements is that the shark bit the man's leg off as if it were a carrot, an assertion that shows its maker had little idea of the strength of the apparatus needed to perform such an amputation. Certainly no shark recorded as having been taken in these waters could possibly perform such an act, though this might happen if a shark thirty feet or more in length happened to catch a man fairly on the knee joint where no severing of the bone was required.
>   The next time the reader carves a leg of lamb, let him speculate on the power required to sever this at one stroke—and the bones of a sheep are much softer than those of a man. [183]

By way of contrast, here is Ron Taylor's description of a white shark that attacked another—written to me in a letter while Taylor was filming Alf Dean, the famous Australian shark fisherman:

> The shark was securely gaffed, and the winch was being made ready to take the carcass on board. Suddenly without warning, one of the other great whites which had been circling the tuna boat constantly, attacked his former comrade. . . . I shall never forget that terrible sight or the sound of tearing bone and flesh.

There is nothing flaccid or soft about a white shark; it is solid muscle, as firm and strong as the rump of a horse. In the photographs that Ron Taylor took of the incident he described, one can see that a bite the size of a basketball was taken from the hooked shark.

People soon became aware of the power of a shark's bite, but no one seemed to know just how strong it really was. In 1965, an ingenious device was invented by James Snodgrass of the Scripps Institute of Oceanography at La Jolla, which was used to measure the strength of a shark's bite. It was called the gnathodynamometer. With Perry Gilbert in a paper published in 1967, Snodgrass wrote: "Quantitative data on the capacity of a shark to inflict damage on both animate and inanimate objects are nonexistent." The gnathodynamometer consisted of a soft aluminum core, wrapped in stainless steel laths, under which were steel ball-bearings. The whole unit was then wrapped in a polyvinyl chloride cover. The pressure on the laths would press the ball bearings into the soft aluminum to a degree that could be measured, thus giving the amount of pressure exerted. Of course, sharks are not in the habit of feeding on polyvinyl chloride, so the devices were made more appetizing by wrapping them with filets of fish. The experiments were performed on tiger sharks, lemon sharks, and dusky sharks, in the shark pens of the Lerner Marine Lab at Bimini, and later on silky sharks in the open ocean off British Honduras. The results were dramatic. One of the duskies was able to apply 30 kilograms of pressure per square millimeter. This would mean a force of 18 metric tons per square inch. On Mohs' scale, used to measure the hardness of metals, a shark's tooth and steel are about the same, and therefore the jaw strength as measured by the dynamometer and the hardness of the teeth themselves are a fearful combination indeed. [214]

It is perfectly easy to distinguish a male shark from a female shark. The males of all species have their pelvic fins modified to form "claspers," which are intromittent organs (from *intromittere*, "to cause to enter") that transfer the semen from the male to the female. All sharks (and rays and chimaeras) practice internal fertilization. Since we know so little about the age of sharks, we have to depend on other crite-

(*Overleaf*) **Plate 4. Carcharodon megalodon, Carcharodon carcharias and Homo sapiens**

ria to determine sexual maturity. A male shark is considered mature if its claspers are enlarged and semi-rigid due to calcification. In many species, the end of the clasper forms a fanlike device, called a rhipidian, and if this can be spread, the shark is considered mature. (This discussion of maturity is based on examination of captured specimens; we know absolutely nothing about how one shark can tell if another one is mature.) A female shark is said to be mature if the nidamentary (shell-making) gland is functional. In most species, these determinants are not absolute, and comparative size becomes the most frequently applied criterion for maturity. For example, analysis of blue sharks, *Prionace glauca*, by Harold L. Pratt of the NMFS Laboratory at Narragansett, has shown that there are few mature males that are less than fifty-nine inches, and that the average mature female is over sixty-four inches.[191] With females, of course, the presence of embryos constitutes an unequivocal assertion of maturity. Accumulated data indicate that in all species of sharks, the females grow larger than the males. (Pratt works with blue sharks collected all over the eastern seaboard, and gets much of his information from the annual Bayshore Mako Tournament in Long Island, where, despite its title, most of the sharks caught are blues.) Stewart Springer noted that adult male sandbar sharks, *Carcharhinus milberti*, from Florida, ranged from seventy-one to eighty-nine inches, while adult females were seventy-two to ninety-two inches long.[219] All the really big white sharks ever caught were females, but Jack Casey's 13.5-foot, 1500-pound specimen (a female) was immature.   (Female sharks have a hymen-like membrane that must be pierced before copulation can occur, and in some species, it is possible to identify a virgin female.)

With very few exceptions, there is little information on the actual mating habits of sharks. The mating of the hornsharks have been observed and described, and a photograph exists of a species of catshark, *Scyliorhinus caniculus*, in the act of copulating. Nurse sharks, *Ginglymostoma*, have been seen mating, and on one rare occasion Dr. Dugald Brown saw the mating of lemon sharks, *Negaprion brevirostris*. We therefore have this extremely limited information on which to base our generalizations about the mating behavior of some 250 species of sharks. In all the above cases, the male grasps some part of the female with his teeth. This fact has led to the assumption that the bite marks frequently encountered on females whose courtship has not been observed are caused by the teeth of males engaged in precopulatory behavior.

The claspers on a male shark normally point rearward. During copulation, they are rotated forward, to permit entrance into the vent of the female. Stewart Springer, who has "seen neither the courtship nor the mating of *Eulamia milberti*," hypothesizes the mating activity as follows:

> *The course of courtship and mating in all of the larger carcharhinids including* E. milberti *probably follows the pattern in which the male persistently follows and occasionally bites the female on the back until she swims upside down. Both claspers probably function at the same time, one entering each oviduct of the female by way of the lateral opening from the cloaca. The contact of the two sharks may be presumed to force the sperm-laden sea water from the siphons into the oviducts.*[219]

Springer assumed that both claspers function at the same time; in their observations of the hornshark, Dempster and Herald found that only one was used.[78] Other observers are equally divided in their conclusions. Dr. Harrison Matthews, who studied the basking sharks of the Hebrides, concluded that these leviathans used only one clasper in copulation, whereas two tope (*Galeorhinus galeus*), killed *in cupola*, were conjoined by two claspers.[162] We have so little to go on; we can only speculate as to the function of the dual intromittent organs.

The claspers themselves, also known as myxopterigia, vary in shape in the different species, being equipped with hooks, spurs, and spines, which presumably serve to keep the clasper (or claspers) in place during copulation. The mating process has been seen in so few species that we can only guess about the others. A small, flexible species such as the catshark is very different from the stiffly muscled mako or the ponderous whale shark.

Although in many cases we are not sure of how sharks are impregnated, we are somewhat better informed about the development of the embryo after fertilization. Here, at least, we can examine the specimens. Sharks are born in three different ways: they either hatch from eggs (oviparity); they are born alive (viviparity); or they hatch from eggs within the uterus, and are then born alive (ovoviviparity). In the oviparous species, the egg case, which is laid in the water after internal fertilization, is usually hard or leathery, and it is often equipped with some sort of tendrils which attach it to plants, rocks, or other stabilizing objects to keep it from floating ashore. (Inevitably some do come ashore; the familiar "mermaid's purse" is the egg case of a skate.) The egg-laying sharks are the hornsharks (heterodontids), the catsharks (scyliorhinids), the whale shark (rhincodontid), and some species of carpet and nurse sharks (orectolobids). The oviparous shark embryo develops within the egg case, much like a bird embryo does, absorbing the nutritive yolk material until it hatches and becomes free-swimming.

Oviparity is relatively uncomplicated; the other variations on the theme of elasmobranch development and parturition are somewhat more complex. Viviparous sharks—sharks that develop within the uterus without the intermediate step of hatching from an egg—are sustained by a placental connection, similar to the one in mammals. The embryo is attached by an "umbilical cord" to a yolk sac, which is in turn attached to the uterine wall. After the yolk sac has been absorbed, the "yolk sac placenta" is formed, and nutrient material is absorbed by the embryo through this placenta, the uterine wall, and the umbilical cord. There are some variations on this system, depending upon the manner in which nutrition is absorbed, but they all depend on the embryo being in contact with the wall of the uterus. Even though this closely resembles the true placental situation in mammals, it must not, as Budker warns, "be too closely compared with the placenta in mammals.... Many authors prefer the term "pseudoplacenta." However, the function is the same, and the similarity nonetheless striking: fully formed young are born, which, during the whole of their intrauterine development, have remained directly in contact with the uterus by means of an umbilical cord and a placenta." [38] Sharks that are known to be viviparous are the hammerheads (sphyrnids), some of the smooth dogfish (triakids), the basking shark (*Cetorhinus*), and some of the carcharhinids, including the blue shark.

On a small white shark fifty inches in length, I saw what I took to be an umbilical scar. Although nothing is known about this species' developmental stages, the presence of the scar would seem to indicate an umbilical connection, and, therefore, viviparity. However, in the porbeagle, a close relative of the white shark,

Bigelow and Schroeder say, "It has long been known that this is an ovoviviparous species, the young lying free in the uterus without connection with the mother. It also seems established that . . . the yolk sac is absorbed and the umbilical cord completely obliterated while the embryo is still very small." [30] It is certainly possible that two members of the same family might differ in their development; it is known that two species within the same genus differ in this way; *Galeus melastoma* lays eggs, while *Galeus polli* gives birth to live young. Even more peculiar is the case of the nurse shark, *Ginglymostoma*, which seems to be either oviparous or ovoviviparous, depending on the circumstances in which it finds itself when the embryos are full term.

The third method of shark development is ovoviviparity, a sort of combination of the other two. In this, the egg is fertilized, passes through the nidamentary gland, where it is enclosed in a soft shell, and is then retained within the body of the female until the yolk sac is consumed. In some species, the embryos, hatched internally, continue to feed on unfertilized eggs as they are produced in the oviduct, until they are born. This oviphagous (egg-eating) condition occurs in the sand tigers (odontaspids) and the porbeagle (*Lamna*), as far as we know; other ovoviviparous species absorb the yolk sac and are nourished by a creamy fluid that is secreted from glands in the uterine wall. The species with the largest recorded number of young is the ovoviviparous tiger shark, *Galeocerdo*, with eighty-two embryos having been found in the uterus of one female. (The figure comes from Bigelow and Schroeder's Cuban associate, Luis Howell-Rivero. He was either very lucky in finding more embryos than anyone else, or Cuban waters are especially conducive to the growth of exceptional specimens.)

Among the more peculiar of the ovoviviparous species are the spiny dogfish, *Squalus acanthias*, which has the longest gestation period of any vertebrate animal, twenty-two to twenty-four months, and the odontaspids, which give birth to only two young at a time, the young feeding not only on the unfertilized eggs, but on unborn embryos as well. One 6.5-inch specimen examined in South Africa had eaten its 1.5-inch sibling. In addition to being cannibals, the young of the sand tigers are also aggressive toward anything else that disturbs their prenatal condition. While performing a caesarian section on a sand tiger, Stewart Springer "encountered an extremely active embryo which dashed around open mouthed inside the oviduct." [223] This is probably the only case on record of a man being bitten by an unborn shark.

All species not mentioned in the previous categories are thought to be ovoviviparous, although in some cases not enough information exists to make a categorical statement. For years it was assumed that the Greenland shark, *Somniosus microcephalus*, was oviparous, since the only specimens taken had thousands of eggs in the oviduct, and no evidence of any sort of internal development. (Bigelow and Schroeder wrote in 1948 that the fact that "none of the females examined have ever been found with embryos supports the general belief that this shark, unlike the other squalids, is oviparous." [30]) In 1954, however, a specimen was discovered to contain ten embryos, so the squaloids were reunited as an ovoviviparous family.

One of the most persistently held beliefs about sharks is that they have to stay in motion to stay alive. As with most other generalizations about sharks, this one is not altogether true, and not altogether false. To begin with, there are some species that spend a lot of time just sitting on the bottom. These are true sharks, not skates or rays, and their gills are located on the sides of their heads. (In the skates and rays, the gill slits are located on the bottom of the head, and there is a water-intake organ known as a spiracle located behind the eye, to provide the oxygenated water to the gills.) Nurse and carpet sharks (orectolobids) sit on the bottom most of the time, and many of the small catsharks are also known to remain stationary on the ocean floor. It is true that some of these species have well-developed spiracles (although in the nurse shark the spiracles are quite small), so it could be said that some of these bottom dwellers make use of the spiracle instead of the gills to move water over the gills. Unlike most of the bony fishes, sharks do not seem to have the necessary equipment to move water over their gills while they are stationary, so they usually have to move themselves through the water to keep a flow of water running over and through the gills. Whenever a large shark is captured for an oceanarium, it is "walked" to stimulate its breathing. This means that one or two people get in a shallow tank with the shark and keep it moving forward through the water until it can obtain enough oxygen in its bloodstream to revive from the trauma of capture and transportation. Usually

this looks more dangerous than it actually is, because the sharks are often moribund, exhausted from their struggles and unable to swim, much less attack anyone.

In 1972, a Mexican diver named Carlos Garcia was diving for lobsters in about sixty-five feet of water off Isla Mujeres, near the Yucatan peninsula. In caves where he expected to find lobsters, he was very surprised to find large sharks, apparently asleep. Garcia later led Ramon Bravo, a professional diver and photographer, to the caves, and Bravo took the first photographs of the "sleeping sharks." He sent some of the photographs to Eugenie Clark, now professor of Zoology at the University of Maryland, and before you could say *tiburon*, she was in Mexico with David Doubilet, a photographer for *National Geographic*, to study and record this phenomenon. Sure enough, there were large carcharhinid sharks (later identified as *Carcharhinus springeri*) motionless on the bottom of the caves. [49]

It may have been all right for the slow-moving orectolobids to sit on the bottom like stingrays, but these were carcharhinids, the ever-moving, always-hunting, pelagic carnivores of the open sea. What were they doing sitting on the bottom? Clark observed that they could be handled and "even lifted gently," and that "they were actively respiring at a rate of between 20 and 28 times per minute." Clark had seen carcharhinid sharks stop swimming once before; she was the director of the Cape Haze Marine Laboratory when Dr. Dugald Brown saw the lemon sharks copulating in the shark pool. While she never saw the sharks mating, she did observe some peculiar behavior, and she wrote: "Once they both stopped swimming and rested side by side for about twenty minutes. Actually, it may be more work for a lemon shark to stop swimming than to swim in slow circles." [50] She knew that sharks sometimes stopped swimming, but this was the first time anyone had ever seen them "sleeping." Clark concluded that they were in a torpid state, possibly brought about by the high oxygen content of the water in the caves, which seemed to contain fresh water springs of some sort. Analysis of these data has not been completed, but it has now been demonstrated that *some* sharks, under *some* conditions, can remain motionless on the bottom. The fresh-water upwellings loosen the parasites on the sharks, and the remoras, which usually were seen only as hitchhikers, were observed picking off parasites. (Clark has discovered the same

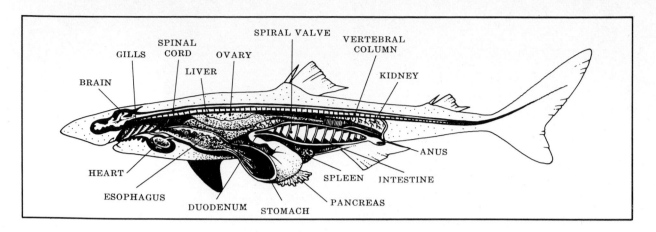

Internal anatomical features of a shark
(*the spiny dogfish,* Squalus acanthias)

phenomenon with the whitetip reef shark, *Triaenodon obesus,* in caves off Japan.)

It is still assumed that most pelagic sharks have to move in order to breathe. Since sharks have no air bladder, they cannot control their density, and because they are heavier than the water in which they swim, they would sink if they did not keep moving forward (a shark cannot swim backward). No one has ever seen a mako, a blue, or an oceanic whitetip stop swimming. (The only time anyone ever saw a motionless live white shark was in an aquarium tank. It sank to the bottom and died after thirty-five hours of captivity.)

Lacking an air bladder, a shark's density-control mechanism is its liver, although it cannot readily change the condition of this organ. The liver in a shark is huge, sometimes as much as 25 percent of the total body weight, but it is usually less—between 5 and 15 percent. A shark's liver serves the normal physiological functions (production of bile, etc.), but it also serves as a fat reserve and a modulator of the shark's overall density. It gives an indication of the general health of the shark. In his detailed study of the sandbar shark, Stewart Springer wrote: "The shark's liver with its high percentage of oil is a good index of its metabolic well-being. The larger fatter livers are found in sharks in good condition while small livers with little oil are frequently found in sharks having severe injuries, sharks in obviously poor condition, or in the males at the end of the mating season." [219] Of all the products available from the shark, the liver has always been the most desirable. In 1937 it was discovered that "the liver of the soupfin (*Galeorhinus zyopterus*) was the richest source of high potency vitamin A oil available in commercial quantities." During World War II, when our supply of cod liver oil was all but cut off by German predation on transatlantic shipping, a full-scale fishery developed in California for this small, plentiful

shark. By 1941, the price had risen from between $40 and $60 a ton to $2,000 a ton. At the same time, there was a substantial shark fishery in Florida, but both coastal enterprises ended when vitamin A was synthesized in 1947. Gavin Maxwell's basking shark fishery in the Hebrides (1945–1948) was established primarily to process the huge livers of these sharks (one liver weighed over a ton).

As shown in the drawing of a spiny dogfish, *Squalus acanthias,* a shark has all the normal equipment for vertebrate functioning, as well as some interesting modifications. First, a shark has no bones. The skull, spinal column, and some fin supports are all cartilaginous, and since there is no rib cage or other supporting structure, the shark is held together, as it were, by its muscle and skin. When a shark is forcibly removed from the water (on a hook, by a gaff, etc.), and then hung up by the tail, it will probably suffer significant internal damage because of the way in which the sensitive internal organs are packed into it. In the water the shark is virtually weightless, but on land or on the deck of a boat, the shark is extremely fragile, especially when on its belly, where there is no muscular protection. It has often been observed that sharks take a long time to die, and there are many stories of a shark that was thought to be dead suddenly "coming to life" and thrashing around dangerously. These behaviors can probably be attributed to reflex muscle action, rather than malicious durability. Bony fishes are supported internally by a skeletal structure, and can withstand a far greater degree of manhandling than a shark.

The stomach of a shark is a "U"- or "J"-shaped organ, which leads through the duodenum to the intestine. The intestine of a shark is equipped with a "spiral valve," which is not a valve at all, but a corkscrew-shaped organ within the intestine that serves to greatly increase the absorptive surface of the intestine without

45

increasing its length. The variations in the design of this interesting system, which is absent in most bony fishes, are almost as numerous as the species of sharks in which they are found.

All fishes have to have a supply of water within their system to remove liquid waste products. If the water in which the fish lives is fresh, the fish does not have to drink; it can absorb the water it needs through its gills. (A stronger solution will flow through a permeable membrane to equalize with a weaker one, by the process known as osmosis.) In saltwater fishes, since blood is the weaker of the two solutions, water would pass *out* of the bloodstream through the gill filaments, if it were not ingested. Therefore, saltwater teleosts have to drink to maintain their water balance. By osmosis, the blood releases the salt back into the sea, leaving a supply of fresh water for the excretory functions. The blood of sharks, however, is a stronger solution than salt water, and therefore, "the end result is that the animal, instead of losing water to the sea water, draws water out of the sea water at no direct physiological expense." Sharks, therefore, do not drink but absorb water through the throat, gills, and other exposed membranes.

Some species of fishes, such as the eel, *Anguilla*, and the salmon, *Salmo*, are relatively salt-tolerant (euryhaline), and they can change their environments with no ill effects. (That, of course, is what they do, as they move from the ocean to the lakes and rivers in which they spawn.) Most species are not salt-tolerant (stenohaline), and placed from one habitat into the other, they will die.

In freshwater lakes and rivers all over the world, the ubiquitous bull shark, *Carcharhinus leucas*, can be found. Bull sharks inhabit Lake Nicaragua, Lake Jamoer in New Guinea, Lake Izbal in Guatemala, and numerous rivers all over the world, including the Amazon, the Ganges, the Zambezi, and the Mississippi. Even though they have been the subject of extensive study, these sharks and their unique osmoregulatory mechanisms are not clearly understood. The principal investigator of this phenomenon, Dr. Thomas Thorson, has written that "individual animals must be capable of adjusting to the change in external medium from full strength sea water to fully fresh lake water."[242] Not only can they perform this seemingly impossible feat (Lineaweaver and Backus suggest that they "ought to become decidedly and perhaps even fatally water-logged"[154]), but they do it at

will. The same individual can swim from the Gulf of Mexico up the Atchafalaya River in Louisiana, or another can come down the Umgeni River in South Africa and enter the Indian Ocean off the Natal Coast. To add further injury to this insult to biological common sense, this shark, with no regard for scientific theory, also cruises the fresh and the salt water locations, biting people more frequently than any other species. One is almost tempted to look for a connection between the insensitivity to environmental changes and the inclination to bite people.

The general view of the behavior of sharks involves isolated individuals, swimming more or less in random locations, hunting for something to eat. Some species, such as the white and the tiger, are rarely found in company with other members of their species, but most other sharks spend some time together with their brethren— at times other than when they are actually mating. Some sharks, such as the smaller squaloids, are schooling fishes, and spend nearly *all* their time with large numbers of the same species. But even the nonschooling sharks congregate at certain times of the year, for mating, pupping, or migration.

Although we can talk about congregations of sharks, we must realize that we know so little about some species that we cannot even make educated guesses about where they go, or what they do when they get there. One of the largest fishes in the sea, the basking shark, *Cetorhinus maximus*, appears off the British Isles in early summer, during which season hundreds of them can be seen at a given time (in *Harpoon Venture*, Gavin Maxwell wrote: "They were packed as tight as sardines, each barely allowing room for the next, layer upon layer of them, huge grey shapes like a herd of submerged elephants"[165]), but in the fall, *they disappear*. No one knows where they go, and they are not seen again until the following spring.

The holes in the fabric of our knowledge of shark behavior are enormous; this "fabric" might be better described as a net—a lot of holes held together by string. We are fortunate that scientists have studied some species of sharks, for this gives us an idea of the behavior of some sharks, and while it is dangerous to generalize, these studies represent a great leap forward over the previous ignorance. Stewart Springer spent years as a commercial shark fisherman, and therefore had the opportunity to record the movements of certain species in his attempts to catch them. He has hypothesized a migratory shark population, to give some cohesiveness to our scattered knowledge of the seasonal movements of sharks:

In this hypothetical population, the young are born in the spring or early summer (each year in some species, in alternate years for others) on specific nursery grounds that are in somewhat shallower water than adults of the population usually frequent. Adult males rarely, if ever, visit the nursery grounds. Females travel either long or short distances to reach the grounds, but actually enter the shallower waters of the nursery only when they are gravid and at full term. The females do not feed while on the nursery grounds. They remain in the nursery area only briefly, and resume feeding a short time after departure—sometimes at no great distance from the nursery grounds, but usually in somewhat deeper water. [226]

Some species separate by sex for migration, such as the sandbar shark, *Carcharhinus milberti*. The females remain close to shore, while the males seem to prefer the cooler offshore waters. No one knows where the mating of large sharks takes place, since the only observations of this activity have taken place in aquarium tanks or pens. It is conceivable that male sharks have some sort of feeding inhibition that occurs simultaneously with their mating activities, since without such a mechanism, the bites that accompany the mating might result in serious damage to the female. (A curious fact about sandbar sharks is that the catch ratio shows five females caught for every male. This might indicate that the females, under no inhibitions during the mating behavior, might attack and kill the males.) During the pupping season, it is the females that do not feed, since they might be inclined to eat their own offspring. For a similar reason, sharks also segregate by size. Shark meat is known to be a favorite menu item of many sharks, and too many small sharks in the vicinity of the larger ones might result in a drastic reduction of the species. (There are no such interspecific inhibitions; a large shark of one species will eat a small shark of another whenever it has the opportunity. Bull sharks show a decided preference for shark meat, and in the case of "Willie," a misnamed female bull shark in the Shark Research Tank at the Oceanic Research Institute

at Durban, she ate sixteen smaller sharks in the tank and was beginning to threaten the divers before they had her destroyed.) It is believed that one of the bull sharks' principal North American nursery areas is the northern Gulf of Mexico, where the pups are dropped. Mature specimens are not caught in these brackish waters, but full-grown males and females are readily taken in the deeper offshore waters in midsummer during the hunting season.

Very little is known about the migratory habits of sharks, since only a few species have been studied, and, as usual, it is not wise to generalize. In addition to Stewart Springer's extensive study of the sandbar shark, the sand tiger, *Odontaspis taurus*, has been reported in large schools off the Carolinas in summer, although their winter whereabouts are unknown. At the Narragansett Laboratory of the National Marine Fisheries Service, Jack Casey and his associates, Harold Pratt and Charles Stillwell, have been accumulating data on the blue shark, *Prionace glauca*, and they are beginning to develop some workable information on migration patterns. Some sharks are not migratory at all, as shown by Dr. John Randall's recent studies (in press) of the reef whitetip, *Triaenodon obesus*, in the Pacific. These sharks have been shown to inhabit the same area for long periods of time, and even to regularly occupy the same caves while "resting." In discussing migration, Springer states that "there are probably as many distribution patterns as there are species." [226] To further complicate matters, some sharks known to be migratory in one region, are nonmigratory in another.

We would expect that members of the same species, in the same general area, would adhere to some sort of observable pattern of distribution. But this is not quite the case. There can be two distinct distribution patterns within a given population: one for the principal population and one for the accessory population. The former is defined as the main breeding population; the latter is made up of individuals or even small groups that have become separated from the main group, and have somehow wandered from their usual geographical range. In his analysis of this phenomenon, Springer writes: "It is possible that sharks of the accessory population are represented in attacks on man more disproportionately to their numbers." [226] Sharks that have gotten "lost," or that have otherwise become separated from the main population, are called "bank loafers" in the

Florida fishery, and catching them is generally unproductive because they do not occur in large enough numbers to make longline sets worthwhile. A shark that has become detached from the main population does not automatically become a "rogue shark," which Dr. Victor Coppleson, the Australian authority on shark attacks, defines as a "single shark . . . which maintains even for years a beat along a limited stretch of shore," and develops a taste for human flesh.[58] With the piscivorous tastes of sharks —given a choice, they will eat fish—the idea of a single shark lurking offshore waiting for human victims seems highly unlikely, but it is possible that the further study of the population dynamics of sharks will give us more information on shark attacks.

There are perhaps 250 species of sharks, although no one is certain of the exact figure. (During the research for this book, I kept a running list of what appeared to be valid species as I encountered them in the literature. When I got to 378, I realized the hopelessness of the task, and quit.) Only a few species come immediately to mind when the word "shark" is mentioned, and these are the large, open-ocean predators. Very few of these are man-eaters (or "man-biters," to be more precise), but still the word "shark" conjures up the image of a lone predator, sculling the water with its tail, staring with lidless eyes in search of something to eat. The hundreds of species that do not fit this romanticized description and have not been implicated in any attacks on anything—except their normal prey—are no less fascinating; perhaps they are even more so because of their diversity and the myriad adaptations they have made to their efficient existence.

The largest fish in the world is a shark. It is a harmless plankton eater, and its name, whale shark, has been confusing people for years. The smallest fish in the world is not a shark (it is the half-inch-long pygmy goby), but the smallest shark is small indeed—it is *Squaliolus laticaudus*, and it is mature at six inches. Between these two extremes, there are sea-roving carnivores over twenty feet long, and luminous sharks only one foot long that hunt in packs. There are tropical sharks and polar sharks, surface feeders and bottom dwellers that may never see daylight, sharks that are restricted to a narrow geographical range, and some that are found in nearly all the world's tropical and temperate waters. There are angel sharks, goblin sharks, carpet sharks, swell sharks, nurse sharks, monk sharks, bramble sharks, silky sharks, cow sharks, bull sharks, basking sharks, frilled sharks, cat sharks, dogfish, hammerheads, porbeagles, and wobbegongs.

In his classic treatise on the anatomy and physiology of sharks, the zoologist J. Frank Daniel said:

> *There lives today a vast group of fishes, some of which are littoral, keeping close to shore; others are nomads of the ocean, roaming vast expanses of its waters; others there are which are pelagic, living near its surface; and still others that are inhabitants of the profound depths into which sunlight never penetrates—these are the sharks, to the man with the nets the most worthless, to the naturalist among the most interesting of living things.*[64]

Sharks are more than just "interesting," they are a marvelously intriguing and fundamental life form that has successfully evaded our most sophisticated scientific and technological efforts to conquer or even to understand them. They are incredibly complex and wonderfully simple at the same time. They are so competent, so beautifully designed for the functions they have to perform, that we cannot help but envy them. They are the masters of their environment in a way that has so far been completely denied us.

THE SYSTEMATICS OF SHARKS

To introduce the sections on the various families of sharks, I intended to list the families and genera in the accepted order, and then to proceed directly to the first group, the primitive sharks. The trouble with that approach became evident immediately: there is no accepted order. A number of authors have listed the orders, suborders, and families, but they all differ materially on the details. Some of the classifications are worldwide in scope, while others are restricted to certain locations, such as the western North Atlantic, California, or Australia. I naively assumed that I could consult the worldwide classifications and the major geographical works, eliminate the duplications, check the various references for synonymy, and produce a current systematic list. I was wrong.

The science of taxonomy is constantly changing. It is unlikely that there will ever be a definitive list of the world's sharks at the species level, and even the family and generic classifications are in a constant state of flux. Some of the reasons for this situation are obvious. In order to categorize animals, you have to be able to compare one with another, to see what the similarities and differences are. Sharks do not lend themselves to easy examination. They are large, and therefore difficult—in some cases impossible—to store. You can get representatives of most bony fishes into jars of formalin, and check one specimen against another when reviewing the classification. (This cannot be done with all the bony fishes; the systematics of the billfishes, for example, has been unresolved for years, and for practically the same reasons. A 1,000-pound swordfish or marlin does not fit into a bottle very easily.) Since some sharks get even larger than billfishes, the problem of storing them becomes almost insurmountable. There is simply no way to store a mature whale shark, basking shark, white shark, or Greenland shark (each of which can attain a length of twenty feet or more and a weight of several thousand pounds), and even the smaller sharks, say those that grow to eight to ten feet in length, and to 400 to 1,000 pounds, present monumental problems. (Some would suggest that whales, which get considerably larger than even the largest sharks, seem to be better understood, but this is not the case at all. Until quite recently, even whalers were unable to tell one species of rorqual from another, and as far as the smaller species are concerned, there are some that have never been seen alive—the only records we have

are of carcasses washed up on the beach. Thus, on the whole, we find that the whales are rather poorly known.)

Most similar sharks are classified according to exterior physical appearance (including such categories as relative position of the fins, size of the gill slits or eyes, color, presence or absence of certain ridges, grooves, barbels, keels, etc.), dentition, vertebral numbers, or the shape of the dermal denticles. These variations occur in every conceivable combination, and they are also likely to change as the shark matures. The proportions of a juvenile shark are often quite different from those of an adult. In order to distinguish one similar species from another, you need good data, plus comparative information on the specimens. Responsible scientists do produce, record, and publish these data, but, unfortunately, sharks are not always caught (or even seen, for that matter) by responsible scientists, and the number of instances where no accurate information exists is sufficient to seriously limit or even invalidate the system.

We are therefore faced with an ever-changing system of shark classification, and while this may appear at first to be impractical or even inept, it is really an excellent example of the viability of the scientific method. Scientists rarely find what they consider to be the final answers to questions—in fact, good science has been defined not in terms of good answers, but in terms of good questions. The science of taxonomy is flexible by definition. To write a definitive answer is to close the door to additions or modifications, and it is only in the interest of the *progress* of taxonomy that anyone systematizes a given group. (If you think the sharks are complicated, consider the plight of the entomologist: no one has any idea how many kinds of insects there are—there may be as many as 230,000 species of beetles, for example—and three-quarters of all living things are insects.)

It is true that some taxonomists have labored long and hard on certain groups of sharks, and the fact that we have any system at all is a testimony to their painstaking and substantial research. The regular discovery of a new species is an exciting prospect (it has been estimated that there are close to 100 new species of fishes discovered every year), and the appearance of a new species should not serve as a dampening influence on our ability to understand the sharks and their relationships with one another. For every species that is synonymized, there is probably a new one already discovered or waiting to be discovered. Usually, new species are small, but not always. The discovery of the coelacanth is of course the most dramatic zoological story of recent years—a lobe-finned fish of a type thought to have been extinct for 60 million years was caught off the east African coast in 1938. The coelacanth gets to be six feet long.

As late as 1966, the second species of mako was described. (Unlike the coelacanth, this species of mako had been seen before, but Guitart Manday published his paper describing it for science in that year.) The common thresher shark, *Alopias vulpinus*, and the bigeye thresher, *Alopias superciliosus*, were long considered the two "good species" in the genus. In 1935, a Japanese ichthyologist described a third species, *Alopias pelagicus*, but somehow, perhaps because it was so rare, it failed to gain the necessary recognition. In their 1975 paper, Bass, D'Aubrey, and Kistnasamy recognized *A. pelagicus* as a distinct species, based on their examination of a specimen caught off Durban,[21] and now there are three. Among the most confusing of the genera are the odontaspids. Since the nomenclatural problems are discussed in some detail in the section devoted to this family, it will suffice here to mention that no one is sure if there are eight, nine, or ten distinct species—and years ago it was being argued that there was only one. All the above-mentioned taxonomic intricacies involve large sharks; the problems with the smaller ones increase inversely with their size. ("Size" is a relative term; the "smaller" sharks can be five or six feet long, and they still don't fit into bottles too well.) There may be 200 species of sharks, or as many as 300. The possible magnitude of variation is symptomatic of the problem, but at the same time it points up the vitality of the art and science of taxonomy.

In the systematic sections that follow, there will be other gaps; taxonomy is not the only area in which our knowledge of sharks is deficient. It is the nature of this book—largely because it is the nature of the sharks—to be somewhat mysterious and unresolved. I had hoped to succinctly summarize our knowledge of sharks, and in a few instances I think I have done so. But in many cases, I have had to resort to convoluted disclaimers, apologies, or plain confessions of ignorance. (In most cases, the ignorance is mine; if I have missed an important reference or misinterpreted a scientific analysis, I cannot blame the scientists or the sharks.)

What follows is a provisional classification of sharks, and then a personal reading of the available information on the various families. My systematic list is scientific only in that it is homogenized from other classifications; I do not represent myself as a systematist, and I have not examined a single specimen with the intention of classifying it in one group or another. I have pored over a lot of lists, however, and I am sure there will be those who disagree with the system I have proposed. That is what taxonomy is all about.

Class Chondrichthyes
Subclass Elasmobranchii
Order Selachii
Suborder Hexanchiformes
Family Hexanchidae (six-gilled and seven-gilled sharks)
  Genus *Hexanchus* (six-gill sharks)
  Genus *Heptranchias* (sharpnose seven-gills)
  Genus *Notorynchus* (broadnose seven-gills)
Family Chlamydoselachidae
  Genus *Chlamydoselachus* (frilled shark)
Family Heterodontidae
  Genus *Heterodontus* (hornsharks)
Suborder Pristioformes
Family Pristiophoridae (sawsharks)
  Genus *Pristiophorus* (five-gill sawshark)
  Genus *Pliotrema* (six-gill sawshark)
Suborder Squatiniformes
Family Squatinidae
  Genus *Squatina* (angel sharks, monk sharks)
Suborder Galeiformes
Family Odontaspidae
  Genus *Odontaspis* (sand tiger, grey nurse, ragged-tooth)
Family Mitsukurinidae
  Genus *Mitsukurina* (goblin shark)
Family Isuridae (mackerel sharks)
  Genus *Lamna* (porbeagle)
  Genus *Isurus* (mako)
  Genus *Carcharodon* (white shark)
Family Cetorhinidae
  Genus *Cetorhinus* (basking shark)
Family Alopiidae
  Genus *Alopias* (thresher sharks)
Family Orectolobidae
  Genus *Ginglymostoma* (nurse shark)
  Genus *Nebrius* (tawny shark)

Genus *Stegostoma* (zebra shark)
Genus *Orectolobus* (carpet sharks, wobbegongs)
Genus *Eucrossorhinus* (wobbegong)
Genus *Sutorectus* (wobbegong)
Genus *Chiloscyllium* (spotted cat-sharks, banded catsharks)
Genus *Hemiscyllium* (epaulette sharks)
Genus *Brachaelurus* (blind shark)
Genus *Heteroscyllium* (Colclough's shark)
Genus *Cirrhoscyllium*
Genus *Parascyllium* (catsharks)
Family Rhincodontidae
Genus *Rhincodon* (whale shark)
Family Scyliorhinidae (catsharks)
Genus *Apristurus*
Genus *Atelomycterus*
Genus *Cephaloscyllium* (swell sharks)
Genus *Cephalurus* (head shark)
Genus *Dichichthys*
Genus *Galeus*
Genus *Halaelurus*
Genus *Haploblepharus*
Genus *Parmaturus* (filetail catshark)
Genus *Pentanchus*
Genus *Poroderma*
Genus *Schroederichthys*
Genus *Scyliorhinus* (catshark, dogfish)
Family Pseudotriakidae
Genus *Pseudotriakis* (false catsharks)
Family Triakidae
Genus *Scylliogaleus*
Genus *Furgaleus*
Genus *Hemitriakis*
Genus *Mustelus* (smoothhound, smooth dogfish)
Genus *Triakis* (leopard shark, smooth dogfish)
Genus *Iago*
Genus *Galeorhinus* (tope, soupfin, school shark)
Genus *Hypogaleus*
Family Hemigaleidae
Genus *Chaenogaleus*

Genus *Hemigaleus*
Genus *Paragaleus*
Family Carcharhinidae (gray sharks, reef sharks, requiem sharks)
Genus *Galeocerdo* (tiger shark)
Genus *Prionace* (blue shark)
Genus *Sciolodon* (sharpnosed shark)
Genus *Loxodon*
Genus *Rhizoprionodon* (sharpnosed shark)
Genus *Aprionodon* (finetooth shark)
Genus *Negaprion* (lemon shark)
Genus *Hypoprion* (night shark)
Genus *Carcharhinus* (gray sharks, reef sharks, requiem sharks, etc.)
Genus *Isogomphodon*
Genus *Triaenodon* (reef whitetip)
Family Sphyrnidae
Genus *Sphyrna* (hammerheads, bonnet-heads, etc.)
Suborder Squaliformes
Family Echinorhinidae
Genus *Echinorhinus* (bramble shark, prickly shark)
Family Oxynotus
Genus *Oxynotus* (prickly dogfish)
Family Squalidae
Genus *Squalus* (spiny dogfish)
Genus *Centroscyllium* (black dogfish)
Genus *Etmopterus*
Genus *Centrophorus*
Genus *Cirrhigaleus*
Genus *Deania*
Genus *Centroscymnus* (Portuguese shark)
Genus *Scymnodon*
Family Dalatiidae
Genus *Dalatias*
Genus *Euprotomicrus*
Genus *Isistius* (luminous shark)
Genus *Squaliolus* (dwarf shark)
Genus *Heteroscymnoides*
Genus *Somniosus* (Greenland shark, sleeper sharks)

PRIMITIVE SHARKS

As George Orwell might have said, all sharks are primitive, but some are more primitive than others. The sharks that bear the closest resemblance to the extinct species are known collectively as the primitive sharks, and they show certain characteristics that make them unmistakable, and totally different from the more "modern" species. There are about 250 species of sharks, and almost all of them have five gill slits. However, one family, the Hexanchidae, includes three genera of six- and seven-gill sharks; and another family, the Notorynchidae, is comprised of one species of seven-gill. (These are *almost* the only sharks with more than five gill slits. The only other is a species of sawshark, *Pliotrema warreni*, with six gill slits, found off the South African coast. It is differentiated from *Pristiophorus*, the "five-gill sawshark," by the number of gill slits.)

The teeth of all the hexanchid sharks are strikingly different in the upper and lower jaws. The upper teeth are similar to those of many other shark species, consisting of a central spire flanked by one or more smaller cusps. The lower teeth are extraordinary, looking not like teeth at all, but like backward pointed combs. One of the cusps is larger than the others, but the remainder (in some species there are as many as ten subsidiary cusps) are smaller and decrease in size toward the posterior portion of the tooth. These lower teeth are large, and both the upper and lower teeth are set in the jaw in multiple rows, the number of rows serving as a species determinant.

Hexanchus griseus

There are now thought to be two species of the genus *Hexanchus*, the bluntnose six-gill *Hexanchus griseus*, and the bigeye six-gill, *Hexanchus vitulus*. They are differentiated primarily by the shape of the snout, the number of rows of teeth in each jaw, the size of the eye and the relative size of the shark itself. *H. griseus* is the larger of the two, reaching a length of fifteen feet and perhaps even more; *H. vitulus* rarely exceeds seven feet. With the exception of these morphological differences, the sharks are similar in biology and behavior. They are dark-

colored, described variously as "coffee-colored," "dark gray" or "mouse gray," and often there is no significant difference between the dorsal and the ventral coloration. They are ovoviviparous, and the number of embryos can range from 7 to 104 in the females examined.

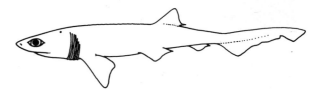

Hexanchus vitulus

The bluntnose six-gill (*griseus*) is a temperate-water species, found in the deeper waters of the Mediterranean (where it is fairly common), both sides of the Atlantic, British Columbia to southern California, Chile, Japan, Australia and South Africa. In an exciting series of experiments with deep-water animals, scientists at the Scripps Institute of Oceanography at La Jolla, California, have observed (by robot motion-picture and still cameras) the feeding of bottom-dwelling fishes, including the large sharks that frequent the deep ocean floor at depths of up to 6,500 feet. In a spectacular photograph accompanying an article about these experiments in *Scientific American*, there is a "fifteen-foot shark" feeding at 2,400 feet in the eastern Mediterranean. Because of its size, color, and location, the shark is almost certainly *Hexanchus griseus*, and therefore represents one of the few photographs of this species alive. (Almost every other picture I have ever seen of this shark was either a drawing or a photograph of a dead specimen. To see a photograph of a living shark adds a new dimension to one's understanding of these primitive animals.)

In Lineaweaver and Backus's *Natural History of Sharks*, there is an interesting story that "exemplifies how errors can be unwittingly propagated time and again."[154] Just as in the case of the apocryphal "36.5-foot" white shark, an anomalous statistic continued to appear in reference to the maximum size of *H. griseus*. In 1846, Jonathan Couch reported a specimen that was "2 feet 2½ inches." Shortly thereafter, mention was made of a specimen 26 feet 5 inches long, captured at Polperro, in Cornwall (the location of Couch's specimen was the same). This monstrous six-gill appears regularly in the literature, even though no specimen was ever taken after that one that even ap-

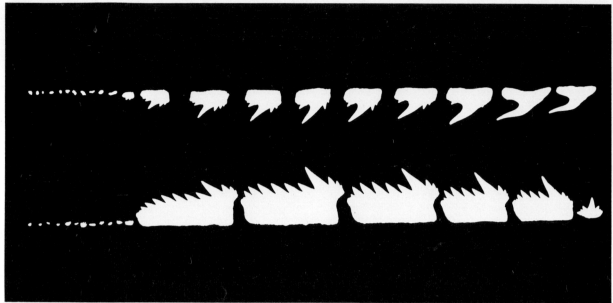

Oceanographic Research Institute, Durban, South Africa

The teeth of the sevengill shark Heptranchias perlo, *showing the characteristic differentiation of the uppers and lowers.*

proached it in size. (It is cited in Bigelow and Schroeder, but with a disclaimer: "One of 26 feet 5 inches was reported from Cornwall many years ago, a giant of its kind *if its size was stated correctly.*") Lineaweaver and Backus propose that 2 feet 2½ inches was converted to 26.5 inches,[154] and later (after Couch's death in 1870), by inadvertence or misinterpretation, written as 26 feet 5 inches.

The common name of *Hexanchus griseus* is six-gill, but it is also called cow shark, mud shark, comb-toothed shark, and bulldog shark. Until 1969, it was thought to be the only species of six-gill shark in the genus *Hexanchus*. Then Stewart Springer and R. A. Waller described a second species, *Hexanchus vitulus*, based on a specimen taken in the Bahamas.[231] Since that time, a number of specimens thought to have been *H. griseus* have been identifiable as *H. vitulus*. *Vitulus* seems to be a warmer-water species, found off Florida, the Philippines, Madagascar and the Kenya coast south to Natal. Like its close relative, *H. griseus*, the bigeye six-gill is thought to be a deep-water species, which may occasionally make excursions to the surface.

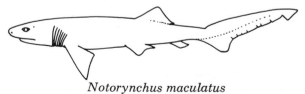

Notorynchus maculatus

The seven-gills are generally similar to the

six-gills, with one obvious difference. There is more confusion about the taxonomy, however, since there are two distinct genera, *Heptranchias* and *Notorynchus*. Like the six-gills, these are primarily differentiated by the shape of the head. (As usual, there were thought to be other species in addition to these two, but at least one of them, *Heptranchias dakini*, was shown to be conspecific with *H. perlo* by Garrick in 1971.[92]) All the hexanchids have only one dorsal fin, set far back, almost over the anal fin. One account mentions "bright emerald-green eyes" in this species, but this characteristic is not mentioned elsewhere. (I have seen one species with startlingly green eyes—the chain dogfish *Scyliorhinus retifer*, that I saw the day they were delivered to the New York Aquarium—see plate 11.) If I had not seen this fish alive, I never would have believed the eye color.) *Heptranchias perlo* is also known as the perlon or perlon shark, perhaps from the French *perle* for "pearl gray." It can be differentiated from the other seven-gill, *Notorynchus*, by its narrow, pointed snout, and its relatively stiff body.

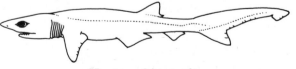

Heptranchias perlo

Notorynchus cepedianus (which used to be known as *N. maculatus*) is the broadnose seven-gill. It can reach a length of fifteen feet and has been described as pugnacious and harmful. (It has been known to attack divers in aquarium tanks. However, this represents an unusual situation, and should not be interpreted as normal behavior.) Its body is much more flexible and supple than that of *Heptranchias*.

This shark is fairly common in the southern hemisphere's temperate waters of Australia, South Africa, India, and South America. It has not been found in the Atlantic or the Mediterranean. It is mouse gray, speckled with dark blotches, although Whitley describes it as having "scattered black and white spots." [253] When Captain Young (see "William Young: Sharky Bill") was operating a shark-fishing station at Pindamar, New South Wales, he reported finding "a seven-gill shark in the net, the only one I ever caught. It was catlike in appearance, with smooth skin and beautiful red and yellow spots, and was about four feet long." [256] (Some of the Australian catsharks [*Hemiscyllium* or *Heteroscyllium*] are brightly colored, but I have never found a reference to a shark— no matter how many gills it had—with red and yellow spots. Biology was not Young's strong suit.) One of the few albino sharks ever seen was a small specimen of *Notorynchus*, captured in San Francisco Bay.

Prominently mentioned in books on sea serpents, the frilled shark can easily qualify for this designation. It is certainly serpentlike in appearance; in fact, it looks more like an eel than a shark. (Its specific name, *anguineus*, comes from the word for eel.) Where other sharks have plain gill slits, this creature has a collar of frills, and its mouth, instead of being underslung as the mouth of a shark is supposed to be, is terminal, that is at the end of the head, as in a snake. Its teeth are three-pronged (trident-shaped). Surely this must be the archetypal sea snake, and it would be—if it ever grew longer than six feet. (In *In the Wake of Sea-Serpents*, Bernard Heuvelmans holds tenaciously to the possibility of "some kind of big *Chlamydoselachus*" [134] to explain some of the more bizarre sightings, but, alas, he produces nothing more than hope.)

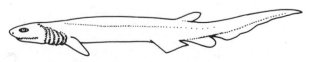

Chlamydoselachus anguineus

Chlamydoselachus anguineus, the frilled shark, is unique among sharks in having the first gill slit completely circle the head on the ventral surface. Whereas in other sharks the left and right gill openings are clearly separated, the first of the frilled shark's six gill slits meets itself under the "chin." Very little is known of this most peculiar-looking elasmobranch, except that it seems to be ovoviviparous, it is most frequently encountered in Japanese waters (where it was first discovered), and it is occasionally taken in deep water off western Europe and southwest Africa.

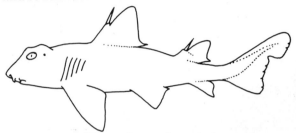

Heterodontus francisci

The heterodontids are reminiscent of some of the earliest sharks in having a large spine immediately anterior to each dorsal fin. This "spinose" condition is characteristic of some of the earliest sharklike vertebrates, among them *Cladoselache* and *Ctenacanthus* of the Devonian Period. The heterodontids, or hornsharks, are distinguished from all other modern sharks by the presence of two spinose dorsal fins and an anal fin. (Other species that have two spiny dorsals have no anal fin, e.g., the dogfishes and other squaloids.) They are peculiar-looking creatures with oversized, knobby heads (accounting for one of their common names, "bullhead") and what are known technically as "strong supraorbital crests," which means a bony arch above each eye. They are bottom dwellers and bottom feeders, with a mouth that is designed for feeding on shellfish. The generic name Heterodontidae, which means "different teeth," is most applicable. In many sharks, such as the hexanchids discussed earlier, the teeth in the upper jaw differ from those in the lower jaw, but the hornsharks have different teeth in *each* jaw. Forward in the jaw are pointed teeth for grasping, and toward the rear are pavementlike teeth for crushing. The diet of the hornsharks consists mostly of oysters and other mollusks.

There are a number of species of heterodontids, similar in morphology and habitat, found in the littoral waters of the world. They include *Heterodontus portusjacksoni* from Australia; *H.*

francisci from California; *H. quoyi* from Ecuador, Peru, and the Galapagos; and *H. ramalheira* from Mozambique and South Africa. They are smallish sharks, usually not exceeding three feet in length, and they are usually a buff color with scattered dark brown spots.

The hornshark is probably best known for its immodesty with regard to its mating habits. Unlike many other species which have never been seen copulating, the hornshark has been observed many times, photographed and documented. Earl Herald, director of the Steinhart Aquarium in San Francisco, wrote this description of their lovemaking:

> *The male had seized the female by the left pectoral fin and was holding on to it firmly with his mouth. The female was lying partially on her left side facing the male and did not appear to be making any great effort to get away from him. In a short time he had manipulated his body so that his tail occupied a position over her back immediately in front of the second dorsal fin. By using her second dorsal spines as an anchor and, at the same time, holding on to the left pectoral fin with his mouth—the mid-region of the body being in a position to move freely—he was able to thrust his right clasper into her vent. The left clasper played no part whatever in the sexual act; it hung loosely in the water.*[133]

For ten years, eggs were laid at the Steinhart Aquarium, but they never hatched. At another California aquarium (The Vaughan Aquarium at La Jolla), eggs hatched between ten months and a year after being laid, but the newborn hornsharks lived only a few months. The eggs of the hornsharks are elongated capsules, with a double spiral flange. When laid, they are a light brown color and pliable, but after a few days in the water, they harden and turn dark brown.

The hornsharks exhibit the closest thing to parental care known in sharks. After the eggs are laid, the female takes them in her mouth and places them in rock crevices, presumably to protect them. They harden in these fissures, making it almost impossible to get them out. In his examination of the habitat of the Port Jackson shark (*Heterodontus portusjacksoni*), A. K. O'Gower wrote that "The eggs must be 'unscrewed' to free them from their ovoposition sites in rock crevices."[187]

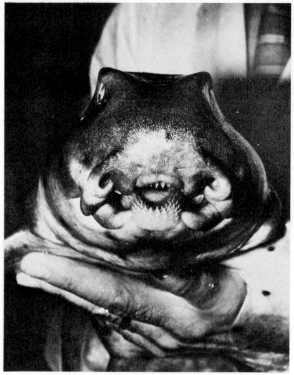

Steinhart Aquarium, San Francisco

Front view of the Pacific hornshark,
Heterodontus francisci.

Two other genera of sharks are included here, not necessarily because they are primitive, but because they do not fit anywhere else. (A 1975 article groups them with the hexanchids, the chlamydoselachids, and the heterodontids, apparently for the same reason.) I have already mentioned the six-gilled sawshark *Pliotrema warreni* as being the only other shark with six gill slits. There are two genera of sawsharks; the other is the more widely distributed *Pristiophorus*, which has the customary five gill openings. (The sawsharks are distinguished from the sawfish, *Pristis*, by the presence of gill slits on the lateral surface. The sawfish, which is a ray, has its gill openings on its ventral surface.) The sawsharks are fairly small, reaching a maximum length of about four feet, including rostrum. This is an extended "saw," studded with lateral teeth, which the shark presumably uses to slash at its prey. (Whitley tells us that in the live-born young, the rostral teeth "lie flat against the side of the snout before birth so that the saw shall not injure the mother."[253]) All the sawsharks have a pair of long barbels located on the underside of the saw, another characteristic

(*Overleaf*) *Plate 5.* **Whale shark** (*Rhincodon typus*)

that separates them from the sawfishes. The six-gill sawshark is found only in South African waters, while the other pristiophorids (there may be as many as three or as few as one species) are found in the deep waters of Japan, Australia, California, and Florida.

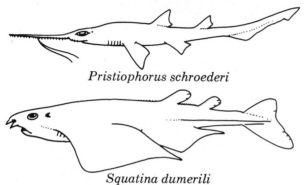

Pristiophorus schroederi

Squatina dumerili

The other family lumped here with the primitive sharks is the Squatinidae, the monk or angel sharks. These flat-bodied sharks are thought to be transitional between the sharks and the rays, since they are compressed bottom dwellers that, to the uninformed, look much like a ray or a skate. Like the sawsharks, however, the angel sharks' gill slits are partly lateral, while those of the rays or batoid fishes are always on the underside. In addition, the pectoral fins of the rays are fused to the side of the head, while those of the angel sharks (and of the sawsharks as well) are free at the anterior edges.

There are eleven nominal species of squatinids, showing anatomical variations that, while requiring close inspection, are, according to Bigelow and Schroeder, "precise enough to be accepted as specific." Each species is also sepa-

Shelton P. Applegate holds a Pacific angel shark, Squatina californica, *after tagging it on the broad pectoral fin.*

rated geographically, thus *Squatina oculata* (from the Mediterranean), *S. australis, S. japonica, S. africana,* etc. The representative of the family found along the East Coast of the United States is *S. dumeril,* named for a French ichthyologist, Auguste Dumeril.

Photographed by an automatic camera at about 3,000 feet in the eastern Mediterranean, a sixgill shark, Hexanchus griseus, *investigates the bait can. This photograph, and those on pages 127 and 164, give us a fascinating look at creatures that no man has seen in their natural habitat.*

Marine Life Research Group, Scripps Institution of Oceanography

The sand tiger, Odontaspis taurus.

SAND TIGERS

The sand tigers (odontaspids) are the embodiment of everything that is confusing, contradictory, and controversial in the study of sharks. Almost everything about them has been in dispute at one time or another, from their nature to their very name.

For a while, the odontaspids were known as the Carchariidae. (For the moment, I shall bypass the equally thorny question of the vernacular names.) In 1948, Bigelow and Schroeder were content to refer to them as Carchariidae [30] (the generic name is *Carcharias*), but more recently, the name *Odontaspis* (which means "snaketooth") has been adopted. Not that it wasn't used before—in 1838, the zoologist Louis Agassiz suggested it—but as these sharks swam silently in the world's shallow offshore waters, their names were changed and changed again. Works written in the 1960s refer to the genus as *Carcharias*, but in 1965 an opinion was published by the International Commission on Zoological Nomenclature (ICZN), re-revising the generic name to *Odontaspis* Agassiz 1838. *Odontaspis* it is then—until someone revises it again.

Now that the confusion regarding the generic name has been eliminated, we can proceed to the specifics. In the western north Atlantic, there is one well-known species, *Odontaspis taurus*. Beyond the familiar waters of the East Coast of the United States, however, nomenclatural chaos reigns. On the West Coast, for example, there is a species known as *O. ferox*, described by Kato, Springer, and Wagner in a paper devoted to the sharks of the eastern Pacific, but known from "only two specimens recorded in the eastern Pacific." The authors then go on to state that "a second species of *Odontaspis* occurs offshore, and is occasionally taken on longlines by Japanese tuna fishermen. This species, *O. kamoharai*, is small, attaining a length of about 1.0m (3.3 feet) and is easily distinguished from *O. ferox* by its large eyes . . . non-denticulated teeth and small second dorsal and anal fins." One would be inclined to conclude from this material that *ferox* is a Pacific species, occasionally confused with another Pacific species. One would be wrong, however. *O. ferox* is in fact a species best known from the Atlantic and Mediterranean, and the redoubtable J. A. F. Garrick (with Leonard Schultz) says in another paper that "the only overlap . . . is between *C. ferox* and *C. taurus*, both of which occur in the Mediterranean and the eastern Atlantic." [93] (This paper was written before the ICZN opinion was published, so *Odontaspis* is still *Carcharias*.)

The same kind of confusion exists all over the world, since this is a fairly common shark in the waters of Australia, South Africa, South America, Japan, India, and China. In these locations, the resident odontaspid almost always has a different scientific name, thus:

Argentina: *O. platensis*
Australia: *O. arenarius*
India and China: *O. tricuspidatus*
Japan: *O. owstoni*
Madeira: *O. noronhai*
South Africa: *O. taurus*

It now appears that there are at least six distinct species of odontaspids. Then along comes Garrick in 1974, with a paper titled "First Record of an Odontaspid Shark in New Zealand Waters,"[89] and which species do you suppose it is? It's *O. herbsti*. *O. herbsti*? It is enough to make the most intrepid researcher throw up his hands.

Incidentally, in America *O. taurus* is called the sand tiger—not to be confused with the tiger shark, *Galeocerdo cuvieri*—but in South Africa *O. taurus* is called the ragged-tooth. The Australian species, *O. arenarius*, is called the grey nurse—not to be confused with the nurse shark, *Ginglymostoma cirratum*.

Everyone agrees on one point, and that is that all the species, however many there are, closely resemble one another. (Garrick says they are "strikingly similar in appearance.") It is really a case of the "splitters" vs. the "lumpers." In taxonomic circles, there are those who would find minute differences to classify a new species or a subspecies (the "splitters") and those who would put similar species together (the "lumpers"). These sharks are very sharky in appearance, with a staring yellow eye, and a mouthful of the wickedest-looking teeth in sharkdom. They reach a maximum length of about ten feet in the Atlantic, but larger ones have been reported in other locations. In some places they are considered harmless, while in others they are considered very dangerous. In American waters, *Odontaspis taurus* is considered "sluggish" and inoffensive. Because *Odontaspis* is unaggressive and fairly easy to catch, it is often seen as an aquarium specimen. In its aquarium habitat it is easily photographed, and this convenience, combined with its evil, snaggle-toothed visage, has made it a popular shark for illustrative purposes. This book uses one, *O. arenarius*, for the jacket illustration; it looks more like a shark is supposed to look than any other species.

Since *Odontaspis* does well in captivity, it is always a popular specimen in aquariums throughout its range. One adult specimen in the Durban aquarium was never known to accept the cut-up fish that the other sharks ate, but "presumably kept her portly proportions by making a meal of the smaller sharks around her at night." As long as I can remember, there have been sand tigers in evidence at the New York Aquarium at Coney Island, and they were kept at the earlier New York Aquarium at Battery Park long before that. At the Taronga Park Aquarium in Sydney, a female grey nurse lived for six years in a 60- by 40-foot pool. She ate 170 to 200 pounds of fish per year, averaging about 50 pounds a month from February to April, but only 3 to 4 pounds a month from May to August, the Australian winter. In 1958, at Marine Studios, Florida, the first sand tiger was born in captivity.

Odontaspis is considered a harmless shark in American waters. Only one attack has been recorded, and this seems to have been provoked. Ranging farther afield in the literature, we discover that it has a totally different reputation in other parts of the world. For instance, J. L. B. Smith, an authority on the fishes of South Africa, describes it this way:

A cunning and quiet scavenger which creeps along the bottom towards the shore, and when stationary in even only 4 ft. of water, the largest specimen is hardly visible against a sandy bottom. If an unwary bather approaches within reach there is a savage rush, and usually another fatality. Even if the victim escapes, the terrible teeth cause fearful lacerations. Probably most shallow water attacks in South Africa are due to this Shark which also penetrates far up estuaries. The jaws of a 10 ft. specimen would easily sever a human head or thigh, those of the largest would easily cut a man in half.[212]

Most of this seems unlikely, as does Smith's assertion that *tricuspidatus*, another species he assigns to South African waters, reaches a length of twenty feet. In the first of his Investigational Reports on shark attacks in South African waters, David Davies, of the Oceanographic Research Institute at Durban, attributed an attack on a swimmer to a ragged-tooth, but he later revised the attribution to the

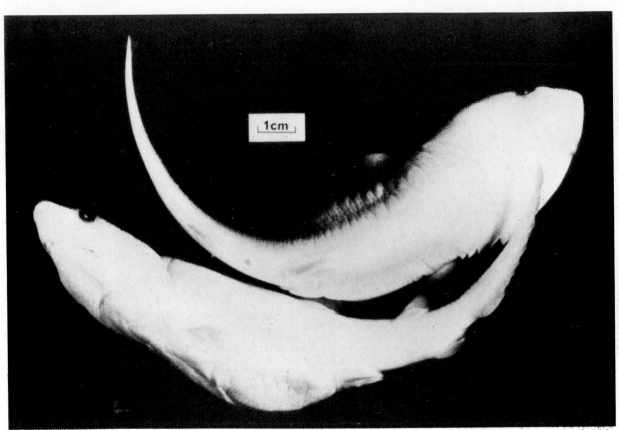

Two embryos of a South African ragged-tooth (Odontaspis taurus),
the advanced state of development before birth. The stomachs are flat, with no visible yolk sac.

bull or Zambezi shark,*Carcharhinus leucas*.[74] The South African odontaspids seem far from the "cunning" man-eaters of Smith's description. At the Durban aquarium in 1966, a program of hand-feeding two small ragged-tooths was inaugurated, in an attempt to discover what they preferred in the way of food. The sharks, named Porgy and Bess, preferred stockfish to tuna, would not eat whale meat or beef, and never bit the hand that fed them.

In Australia, the species is *Odontaspis arenarius* (grey nurse), and its reputation varies, depending on the source. Victor Coppleson in *Shark Attack* includes *Carcharias arenarius* in the category of sharks to be "regarded with suspicion, or which have had attacks attributed to them."[58] Ben Cropp, a shark-killer, whose books detail his abilities to spear, poison, stab, explode, shoot, and otherwise dispatch all sorts of sharks, spent a great deal of time in pursuit of grey nurses, because they were "placid ... and easy to spear."[62] Valerie Taylor, who, with her husband, Ron, accompanied Cropp on some of the early shark-killing and filming expeditions, wrote this to me in a letter:

> *It has been my experience that the Grey Nurse is a harmless shark, as far as attacking man is concerned. It will not attack man. This does not mean it will not defend itself. I am sick to death of skindivers saying how they were attacked by a Grey Nurse after they had speared it. In every case the poor creature was trying to escape and the diver got in the way.*

The shark seems to be a victim of its appearance; it looks as if it ought to be dangerous, and therefore people are more than willing to consider it so. (See Plate 3.)

I think it is safe to assume that a description of one species is a description of all species of *Odontaspis*. The variations noted by Bigelow and Schroeder and Garrick are minor, usually having to do with tooth morphology, and, less

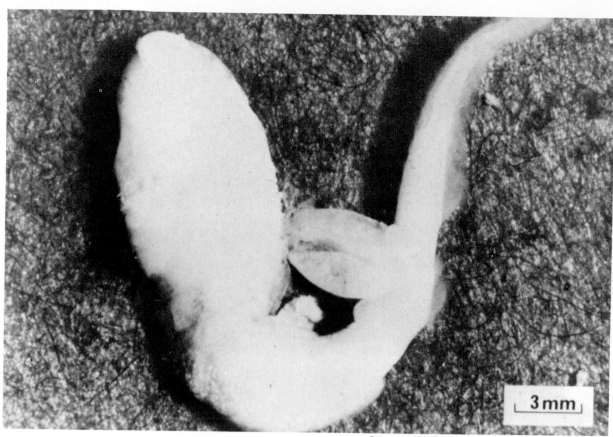

Oceanographic Research Institute, Durban, South Africa

*One of the embryos in the previous photograph (page 62), had consumed
a smaller unborn embryo. This pre-natal cannibalism is most unusual.*

frequently, with color. Since the color of sharks varies considerably within a given species, unless there are major color differences, this would not seem to be a good determinant. All odontaspids are grayish brown above, lighter below, and they often have a series of irregular dark spots on the flanks. They have a pointed, slightly upturned snout, and teeth that are always erect and decidedly "fanglike." The fins are heavy and fleshy, often tipped with black on the posterior margins. The first dorsal is situated fairly far back (it originates behind the posterior margins of the pectorals), and it is close to the second dorsal, which is almost as large as the first. The base of the tail is stocky, and its movement, at least in aquarium specimens, is slow and steady. In the wild, however, they must be capable of swift rushes, since they feed on such speedsters as bluefish and bonito. They are almost omnivorous, and examination of the stomach contents has shown that they feed on many other fishes, including slow swimmers and bottom dwellers, and occasionally even crabs. Bigelow and Schroeder maintain

that "there is no reason to suppose that this species ever attacks large prey."

Odontaspids are ovoviviparous, which is the common method of parturition in most of the galeoid sharks, but the embryos are also *oviphagous* ("egg-eating"), which is uncommon in any creature. Two embryos develop in the uterus, one in each side. Each embryo then consumes the eggs as they come down the oviduct, accounting for their large size at birth (about three feet). Sand tiger embryos can be dangerous before they are born, as can be attested to by Stewart Springer, who was bitten by an unborn specimen while he was examining a gravid female.[223]

Odontaspids have developed a peculiar habit in aquariums. They rise to the top of the tank to gulp a mouthful of air, which, retained in the stomach, acts as sort of a swim bladder. It is not known if they do this in their natural habitat, and no other species is known to do it, in the sea or in captivity.

Goblin shark, Mitsukurina owstoni.

MITSUKURINA

In the nineteenth century, the fossil remains of a Cretaceous sharklike vertebrate were found in the Syrian chalk beds and elsewhere. It was classified as *Scapanorhynchus*, meaning "shovel-snout," because of its strange overhanging beak. Unlike the rostrum of a sawfish or the bill of a marlin or a swordfish, this strange protrusion seemed unrelated to the mouth; it is not an extension of the upper lip, but more like a greatly elongated nose, or even a horn emanating from the forehead. This fossil shark had a proper set of jaws, independent of the strange protuberance. It was classified with other archaic sharks, and those who follow the doctrine of natural selection assumed that it had become extinct millions of years ago, to be replaced by other, more successful sharks.

In 1898, a specimen of an odd-looking shark was brought to the attention of Dr. David Starr Jordan, then president of Leland Stanford University, and a leading authority on the fishes of Japan. Jordan belived that the shark was new to science, and since he could not place it in any known family, he created a new one for it. He named it *Mitsukurina owstoni,* after Professor Kakichi Mitsukuri, a Japanese ichthyologist, and Alan Owston, a natural history dealer from Yokohama. Mitsukuri had been the first to examine the shark, and Owston had been instrumental in obtaining the specimen from local fishermen. Jordan's designation was not destined to last, however, since upon publication, paleontologists were quick to notice that this "new species" was, in fact, a very old species; it was the same animal as the Cretaceous fossil shark *Scapanorhynchus*, thought to have been extinct for 100 million years. By 1910, the necessary revision had been published, and the living shark and the fossil shark shared the same name, *Scapanorhynchus*.

(This sort of name-swapping and -changing is hardly unique to the sharks; zoologists in vari-

64

ous disciplines are constantly changing the names and affiliations of mammals, birds, fishes, and invertebrates.)

In the February 26, 1910, issue of *Scientific American*, Dr. L. Hussakof added *another* species to the genus *Scapanorhynchus*.[139] He had compared "several" of the known specimens at Columbia University and the American Museum of Natural History, and among them he found one that he considered to be so different from the rest that he felt it should be a different species. It had a less-protruding jaw, a very much smaller spiracle, and the eye was located further forward in relation to the mouth. If these differences could have been shown to exist in more than one specimen, they would probably have been sufficient to identify a new species. Only one of the specimens showed these variations, and in the illustrations that Hussakof used to show "the examples of the degrees of difference which are used by specialists to distinguish species of fish," the new species simply looks deformed. Since *Scapanorhynchus* looks deformed even in normal specimens, it is difficult to say that one specimen is more deformed than another. The "new species" was named *S. jordani* after Dr. Jordan, but it seems to have vanished from the literature, and we are left with the monotypical genus *Mitsukurina*. (Somewhere along the line, *Scapanorhynchus* got changed back to *Mitsukurina*, which remains the name today. The early name for the fossil shark, *Scapanorhynchus*, is also considered valid, so after all the confusion it was decided that the two were different species after all, one extinct and one living.)

The Japanese fishermen who caught the first specimen of *Mitsukurina* in the "Black Current" off Yokohama called it *tenguzame*, which means "goblin shark." This has become its common name, although very few people besides ichthyologists and shark-book authors ever get a chance to use it. The shark is extremely rare, found only in deep water off Japan, South Africa, perhaps off Portugal, and, in one strange instance, in the Indian Ocean, cable malfunction necessitated the raising of the cable, and an awl-like shark's tooth was found embedded in the wire covering. The cable had been at 750 fathoms, and the tooth belonged to a goblin shark.

The shark is thought to have been feeding on some sort of animal life growing on the cable at that depth, but very little else is known of its feeding habits. Its awl-like teeth and protrusible jaws seem to indicate that it is a fish eater, but this is only a supposition. (It probably needs protrusible jaws to feed at all, given the nature of its forehead appendage. This seems a self-handicapping situation, so perhaps the protrusion serves some other, less problematical function.) The first known *tenguzame* was a 3.5-foot male, but subsequent specimens have been as long as 14 feet.

This seems to me the strangest of all the sharks. It looks like some kind of prehistoric survivor, an experiment in shark design that doesn't seem to work. And yet, by definition, it does work. *Triceratops*, the dinosaur with three horns, is long gone, as are *Pteranodon* and hundreds of other "impossible" animals. There is little that can be said about this mysterious shark, because so little is known about it. And yet, we have the most curious, incontrovertible fact of all: *Mitsukurina* lives.

The most infamous of the mackerel sharks, the great white.

THE MACKEREL SHARKS

The mackerel sharks, also known as Isuridae or Lamnidae, are probably the most notorious of all shark families. There are only three genera, *Carcharodon*, *Lamna*, and *Isurus*, but in these genera can be found the most infamous, the most powerful, and the most graceful of all the sharks.

Two species of *Carcharodon* are discussed here —the mighty *Carcharodon carcharias*, the great white shark, and the incredible *Carcharodon megalodon*. Two species of porbeagles are discussed—the Atlantic, *Lamna nasus* and the Pacific, *Lamna ditropis*. And two species of makos are discussed—the shortfin, *Isurus oxyrinchus*, and the longfin, *Isurus paucus*. All these sharks have enough in common to classify them as a single family: they share the same fusiform, tapered shape, and the same pointed snout. They all have laterally flattened caudal keels (although the porbeagle has a secondary caudal keel as well), their tails are almost equally lobed and muscular, and they have an insignificant second dorsal fin. They all swim stiffly, flexing only the tail that is strengthened by the muscular keels, and they are capable of incredible speed. Some say the mackerel sharks are the fastest animals in the sea. They are

similar enough so that a layperson might confuse one species with another (the first mako caught in British waters was thought to be a porbeagle), but they are different enough so that anyone made aware of the differences will never confuse them again.

More is known of some of them than of others. On the basis of some limited information on embryo porbeagles and makos, we have attempted to generalize about the family, but it does not necessarily work. We need more than mere suggestions to empirically determine the breeding cycle of the white shark. More than one species has proven exceptional within the generic rule of its own kind. Two of the genera, *Lamna* and *Isurus*, have sharply pointed, bladelike teeth, with smooth cutting edges. *Isurus* has two recurved, smaller teeth in the middle of each jaw, while *Lamna* does not. The teeth of the porbeagle are cusped at the base; those of the mako are not. But the teeth of the white shark are different from those of any other member of its family, different from those of any other shark. If the body form were not so similar, surely the unique formation of the teeth would be sufficient to set *Carcharodon carcharias* in a family of its own. This might be logical for a species that grows more than twice as big as its relatives and that cannot be understood as a member of a living genus; it is a relic of the past, a somewhat smaller version of the extinct *Carcharodon megalodon*, the greatest predator that ever lived.

The makos and the porbeagles are known to be "warmblooded." Heat from the blood is retained within the body, rather than being lost through the gills, as it is in most other sharks and bony fishes. This enables makos and porbeagles to use their muscular power to best advantage. Francis G. Carey and John M. Teal of the Woods Hole Oceanographic Institution studied this phenomenon in the mako and the porbeagle. They wrote:

> *We are impressed with the similarities between tuna and the lamnids and with the number of features which can be related to the requirements of high-speed swimming. Both groups of fish have heavy, streamlined bodies, shapes which give room for a large bulk of muscle, yet offer low drag. Their caudal fins are thin, hard and of lunate shape and they beat with short rapid strokes, making an effective high-speed propulsion system.[42]*

However, since the only sharks that were examined were makos and porbeagles, Carey and Teal also wrote, "We expect that the third member of this family, *Carcharodon*, will also be found to be warm-blooded when we have an opportunity to measure its temperature."

A lot is expected of the white shark, but it has shown a strong tendency toward nonconformity. It is not easily weighed or measured, and it has never been examined in a gravid condition. Not much more is known of its relatives. They are certainly caught more frequently—Long Island has its mako tournaments, and the porbeagle is a prized game fish in British waters. And a few embryos of the mako and the porbeagle have been examined. Is it not a measure of the elusiveness of these sharks that it was not until *1966* that the second species of mako was discovered? The white shark is considered to be so rare that a documentary film was made about the search for it, and then a book was written about the making of the film. Stewart Springer wrote, "In the Florida shark fishery, over a period of 10 years, only 27 white sharks in 100,000 large sharks of all species were recorded."[218]

Of all the distinguishing characteristics of the isurids, perhaps none is more noteworthy than the eye. In all the species, it is deep black and expressionless, malicious in its simplicity and wiser than the staring eye of the other large sharks. We will probably never know for certain, since not one of the isurids has ever been kept alive in captivity, but they have about them a look of complacent, silent intelligence. Perhaps they know that we will never know them.

PORBEAGLE

Gavin Maxwell, after a day at sea fishing for basking sharks, put into the Scottish port of Lochmaddy. After cleaning up, he went to the local hotel. There, a "conventionally tweeded and white-moustached figure," obviously a fisherman, asked him if he had had any luck. Maxwell replied that he'd got "four, two large and two small." The white-mustachioed gent assumed that Maxwell was talking about sea trout, and asked what the biggest weighed. With a straight face Maxwell replied, "He's not weighed yet, but I think he'd be about six thousand pounds."[165]

This proves, I think, that in fishing, as in many other areas, everything is relative. In English waters, the porbeagle is considered the premier shark to catch, but in other parts of the world it is considered a nuisance, or at best a poor substitute for its more glamorous relative, the mako. In *The Rubby-Dubby Trail: Shark Fishing in British Waters*, Trevor Housby sings the praises of the otherwise lowly porbeagle, calling them "great fish" and "monsters" and listing them first on his list of sharks in British waters.[138] One man's monster is another man's minnow, however. The biggest porbeagle caught on rod and reel was 8 feet 4 inches long, weighed 366 pounds, and was caught off Montauk, Long Island.

If a shark can be said to have problems, then the porbeagle has them. It has a funny name, which cannot really be said to be the porbeagle's problem, and it was nearly eradicated in an area of the North Atlantic—which certainly *is* the porbeagle's problem. First the name: The *Oxford English Dictionary* (OED), our primary source of information on the origin of words, tells us that the derivation of the word porbeagle is unknown, but that it comes from a Cornish dialect and made its first recorded appearance in Borlase's *History of Cornwall* in 1758. This apparent lack of information on the origins of the

Porbeagle, Lamna nasus. *Note the white spot at the base of the dorsal fin and the secondary caudal keel.*

word has not stifled speculation and guess-work, and numerous theories have been advanced. Frank Mundus, in *Sportfishing for Sharks*, says, "This shark's unusual name has been traced . . . back to two Old French-language words meaning 'hog nose.' "[175] (As we shall see, this is a good guess for the meaning of the scientific name, *Lamna nasus*, but it has nothing whatever to do with porbeagle.) Norman and Fraser, in *Giant Fishes, Whales and Dolphins*, have no trouble with either the scientific or the vernacular names:

> *The scientific name* Lamna *is derived from a Greek word for a horrible monster of man-eating tendencies, a creature used by the ancient Greeks to terrify naughty children. The term "Porbeagle" is simply a combination of porpoise and beagle, and refers to the porpoise-like appearance and active, predaceous habits.*[184]

Would that it were that easy. Porbeagles do not look at all like porpoises, and the beagle is one of the last dogs you would choose if you wanted to suggest "predaceous habits." (Incidentally, the OED gives this as the origin of the word "porpoise": *porcus pisces* = hog-fish or fish-hog. The origin of the word "beagle" seems to be lost forever.) In yet another work, Lineaweaver and Backus quote the above definition by Norman and Fraser, but also give another definition. They say that *Lamna* means "a large shark like a large boar."

It is all terribly confusing, since the porbeagle has other common names in addition to its controversial one, including mackerel shark, bonito shark, and salmon shark, derived from its preying upon, rather than its resemblance to, these fishes. The value of Linnean binomial nomenclature is obvious in a situation like this; in one location it's a porbeagle, in another it's a salmon shark, and off the coast of Maine, it's a bluedog. If it's a shark with a conical snout, sharp, narrow teeth, a symmetrical tail, and a double keel at the base of the tail, it's *Lamna nasus*. That is, if it's found in the Atlantic. If it's found in the Pacific, it is *Lamna ditropis*, the Pacific porbeagle. *Ditropis*, by the way, means "double keel," and of course *nasus* means nose, both of which refer to the salient characteristics of the species. This double keel is unique to the genus *Lamna*. The upper, wide keel is similar to that of the other mackerel sharks, but the second and smaller keel, located on the lower lobe of the tail fin itself, occurs only in the porbeagles. Some bony fishes have keels, including some of the mackerel-like fishes (the scombroids) and the billfishes, and these fishes are characterized by a symmetrical tail, and a graceful, stream-lined shape which gives them great speed in the water. The sharks that feed on these swift swimmers are similarly designed, and they are known as the Isuridae, a name that means "equal tails." Members of this family are the white, the makos, and the porbeagles. (It is difficult to write about the mackerel sharks without some degree of repetition; much of what we know about one species has come from observations of the other species. The discussion of the breeding habits of the mako, see p. 76, incorporates material on the porbeagle —in fact, it is *derived* from the porbeagle data— and the peculiar warmbloodedness that contributes so significantly to muscular efficiency also appears in the section on the mako, and is mentioned again in connection with the great white.) Other characteristics that exemplify the mackerel sharks are a very small second dorsal fin and a torpedo shape that is similar to the scombroids in profile, but not so laterally compressed.

The other members of the family have usually overshadowed the porbeagle and therefore deprived it of its just recognition. The porbeagle's big and redoubtable relative, *Carcharodon carcharias*, the white shark, is the most notorious of all sharks—as much as twenty feet of carnivorous terror, weighing a ton or more, and with a nasty reputation for attacking people. Closer in size and temperament to the porbeagle is the mako, which can reach a maximum length of twelve feet, and is recognized as the most spectacular jumper in the sea, and is therefore a much sought-after game fish.

There is no problem in differentiating the porbeagle and the great white—the white is usually lighter in color (but not white), while the porbeagle is usually a dark bluish or brownish gray above, fading to white below. It is often makos that are mistaken for porbeagles, but the mako is a more slender fish, and it is a rich blue color above. The porbeagle also has a white patch at the posterior base of the dorsal fin (see Plate 8). On that subject, Frank Mundus says:

> *A season or so ago a skiff passed the* Cricket II *offshore towing a shark by the tail. We hailed her pilot and asked him what he had. "A mako," he called, slowing down. From that distance it could have been, for all we knew. But then he lifted the fish part way out of the water, and we saw the telltale patch of white on the rear edge of the first dorsal fin at its base, a sure sign in fast identification of this species. We didn't correct the guy then, and moved on.*[175]

Mundus relates how the fisherman later continued to insist that he had caught a mako, and how he (Mundus) would not bet with him, because "it would have been like taking candy from a baby." It is always refreshing to read of the code of honor that exists among fishermen.

The teeth of the mackerel sharks are interesting for reasons other than their use as a genus determinant. Most sharks have teeth that differ in the upper and lower jaws. This differentiation is based on the separate functions that the jaws perform. The lower teeth are often narrower and more pointed, and they are used to pierce and hold the prey, while the broader serrated upper teeth are protruded, and the head is twisted, thus removing a bite of flesh. In other words, the sawlike edges of the upper teeth function as a knife, while the lower teeth serve to hold the prey, much in the manner of a person carving a roast with a knife and fork. (This arrangement presupposes a prey animal too large to be engulfed in one gulp.) In the jaws of the mako and the porbeagle, both the upper and lower teeth are narrow and smooth-edged, which would indicate that both sets are used for grasping and that the prey is swallowed whole. This is borne out by many studies of the stomach contents of mackerel sharks, which show many fish more or less undamaged, except for the stablike puncture wounds made by the teeth. Of course, there are bound to be exceptions, and all these sharks can and will take a bite when necessary. White sharks have been found with half a seal or half a porpoise in their stomachs, and others have been examined with a whole seal inside. In any case, the white shark has serrated teeth in both the upper and lower jaws, and is often seen feeding on the carcasses of dead whales, an activity that would require biting the prey rather than swallowing it whole. The teeth of the porbeagle are pointed and narrow, and they differ from those of the mako by the presence of small cusps on either side of each tooth.

The fishery alluded to earlier that threatened the North Atlantic population of the porbeagle was conducted by the Norwegians. It was a longline operation, producing at its height in the 1960s some 9 million pounds of porbeagle per year. This catch was shipped almost entirely to Italy, where the shark meat (known as *smerglio*) was extremely popular. Soon the catch figures began to diminish, demonstrating that a shark population could be "fished out" in a given area where the species is nonmigratory. The depletion of the "resource" was also a function of the low fecundity rate of the porbeagle. An animal that produces only two to four young per year cannot suffer vast depredations on the adult population without drastic effects. (This has always been the problem with commercial fishing for large sharks; eventually the fishermen have to range so far afield to maintain the catch quotas that the cost of fishing begins to outweigh the profits.) When the North Atlantic fishery was no longer profitable, it was suspended.

Porbeagles are pan-oceanic, having been reported in the North Atlantic, the North Sea, off England, Scotland, Iceland, Newfoundland, New England, and from corresponding latitudes in the southern hemisphere. (There is the possibility that there are two more species of *Lamna*—*L. phillipi* and *L. whitleyi*—both from southern oceans, but we will leave this argument to the taxonomists, since the situation is confusing enough already.) All the porbeagles can be characterized as temperate or even cold-water species. This is one of the reasons that there have been no documented attacks on swimmers; even though the porbeagle is certainly capable, there are just not very many people in the waters where the porbeagle lives. Housby gives two instances of possible porbeagle attacks in British waters, both in 1971,

and both indefinite as to the species. The Shark Attack File has no recorded porbeagle attacks.

Given its illustrious relatives, it is no wonder that the porbeagle has been given short shrift. The shark with the funny name has not been incriminated in unprovoked attacks on humans, and it does not perform elaborate high jinks when it is hooked. It may appear to be the poor relation of the more flamboyant mackerel sharks, but it is a full member of the family, a swift and capable hunter. The porbeagle is not as deadly as the white or as graceful as the mako, but it is among the fastest swimmers in the sea, and therefore it ranks at the very peak of the food chain. It is the "top predator" in its own territory.

MAKO

The mako is the quintessential shark. It is probably the most graceful of all sharks, the most beautifully proportioned, the fastest, the most strikingly colored, the most spectacular game fish, and one of the meanest-looking animals on earth.

Like its close relatives, the great white and the porbeagle, the mako has a homocercal (equal-lobed) tail, and a horizontally flattened keel at the tail's base. They all are gracefully streamlined, with a conical snout, dark eyes, small second dorsal fins, and the aforementioned tail shape. The dark eyes give them a look of intense intelligence that they may not possess, as well as the bold look of another group of superbly designed predators, the falcons.

The keels of the mackerel sharks are fascinating and mysterious structures. They show a compression in the dorso-ventral plane of the entire base of the tail, also called the caudal peduncle. It is assumed that this modification is related

to speed and power in swimming, since it significantly adds to the musculature of the tail structure, the shark's means of propulsion. Among the sharks, the mackerels show the most pronounced keels, but other species, not normally associated with fast movement, also have this modification. The whale shark and the basking shark, two plankton feeders that are characterized by slow and ponderous movements, have keels on their tail structure, and the tiger shark, not known for speed, also shows this characteristic. Many of the scombroid fishes (tuna, mackerel), and the billfishes (marlin, sailfish), have one or more small keels, but the broadbill swordfish is the only teleost that shows a development that is in any way similar to that of the mackerel sharks. In my paintings of the mako I have tried to show this unique structure by "twisting" the shark, rather than painting it in profile. In the painting of the longfin mako (see Plate 2), one can also see the keel of the broadbill, depicted as the prey of the shark.

Plate 6. **Mako shark** (*Isurus oxyrinchus*)
(*Overleaf*) *Plate 7.* **Great white shark** (*Carcharodon carcharias*)

Variation on the theme of the flying mako (see Plate 6, p. 71). This one is hooked.

Another characteristic that separates the isurids from all other elasmobranchs is their ability to conserve body heat and maintain a body temperature that is considerably higher than the ambient water. It has long been known that certain scombroid fishes, especially tuna, have this ability, but in 1968 two Woods Hole biologists, Carey and Teal, were the first to mention this phenomenon in sharks.[42] Only makos and porbeagles were tested, but white sharks, the third member of the family, were examined, and showed the same structural modifications, so it is safe to assume that they share this ability. According to Carey and Teal, heat is conserved by a "set of countercurrent heat exchangers located in the circulation between the gills and the tissues. The heat exchangers form a thermal barrier which permits the flow of blood but blocks the flow of heat." The authors conclude that there is a threefold increase in the muscle power for every ten degrees Centigrade rise in body temperature. A mako that can jump fifteen to twenty feet in the air requires a starting velocity of 22 miles per hour. I have recently read, in a popular book on sharks, that makos can catch swordfish "capable of speeds up to 60 miles an hour," but this seems a bit excessive for both the shark and the swordfish.

Since no female white shark has ever been taken in a gravid state, we can only assume that the

Plate 8. **Porbeagle** (*Lamna nasus*)

Mako sharks.

reproduction and parturition of the white is similar to that of the mako and the porbeagle. A pregnant mako has been examined, and it was found to contain ten embryos, five male and five female, ranging in size from 25 inches to 27.5 inches. It can be assumed that these embryos were close to term, since there have been free-swimming makos caught that were 31.5 inches long. According to Bigelow and Schroeder, porbeagles are ovoviviparous (eggs hatch in the female, and are not otherwise attached), and they are nourished *in utero* by "swallowing unfertilized eggs which lie close to it in the uterus, the result being that the stomach becomes enormously swollen by the masses of yolk so swallowed, forming a so-called 'yolk stomach.' " We can suppose that the same applies to makos.

Almost all sharks are dark above and lighter below, but few show the dramatic contrast between the rich ultramarine dorsal surface and snowy underbelly of the mako, often separated by a band of silver. A profile portrait of the mako shows this shark to best advantage, emphasizing the conical snout which is so uniquely pointed. This characteristic has resulted in one of its vernacular names, sharp-nose mackerel shark. Other common names include blue pointer, mackerel shark, and bonito shark. Makos have particularly long teeth, which are not serrated like those of their infamous cousin, the great white, nor are they cusped like those of their relative, the porbeagle. The teeth of a big mako are huge, resembling curved knives set into the jaw. They are also flattened on the forward surface, which increases this knifelike impression. Smaller specimens have more rounded teeth, so it takes a big mako to display the full and frightening implications of these teeth. Ernest Hemingway had obviously seen big makos, and he describes one in *The Old Man and the Sea:*

He was a very big Mako shark built to swim as fast as the fastest fish in the sea and everything was beautiful about him except his jaws. His back was as blue as a sword fish's and his belly was silver and his hide was smooth and handsome. He was built as a sword fish except for his huge jaws which were shut tight now as he swam fast, just under the water with his high dorsal fin knifing through the water without wavering. Inside the closed double lip of his jaws all of his eight rows of teeth were slanted inwards. They were not the ordinary pyramid-shaped teeth of most sharks. They were shaped like a man's fingers when they are crisped like claws. They were nearly as long as the fingers of the old man and they had razor-sharp cutting edges on both sides. This was a fish built to feed on all the fish in the sea, that were so fast and strong and well armed that they had no other enemy.[131]

(In his office at the Mote Marine Laboratory in Sarasota, Florida, Perry Gilbert has the enormous jaws of a 1,000-pound mako. It was caught at Cojimar, Hemingway's old fishing village in Cuba.)

The teeth of most sharks are laid back when not in use, and the opening of the mouth brings them into an upright position. This occurs to a limited extent with the mako, but its lower teeth are always erect and serve to give this shark, in life as well as in death, a snaggle-toothed and fearful visage. It is the stuff of which nightmares are made. For the big game fisherman, mako fishing is the stuff of which dreams are made. Capable of spectacular gymnastics and at the same time one of the few fish whose actions can be decidedly aggressive, the mako brings an added dimension to game fishing. Makos charge boats, sometimes jump right into them, and generally provide a level of excitement beyond that of the ordinary game fish experience. In mako fishing, you might lose not only your fish, you might lose your rod or even your arm. It is perhaps the only type of big game fishing where there is a real element of personal danger.

Writing a firsthand account of mako fishing off Nantucket, Jerome E. Kelley described his wild experience:

A black shape came boiling out of the water directly at me. Whack! the mako hit where it hurt—across the ribs and stomach. The Egg Harbor's cockpit was a

good 13 feet long and I was thrown the length of it.

I lay against the cabin door trying to get my breath back. Not eight inches from my left foot was the gasping mouth of the shark, filled with rows of razor sharp teeth. His malevolent eyes, I thought, were viewing me rather intently. Helplessness was hardly the word for my predicament. I could see, I could hear, I could think, but I couldn't move.

Suddenly the shark came to life and so did I. For the next two or three minutes it was a deadly game of ring-around-the-rosie in the cramped cockpit. The outcome of the game was finally decided by five or six blows from a baseball bat. The score: three fractured ribs for me; a badly lacerated elbow for Bill; one very dead 286-pound mako shark.[147]

Frank Mundus, fishing out of Brielle, New Jersey, before he moved to Montauk, tells of an even more frightening episode in his *Sportfishing for Sharks:*

As the mako zoomed through the air on a parabolic trajectory he came down squarely across one of the two anglers' rods. Down the rod slid the shark's bulk, shearing off rod guides as it went. The startled fisherman, seeing a few hundred pounds of mako about to be deposited in his lap, had the presence of mind to try to get the hell out of there. He jumped out of the fishing chair, going over backward, and landed on his head on deck, almost breaking his neck. The mako slid into the cockpit and promptly took over. The first thing he did was smash a rod butt.

Pandemonium broke loose. The shark went berserk. Bouncing and twisting violently, he slammed his way from gunnel to gunnel. He smashed fishing chairs; he sent chum cans flying to spew their contents all over the place; and with a passing swipe he tore a rod holder off a coaming. All hands beat a hasty retreat to the cabin and barricaded themselves behind the companionway door. Seconds later the mako crashed against the door, knocking its knob out by the roots.[175]

It is difficult at best to judge heights from the water, but there seems to be a general consensus that a fighting mako can jump at least twenty feet out of the water. Less conservative estimates give him credit for thirty-foot leaps. Zane Grey, who revered and respected the mako as much as any other fish, once calculated that one mako jumped "fifteen feet above the boat."

If it can be said that one man is responsible for the popularity of a single game fish, then it must be said of Zane Grey and the mako. In the annals of popular literature, Grey was well known for his novels of the American West. He wrote fifty-four novels (over fifteen million copies were sold), and many of them are still in print as paperbacks.

For the May–June 1934 issue of *Natural History* magazine, Grey wrote an article titled "The Great Mako." [110] In a prefatory note, Dr. E. W. Gudger of the American Museum of Natural History said: "It is the first account ever published . . . of a shark that leaps when it is hooked." The photographs accompanying the article "illustrate for the first time this leaping fighter of the South Seas." Anyone who has ever tried to anticipate the spot at which a hooked fish will emerge from the water will understand the difficulties involved and realize that for 1934, these photographs are spectacular. (In fact, they are pretty good even for today—I have not seen many better photographs of leaping makos.)

The mako's tendency to leap when excited is demonstrated remarkably by an incident that took place in Puerto Rico in 1956. A fisherman cleaning fish on the beach noticed two sharks patrolling within twenty or thirty feet of shore. When one of the sharks came close enough, a man named Robert Strong waded into the shallow water and fired a speargun at it. The shark swam for deeper water, shook out the spear and then turned and headed back toward shore, where it launched itself out of the water and landed on the sand in front of Strong. The shark managed to return to the water on a receding wave, so capture or even definite identification was impossible, but from Strong's description, and from the high-flying antics of the shark, there is every reason to believe it was a mako.

Zane Grey did his mako fishing in New Zealand waters, particularly off North Island. Prior to his much-publicized exploits, sharks had not been considered game fish at all. Then, for many years the mako was the only shark on the International Game Fish Association's (IGFA)

list, but now six more species are included: the blue, porbeagle, hammerhead, thresher, tiger, and white.

Makos are worldwide in distribution, favoring tropical and temperate waters. They do not school, and they are never seen in very large numbers. One area in which they seem to be fairly plentiful is the Atlantic Ocean just south of Long Island. For more than ten years, the Bayshore Tuna Club has held a mako tournament here, and the catch, while never as plentiful as the blue sharks or the sandbars, has not been insignificant. For example, in 1975, there were 50 makos caught, 120 blues, and 110 sandbars. Makos are also caught off the coasts of England, as related by Trevor Housby in his 1972 *The Rubby-Dubby Trail: Shark Fishing in British Waters*. ("Rubby-dubby" is the equivalent of our chum, only it is not ladled overboard, but rather hung in the water in a cheesecloth bag to disperse the oil slick.) Housby discusses only four species of sharks: the porbeagle, the blue, the thresher, and the mako. Makos in British waters seem to attain a respectable size; the current record is a 500-pound fish caught by a Mrs. Yallop off Looe in Cornwall, and Housby tells of even larger fish that were hooked but got away before they could be brought to gaff. [138]

The mako is always included in lists of potentially dangerous sharks, even though the number of authenticated reports of unprovoked attacks seems to be quite low. In the Shark Attack File, a total of eighteen attacks are attributed to makos, but as David Baldridge says, "More often than not, identifications were made on the weakest of evidence, and were . . . no more than snap judgements made by casual observers." [17] In the category of "attacks on boats," the mako is the undisputed leader, according to J. A. F. Garrick and Leonard P. Schultz in "Potentially Dangerous Sharks," published in *Sharks and Survival*. [93] As of this writing, Dr. John Randall of the Bishop Museum in Hawaii is preparing a paper on a mako attack in the Red Sea. Randall is an acknowledged authority on sharks and their identification, so there would seem to be no question about the species in this instance. Randall said (in a letter to me) that he is writing the paper "with a Dr. Levy, the physician who treated the patient, who barely survived."

Like the porbeagle, the mako tends to inhabit deeper waters than the great white. Another way of saying this is that there have been fewer recorded instances of makos in the vicinity of swimmers. (White sharks feed on seals and sea lions as well as fish, and these marine mammals are often found close to shore. Makos and porbeagles are piscivorous, and they habituate the areas where their prey is found.) Makos seem to have a particular affinity for the flesh of billfishes, especially the swordfish. There are numerous records of makos caught with a broken sword of a marlin or a swordfish in their flesh, and one case where an entire swordfish weighing 120 pounds was found in the stomach of a 730-pound mako.

The world's record makos come from New Zealand waters, although there seem to be good-sized specimens throughout their range. (The 1,000-pound Cuban fish whose impressive jaws are now in Perry Gilbert's office was taken by commercial fishermen.) The word "mako" is of Maori origin, although its meaning is unclear. It is probably the Maori name for that particular shark, and not, as has been suggested, a corruption of the English word "mackerel." During his three seasons in New Zealand, Zane Grey caught "in the neighborhood of seventy makos."[110] He kept careful records, and his largest was 580 pounds, of which he says, "The last began to get into a class with big mako." The all-tackle mako record, listed in the IGFA Record Book, is a 1,061-pound fish caught off Mayor Island, New Zealand.[140] Records such as this indicate only fish brought to gaff under strict IGFA regulations; there are a lot of bigger fish that are not successfully boated. As Zane Grey put it, "The mako is a fish that often gets away." Reliable estimates of the largest makos run to a weight of 1,300-plus pounds, and a length of over 13 feet. (The 1,061-pound shark was 12 feet 2 inches long.)

Much has been written about the gigantic ancestor of the white shark, the fifty-foot *Carcharodon megalodon*, with the six-inch teeth. The mako also has some extinct relatives, and these, while smaller and less notorious than *megalodon*, are equally impressive. Very little work has been done on these fossil isurids, but their existence is verified by some spectacular teeth in my collection. Identified variously as belonging to *Isurus hastelis*, *I. mantelli*, *I. retroflexa*, *I. willsoni*, and *I. desorii* (some of which are surely synonyms), these are triangular teeth, some of which are larger than the largest known teeth of the white shark. In contrast to the serrated teeth of *Carcharodon carcharias*, these teeth are absolutely smooth on the edges, and even though I am reluctant to use the overworked term in reference to shark's teeth, these are literally "razor-sharp." These fossil teeth, all of which came from Miocene deposits in North Carolina, suggest makos in the twenty-foot class; a conservative estimate suggests a weight of 4,000 pounds for a fish this size.

For a fish that seems fairly easy to identify, the mako has had a long history of misidentification, reclassification, and name-changing. (I suppose it must be pointed out that it is not *that* easy to identify; the first mako caught in British waters was called a porbeagle.) At first it was thought that there were many separate species, including *Isurus oxyrinchus*, *I. glaucus*, *I. tigris*, *I. mako*, *Isuropsis dekayi*, *Lamna oxyrhynchus*, and many, many others. (Not all of these represented different species; they were often revised names for the same species.) By the 1930s, the confusion seems to have been markedly reduced, and there were two recognized species, *Isurus oxyrinchus* from the Atlantic, and *Isurus glaucus* from the Pacific. The two were segregated for many years, and in 1936 one author-fisherman, Hugh D. Wise, remarked: "Sooner or later, your guide will probably tell you that you have caught a Mako. I hope he will be right, but more likely you will have caught a Mackerel Shark or a Porbeagle. I have never seen a Mako in our Atlantic, and I do not believe there are any there."[225] Bigelow and Schroeder recognized two species in 1948, but noted that "the ranges of *glaucus* and *oxyrinchus* seem to be continuous around the Cape of Good Hope."

In 1967, J. A. F. Garrick of the University of Wellington, New Zealand, published a paper titled "Revision of Sharks of Genus *Isurus* with Description of a New Species." In this account, Garrick concludes that "the 12 nominal species of *Isurus* represent only 1 worldwide species."[90] (More on the "new species" shortly.) This taxonomic revision is based on a thorough examination of the published material, including illustrations and the specimens originally described, whenever possible. Variables in the earlier material had to do with location (where the specimen was originally caught), size and shape of the dorsal fin, number of vertebrae, and number of teeth. Some 150 years after the first publication of the name and description of *Isurus oxyrinchus*, the name was settled, and surprisingly enough, it was exactly the name that was first bestowed on the animal by Constantine Rafinesque, in 1810. The correct full name is *Isurus oxyrinchus* Rafinesque 1810.

Garrick was able to synonymize all the earlier species except one. There were records of a mako with extremely long pectoral fins that could in no way be combined with the others. This was a relatively uncommon fish, known primarily from Japanese longline fishermen in the tropical Indian and Pacific Oceans, but also found in the warmer parts of the Atlantic. It differs from *I. oxyrinchus* in that the pectoral fins are as long as the head, while in *oxyrinchus* and other species, the pectorals are not more than 70 percent of the head length. There is also a "dusky" coloration on the underside of the snout, darkening in direct proportion to the increase in size of the fish, and a difference in the teeth. The eye of the "longfin mako" is larger than that of the shortfin, suggesting a deeper-water habitat. In 1967, Garrick named this new (longfin) species *Isurus alatus* (from the Latin for "winged"), but in 1966, Cuban ichthyologist Guitart Manday also published a paper describing the species, and he had named it *I. paucus*. Since Manday's paper was published first, the name he suggested has priority.

I have seen one of the few films ever made of a free-swimming mako. It was taken by Dr. Scott Johnson off Catalina Island in California, while he was in a submersible, filming the reactions of blue sharks to certain repellent devices. (In this film, there is also the surprising sight of a California sea lion feeding among the blue sharks. Johnson told me that this often happens.) Blue sharks are slim, sinuous swimmers, turning and twisting by using their long, curved pectoral fins. By contrast, the mako is a stiff-bodied swimmer, propelling itself through the water with short strokes of its thick, powerful tail. In contrast to the white-rimmed, staring eye of the blue shark, the black eye of the mako looks deep, serious, and menacing. When seeing a mako in its own element, one has the overall impression of blue muscular efficiency.

The author dissecting a 4-foot-long white shark at Sakonnet, Rhode Island.

GREAT WHITE SHARK

I have seen only two great white sharks; neither was great, and neither was white. The first was caught during a mako tournament off Bayshore, Long Island, and was brought in dead. The second was caught accidentally in the trap nets of Rhode Island fishermen, and it was also dead when I saw it. Both sharks were about four feet long, were a dark brownish gray above and white below, and had the signs of a faint umbilical scar on the chest between the pectoral fins, indicating that they were not more than a few months old. One was a male and one was a female.

The white shark, *Carcharodon carcharias*, even at the age of a few months, is larger than many other species full-grown. It is a completely functional predator, a perfect small-scale version of the massive creature it will become. When I received a telephone call from the local fishermen in Rhode Island (I had left a note asking to be notified if any sharks were brought in), I asked what kind it was, and I was told it was "just a gray shark." I almost said that I was not interested in "just a gray shark"

(which I thought would be a blue or a sandbar), but I realized that since they had taken the trouble to call, I ought to pay them the courtesy of responding. When I arrived at the docks, I asked where the "man-eater" was, knowing that it was no such thing. The fishermen indicated that it was behind a pile of boxes on the pier, and when I saw it, I gave an involuntary start—it *was* a man-eater, a great white shark. Four feet two inches long, it weighed 51 pounds. When I explained that this was indeed a white shark, I was told that I had probably seen *Jaws* too recently; white sharks were huge monsters; there were no white sharks in Rhode Island; and how did I know, anyway? I pointed out the characteristics that identified this as a white and no other species: The snout was conical and not flattened. The teeth were triangular, serrated, and proportionally large. (In this four-foot specimen, the largest tooth measured just under three-quarters of an inch in length; in the largest specimens, the teeth are over two inches long.) The eye was black, with no visible pupil; the fish itself was a dark gray-brown, and its undersides were white. On the lower surface, the pectoral fins were tipped with black, and at the axil (corresponding to the human armpit), there was an oval black spot. At the base of the tail were the flattened keels that are characteristic of the family, and the upper and lower lobes of the tail were almost equal in size. (The other members of the family are the mako and the porbeagle, but their teeth are different, their pectorals are not black-tipped, and they have no axillar spot.) Once you have seen a great white, you will never mistake it for any other shark. (See Plate 7.)

Perhaps it is because of the aura of fear and mystery that surrounds this, the most formidable and infamous of all the sharks, that there is a shock of recognition when you actually see one. It is an event that permanently imprints itself on your mind: this is it; this is the man-eater. Even beyond the identification of the characteristics or the sense of seeing this fabled killer, there is something else, something that hits you even when you are looking at a dead juvenile lying on a fish dock. Even in death, the white shark exudes strength and power, though its jaw is slack, its teeth protruding, and its eyes glazed. It looks heavy, solid, and immensely strong, and its proportions are perfect. It does not look like a baby shark—it does not look like a baby anything. But this one was a baby, and it might have grown to nineteen feet long and weighed a ton and a half.

There is a curious record book kept on white sharks; in addition to a book on maximum-size fish, there is also a book on the smallest ones. This is done because our information on white sharks is so limited that we have no idea how big they are when they are born, and therefore the smallest ones caught are assumed to be close to the size at birth. No gravid female has ever been taken, and, with one curious exception, there is no information at all on the method of parturition, the number born at any time, the locations where they are born, or the size of the female at sexual maturity. The one exception is mentioned in a 1938 publication by Norman and Fraser and concerns a female taken off Alexandria in the Mediterranean. "When it was cut open, 9 young were discovered inside, each 2 feet long and weighing 108 lb."[184] This reference is included in Bigelow and Schroeder, but with the disclaimer, "The stated weights of these embryos . . . were obviously in error." This is the only reference to great whites *in utero*, and since it is so far off the mark, it probably ought

to be considered a typographical error or a misidentification of the species. The present record for the smallest great white is 36 pounds at 51 inches. This specimen, caught in 1974 off Bayshore, is in the freezer of the National Marine Fisheries Service Laboratory (NMFS) at Narragansett, Rhode Island. It is guarded by Jack Casey (see "Jack Casey: The Shark Tagger"), a fisheries biologist who specializes in shark research, concentrating on population dynamics and migration. Just as maximum records are regularly exceeded, minimum sizes are constantly being reduced. In 1948, Bigelow and Schroeder gave the size of the smallest living specimen as "about five feet long."

The *largest* great white shark is another problem altogether, much more dramatic of course, but here, given the nature of the problem, the records are full of misinformation, typographical errors, and wild exaggerations. When a fish weighs over a ton, as large white sharks do, it is a difficult proposition to weigh it at all, let alone to weigh it accurately. Very few docks are equipped with the scales necessary to perform this task, and it is understandably difficult to transport the fish to a location where there is a scale equal to the job. We therefore find that the weight of many of the larger whites has been guessed or estimated using some length-weight formula that is often not revealed. For example, the shark that Frank Mundus harpooned off Montauk, Long Island in 1964 (which, incidentally, was one of the "real" elements that Peter Benchley incorporated into his novel *Jaws*), was reported to have weighed 4,500 pounds. The sign that accompanies the mounted head of this specimen in Salivar's Dock, a restaurant in Montauk, gives this as the unequivocal weight. It seems curious that it is such a round number, and we discover from Mundus's own book, *Sportfishing for Sharks*, that the fish was never weighed at all. It was only measured, and then the "tonnage" was estimated, "based on known length-girth-weight relationships."[175] I have seen this head, and there is no question that it was an enormous fish—it was seventeen feet long and thirteen feet in girth. The figure of 4,500 pounds, however, has entered the literature without the fish ever having been weighed.

The business end of a 16½-foot-long white shark caught off Southern California in 1975.
Charlie Van Valkenburgh, Sea World

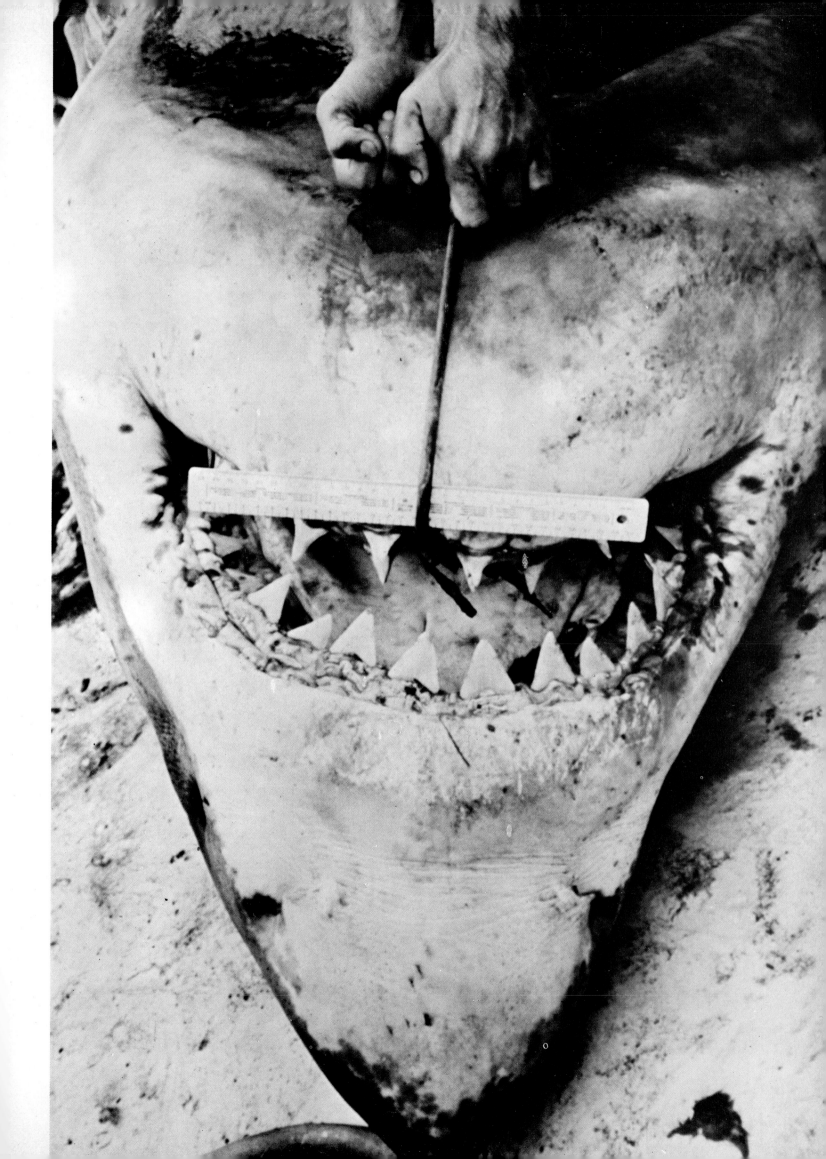

(RE)

Great white shark and sea lion in California kelp.

(The female shark that was supposed to have contained those 108-pound embryos was reported to be 14 feet long and to weigh 2.5 tons. Even if the figures were remotely possible, which they are not, it is difficult to imagine that the town of Agamy, where the fish was caught, had the facilities to weigh anything in the 5,000-pound range.)

Other large specimens have been subjected to this same sort of guesswork. Jack Casey had to guess at the weight of his 14.5-foot white—again, there was no scale that was adequate. (He now maintains that he should have cut it up into 50-pound chunks, added a percentage for the blood and other fluids lost in the butchering process, and thus produced a fairly accurate weight. He did not do this, and therefore his guess of 1,500 pounds—probably on the conservative side—is the only weight we have.)

It is Casey who has been programming the weights and sizes of white sharks. Using a sophisticated computer program, he has plotted the curve with maximum deviation of *Carcharodon carcharias.* He has incorporated a considerable amount of data; it includes the records of the Game Fishing Association of Australia, the records of the International Game Fish Association, his own NMFS data assembled from communication and correspondence with fishermen and scientists around the world. Since the tail of a shark can be pulled out of position to increase the animal's length, Casey uses the "fork length," the measurement from the tip of the snout to the fork of the tail. Where this has not been done, the other measurements are converted from the original number by a factor of approximately 7 percent. From the data fed into it, the computer produces the "line of best fit," a curve that begins to rise sharply with the larger fish. The weight increases roughly by a cube of the length, so for sharks in the 2,000+ class, the line rises almost vertically.

The largest recorded sharks include Mundus's 1964 specimen, a 15-foot, 3,031-pound female caught in California in 1958, a 2,875-pound fish harpooned off Peru, and two specimens, 3,150 and 3,440 pounds, harpooned during the summer of 1975 off the California coast. All of the largest specimens were females; females are usually larger than males. (Both of the 1975 California specimens had substantial prey animals in them when they were examined; the larger one had the "posterior quarter of a northern elephant seal present.") The largest fish ever caught on rod and reel was a white shark weighing 2,664 pounds. When fishing for white sharks, they are chummed alongside the boat with whale oil, fish, and blood. They are also fed hunks of horsemeat or sheep, in an attempt to get them to take the hook. There is a question as to whether the record fish are weighed with or without the chum, or if a shark with a 400-pound seal in it should have that added to its total weight.

The two best-known (or at least the most publicized) giant sharks are not included above. The first is a shark whose jaws reside in the British Museum (of Natural History). The tag on these jaws reads "36.5 feet. Port Fairy, Australia," and the shark was caught prior to 1870, the year in which the information was first published in Günther's *Catalog of Fishes in the British Museum*.[122] For years, this record stood unchallenged, and it was the basis for much speculation and exaggeration. (If there was a 36-foot shark, why not a 37? 38? 40?) In most scientific and popular works, the maximum size of the great white shark was given as 36.5 feet. Finally, someone took it into his head to measure this famous jaw. In 1962, Perry Gilbert, one of the world's leading authorities on sharks, went to the British Museum and requested the Port Fairy jaws. He measured the jaws and teeth, and realized that they were about the same size as a set he had measured in Durban, which was known to have come from a shark that was 16.5 feet long. Gilbert therefore concluded that "the figure of 36.5 feet, so widely quoted, was probably a printer's error."[100]

The second famous giant white shark is a 21-footer mentioned in Bigelow and Schroeder as having been reported by Luis Howell-Rivero. Neither Henry Bigelow nor William Schroeder saw this specimen; they relied on the reports of Howell-Rivero, a respected Cuban ichthyologist. Bigelow and Schroeder "received a good photograph, apparently of this specimen, with weight stated at 7,302 pounds, from Ollyandro del Valle." In his paper debunking the myth of the 36.5-foot shark, Gilbert refers to the Cuban specimen as "the largest great white shark that has ever been measured," and we have no reason to doubt the length because it seems within the realm of possibility, and also because it is fairly easy to measure something 21 feet long. It is the weight of this fish that troubled me, since it is some 4,000 pounds heavier than any other white shark, but only two feet longer than the next longest, a 19-footer measured by David Davies in Durban. Two tons is a lot of shark to fit into two feet.

I asked Jack Casey to check the weight of this shark on the computer by comparing the weight with that of other known specimens. On the graph, most of the specimens follow the curve

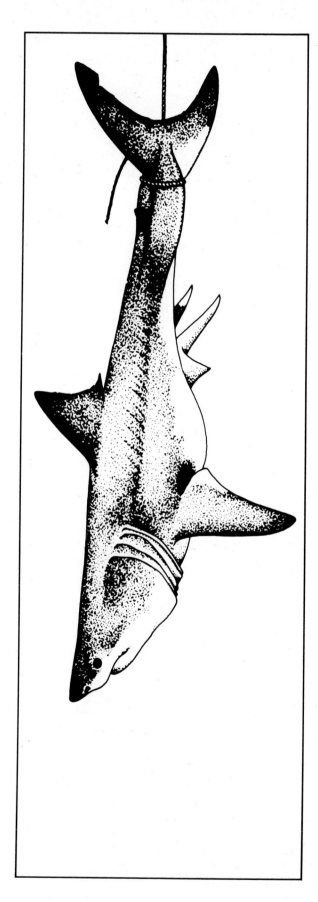

Grace and power in motion—the great white shark in Australian waters.

pretty closely, with expected deviations that have to do with sex, condition, recent feeding, and so forth. For the 21-foot shark, we got a figure of 4,100 pounds, with a possible variation of 13 percent. Adding the 13 percent (533 pounds) to the 4,100-pound figure, we got a maximum total of 4,633 pounds, a difference of 2,669 pounds from the weight given by Howell-Rivero. The 7,302-pound figure is simply incompatible with the known data, and I therefore suggest another error, perhaps in the transmission of information from Howell-

Rivero to Bigelow and Schroeder. (The reference to the photograph, "apparently of this specimen," prompted me to write to the Museum of Comparative Zoology at Harvard, where the papers of Bigelow and Schroeder now reside. After considerable correspondence, I was told that "there is still no photograph of *Carcharodon carcharias* of Howell-Rivero—I fear this is a lost cause.")

The literature on great whites is full of references to larger ones than the recorded maximum. There have been sightings of sharks that range in size from twenty-two to thirty feet, usually calculated by measuring a submerged shark against the boat in which the observer sits. In his book *Shark for Sale*, an account of his shark-fishing experiences in the Seychelles, William Travis tells of hooking a huge shark, which was hauled up "foot by foot," to "see how tired the brute was." By measuring the shark against a mark scratched on the bulwark of his shark-fishing boat, Travis concluded that the fish was twenty-nine feet long. The brute was not very tired, however, because it "made a determined dash ahead, swung round the anchor chain, baulked as the line caught on it and then, with one savage lunge of its head, snapped the rope as if it were a strand of cotton." [246]

There are too many stories of gigantic white sharks to discount them all, and although in many instances no measurements were taken, reliable observers actually saw the fish. We cannot discard every observation without supporting evidence as just another "fish story." One observation is even documented by a photograph, but since there is nothing in the picture to give it scale, we have to take the author's word that "this monster Queensland white shark would have been about twice as big as the present rod and reel record." The author is Peter Goadby, one of the most respected men in Pacific big-game fishing. [105] In 1954, Alf Dean, the holder of the current white shark record, fought a shark for five and a half hours, when the hooks finally pulled out. The shark was estimated to weigh 4,000 pounds.

Many other tales of "the one that got away" are also to be encountered. The chances are that if a fish can weigh 3,000 pounds, another of the same species can weigh 3,500 pounds. If there is one 21 feet long, there is probably another 23 feet long. After examining the Port Fairy jaws at the British Museum in 1972, Dr. John Randall wrote a paper titled "Size of the Great White Shark *(Carcharodon)*." [196] He came to the same conclusion as Perry Gilbert as regards the erroneous label on the jaws, but he also postulated the existence of larger sharks: "Bites on whale carcasses found off Southern Australia suggest that white sharks as long as 25 or 26 feet (7½ or 8 meters) exist today." So far, not one of these monsters has been caught.

This might not be a function of their elusiveness as much as of their immensity. It is hard to imagine a man reeling in a fish that weighs more than a small car, and there is no longline gear in use that can hold a two-ton shark. There have been numerous reports of commercial lines torn and hooks straightened, as if by a fish of great weight. Stewart Springer wrote: "The power of a large white shark is difficult to estimate. In the fishery these sharks were able to break wire rope or chain having a breaking strength of approximately 3,800 pounds." The extent to which these giants have captured the imagination of writers can be seen in a well-known book on fishes (Herald, *Living Fishes of the World*): amid the references to the 36.5-foot shark and the 20- and 25-foot man-eaters, a 17-foot-long specimen weighing 2,800 pounds is referred to as a "small shark." [132]

The most extraordinary story is told by D. G. Stead, in *Sharks and Rays of Australian Seas*. The account has been quoted frequently, often to demonstrate the existence of *Carcharodon megalodon*, the giant extinct relative of the white shark, but it is sometimes used as an illustration of the great size to which the white shark can grow. Stead maintains that this is "the most outstanding of all stories relating to the gigantic forms of this fish that has ever come to light." With that statement there can be no disagreement, but the story itself is somewhat more difficult to accept:

The men had been at work on the fishing grounds which lie in deep water—when an immense shark of almost unbelievable proportions put in an appearance, lifting pot after pot containing many crayfishes, and taking in, as these men said, "pots, mooring lines and all." These crayfish pots, it should be mentioned, were about 3 feet 6 inches in diameter, and frequently contained from two to three dozen crayfish, each weighing several pounds.* The men were all unanimous that this shark was something the like of which they had never dreamed of. In company with the local

---

* Lest the reader infer that the size of the crayfish is also greatly exaggerated, the word "crayfish" is used in Australia to denote the spiny lobster, a creature that can easily weigh several pounds.

(Overleaf) Plate 9. **White shark** *(Carcharodon carcharias) and* **sea lion** *(Zalophus californianus)*

© RICHARD ELLIS - 1975

Fisheries Inspector I questioned many of the men very closely and they all agreed as to the gigantic stature of the beast. But the lengths they gave were on the whole, absurd. I mention them, however, as an indication of the state of mind which this unusual giant had thrown them into. And bear in mind that these were men who were used to the sea and all sorts of weather, and all sorts of sharks as well. One of the crew said the shark was "three hundred feet long, at least!" Others said it was as long as the wharf on which we stood— about 115 feet! They affirmed that the water "boiled" over a large space when the fish went past. They were all familiar with whales, which they had often seen passing at sea, but this was a vast shark. They had seen its terrible head which was "at least as large as the roof of the wharf shed at Nelson's Bay." One of the things that impressed me was that they all agreed as to the ghostly whitish color of the fish.[234]

Besides crayfish pots, what does a white shark eat? Disregarding for the moment the refuse that is sometimes found in the stomach of a captured shark,   we find that white sharks are carnivores on a large scale, feeding on squid, fish, and sea mammals when they are available. The sharks are sometimes observed feeding on the carcasses of harpooned whales, and some of the stories of giants come from these situations. The largest shark recorded by David Davies, director of the Oceanic Research Institute (ORI) in Durban, was a 19-footer harpooned "in the whaling grounds approximately 100 miles off Durban." (It was the reported presence of large white sharks in South African waters that encouraged Peter Gimbel to take his "Blue Water" expedition there in 1969, and it was a 16.5-foot specimen that Perry Gilbert examined at the ORI that caused him to question the 36.5 figure for the British Museum specimen.)

In 1960 off Block Island a dead whale was floating, attended by scores of large sharks, including whites. Jerome E. Kelley, a fisherman and writer who was there, says that he saw "12 to 15 of the biggest white sharks I had ever seen. . . . I'm certain that the smaller sharks attending this grisly party were at least 12 feet long, with the larger ones exceeding 15 feet."[147] Frank Mundus was also at this "grisly party," and he recorded this entry in his log for July 5:

This was the day we saw three big whites feeding on the carcass of a dead blue whale....We harpooned one of the feeding monsters. Estimated weight was 3,500 lb.[175]

Someone once told me that they had taken movies of this occasion, and insisted that some of the sharks were longer than his boat—thirty-six feet. The quality of the film and the size of the sharks diminished as I pressed to see the film. Finally I discovered that the film was of very poor quality, and only a few seconds long, and taken on an overcast day—and it was probably lost anyway.

Besides whales, white sharks also eat other sharks. A huge female (16 feet 9 inches, 2,820 pounds) that was harpooned in Monterey Bay, California, in 1957 was feeding on a dead basking shark that was tethered to a 55-gallon drum. When the white shark was examined, it had a 27-pound chunk of basking shark lodged in its throat. A white shark that had been ravaging a longline was finally hooked itself, and was found to have eaten two sandbar sharks, one six and the other seven feet long, which it had obviously torn from the hooks. Other sharks that have been found in the stomachs of whites are gray smoothhounds *(Mustelus californicus)*, spiny dogfish *(Squalus acanthias)*, soupfins *(Galeorhinus zyopterus)*, and one porbeagle *(Lamna nasus)*. White sharks eat all manner of fish—fast swimmers, slow swimmers, and bottom feeders including skates and rays. The larger sharks require larger food, and this often leads them to pursue the marine mammals, including seals, sea lions, porpoises, and sea otters. With the exception of the Cetacea (whales and dolphins), all other sea mammals come ashore to breed, and must therefore approach land, at least some of the time. It is interesting to note that the cold-water areas in which white sharks are found most commonly— California, South Australia, South Africa, and parts of New England and the Canadian Maritimes—all support large populations of seals or sea lions. Sea otters have been killed by white sharks, but it seems that they are rarely eaten. In 1957 and 1958, twenty-four dead sea otters were found washed ashore in northern and central California. Some were headless, others were intact, but they all were scarred by deep gashes. One bore the unmistakable signature of *Carcharodon carcharias* in one of the gashes, a serrated tooth fragment. We can only speculate as to why the otters were killed and not eaten, but the reason may have to do with the strong odor they secrete. Sea otters are mustelids, related to weasels and skunks, and they can emit a powerful odor, which may have repelled the sharks.

Low on the list of items on the shark's menu is the boat; yet white sharks are infamous for their attacks on boats. We might expect a hooked white shark to attack a boat, since the frenzy that accompanies the pain of a large hook (assuming that sharks feel pain) could result in an attack on anything within range. However, white sharks have attacked boats for no apparent reason. Off Capetown in 1960, a white shark (identified by a tooth fragment it left in the boat) charged and bit a 24-foot fishing boat leaving an 18-inch hole—fortunately above the waterline. Frank Mundus also had a white shark charge the *Cricket II*, but it swam away after ramming her in the bow. In one instance, a white shark estimated at 12 feet and 1,000 pounds attacked and sank a dory off Cape Breton Island, Nova Scotia. The shark did not pursue the attack on the two fishermen who were dumped in the water, but one of them drowned before help arrived.

The great white is the shark most often implicated in attacks on humans, and it is *always* number one on the list of dangerous sharks or man-eaters. People have died as a result of white shark attacks, but very few have actually been eaten, either whole or in part. Perhaps this is splitting hairs, but I believe that it is necessary to draw a distinction between death as a result of excessive bleeding after being attacked by a shark, and death as a result of having a portion of one's anatomy ripped off and swallowed. Researchers on the subject of shark attacks are interested in this distinction, since the discovery of the motive of a shark attack is necessary to its prevention.

There are some recorded instances where swimmers and divers who have seen white sharks in the water have not been molested. (Of course, we can never know how often divers have *not* seen white sharks when they were present, so the information we have is somewhat one-sided.) Cousteau tells of three instances when white sharks saw him and fled;[59] Stan Waterman once jumped in the water off the Great Barrier Reef to find himself face to face with a white; and Don Nelson tells a chilling story of being stalked by a white in Florida waters.[179] Far more dramatic—and far more frequent—are the descriptions of white shark attacks.

Given the white shark's habit of cruising inshore as well as off, the increase in the number of recreational swimmers and divers, and the shark's nefarious reputation, one would expect the number of documented attacks to be extremely high. After exhaustive research, based on thousands of reports, clippings, and letters from all over the world, the Shark Attack File shows only thirty-two attacks that are attributed to the great white shark (see table). (The file contains data only up to 1969, the year that funding was cut off, so any attacks that took place after that are not recorded, at least not officially.) Whites have always been considered the most dangerous of sharks, and there is a tendency to ascribe any attack to this species if the shark is not seen. Since *Jaws*, however, practically every shark is automatically assumed to be a white, and if there is an attack, the white is almost certain to be held responsible.

There have certainly been more than thirty-two white shark attacks. Often the victim is lost, but, more frequently, the shark is not identified. When one is in the water, being bitten by a large fish, the desire to know the name of the fish is usually displaced by the desire to escape. Since we can only speculate on those attacks where the attack shark was not identified, I propose to restrict this discussion to the thirty-two known attacks. They took place from 1916 to 1968, from New Jersey to California, from Australia to Argentina. (It must be pointed out that not even all of these attacks are definitely attributable to the white shark; in the Shark Attack File, the entry for attacking species was often based on an amateur identification. Whenever someone even said they knew what kind of shark it was, it was so recorded in the file. This is particularly important in the case of the 1916 New Jersey attacks, discussed below and at length in the chapter "Shark Attack.")

A careful examination of the records leads to some interesting conclusions. Of the thirty-two attacks, at least seven are open to question as to the attacking species. There is no reason whatever to attribute the first two 1916 New Jersey attacks to a white shark. The only reason for having done so is that a white shark was caught in Raritan Bay, south of New York, two days after three people were attacked, two of them fatally, in Matawan Creek. Aside from

being inland, where white sharks are not known to go, Matawan Creek is seventy-five miles from the site of the first attack, Beach Haven, New Jersey. The white shark was held responsible for the Matawan attacks because it was caught near the scene of the crime, and on this flimsy evidence, plus an acceptance of the "rogue shark" theory—since the five attacks occurred within a ten-day period, it was assumed that one shark was responsible.

Two other attacks that have been attributed to the white shark are also debatable. In the case of the attack on Robert Pamperin, an observer described the shark as having a tail with an upper lobe much longer than the lower lobe, which would be characteristic of a tiger shark or even another large carcharhinid, but not a white. In the case of Tony Dicks, the figures given for the length and weight of the shark (which was killed), are 9 feet and 280 pounds. According to the records of the Game Fish Association of Australia, white sharks in the 108- to 112-inch range (9 feet to 9 feet 4 inches) weigh between 506 and 614 pounds.

Subtracting the seven attacks from the total of thirty-two, we are left with twenty-five documented attacks, and some of these are probably questionable as well. The great white shark has always been held to be the most dangerous of sharks, but the facts do not bear this out. The east coast of Australia, far and away the most dangerous area in the world as far as shark attacks are concerned (before meshing was instituted as a means of prevention) is not a frequent habitat of the white shark. In addition, this coast is marked by numerous rivers that flow into the Coral Sea, a circumstance known to be attractive to carcharhinid sharks. The Natal coast of South Africa, second in worldwide attacks (again, until mesh nets were installed), is also characterized by the large number of rivers that run to the sea. White sharks are not common here either—since 1964, only 2 percent of the sharks caught in the nets of the Natal Anti-Shark Measures Board have been whites. Dr. David Davies attributed the 1960s attacks to the bull shark (known then as the Zambezi shark) and it is reasonable to assume that many of the attacks that preceded Davies' investigations were committed by the same species.

The flat black eye and conical snout of Carcharodon carcharias, *the great white shark.*

The white shark is relatively easy to identify; that is, if one is able to describe the attacking shark, one or more of its determining characteristics might be noted (pointed, conical snout, black eyes, triangular teeth, white underbelly, homocercal tail, etc.). The bull shark, however, looks just like a shark; it has no distinguishing features except that it lacks a ridge between the dorsal fins, and very few observers would pay attention to that. *Carcharhinus leucas,* the bull shark, has been indicted in dozens of attacks all over the world, in fresh as well as salt water. (Until it was synonymized to one worldwide species, it was the Zambezi shark, the Lake Nicaragua shark, the Ganges shark, the Java shark, and perhaps a dozen more names from various locations.) Even in the Shark Attack File, where identifications are often vague, the total number of attacks attributed to the bull shark, with its various names and from its various locations, is thirty-seven. I have suggested elsewhere that a bull shark was responsible for the Matawan Creek attacks, because of its preference for fresh water, and its habit of attacking people.

Of the thirty-two white shark attacks, an incredible 37.5 percent occurred on a stretch of the California coastline less than 120 miles long (measured in a straight line between the two terminal points). This zone extends north and south from the city of San Francisco, from Tomales Point at Bodega Bay in the north, to Santa Cruz and Monterey Bay in the south. The area also includes the Farallon Islands, about 30 miles west of the city of San Francisco, a popular area for abalone diving, and the home of a colony of sea lions. It appears that if San Francisco were to slide into the sea, as some predict it will, there would be even more to worry about than mere earthquakes, fires, and tidal waves. According to the statistics, the city and its environs have easily won the unwanted title of White Shark Attack Capital of the World. South Australia is a poor second, with four attacks by white sharks, only one of which was fatal. Of the twelve attacks that took place in a California, two resulted in the death of the victim.

One attack that is not included is the notorious hoax that appeared in *Life* magazine in June 1968. During the making of a grade-B thriller called *Shark!* a drugged bull shark was pulled through the water and brought into contact with a diver. Ketchup and other liquids were released into the water at the moment of contact, and the cameras were rolling. It was a perfectly harmless sequence in which no one was hurt except the shark, which subsequently died. In *Life*, a series of photographs appeared, under the headline "Shark Kills a Man." The shark is obviously not a white, since it has a relatively large second dorsal fin, and a flattened rather than a conical snout. In the caption that accompanied the photographs (three of which are reproduced at right), the hapless stunt man, "Jose Marco" was supposedly attacked and killed by a "huge white shark," that had somehow gotten through the protective netting. It was reported that Marco died in a hospital two hours after the attack.

Dewey Bergman, a diver and dive-shop operator with a professional interest in Isla Mujeres, investigated the "incident," and in an article in *Skin Diver* magazine in 1969, wrote that he could find no record of any shark attack, no one named José Marco, and no hospital records of any such occurrence.[28] The people at *Life* later admitted that they might have been the victims of a publicity stunt, but never published a correction.

The number of survivors of attacks by great whites—about two out of three—seems to support the theory that the shark was not trying to eat its victim. Surely a creature capable of biting a seal or a porpoise in half would not grasp its prey in an almost gentle bite. "Gentle" is a relative term, of course, but sharks, whose bite is measured in tons per square inch, and who can take a 30-pound bite out of a whale as easily as a person bites a peach, can certainly do more damage than they have done to divers. In at least two instances (one involving Frank Logan and the other, Rodney Fox), the man's

The shark attack that never happened. Photographs purporting to show an attack on a stunt man by a great white shark actually show a drugged reef shark (probably Carcharhinus springeri*), a diver, and lots of ketchup. The photographs were promotional material for a Hollywood film, but they were printed in various magazines as if there had been a real attack.*

Heritage Enterprises

94

entire torso was in the shark's mouth, and the man survived. We do not know why the shark released its victim in these cases, but we can assume that the shark did not intend to eat the man. The white shark cannot be such an inefficient feeder that its prey, once in its mouth, escapes approximately two out of three times. If this were the situation, the sharks would have died out years ago, and since they have been around for tens of millions of years, they must be doing something right.

There is a new "sport" available to a select few who have the proper combination of time, money, skill, and equipment, not to mention the desire to look the white death (as it is called in Australia) straight in the eye. The sport is diving with the great white shark, intentionally. The shark cage is the single piece of equipment that is indispensable. A primitive version was used by Peter Gimbel off Montauk in 1965, where he filmed the graceful blue sharks in action under water. His short film, called *In the World of Sharks*, and the still shots of sharks feeding on the carcass of a porpoise made Gimbel's reputation as a "shark man," and created in him the great desire to film the white shark in its native waters.

On board the *Saori*, the boat they had chartered for the South Australian filming of *Blue Water, White Death*, were Gimbel, Ron and Valerie Taylor, Stan Waterman, Peter Matthiessen, and Rodney Fox. (Both Waterman and Fox are statistics in the Shark Attack File; Waterman is number 766 for an incident that took place in the Bahamas with a tiger shark, and Rodney Fox is number 1235, the celebrated survivor of a white shark attack at Aldinga Beach.) Waterman and Gimbel, experienced film makers, had never been in the water with a white shark. The *Saori* was anchored over the aptly named Dangerous Reef, trying to attract whites with whale oil and ground fish. When the sharks arrived, Gimbel, Waterman, the Taylors, and Matthiessen descended in the cages. In *Blue Meridian*, Peter Matthiessen describes his first view of a white shark in the water:

> The shark passed slowly, first the slack jaw with the triangular splayed teeth, then the dark eye, impenetrable and empty as the eye of God, next the gill slits like knife slashes in paper, then the pale slab of the flank, aflow with silver ripplings of light,

> and finally the thick short twitch of its hard tail. Its aspect was less savage than implacable, a silent thing of merciless serenity.[164]

The footage made at this time was the first ever taken of white sharks from an underwater vantage point. Matthiessen calls it "surely the most exciting film ever made under water."

Since *Blue Water, White Death*, other films have been made of the white shark under water. These are unquestionably exciting, as is any view of such a mysterious and terrible predator, but they are an anticlimax to Gimbel's film. He did not know what the white sharks would do to his cages; all subsequent film makers had seen his film.

Perhaps the great white shark is not the man-eating monster it has always been thought to be. It does attack people; that cannot be denied. But it does so infrequently, and the victims survive in a fairly high percentage of the cases. (Of the four white shark attacks in South Australia from 1961 to 1964, Geoffrey Corner was the only fatality, and that was because an artery was severed. The Shark Attack File indicates that Corner was attacked by "a 14-foot bronze whaler," but the attack has been attributed to a white shark anyway, because of the location, and also because bronze whalers do not get to be fourteen feet long.) The white shark is a great and frightening beast, even if the reports of 25-footers prove to be unfounded. A fourteen- or fifteen-foot specimen is capable of swallowing a seal or a porpoise, or biting a person in half. The thought of being in the water with this monster is almost as terrifying as the fact, and this has been more than sufficient to establish its reputation as the archetypal man-eating shark. I suggest that the overwhelmingly evil reputation of this shark is undeserved. It is far from a friendly house pet, but it is probably just as far from the hysterical stereotype we have been given—of a huge, voracious monster, lying in wait to eat us all.

The great white shark is a holdover from earlier times; times before people decided to make the ocean their playground. *Carcharodon carcharias* is at best a rare species, and is probably even an endangered one in terms of numbers. Directly, people are killing off as many as they can; we are currently in the midst of a shark-slaughtering frenzy, and "indirectly," as Stewart Springer wrote, "the competition with man has already consigned the white shark to oblivion by destroying the seals, sea turtles and whales that are the white shark's natural foods."[216] There are those who would not mourn the white shark's passing, but I am not among them. I admire this great animal for its grace, its size, its power, its "merciless serenity." Not many people have killed white sharks in the sharks' environment, but when the man is on a boat, with a harpoon or a fishing rod, the odds are very much against the shark. Not even the great white shark can endure the onslaught of the most complete and deadly predator the world has ever known.

I am reminded of the reputation of the killer whale. For years people feared this creature, calling it the most savage of all the animals in the sea. (It is, incidentally, one of the few animals known to attack the white shark.) It was reported that killer whales knocked men off icebergs so that they could eat them; they tore the tongues from the living baleen whales; they swallowed dozens of whole porpoises and seals. Even its name characterized it as one of the sea's great villains. In 1965, a 22-foot male was captured near the town of Namu, British Columbia. Almost everyone knows the story of this whale, which turned out to be an intelligent, sensitive creature, not a seagoing homicidal maniac. In 1968, I visited Sea World in San Diego, California, where "Shamu," the second killer whale in captivity was on exhibition. As part of the show, the trainer brushed Shamu's teeth with a huge toothbrush, *and then he put his head inside her mouth.* Everything I knew, or thought I knew, about killer whales was being changed before my eyes. I remember thinking at the time that it was as if someone were trying to kiss a king cobra. I am not suggesting for a moment that anyone should attempt to brush the teeth of a white shark, or put his or her head in the shark's mouth—in fact, I am not even suggesting that anyone in his right mind would want to be in the water, unprotected, with a white shark. My point is that as with the reputation of the killer whale, that of the white shark is probably grossly overdramatized. Like the killer whale, however, the white shark is a massive predator, and those who would stray so far from their own territory are inviting conflict with these car-

nivores. Scott Johnson, the developer of the Shark Screen and other protective devices, wrote in a letter to me: "I think [sharks] were in the ocean first and we are the intruders there. If we get attacked by sharks while swimming or diving, it's our fault; the shark is probably just defending its property and we can't blame them for that." A Hollywood promoter is now trying to arrange a battle "to the death" between Ben Cropp, "the world's foremost shark fighter," and a great white shark, to be shown on closed-circuit television. This "event" would presumably make a lot of money for the promoter. I don't know about Ben Cropp, but the white shark deserves better than this.

Only once has a white shark been kept in captivity, and this specimen, an 8.5-foot male, died thirty-five hours after being placed in a tank at Marineland in Florida. It had been hooked and taken alive, but when it was put in the tank, it lay on the bottom, not moving, until it died.

In the summer of 1975 (the summer of *Jaws*), some fifteen white sharks were harpooned off the California coast. Five of these, ranging from six to sixteen feet in length, were obtained by Sea World in San Diego and put on exhibition. Sea World has branches in Orlando, Florida, and Cleveland, where the sharks were exhibited in room-sized freezers with glass sides—huge dead animals suspended from the ceilings, with teeth bared, and clouded frozen eyes.

We see this animal dead, or we see it as a primordial terror, but we know almost nothing about it as a living creature, feeding, hunting, mating, propagating. One of the most awesome creatures on earth still swims the world's oceans, unknown and spiritually unconquered. The discovery of its breeding grounds or mating habits will not dull the razor-serrations of its teeth, nor will it change the centuries of calumny that the white shark has endured. But before we eliminate this animal from the earth, perhaps we ought to know a little more about it. It is our ignorance of the white shark, not its actual habits, that has been responsible for our attitudes toward it. Bertrand Russell wrote: "Fear is the main source of superstition, and one of the main sources of cruelty. To conquer fear is the beginning of wisdom, in the pursuit of truth as in the endeavor after a worthy manner of life."

ATTACKS ON SWIMMERS AND DIVERS BY THE GREAT WHITE SHARK (*CARCHARODON CARCHARIAS*) AS RECORDED IN THE SHARK ATTACK FILE

SAF#	DATE	NAME OF VICTIM	LOCATION OF ATTACK	FATAL
202	July 2, 1916	Charles Vansant	Beach Haven, New Jersey	yes
399	July 6, 1916	Charles Bruder	Spring Lake, New Jersey	yes
204	July 12, 1916	Lester Stilwell	Matawan Creek, New Jersey	yes
205	July 12, 1916	Stanley Fisher	Matawan Creek, New Jersey	yes
206	July 12, 1916	Joseph Dunn	Matawan Creek, New Jersey	no
222	July 25, 1936	Joseph Troy	Buzzard's Bay, Massachusetts	yes
355	Aug. 23, 1943	Sailor	Gulf of Panama	yes
236	Dec. 7, 1952	Barry Wilson	Point Aulone, California	yes
255	Jan. 22, 1954	Alfredo Aubone	Buenos Aires, Argentina	no
240	Dec. 6, 1955	James Jacobs	Pacific Grove, California	no
372	May 7, 1959	Albert Kogler	Baker's Beach, California	yes
382	May 30, 1959	Tony Dicks	Port Elizabeth, South Africa	no
376	June 14, 1959	Robert Pamperin	La Jolla, California	yes
554	Dec. 4, 1959	James Hay	Bodega Bay, California	no
683	April 24, 1960	Frank Gilbert	Tomales Point, California	no
686	May 19, 1960	Suzanne Theriot	Santa Cruz, California	no
842	March 12, 1961	Brian Rodger	Aldinga Beach, Australia	no
1220	1961	Manfred Gregor	Ricchione, Italy	no
917	Aug. 20, 1961	David Vogensen	Bodega Bay, California	no
1115	Nov. 11, 1962	Leroy French	Farallon Islands, California	no
1122	Dec. 9, 1962	Geoffrey Corner	Caracalinga Head, Australia	yes
1235	Aug. 12, 1963	Rodney Fox	Aldinga Beach, Australia	no
1247	Jan. 11, 1964	Jack Rochette	Farallon Islands, California	no
1266	Feb. 5, 1964	Leslie Jordan	Dunedin, New Zealand	yes
1344	Nov. 29, 1964	Henri Bource	Lady Julia Percy Island, Australia	no
1347	Dec. 13, 1964	John Harding	Wooli, NSW, Australia	no
1406	Feb. 26, 1966	Raymond Short	Coledale Beach, NSW, Australia	no
1449	March 9, 1967	William Black	Dunedin, New Zealand	yes
1452	March 19, 1967	Len Jones	Paradise Reef, South Africa	no
1463	Aug. 19, 1967	Robert Bartle	Jurien Bay, Australia	yes
1561	July 27, 1968	Frank Logan	Tomales Point, California	no
1647	Sept. 6, 1969	Donald Joslin	Tomales Point, California	no
1474	May 28, 1972	Hellmuth Himmrich	Tomales Point, California	no

Notes

The entries in the table are in order of occurrence. The file numbers represent the order in which the information was received.

Although Theo Brown is recorded in the SAF as having been attacked by a shark once (SAF #1100, in 1955, while trying to set an underwater endurance record), in his own book, Sharks, The Silent Savages, *he records another attack, this one by a white shark. He shot the shark with a speargun, which made him the*

only other person (John Harding also did it) to parry the attack of a white shark without injury.[37]

The attack on Hellmuth Himmrich (SAF #1474, above) took place after the Shark Attack File had been officially closed. Information was sent to the Mote Marine Lab, however, and the data are included in Baldridge's book, Shark Attack, *but not in the report that preceded it.*[16] *With the Himmrich attack, the total comes to thirty-three, but the data analysis was based on the thirty-two previous attacks.*

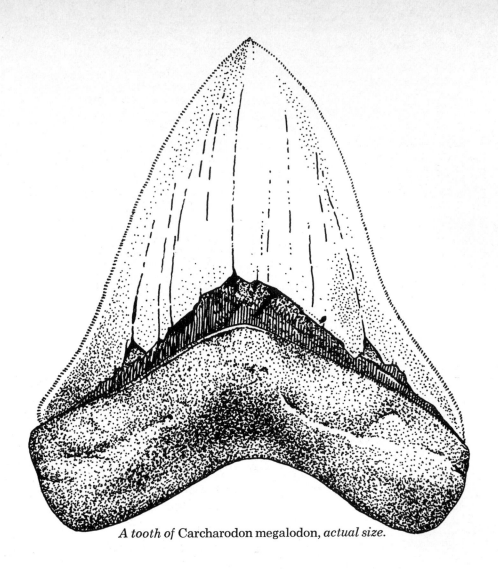

A tooth of Carcharodon megalodon, *actual size.*

CARCHARODON MEGALODON

On my desk as I write this is a shark's tooth. Measured vertically from the base to the point, it is a shade over five inches long. It weighs over eleven ounces, almost three-quarters of a pound. It is a fossil of course, and while the root is rough and stonelike, the blade portion is smooth and striated, not unlike a recent tooth. It is a soft, brownish gray color, with the subsurface inner gleam of enamel. The tooth has one curved face and one that is almost flat, although careful examination shows that the "flat" side is curved as well, but more subtly. The convex surface of the tooth is in fact the inner face, but it looks to be the opposite; almost every untrained observer assumes that the curve of the tooth should follow the natural curve of the jaw, but this is not the case. Sharks' teeth often look like they are in backwards. The reason for this is not immediately apparent: the teeth originate "upside down" in the membrane of the jaw, and it is in *this* configuration that they must conform to the curve of the jaw. (On one occasion, Peter Benchley and I were perched on ladders in front of the huge reconstructed *megalodon* jaw in the American Museum of Natural History, making a television program. When we looked at the fossil teeth that were set in this eight-foot-high plaster model, we both thought that all the teeth had been put in backwards. We were fully prepared to make our startling discovery known to science and correct the mistakes of the poor museum preparators who had committed such a foolish error. Later, I mentioned our discovery to Perry Gilbert at the Mote Marine Laboratory, and he showed me the jaw of a great white shark in which the teeth were oriented the same way. I was, fortunately, disabused of my inclination to correct the paleontologists of the Museum of Natural History—at least on this count.)

The tooth before me is finely serrated on its cutting edges, with some fifty serrations to the inch. On the inner surface of the tooth, between the stonelike base and the polished triangular blade, there is a chevron-shaped area that is dark brown. This "scar" and the very small size of the serrations are the characteristics that identify this tooth as that of *Carcharodon megalodon*, an ancestor of the great white shark, and the largest predatory fish that ever lived. The label in the museum that accompanies the jaw in which Benchley and I made our nondiscovery reads:

THE JAWS OF A GIANT
EXTINCT SHARK

Most of the oceans during middle and late Tertiary time were inhabited by a giant shark named Carcharodon megalodon, *a close relative of the living white shark or man-eater.*

The jaws suspended above have been restored in plaster to hold the fossil teeth of this giant shark. The size of the jaws was determined on the basis of the tooth-jaw proportions in the modern relative, and the same number of teeth was used in the restoration as in the living form. All the teeth from a single individual of Carcharodon megalodon *have not been found together, but it is probable that the extinct and living species have about the same number of teeth in each jaw.*

As restored, the jaws measure nine feet across. The largest teeth average six inches in height. It is estimated that this giant shark reached a length of approximately forty-five feet.

The reconstructed jaws of Carcharodon megalodon *in the Hall of Fossil Fishes at the American Museum of Natural History in New York.*

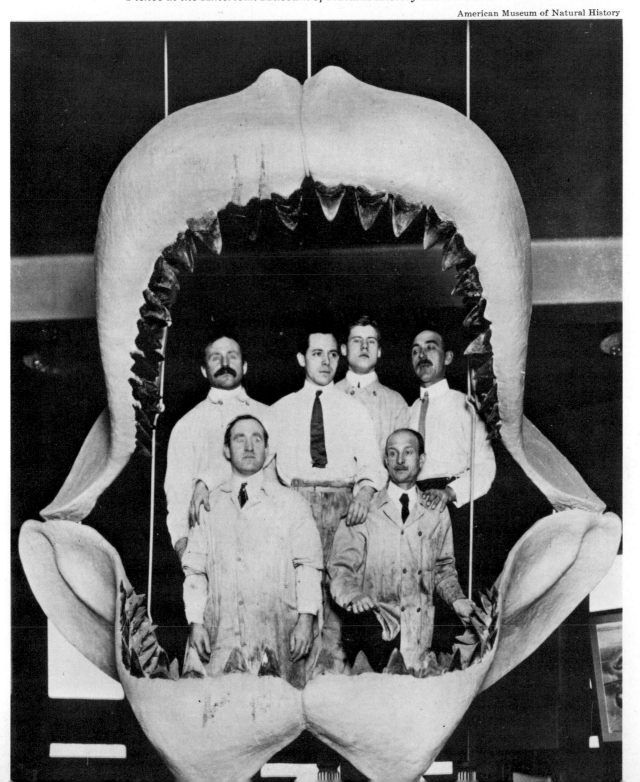

It is perfectly obvious in looking at this jaw that it belonged to a fish considerably longer than forty-five feet. (In the television program that was being filmed when Benchley and I were sitting in front of the jaw, one sequence had Benchley sitting *in* the jaw in an easy chair with a standing lamp next to him, which he was to turn out at the conclusion of the program. The chair, the lamp, and Benchley were all easily contained in the jaw.)

This is the same jaw that has been shown in virtually every shark book, with a few stern-faced gents in lab coats standing in it to give an idea of its immense size. An attempt to visualize a 45-foot fish attached to this jaw produces a ludicrously out-of-proportion creature with an enormous head. This could have been possible, of course, but it is less likely than two other possibilities: one, that the fish was really much larger than 45 feet, or, two, that the jaw reconstruction is incorrect. It is easy to imagine a 75- or 100-foot shark with jaws "nine feet across," and that has been the general reaction to this spectacular exhibit. References abound to gigantic sharks, from 50 to 120 feet long. (A recent popular publication, *Shark Safari* by Hal Scharp, assigns a possible length of 120 feet to *megalodon*, and demonstrates its size by illustrating the shark next to a 45-foot trailer truck and claiming that the shark "could almost engulf the entire truck within its gigantic jaws!"[204])

Since the teeth are undeniably authentic, the possibility of error cannot exist with them, except insofar as their interpretation is concerned. Perhaps the model jaw is too big. This, which is a less dramatic possibility than the misinterpretation of the size of the fish, turns out to have been the actual mistake. While Benchley and I were eager to fault the preparators who put the teeth in backwards, the real fault lay with the paleontologists who established the size of the jaw itself. Examination of the jaws of white sharks show that the largest teeth (the second anterior upper) are approximately the same height as the part of the jaw from which they protrude, and in some cases the tooth is even larger. For reasons lost in the files of the museum, it was decided to make the jaw thickness almost *four times* the height of the tooth. A comparison of jaw height to tooth size has shown that the jaw is at least one-third too large, and further comparison of these teeth with those of a white shark also

shows that the fossil teeth in the rear of the jaw are far too large.

In a recent analysis, Dr. John E. Randall has dismissed the theory of a 100-foot shark, and brought the size back down to where the museum said it was in the first place: "The size of extinct *Carcharodon* has been grossly exaggerated. Based on a projection of a curve of tooth size of recent *Carcharodon carcharias*, the largest fossil Carcharodon were about 43 feet (~ 13 meters) long." Forty-three feet! The largest great white authoritatively measured was less than half that length (twenty-one feet), and this is an anomaly, since no others have been recorded at over nineteen feet. No one can accurately ascertain the weight of a 43-foot *megalodon*, but plotting the length-weight ratio of white sharks, a figure of about 28,000 pounds seems not unlikely. It hardly seems necessary to exaggerate the dimensions of this gigantic predator; a fish this size could swallow a horse. (See Plate 4.)

There are those who would believe that *megalodon* still exists, cruising at great depths and feeding on giant squid and other deep-sea creatures. It seems unlikely at best, since there is no evidence to demonstrate its existence, and the strongest argument is that we cannot prove its nonexistence. It is obviously easier to show that something exists than to prove that it does not, and the 1938 discovery of the coelacanth, a lobe-finned fish thought to have been extinct for 50 million years, is usually cited by those who would argue that there are probably sea creatures still unknown to science. Dr. J. L. B. Smith, the discoverer of the coelacanth, said in *The Sea Fishes of Southern Africa*: "These monsters [*megalodon*] may still live in deep water, but it is better to believe them extinct."[212]

In *Blue Meridian*, Peter Matthiessen's chronicle of the making of the movie *Blue Water, White Death—The Search for the Great White Shark*, there is an acknowledgment to "James F. Clark of the Museum of Comparative Zoology at Harvard for permission to paraphrase his arguments in support of the hypothesis that the white shark's gigantic relative, *Carcharias* [sic] *megalodon*, still exists."[164] This reference, in an otherwise accurate and extremely well written book, is unfortunate, since it implies that Clark was on the staff of the museum at Harvard, while, in fact, he was just a student there. His "arguments," submitted in a paper for Biology 130, were titled "Serpents, Sea Creatures and Giant Sharks."[54] Mr. Clark has been kind enough to send me a copy of the paper, and it makes for fascinating reading, although he errs in one basic assumption when he states that there is no difference between the teeth of *Carcharodon megalodon* and those of *Carcharodon carcharias*, except for size, which "can no longer be regarded as a species distinction." My intent is not to criticize an unpublished biology paper, but only to demonstrate the ease with which misinformation can creep into popular literature. Regardless of size, the teeth of *megalodon* and those of *carcharias* are differentiated by the large size of the triangular scarred area and the size of the serrations, and these differences are "obvious, constant, and present no problem in differentiating the two," according to a letter I received from Dr. Shelton P. Applegate, a distinguished vertebrate paleontologist and the acknowledged expert on *megalodon*.

If we accept the assumption that the great *megalodon* is extinct, and has been for some time, we must address the much more difficult problem of the causes of its extinction. Overspecialization, of which gigantism is one example, has often proved to be an evolutionary dead end, and many living creatures can number among their ancestors gigantic versions of themselves. Some that come to mind immediately are *Deinosuchus*, a fifty-foot crocodilian of the Cretaceous Period, and *Archelon*, a twelve-foot-long turtle. There are many other examples of giant ancestors of smaller descendants, but the progression from larger to smaller does not automatically obtain. The great puzzle of extinction still remains largely unsolved, and grade-school explanations of "climatic changes" or "brains too small" do little to provide a solution. Dinosaurs, usually cited as examples of biological obsolescence, dominated the earth for over a hundred million years, far longer than any other vertebrate group to date.

Any solution to the problem of *megalodon*'s disappearance is speculatory at best, but we can assume that it had to do with the availability of prey, climatic changes, continental drift, evolutionary variation, probably some still-undiscovered factors, and undoubtedly a combination of all these elements. One suggestion has it that the giant sharks fed on primitive whales *(Cetotheres)*, but since the whales exist today (albeit marginally, thanks to the preda-

tion of the most efficient of all evolutionary determinants, humans), it seems unlikely that the predators were eliminated while their prey continued. Water temperatures, and for that matter the location of the water as well, have changed considerably over the last 20 or 30 million years, but by the Tertiary Period (some 65 million years ago), most families of sharks had become firmly established.

At first analysis, the concept of survival of the fittest seems the least likely solution to the problem, since it is difficult to imagine a more "fit" predator than *megalodon*. But perhaps, as in the case of other great predators, factors combined to reduce the availability of large prey, and the smaller predators became that much more efficient. Surely, one of the most terrifying predators ever to have lived was *Tyrannosaurus rex*, but the "king of the tyrant lizards," twenty-five feet tall and with six-inch teeth, has gone the way of *megalodon*. (It is interesting to note that *megalodon* was probably bigger and heavier than *T. rex*, and was probably second only to the sperm whale as the largest predator that ever lived.)

We must conclude that we do not know why the great *megalodon* disappeared, but we probably can be thankful that it did. Forty-foot predatory sharks cruising the oceans of the world would be a significant deterrent to swimming, sailing, and almost all other activities involving close contact with the ocean.

At present, the only activities that involve *megalodon* are speculation on its existence and searching for its spectacular teeth. A great many of these teeth have been discovered, indicating a sizable population at some time in the past. The teeth are found most frequently in certain areas of the West Coast of the United States, including California (notably, an area near Bakersfield known as "Sharktooth Hill"), and in scattered localities on the East Coast, such as Cape Cod, Chesapeake Bay, North Carolina, and on both coasts of Florida (especially an area around Venice). These localities do not only yield the teeth of *megalodon*, but other fossils as well, including whale vertebrae and smaller sharks' teeth. There are some areas where a visitor can pick up dozens of small fossil sharks' teeth, but the dramatic *megalodon* teeth are becoming increasingly rare. They are now sought by divers and professional collectors, and they are the occasional by-products of ocean-floor mining investigations.

The giant teeth of *megalodon* were discovered on the ocean floor as long ago as 1873, and by relatively unsophisticated methods. On the British *Challenger* expedition, the first major oceanographic research voyage, manganese-encrusted teeth were dredged from depths of over 2,000 fathoms. The *Challenger* teeth have been the subject of much discussion, since they frequently enter the literature without their coating of manganese dioxide, and are therefore responsible for occasional references to *fresh* teeth of *megalodon*. One such reference, for example, can be found in Smith's *Sea Fishes of Southern Africa*, where he refers to "teeth 5 ins. long [that] have been dredged from the depths, indicating sharks of 100 feet with jaws at least 6 feet across."[212] Notice that Smith does not mention *fossil* teeth. The teeth found during the *Challenger* expedition were all manganese-encrusted, and were all fossils. All the *megalodon* teeth I have seen have been discolored (from the original white), ranging from brownish buff to black, and I have never seen a reference to a white tooth much more than two inches high.

The time of *megalodon*'s disappearance is also problematical. Various estimates have been published, from 30 million years ago to less than 50 thousand years ago. The more-recent estimates are based on microscopic analysis of the manganese layer, and dramatically reduce the previously accepted figures. If these assumptions are correct, *Carcharodon megalodon* became extinct at approximately the time that humans first inhabited the North American continent. The true answer probably lies somewhere in between.

Like present-day sharks, *megalodon* had a completely cartilaginous skeleton, and therefore left no fossil record of any parts except teeth and an occasional vertebral centrum (vertebral centra are disc-shaped bodies that surround the spinal cord, and are subject to some calcification). Thus our evidence of the largest predatory fish that ever lived consists only of the teeth and an occasional section of the backbone.

Vertebrate paleontology is a science that is based to a certain extent on the reconstruction of animals from their fossilized remains. Sometimes paleontologists are fortunate enough to find complete skeletons, which obviously simplifies the process of reconstruction. More often,

however, only isolated bones or teeth are found, and like a kind of jigsaw puzzle, complete animals are postulated on the basis of a tooth, a jawbone, or a pelvic fragment. It is therefore not only possible, but it is accepted scientific practice, to suggest the size, shape, and evolutionary relationships of a fish from dental evidence alone.

The teeth of *megalodon* (and of other extinct members of the genus *Carcharodon*) are oversized replicas of the teeth of the only living member of the genus—*Carcharodon carcharias*, the great white shark. The differences mentioned earlier (smaller serrations, the dark triangular area between the base and the blade, and the size of the fish), are enough to differentiate the sharks on the species level, but the gross morphological characteristics (larger serrations, triangular shape) are sufficient to suggest a very strong relationship between the extinct *megalodon* and the recent *carcharias*. We can therefore assume that the considerably enlarged body of *megalodon* was close *in form* to that of *carcharias*. *Megalodon* probably had the same fusiform, tapering body, the same flattened caudal keels, and the same homocercal tail lobes. Extrapolating from the proportions of a large white shark, we can deduce that a 45-foot *megalodon* would have had a tail that was almost 15 feet high, pectoral fins 8 feet long, and a dorsal fin that stood 6 feet tall.

Other members of this genus, characterized by the evidence of triangular serrated teeth, are *Carcharodon sulcidens*, often found in South Africa, and *Carcharodon angustidens*, also known as *C. auriculatus*, and found in North Carolina, Florida, and Belgium. I have seen one reference to another species, *C. landenensis*, from Oued-Zem, Morocco. This tooth is characterized by the larger serrations of a *carcharias* tooth, but it is flanked by multiserrated cusps. The other species are differentiated by their differing proportions and by the presence of single lateral cusps on some of the *angustidens* teeth. In younger specimens of the white shark, all the lower teeth show these cusps, and some of the upper ones do also. The likelihood is that these other species resembled *megalodon*, but were somewhat smaller. The three genera of sharks classified in the Isuridae today, the white, the mako, and the porbeagle, have teeth that show greater differences than those of any members of the genus *Carcharodon*, extinct or living. In other words, *C. carcharias* is a very close relative of *C. megalodon*.

THE BASKING SHARK

The first clear and entire view of a basking shark is terrifying. One may speak glibly of fish twenty, thirty, forty feet long, but until one looks down upon a living adult basking shark in clear water, the figures are meaningless and without implication. The bulk appears simply unbelievable. It is not possible to think of what one is looking at as a fish. It is longer than a London bus; it does not have scales like an ordinary fish; its movements are gigantic, ponderous, and unfamiliar; it seems a creature from a prehistoric world, of which the first sight is as unexpected, and in some ways as shocking, as that of a dinosaur or iguanadon would be.[165]

Gavin Maxwell, a man usually associated with otters *(Ring of Bright Water)*, wrote these words in 1952. They appeared in his first book, *Harpoon Venture*, which was a chronicle of his experiences as a commercial shark fisherman in the waters of the Hebrides from 1945 to 1949.[165] Maxwell fished for the basking shark, *Cetorhinus maximus*, because he believed that this enormous creature could provide enough liver oil to make a profitable industry for the Island of Soay. (The liver of a single basking shark, sometimes as much as 20 percent of its total weight, might provide as much as 500 gallons of oil.) The venture failed for many reasons, not the least of which concerned an attempt to utilize all the by-products of the shark, including the skin, the flesh, and the fins. In *Harpoon at a Venture* (published in America as *Harpoon Venture*), we learn a great deal about the second largest fish in the world. (The largest is the whale shark, *Rhincodon typus*, with accurate recorded lengths of up to forty feet. Maxwell saw hundreds of basking sharks during his four-year adventure, and estimated the largest one at "upwards of forty feet.")

Like the whale shark, the basking shark is a huge, slow-moving plankton feeder. Also like the whale shark, the basking shark is the sole member of a family created especially to accommodate it. The shark is called *Cetorhinus maximus*, and the family is the Cetorhinidae. The name *Cetorhinus* comes from *cetos* meaning "whale," and *rhiny*, meaning "shark" or "rasp." There is, therefore, the possibility that the scientific name of the basking shark,

Cetorhinus, translates as "whale shark" but it is best not to dwell too long on the exact translation of scientific names. In any event, the *maximus* part of the basking shark's name is clear: it means "great," and there is no dispute about that. One 29-foot specimen weighed in pieces at the Soay station totaled over six tons, with the stomach contents estimated at another ton. Other documented weights for basking sharks are 6,580 pounds at 28 feet, and 8,600 pounds at 30 feet. In 1969, a 27-foot specimen weighing 4,400 pounds was captured by commercial fishermen in the Gulf of Mexico near Siesta Key, Florida. This, the first instance of a basking shark in the warm waters of the Gulf, considerably extended its known range. For the most part, basking sharks are found in colder waters, primarily in the North Atlantic. They are also found in corresponding low latitudes in the North and South Pacific waters, but with the exception of the Gulf of Mexico occurrence, there have been no reports from tropical climates.

The basking shark is much more "sharky" than the whale shark, its rival for the title of world's largest fish. It is uniformly dark in color, sometimes with lighter or whitish undersides, and in profile (but not in dentition), it is similar to the mackerel sharks. It has a lunate caudal fin, a high, triangular dorsal fin, and a pointed snout. The eye of a basking shark is small, like the eye of a pig, which gives it a somewhat stupid look. In its gross morphology, its most dramatic characteristics are the enormous gill slits. There are five, as in most sharks, and they extend the full length of the profile, almost meeting below the head. This gives the shark a most peculiar appearance, as if it were nearly decapitated. (See Plate 10.)

These gill slits are extremely necessary to the shark's *modus operandi*, since it feeds on plankton by swimming through the water with its mouth and gills opened wide. On the inside of the gills is a series of long, quill-like gill rakers, which serve to trap the minute animals and plants as the water washes out through the gill slits. While feeding, the basking shark swims at about two knots per hour, and this enables it to eat and breathe in the same motion. The water carrying the plankton also passes over the gill arches, which absorb the oxygen that the fish requires.

(Overleaf) Plate 10. **Basking sharks** *(Cetorhinus maximus)*

RICHARD ELLIS -75

Gavin Maxwell, courtesy of James Maxwell Watt, Esq.

The basking shark fishery at the Isle of Soay in the Scottish Hebrides.

On rare occasions, basking sharks without gill rakers are taken. This infrequent occurrence has led to theories of hibernation (since the fish obviously cannot eat without its feeding apparatus), or annual replacement of the gill rakers. Some scientists feel that during periods when food is scarce, the sharks descend into deeper water for a protracted period of inactivity. At present, our knowledge of the habits of the basking shark is restricted to the observations that can be made from the surface or from above. In the late forties a basking shark fishery was conducted off the coast of California, using spotter planes to locate the sharks.

The smallest basking shark known was about five feet long, but we do not know if this was a newborn shark or a juvenile. It is assumed that basking sharks are viviparous (live-bearing), but since no gravid female has been seen since 1776, and the accuracy of this identification has been questioned, we must admit to almost total ignorance on the subject of reproduction in *Cetorhinus maximus*. Even though Matthews' paper (1950) on the subject of reproduction in basking sharks is lengthy, it consists mostly of histological examination of the testes, claspers, and ovaries, and does not explain much more about the mysteries than we could have assumed from simple observation. Matthews, who studied the specimens brought in by Maxwell's Hebridean shark fishery, noted the extraordinary ratio of males to females that were caught: for each male, there were between thirty and forty females! He concludes his discussion in this manner:"

> *Where are the other males? Do they habitually swim at greater depths and come to the surface only in quest of the females? Are they shyer of the predaceous fishermen? Or is there a social structure in the population so that the dominant males hoard harem schools of females and keep their rivals at a distance? Some fortunate naturalist may one day be able to find the answers to this and many other riddles about these interesting creatures.*

Young basking sharks differ from adults in one significant feature. They have an elongated snout, often with a hornlike protuberance on the end. While the mature sharks have an ordinary-looking head, some young specimens have a snout so long that it is said to resemble a short trunk.

C. maximus is usually described as brownish or blackish in color, but Gavin Maxwell describes them thus: "Looking down from the foredeck of a boat, the body never looks darker than the water surrounding it, always lighter, and of an umberish color with darker markings." The dorsal fin seen projecting above the surface of the water usually appears black, but this may have to do with the drying of the mucous covering when the shark is not in the water. This mucous covering (the purpose of which is not known) dries to a blackish color when exposed to the air, and this probably accounts for the discrepancy in the descriptions of the fish. In addition to confusing observers, this covering is unpleasant to touch and smells awful. The skin of the basking shark is covered with minute denticles, which, unlike those of most other sharks, seem to be arranged in a haphazard fashion. In other species, these dermal denticles point toward the tail, giving the fish a smoothness of texture when rubbed in that direction and the feeling of rough sandpaper when rubbed toward the head, or against the grain. On the basking shark, the skin is rough to the touch in every direction.

One of the truly extraordinary aspects of this fish is its occasional tendency to leap completely out of the water, no mean feat for a fish whose weight is calculated in tons. This sort of behavior is usually associated with feeding fishes, or with game fishes that are hooked. Basking sharks are susceptible to parasites such

as copepods, sea lice, and lampreys, and it might be to dislodge these bothersome creatures that the sharks breach. All the species of great whales are known to leap clear of the water, and their actions may be similar in nature to those of the basking sharks. They may all be trying to loosen the parasites, or they may be communicating with one another by the great crashing sound of their reentry.

The size attained by basking sharks, their habit of swimming on the surface with the dorsal fin and part of the tail exposed, and another habit that seems unique in sharks—swimming at the surface in single file, nose to tail—have given rise to many tales of "sea serpents," which prove to be basking sharks, alone or in company, living or dead. Maxwell reports that he has "several times seen three or more large sharks swimming nose to tail, following each other for long distances and sometimes in circles, and these an inexperienced observer would almost certainly mistake for one creature of great length." P. F. O'Connor, another shark fisherman of the Hebrides, discovered that the snouts of many of the fish he captured were rubbed raw "by the continuous grinding against the sharp denticles on the hide of the beast in front." Both Maxwell and O'Connor were fishermen, not scientists, but it is not only fishermen's tales or popular literature that includes references to basking sharks as sea monsters. In Bigelow and Schroeder, there is a section in the discussion of the basking shark titled "Basking Sharks Reported as Sea Serpents or Other Monsters." With true scholarly caution, the authors introduce this section with these words: "Without entering into the controversy regarding the so-called 'sea-serpent,' we may point out that the Basking Shark has formed the demonstrable basis of sea serpent stories on several occasions."

More frequent than reports of unidentified monsters at sea have been the reports of the remains of mysterious gigantic carcasses washed up on shore. In his book *In the Wake of Sea Serpents*, the Belgian zoologist Heuvelmans devotes an entire chapter to "all the stranded monsters that have proved to be basking sharks." Included in this chapter is a lengthy discussion of the "Stronsa Beast," a *cause célèbre* in 1808 and thereafter. It had washed up on the beach at Stronsa (now spelled Stronsay), in the Orkneys, and was identified as a sea snake with a mane like that of a horse, a long neck, six legs, and a total length of some fifty-five feet. It was given the scientific name *Halsydurus maximus* ("great sea-snake") and, for a while, a new creature was known to the world. When sections of the vertebral column, parts of the skull, and pieces of the skin were examined, it became clear the *Halsydurus* was our old friend *Cetorhinus* after all. It seems that in decomposition, the basking shark leaves remains that can easily be mistaken for a sea monster, since the great gill arches slough off first, leaving the small skull on the anterior end of the long vertebral column. The pectoral fins, pelvic fins, and claspers (in a male shark) could all be mistaken for legs, and if the lower lobe of the tail rots off first—as it would tend to do, since vertebrae are only present in the upper lobe—it is quite possible to see the remains of a large basking shark as a sea monster. (The "mane like that of a horse" is probably the result of the fraying of the cartilaginous supports of the dorsal fins.)

Basking sharks seem to be the only species of sharks that wash up on shore with any degree of regularity. Why this is so is problematical, since no sharks have an air or swim bladder, and they are supposed to sink when they die. It may be that they are not washed up dead, but rather they are stranded, in the manner of the whales. Beached whales, however, are sometimes found alive, while no basking shark has been discovered on land in any condition other than

advanced decomposition. Of course, whales breathe air, and therefore would stay alive longer out of the water, but even so, there are few reports of stranded leviathans that were identified as basking sharks. The decomposed carcasses of basking sharks have been found on the beaches of Cape Cod, Norway, Scotland, France, and Australia. Only the giant squid has engendered more sea-serpent tales.

I had occasion to examine the remains of an unknown animal that had washed up on a beach in Rhode Island. My final identification of the animal was made easier by a photograph that appeared in a local newspaper. I was told by a friend that "some huge thing" had washed up on a neighboring beach, and "it was not a whale." I went to look for the remains, but all I could find were a few large cartilaginous vertebrae. These were sufficient to identify it as a large shark, but I was not sure of the species until the next day, when an article appeared in the local weekly newspaper, showing our trap fishermen at work. Accompanying the article was a photograph of the fishermen hauling in an eighteen-foot basking shark. When I asked the fishermen what they had done with the shark, they told me it had gotten fouled in the net and was dead when they hauled it in. They cut it loose, and less than a mile from where it was caught, I found its remains.

THRESHER SHARKS

There is a story told about the relationship between the thresher shark, the broadbill swordfish, and the whale. It seems that the thresher would circle the unlucky whale, slapping at the water with its sickle-like tail, and beating the surface of the ocean into a froth to further confuse the victim. While the whale was thus distracted, the swordfish would pierce the hapless whale in a vital spot and kill it. This cooperative venture was apparently undertaken because neither the thresher nor the swordfish could handle the large whale separately. The results of this cooperation would appear to be a cetacean feast for the participants.

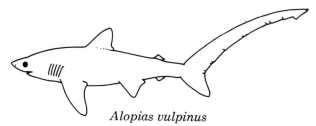

Alopias vulpinus

Unfortunately, neither the swordfish nor the thresher includes whale meat in its regular diet, so this whole operation would seem a rather unnecessary, if not downright wasteful, thing to do. The fable does point up an interesting comparison between the two alleged conspirators: both have an abnormally elongated appendage, the swordfish in the forward position, and the thresher in the aft. We have a pretty good idea of the uses the swordfish (or the marlin or the sailfish) makes of its elongated snout, but the thresher's tail is a little more problematical. Generally, the tail is about equal in length to the body of the fish, and since a thresher can achieve a total length of twenty feet, that means ten feet of shark body and ten feet of tail. Among the uses suggested for this tail are the following, in descending order of credibility: it is used to round up fish into a compact school, which the shark then feeds on; it is used to flip fish out of the water and into its mouth; it is used to slap seabirds sitting on the surface, so the shark can then gobble up the stunned birds. There are "eyewitness" reports of these actions, and somewhat less well-documented stories about truly bizarre uses to which the tail has been put. One story, quoted by someone who said the story was told to him, tells of a longline fisherman who had hooked a large shark, and when he leaned over the gunwale to see what it was, the tail of a thresher (for that is what it was) came whipping out of the water and decapitated him.

Most sharks have only one offensive apparatus: their mouths. Even sharks with relatively small teeth (like threshers), use their teeth to capture their prey, to fight, or to defend themselves. It is therefore somewhat surprising to hear, even in theory, of a shark that uses its tail as a food-gathering device or as an offensive weapon. The only other higher animals that come to mind that use their tails for anything other than hanging from trees, or wagging as some sort of an instinctive signal (such as cats, dogs, deer, etc.), are crocodiles and porcupines. Crocodiles have been known to sweep their victims into the water with a swipe of their powerful tails, and porcupines swing their quill-studded tails in defense against predators. Both these animals use their tails in the air, where resistance is considerably less than in the water. This is not to say that threshers do *not* use their tails as a weapon or as a food-gathering device, but proof is sorely lacking. Threshers are usually found offshore, and I do not think their feeding process has ever been observed, except at the surface and from a distance. (See Plate 12.)

In a discussion of the morphological excesses sometimes seen in sharks, especially the "hammer" of the hammerhead and the tail of the thresher, Paul Budker seriously questions the "food-gathering" explanation. He points out that "the thresher could do just as well as related species without somersaults and other antics and without behaving like a sheepdog."[38] Moreover, the fishes that the thresher is supposed to be concentrating into a tight school "are renowned for their gregarious habits and surely need no stimulus to form shoals of tightly packed individuals." Most of those who have speculated on the function of a thresher's tail have assumed that it *could* be used to herd small fish into tight schools, and therefore that it *should* be so used. This is specious, unscientific reasoning, and the facts as we know them do not support this idea. (Budker sees the tail as an overspecialization, like the elongated head lobes of the hammerheads.) If there is indeed a "purpose" to this extreme elongation of the tail, we do not know what it is.

We do know that a shark's source of propulsive power is its tail, the other fins serving as planing, stabilizing, or steering devices, so some connection must be drawn between the threshers' extraordinary appendage and their forward motion. If the tail is strong enough to accomplish even some of the wondrous feats ascribed to it, then it surely must add to the sharks' speed. It may also have something to do with a "circling" motion; even if the sharks do not actually herd the prey fish into tightly packed schools, they accomplish this defense on their own, and it may be necessary for the sharks to surround a small school. Threshers feed on menhaden, shad, herring, and mackerel, and they catch them with their teeth.

There are at least two species of threshers. The most common and best known is the common thresher, *Alopias vulpinus* (whose names mean "fox fox" in Greek and Latin, respectively—names presumably derived from its long tail). The bigeye thresher, *Alopias superciliosus*, has a much larger eye, suggesting a deeper-water habitat, fewer teeth in the jaws, and a dorsal fin set much further back. Bass, D'Aubrey, and Kistnasamy describe a third species, *Alopias pelagicus*, which has smaller teeth than the previously identified species; in their report they describe and illustrate a specimen taken off Durban.[21] Because of their unique appearance, threshers have been given a variety of colorful and descriptive names, including fox shark, foxtail, swingletail, and sickletail.

Threshers are found throughout the temperate waters of the world, and are occasionally listed as potentially dangerous, but the only danger seems to be from the whipping tail on the deck of a fishing boat. Frank Mundus refers to the thresher as "the grim reaper of the sea,"[175] although from reading his account of this shark, it is difficult to see why. The only reference to an injury sustained by any fisherman is the story of the man who was decapitated by a thresher's tail, and this is a second- or third-hand story.

Threshers are listed as game fish by the International Game Fish Association, with most of the heavy-tackle specimens coming from New Zealand, while the light-tackle specimens have been caught in California waters. The current record is a 739-pound fish, caught off Tutukaka, New Zealand, in 1975. It was 15.5 feet long. Earlier records show a 922-pound specimen, also from New Zealand, but this one was caught on untested line and is therefore ineligible for the record books. Threshers are not common anywhere, but are considered prime game fish wherever they can be found. In British waters they are eagerly sought (although rarely caught), and they receive regular mention in books about big game fishing in New England, California, Australia, and, of course, New Zealand. Zane Grey, writing about the thresher in New Zealand waters, called it "exceedingly stubborn. Comparing him with the mako, he is pound for pound, a harder fish to whip."

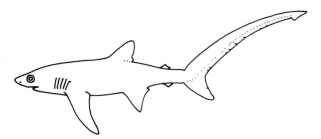

Alopias superciliosus

NURSES AND WOBBEGONGS

There is only one orectolobid shark in American waters, and it is a drab, slow-moving, generally inoffensive creature known as *Ginglymostoma cirratum*, the Atlantic nurse shark. (The origin of the name nurse shark is obscure, although I have read one reference by Hodgson to a specimen "sucking violently on the end of the chemical outlet tube," thus giving "an ear-splitting demonstration of the appropriateness of its common name."[137] The Australian grey nurse, *Odontaspis arenarius*, is no relation, and its name is equally obscure.) *G. cirratum* is common in the tropical waters of the western Atlantic, and it is also a common inhabitant of aquariums and oceanariums. Eugenie Clark said unequivocally in 1963 that "*Ginglymostoma cirratum* is the shark most successfully kept in captivity."[52] The record for a shark in captivity—twenty-five years—is held by a nurse shark in Chicago's Shedd Aquarium. In the wild as well as in a tank, the nurse shark is a bottom feeder, but it can be conditioned to come to the surface for food.

The prominent nasal barbels and small eyes of the nurse shark would seem to indicate that it uses its sense of touch more than its sense of vision to locate food. In tests conducted at the Lerner Marine Laboratory in Bimini, however, nurse sharks proved especially adept at locating a food source by their sense of smell. These experiments, conducted in a fenced-in area of the Bimini lagoon, involved fish juices being re-

leased from a tube (it was at this time that the shark mentioned above "nursed" on the tube) into water in which an offshore current was running. Much to the surprise of the observers, the nurse shark was better able to locate the source of the odor trail than a lemon shark, a carcharhinid species that was supposed to be more sensitive to the odor of moving prey.

For the most part nurse sharks feed on shrimps, crabs, spiny lobsters, and sea urchins, but they occasionally bestir themselves to catch a fish. Like the other orectolobids, the nurse shark can and does spend a great deal of time on the bottom or in underwater caves. It obviously can breathe while stationary, and does not have to move to keep water circulating over its gills.

Because of its sedentary habits, its abundance, and its preference for fairly shallow waters, the nurse shark is the shark most often encountered by divers in the Florida-Caribbean region. A nurse shark resting on the bottom does not look very "sharky," and many people have tried to tease it, poke it, or even ride on it—often with disastrous results. There are numerous cases on record of nurse sharks turning and biting their tormentors, and they are quite capable of inflicting a nasty wound. Even a small specimen can be dangerous; a thirteen-year-old boy had his arm severely mauled after he grabbed the tail of a 2.5-foot nurse shark. This shark is known to reach a length of 14 feet (10 feet is

An adult nurse shark, Ginglymostoma cirratum, *eating a smaller member of the same species, off the New Jersey coast. The nasal barbels are particularly noticeable.*

considered a good-sized adult, however) and weigh upwards of 350 pounds, and it is therefore the better part of valor to leave them alone, no matter how placid they look sitting on the bottom. In one instance, Peter Gimbel and Peter Matthiessen were diving in the "blue hole" in Nassau, when they decided to explore a cave in the wall. Without knowing it, they had cornered a large nurse shark, which bolted by them in its attempt to escape. Matthiessen wrote: "There was much less danger that it would attack than that it would knock us senseless against the coral or cut us up with the placoid scales of its rough hide in a charge to freedom through the narrow passage."[164]

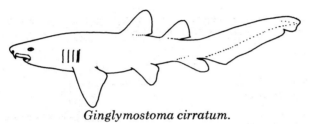

Ginglymostoma cirratum.

A number of incidents have been reported of divers being attacked by nurse sharks that were annoyed, but perhaps none is as peculiar as Eugenie Clark's story (in *The Lady and the Sharks*) of Beryl Chadwick, who was feeding the sharks at the Cape Haze Marine Lab in 1956:

Beryl brought a class of schoolchildren onto the dock beside the shark pen to show them his favorite shark, Rosy. The big old nurse shark was at the bottom of the pen and couldn't be seen. Beryl, who often called her up this way to feed her, splashed his hand on the water while kneeling on the feeding platform. He let his hand dangle over the side some distance above the water and turned for an instant to say something to the watchful children. Rosy lifted her head out of the water and touched Beryl's hand. It was such a smooth gentle-looking maneuver that it could have been mistaken for a kiss. But the end of one of Beryl's fingers has been a quarter of an inch shorter ever since.[50]

An unusual feature of the nurse shark is the apparent ambiguity in the manner in which the young are born. According to Breder and Rosen, there is "some question as to whether ... the nurse shark, *Ginglymostoma*, sometimes lays eggs or always hatches them within the body. Possibly either is done, depending on

various conditions."[35] Nurse sharks give birth to small pups (eight or nine inches long at birth) which have a large "yolk stomach" which they gradually absorb. On my last visit to the Mote Marine Laboratory, Pat Bird, the aquarist, was hand-raising a number of baby nurse sharks that had hatched from eggs taken from the mother. All was going well until a sudden cold snap dropped the water temperature, and all but one of the babies died. As of March 1976, this one is doing fine, and if it survives, it will be the first nurse shark successfully raised in captivity. (This may sound odd for a shark that does so well in captivity, but in the past, whenever nurse sharks were born in an aquarium tank, they were eaten by other sharks almost immediately.)

Among the characteristics which identify this shark are its brownish color (juvenile nurse sharks are reddish or yellowish brown, with a series of irregular dark spots, that disappear with maturity), nasal barbels, a groove connecting each nostril with the mouth, large rounded fins, and a long tail with almost no lower lobe. (The name Orectolobidae comes from the Greek *orectos*, meaning "stretched out," and *lobos*, meaning "lobe," referring to the tail.) The fourth and fifth gill slits are often so close together that they appear as one—untrained observers sometimes think they have discovered a "four-gilled shark" when they notice this.

While *Ginglymostoma cirratum* is the only member of the family in the Western Hemisphere, there are two other sharks that resemble it so closely that the three were once thought to comprise a single species. *Ginglymostoma brevicaudatum* and *Nebrius concolor* are quite similar to the Atlantic nurse shark, differing primarily in size and tooth morphology. *G. brevicaudatum*, true to its name, has a smaller tail than *cirratum*, and its dorsal fins are almost equal in size, while the second dorsal of *cirratum* is considerably smaller than the first. *Brevicaudatum* is found in South African waters. In Australia, *Nebrius* (= *Nebrodes*) *concolor* was known as the tawny shark, or "Madame X," according to G. P. Whitley, who wrote: "For a long time the identity of this shark was in doubt. Fishermen reported a shark which coughed and spurted water at them in Queensland, but no specimens were forwarded for classification. The shark was therefore dubbed 'Madame X' and the name stuck."[253] This species is also found in South Africa, and Bass, D'Aubrey, and Kistnasamy, in a publication in

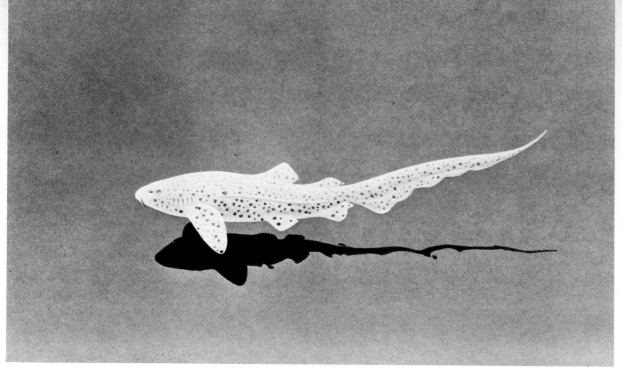

Stegostoma varium, *the zebra shark.*

which the synonymy is briefly reviewed, give the delightful "giant sleepy shark" as the local common name. [21]

The orectolobids are characterized by the long nasal barbels and the grooves which connect the nostrils to the mouth. If not for these characteristics, it would be very difficult to differentiate these sharks from the Scyliorhinidae, the catsharks.* One species that adds to the confusion is *Chiloscyllium*, known in Australia as the brown-banded catshark, and in South Africa as the blue-spotted catshark. These two sharks, which may be conspecific, are presently classified as orectolobids. They reach a length of about three feet, and are variously marked with dark bands or blue-white spots.

Other orectolobids which have not been clearly identified as to species or even genus are *Brachaelurus* (found in Australia and known, for a reason that I have been unable to discover, as the "blind shark"), *Heteroscyllium colcloughi* (known from only one specimen from Queensland), and *Hemiscyllium sp.*, the epaulette sharks, sometimes classified as catsharks, sometimes as orectolobids.

_____

* Like the carcharhinids, the catsharks (Scyliorhinidae) are currently being revised, and the revision will not be available until after this book has been completed. Stewart Springer, who has been working on the revision for over ten years, has kindly helped me with the section on the Scyliorhinidae, but for the orectolobids, I have had to rely for the most part on already published material, which is confusing and contradictory, at best. I have used Whitley's 1940 *Fishes of Australia, Part I, Sharks, etc.;* Bigelow and Schroeder's 1948 key to the genera of orectolobids in *Fishes of the Western North Atlantic;* and Bass, D'Aubrey, and Kistnasamy's *Sharks of the East Coast of Southern Africa, IV,* 1975. These works cover a period of thirty-five years, and obviously more work is needed to clarify a most muddled situation.

There may be only one representative orectolobid in North American waters, but a most varied and colorful population of orectolobids inhabits Australian waters, including carpet sharks, zebra sharks, epaulette sharks, and wobbegongs.

Stegostoma varium, the zebra shark, is built along the lines of a nurse shark, except that where the nurse shark is a mousy grayish brown, *Stegostoma* is yellowish white with dark brown spots, with a series of longitudinal ridges similar to those of the whale shark (to which it is not related). The name "zebra," which seems inappropriate at best for a spotted shark, was probably first applied to the juvenile of the species: young zebra sharks are dark brown with white stripes. (It should be pointed out that another vernacular name for this species is "leopard shark," which would apply to the adult, but not to the juvenile.) The spiracles of this shark, located behind the eyes, are larger than the eyes. With the exception of the thresher, *Stegostoma* has a tail that is proportionally the longest of any shark, with the upper lobe (there is only a hint of a lower caudal lobe) accounting for as much as 50 percent of the shark's total length. This shark reaches ten or eleven feet in length and, like the other orectolobids, it spends most of its time resting on the bottom. *Stegostoma varium* is found in the waters of the western Pacific, Australasia, and the Indian Ocean.

As far as I can tell, Whitley's *Fishes of Australia, Part I, Sharks, Etc.*, published in 1940, is the latest word on the wobbegongs. While it is an interesting book, full of odd anecdotal material and photographs, and occasionally illustrated with Whitley's own drawings, it leaves much to be desired as a definitive work on a group as interesting as the wobbegongs. According to Bigelow and Schroeder, there are three genera: *Eucrossorhinus*, *Orectolobus*, and *Sutorectus*. All three are bottom-dwelling, somewhat flattened sharks, with a series of fleshy lobes or fringes around the mouth. Some are oviparous, laying large, leathery eggs, and others, according to Whitley, are viviparous.[253]

The wobbegongs, also known as carpet sharks, are brightly colored, well-camouflaged sharks that spend their days lying on the bottom looking like rocks, weeds, and coral, and their nights looking for food. They have spots, stripes, rings, blotches, and many combinations of the foregoing, all of which make them very difficult to see as they lie motionless on the bottom. Among the species recognized are *Orectolobus maculatus* (the largest of the wobbegongs, which reaches a length of 10.5 feet); *O. ornatus*, the banded wobbegong; *O. wardi*, the northern wobbegong; *Eucrossorhinus ogilbyi*, the tasseled wobbegong; and *Sutorectus tentaculatus*, the cobbler carpet shark. I am not sure if all these species are valid, but everyone seems to use Whitley as a reference, and this list comes straight from his book. (It must be open to question, because his use of the scientific name of the other genera is almost totally outdated; it is difficult to find a single name that is in use today. However, until someone revises Whitley's nomenclature, it will have to apply.)

The various wobbegongs range in size from 3 to 10.5 feet, and are considered to be dangerous if provoked. (To provoke a wobbegong, all you have to do is walk around rocky areas; sooner or later you'll step on one.) One look at the mouth of a wobbegong will confirm the potential danger; there are row after row of "long, cruel, tearing teeth" (as Whitley describes them), and it is obvious that these teeth can inflict serious wounds on the poor unfortunate who disturbs one of these sharks. The Shark Attack File lists only one authenticated wobbegong attack, but contains fourteen "unauthoritative" attacks, and given the distinctive appearance of these sharks, it is very likely that at least some of the sharks were wobbegongs. (In a curious footnote, Whitley introduces a new species, *Eucrossorhinus dasypogon* [Bleeker], "from the East Indies and New Guinea," and says that this fish, locally called *gotadoeoeo*, "attacks and generally kills the natives.")

WHALE SHARK

The largest fish in the world has a name that is guaranteed to confuse anyone but the experienced ichthyologist. It is called the whale shark, which is something like calling an animal a "cat-dog," or a "bird-snake." It sounds like it might be either a whale or a shark, but we are not really sure which. It is no relation whatever to the whales, which of course are mammals, and *Rhincodon typus* (to eliminate the confusion, at least for the moment, by using its scientific name) is a fish. It has gills, breathes water, and does not come up for air. It is a shark, which means that in addition to the above characteristics, it has five gill slits, a multitude of teeth, skin that is composed of dermal denticles, and a cartilaginous skeleton. The "whale" portion of its common name simply serves to comment on its size.

The whale shark, however, is unique among the sharks, unique among the fishes, and even unique among the vertebrates that inhabit the sea. First of all, it is gigantic when fully matured. We are not sure how big it can get—but more on that later. Suffice it to say here that it is a very big fish indeed, bigger than any other fish that swims. It is one of the few sharks whose mouth is in the "terminal" position, meaning that it is located at the front of the head rather than being underslung, as is the case with most other species of sharks. It might be assumed that the largest fish in the world would have little need of camouflage; in fact, it is almost impossible to imagine this behemoth hidden at all, especially since it inhabits the open ocean, where no plants grow. And yet, the whale shark is covered in an intricate pattern of dots and stripes arranged in a very regular grid —a pattern that is unmatched anywhere else in nature. Starting at the broad head, the great fish is covered with a closely spaced pattern of dots, usually yellowish or white on a darker background. (The fish has been described as varying from dark gray to reddish or greenish brown on the back and sides, but most observers content themselves with a simple "brown" or "brownish.") From the snout to the pectorals, the dots are small and close together, but random in their placement. Above the pectorals, a more organized arrangement begins to appear, consisting of vertical rows of large dots (two to three inches in diameter), separated by vertical stripes. There are also strong horizontal ridges, which heighten the grid or checkerboard effect. The whale shark is lighter below, as are most sharks, and the tail is also spotted, but less densely than the foreparts. And if all this were

not enough to differentiate this shark from all other sharks, it does not have the caudal notch that appears in every other large selachian. This peculiar "cut," located near the top of the upper lobe of the tail fin, is visible on the tails of almost all other sharks, and no one seems to have the slightest idea of its purpose or function, if indeed it has one. It is probably unnecessary to assign a clear use to every lump, bump, and notch, but it seems unlikely that millions of years of evolution would have retained unnecessary structures. The likelihood is that there is (or was) a reason for this notch in the tail fin, but we have not found out what it is yet.

In its external appearance, *Rhincodon* (which means "rasp-tooth") *typus* is nothing if not surprising. One's first impression is usually of disbelief—is *anything* really this big? Add to this the bizarre coloring, and you end up thinking that no such creature can possibly exist. In *Kon-Tiki*, Thor Heyerdahl writes of the expedition's first encounter with a whale shark:

> *Knut had been squatting there, washing his pants in the swell, and when he looked up for a moment he was staring straight into the biggest and ugliest face any of us had ever seen in the whole of our lives. It was the head of a veritable sea monster, so huge and so hideous that if the Old Man of the Sea himself had come up he could not have made such an impression on us. The head was broad and flat like a frog's, with two small eyes right at the sides, and a toadlike jaw which was four or five feet wide and had long fringes hanging from the corners of the mouth. Behind the head was an enormous body ending in a long thin tail with a pointed tail fin which stood straight up and showed that this sea monster was not any kind of whale....*
>
> *When the giant came right up to the raft, it rubbed its back against the heavy steering oar, which was lifted up out of the water, and now we had ample opportunity of studying the monster at the closest quarters—at such close quarters that I thought we had all gone mad, for we roared stupidly with laughter and shouted overexcitedly at the completely fantastic sight we saw.*[135]

The whale shark is usually a rare and solitary animal, although there have been instances in which more than one has been seen at a time,

(Overleaf) A young whale shark photographed with divers in the waters off Bermuda.

Edwin J. Gould

and even some occasions when small schools have been sighted. They are usually slow-moving, inquisitive creatures, and they have a tendency to hang around boats and divers, making no effort whatever to get away. That the creature is capable of swift movement is demonstrated by its actions after one crew member of the *Kon-Tiki*, "encouraged by ill-considered shouts," harpooned the great shark:

> *Then in a flash the placid half-wit transformed into a mountain of steel muscles. We heard a swishing noise as the harpoon line rushed over the edge of the raft, and saw a cascade of water as the giant stood on its head and plunged down into the depths. The three men who were standing nearest were flung about the place head over heels and two of them were flayed and burnt by the line as it rushed through the air. The thick line, strong enough to hold a boat, was caught on the side of the raft but snapped at once like a piece of twine, and a few seconds later a broken-off harpoon shaft came up to the surface two hundred yards away.*[135]

On another occasion, a fishing instructor harpooned a 32-foot specimen in the Arabian Sea, and after lashing two steel-hulled boats together (measuring 32 and 27 feet long, respectively), the instructor, a Mr. Illugason, and his fifteen students, were towed for three hours, "at a speed of five knots."

An American ichthyologist, Dr. E. W. Gudger of New York's American Museum of Natural History, had an ongoing preoccupation with whale sharks, and tracked down every report, rumor, or suggestion of their occurrence, resulting in the publication of dozens of papers with such titles as "The Whale Shark in the Gulf of California,"[116] "The Food and Feeding Habits of the Whale Shark,"[113] and "The Whale Shark Unafraid."[117] It was Gudger who obtained the 17-foot 4¾-inch specimen which was exhibited in 1931 in the Hall of Fishes at the AMNH, and now, slightly refurbished and repainted, it hangs there still.

Many of Gudger's accounts had to do with a whale shark being rammed by a ship ("Whale Sharks Rammed by Ocean Vessels"[118]), and this does not seem to be an altogether uncommon occurrence. The great fish seems to be unwilling to get out of the way of anything, and this recalcitrance often results in damage to the shark, the ship, or both. There have been accidents of

this sort on a more or less regular basis, since the largest fish in the world was discovered off the coast of South Africa in 1828. This huge animal, unknown to science until the first quarter of the nineteenth century, with a habit of getting in the way of ships on the open sea, surely was the basis of many sea monster stories. In 1905 the liner *Armandale Castle*, J. C. Robinson, captain, collided with a "large fish" which could not be identified by any observer. An illustration published in a contemporaneous account clearly shows that the large fish is a whale shark, complete with spots, ridges, and an unnotched tail. The size is given at "not less than 57 feet in length."

This brings us to the interesting question of the maximum size of *R. typus*. A careful search of the literature reveals many references to 32- to 38-foot specimens, and a great deal of speculation about how big they *might* get. In Baja California waters, William Beebe saw a 42-footer from a boat, harpooned it, but could not bring it in. Again off Baja California, Conrad Limbaugh reported diving with a specimen "estimated to be 35–42 feet long."[153] Bernard Heuvelmans, in *In the Wake of Sea-Serpents*, refers to several giant specimens, such as one "53 feet long that was measured at Kommetje Bay in South Africa, and there are even some 60 to 65 feet long, like the one which was caught in a bamboo fish-trap at Koh Chik in the east of the Gulf of Siam in 1919 but could not be measured accurately by a qualified person."[134] These are the only references I have ever seen to these specimens, and without some corroboration, I am little inclined to accept them as fact.

I suggest that whale sharks are mature at thirty-five to forty feet, and probably don't get much past forty. (There seems to be an inclination to assume that if a fish can get to be forty feet long, it ought to be able to reach fifty, and therefore sixty. This tendency to assign infinite growth to certain fishes is nowhere more evident than in the sharks, and particularly in the case of the extinct *Carcharodon megalodon*.) At forty feet, the whale shark is in fact larger than a small whale—the minke whale, smallest of the baleen whales, does not exceed thirty feet in length. An 1870 specimen from the Seychelles is included in Bigelow and Schroeder, and at forty-five feet it is the largest recorded in the scientific literature. (It is incorporated as a footnote, and the authors are quick to point out that they did not see this specimen.) Others in Bigelow and Schroeder are given as "6–34 feet

Plate 11. **Chain dogfish** (*Scyliorhinus retifer*

(*Overleaf*) *Plate 12.* **Thresher shark** (*Alopias vulpinus*)

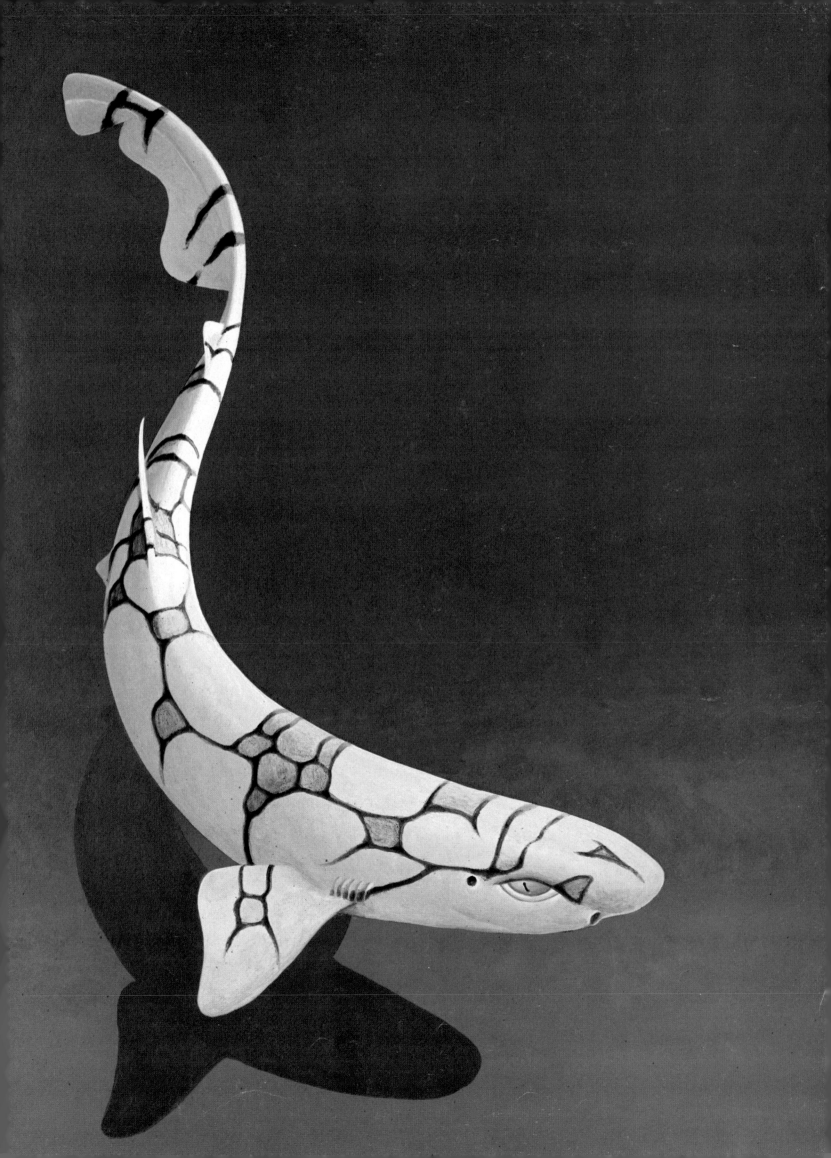

© RICHARD ELLIS · 1975

recorded for Cuban specimens, 18–34 feet for Florida examples, and 31.5 feet for one taken at Fire Island, New York. . . . The estimated weight for a 38-foot whale shark taken off Knight's Key, Florida, in June 1912 was 26,594 pounds." Perry Gilbert told me that he had once seen three whale sharks together in the Gulf of Mexico; he said they were about thirty feet long. When I asked him about the fifty- or sixty-foot sharks that are supposed to exist, he told me that he thought thirty-five to forty feet was about the maximum.

When Bigelow and Schroeder published their monumental work in 1948, they said of the whale shark: "The size at sexual maturity is not known, nor is the size at birth." Under the subheading "Developmental Stages," there is this statement, which sums up all that was known at the time regarding the parturition of the whale shark: "Sixteen eggs have been counted in a specimen from Ceylon, these being of the 'same form as in dog fish.' Whether or not these hatch before birth is not definitely known."

In 1955, J. L. Baughman published a paper describing an event that shook the shark world.[23] Dredged up 130 miles south of Port Isabel, Texas, was a leathery egg case, the likes of which had never been seen before. It looked very much like the egg cases of other sharks and rays, but this one measured twenty-seven by sixteen inches! Odell Freeze, a shrimp trawler who had found the case in one of his nets, "felt something alive and kicking inside." He carefully cut open the case and revealed a perfectly formed whale shark embryo, 14.5 inches long, and complete with wide snout, stripes, spots, and lateral ridges. It was thus determined conclusively that whale sharks lay eggs. This was the first and last time that the egg case of a whale shark had been recovered.

In "The Maintenance of Sharks in Captivity," Eugenie Clark gives the following reference:

FAMILY RHICONDONTIDAE Whale Sharks *Dr. Hiyama informs me that a whale shark weighing several thousand pounds was exhibited alive for several months, many years ago, at the Mito Aquarium. It was kept in an open aquarium. A small bay was separated by a "net septum" from the open sea, and dolphins, small whales, and sharks were exhibited here. This whale shark is apparently the largest maintained in captivity for any length of time.*[52]

Obviously, this was a small whale shark, since it only weighed "several thousand pounds." The problems involved in feeding a fish that weighs a couple of tons must be significant.

For the whale shark at liberty, however, the problems are minimal. It has teeth—some three to five thousand—but they are minute, averaging about 3 mm in length, and are of no use for chewing or biting. (Precisely what function they do serve is unknown at this time.) The teeth are arranged in over 300 "dentary bands." It is thought that the whale shark feeds primarily on small animals such as plankton and schooling baitfish, which it inhales into its great maw (the mouth of a 35-foot shark is about 6 feet across), and then flushes the water out through its gill slits. The food is retained by a series of gill rakers and strainers that extend into the throat.

There have been accounts of whale sharks feeding in a *vertical* position, with their mouths at or above the surface of the water. They bob up and down, in fifteen- to twenty-second cycles, pausing at the surface to let the water rush into their mouths. While on the research vessel *Oregon*, Stewart Springer reported that he saw "several . . . tuna leap into the mouth of the shark at each cycle." Since the shark then descended below the surface in a flurry of foam, Springer was unable to tell if the shark retained the tuna. Stewart Springer is one of the world's leading authorities on sharks, and his remarks —especially those that are based on firsthand observation—are not to be taken lightly. He said in 1957, "I am inclined to believe that the whale sharks did swallow a considerable number of tuna although I would be much more certain if we had caught one and found tuna in the whale shark's stomach."[217]

Whale sharks are found in all the tropical waters of the world. As with many tropical species, an occasional stray wanders into colder waters. The northernmost record is in the vicinity of New York (Fire Island, 1935), and the southern limit seems to be South Africa. Interestingly enough, the first whale shark ever seen by science, the one harpooned off Table Bay, South Africa, in 1828, was far south of its usual range. They are not common anywhere, although this apparent rarity may be more a

Plate 13. **Bull shark** (*Carcharhinus leucas*)   **123**

function of its deep-water existence than its possibly low population. A whale shark at the surface is hard to miss, but there may be large numbers of these great creatures feeding on plankton below the surface, and therefore unknown. Because they are not likely to take a baited hook, the only ones that are seen are those that are sighted at the surface. In all, there have been about one hundred sightings of whale sharks recorded. They are most frequently reported from the Indian Ocean (between the Seychelles and Mauritius), off Southern California, the Philippines, and the Bay of Bengal.

Hans Hass, a pioneer underwater scientist, diver, and photographer, was looking for a manta ray to photograph in the Red Sea. One of his boatmen sighted a fin that "looked like the dorsal fin of a shark, only much larger." Unaware of what it was, Hass entered the water:

> *Under water I could see nothing, only empty, blue, bottomless sea.... At last, however, I perceived some blurred outlines. The veil lifted and I was able to see quite clearly. What I beheld was so extraordinary that I hung motionless in the water. Ahead of me was gliding along a shark fully twenty-five feet long. His whole gigantic body was flecked with hundreds of white spots.*[127]

Hass rode the shark by hanging on to its dorsal fin and the tail. He said, "The tail took me six feet to the left, then six feet to the right. But the movements became more rapid. Obviously the beast was vexed." Then he had his companions hitch a ride to give a sense of scale to the photographs. His were the first photographs ever taken of a whale shark under water, and since that historic day in 1950, divers and

photographers all over the world have hoped for the opportunity to experience the gentle magnitude of this checkerboard giant.

Ben Cropp, an Australian diver and film maker, filmed *R. typus* in the Tasman Sea, off Montague Island. He claims to be the second man to film the whale shark under water: "The photos, blown up from the sixteen-millimeter color movie film, made front pages in newspapers around the world, and appeared in the top magazines."[62] Ron and Valerie Taylor also filmed the whale shark, and in 1967 Jacques Cousteau made a film of his divers hanging on the dorsal fin of a whale shark.

In September 1974, Edwin Gould, his wife Sydney, Wolfgang Sterrer (the director of the Marine Biological Station in Bermuda), and several other divers were diving the Argus Tower, some thirty miles off shore. From out of the gloom there appeared an enormous creature, obviously a shark. Sydney Gould recalls her initial feeling of terror as she watched the measured approach of this giant spotted beast, but her husband managed to inform her of its harmless nature by hand signals. She approached the great fish and swam with it in the accepted fashion (hanging on the dorsal fin, peering into the great mouth), to the delight of the underwater photographers.

I have also benefited from their experience, since it is Sydney that I painted swimming with the whale shark (see Plate 5). It was an unexpected bonus to have such a lovely model. I worked directly from the Goulds' photographs, and I am grateful for their help. Ordinarily, I am not inclined to title my paintings, but I could not resist calling this one *Portrait of a Lady with a Large Fish.*

CATS AND DOGS

The inherent weakness and confusion of common names is nowhere more obvious than in this large and diversified group. There is no vernacular name that can encompass them all; every time we try to categorize them, one or another genus escapes pseudonymously, to reappear elsewhere in the literature. The family Scyliorhinidae is known collectively as the catsharks, but individually some of them are known as dogfish (not to be confused with the true dogfish, the Squalidae, which are characterized by the absence of an anal fin, and are confusing enough on their own).

As of this writing, Stewart Springer is revising the scyliorhinids, and as with my discussion of the carcharhinids, which Garrick is currently revising, my premature (and probably erroneous) discussion of the scyliorhinids will be a case of "too little, too soon." I will do my best, however, making use of the information at hand, which is none too plentiful. Gilbert Whitley's *Fishes of Australia, Part I, Sharks, etc.*[253] contains all sorts of exotic genera and species, not all of which will survive Springer's revision.* Three genera are listed in Bigelow and Schroeder: *Scyliorhinus, Apristurus,* and *Galeus.* (Other families to be included in this loose confederation are the Pseudotriakidae, the false catsharks; and the Triakidae, the smooth dogfishes.) Because of the variety and generally confusing classification of the various genera, I think it safest to treat each one separately, on the assumption that, in time, the proper relationships will be published.

The scyliorhinids do not have a nasal groove connecting the nostril with the mouth, a characteristic that separates them from some of the smaller orectolobids, such as *Parascyllium* and *Chiloscyllium.* Other identifying features of scyliorhinids are small size, the presence of a spiracle, and, usually, a deep-water habitat. According to Bigelow and Schroeder:

> *The family includes numerous species of small sharks in tropical and temperate latitudes, from both shoal water and deep. Although it embraces two of the most common and best known of the European sharks (*Scyliorhinus caniculus *and* S. stellaris, *the so-called spotted dogfishes), the centers of abundance for both genera and species are the western Pacific, Australasian region and the Indian Ocean to South Africa. It is represented in the western North Atlantic by only a few, little-known deep-water species.*

The "most common and best known" species in European waters, *S. caniculus* and *S. stellaris,* are extremely abundant in the eastern Atlantic, being taken in large numbers in the nets of commercial fishermen. In the western North Atlantic there are also two species, *S. torrei* and *S. retifer.* These small sharks (maximum length is about three feet) are all very similar; they are differentiated by minor, but constant, morphological variations (e.g., the distance between the nasal flaps; the location of the origin of the first dorsal fin)—and by color variations, which are the primary means of identifying the various subspecies. In 1948 Bigelow and Schroeder had *S. retifer* and *S. boa* as different species, but by 1970 these had been synonymized by Springer, who had identified three more subspecies, all morphologically homogeneous, but with completely different color patterns. The five subspecies are:

Scyliorhinus retifer retifer: Net-like pattern on cream-colored ground.
Scyliorhinus retifer meadi: Saddle-like blotches; no black or white spots in color patterns.
Scyliorhinus retifer boa: White spots in saddle blotches.
Scyliorhinus retifer haeckelii: Numerous small black spots in saddle blotches.
Scyliorhinus retifer besnardi: Large black spots; indistinct saddles.[220]

The other distinct species in the western North Atlantic is *Scyliorhinus torrei,* which is very similar to *S. retifer,* but is mature at a much smaller size. The American scyliorhinids have been collected in the Gulf of Mexico, the Caribbean, and off the East Coast of the United

---

* Springer points out the difficulties in separating the families of Scyliorhinidae and Triakidae, finally resorting to the "arbitrary" device of separating them by the location of the base of the first dorsal fin. The triakids are an example of a genus in which new species are regularly placed, often for no better reason than they do not seem to fit elsewhere. In a 1968 paper describing a new species, *Triakis fehlmanni,* Springer referred to the family as "an uneasy assemblage," and then noted that "this is an understatement in view of the remarkable diversity of the group. . . . The addition of the new species places more strain on currently used definitions of genera and families of sharks and emphasizes the need for review of characters that are traditional for their recognition."[227]

States as far north as Long Island. They are bottom-dwelling creatures, and the depths at which they are usually found would indicate a life of nearly perpetual darkness. (Even the deepest-water sharks come to the surface occasionally, usually in pursuit of prey.) They are among the sharks with a pupil that can be increased or decreased in size—depending on the amount of light present—from a round circle to a narrow slit. We are used to seeing this sort of pupillary contraction in cats, where the slit is vertical, but in the scyliorhinids, the slit is closer to the horizontal axis. It was a subspecies of *Scyliorhinus retifer* that I saw at the New York Aquarium (probably *S. retifer retifer*, known as the chain dogfish, because of the chainlike pattern of its dark brown markings), and I was surprised not only by the almost horizontal slit of the pupil—it was broad daylight, probably an unfamiliar condition for this little shark—but also by the bright emerald-green color of the iris. (See Plate 11.)

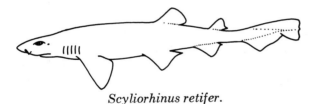

Scyliorhinus retifer.

There are catsharks that have been bred successfully in captivity. In the Dusseldorf Aquarium in May 1954, five specimens of *Scyliorhinus stellaris* (then known as *Scyllium catulus*) were obtained from Monaco. Their mating activities could not be observed because of concrete blocks in the tank, but eventually one of the females began to swim around a stick in the aquarium, a tendril appeared from her vent, and an elongated egg was pulled from the mother's body. She continued to swim in circles, until more of the threads were wrapped around the stick. Nine months later, the eggs hatched, and as of 1963, twenty-one babies had been successfully raised. (They were not left with the adult sharks, but were shielded from them by a plastic screen, or removed from the tank altogether.)

The Australian and South African catsharks, as brightly colored as any group of sharks in the world, are almost chaotic in their taxonomy. Whitley assigns almost every individual a separate genus, and these include *Aulohalaelurus*, *Asymbolus*, *Juncrus*, *Figaro*, and *Actelomycterus*. In South Africa, where the catsharks

Zoologische Garten Leipzig

The egg case of Scyliorhinus stellaris *that was laid and hatched in a German aquarium.*

are commonly known as *skaamoogs*, or "shy-eyes," from their habit of curling their tails over their eyes when they are brought out of the water into the light, there are almost as many nominal genera, including *Poroderma*, *Holohalaelurus*, *Haploblepharus*, and *Pentanchus*. Some or all of these may be valid species. In any event, they are all small, elongated sharks, usually with a distinctive color pattern of spots, saddles, blotches, or even stripes.

Halaelurus seems to be a good genus from the eastern and western Pacific, as well as for South Africa. In Kato, Springer, and Wagner's *Field Guide to Eastern Pacific and Hawaiian Sharks*, there are three species listed, complete with illustrations and a coherent key to their identification.[146] These are *Halaelurus canescens*, *H. bivius*, and *H. chilensis*, all from the cooler waters of Chile and Peru. *H. natalensis* is given in Smith's *Sea Fishes of Southern Africa* as "an

The false catshark, Pseudotriakis microdon, *feeding on a baitfish at a depth of 2,100 feet in the waters of Aldabra Island off East Africa. This shark is seldom seen, and a photograph of a living specimen is rare indeed.*

unmistakable species, fairly common in the trawl," and in a paper published in 1971, Springer named yet another species, *H. dawsoni,* from New Zealand.[220]

An apparently monotypical species is also found in the eastern Pacific; this is the peculiar "head shark," *Cephalurus cephalus,* in which the gill slits and the pectoral fins are so far from the snout that the shark seems to be mostly head. It is about a foot long, and is known only from a couple of specimens from the Gulf of California and the Revillagigedo Islands.

Cephalurus cephalus.

The widely distributed genus *Apristurus* is comprised of small, deep-water sharks, perhaps as many as thirteen species, but probably fewer. They are characterized by a long, dorsally flattened snout with prominent nostrils, and gill clefts in which the gill filaments are exposed. They are usually dark brown to blackish in color, and are presumed to be oviparous. The various species from the coastal waters of the United States are the Atlantic catshark, *Apristurus atlanticus;* the brown catshark, *A. brunneus;* the deep-water catshark, *A. profun-*

dorum; and one with no common name, *A. laurussoni.* Other species exist in the waters of South Africa and possibly Japan and the East Indies. A Pacific species is known as *Apristurus spongiceps.*

In a number of popular books on sharks, the story is told of the strange shark that washed ashore at Amagansett, Long Island, on February 8, 1883—a shark whose like had not been seen before in the United States. A couple of specimens had been recorded in Portuguese waters before 1883, so it was not totally new to science. It was *Pseudotriakis microdon,* the false catshark, a rare, deep-water creature that is hardly ever found close to shore—in fact, it is hardly ever found at all. Other scattered locations of this species include the waters off Iceland, the Cape Verde Islands, and Manasquan, New Jersey, where another American specimen was taken in 1936. It has an equally rare Pacific counterpart, *Pseudotriakis acrages,* which for some reason the Japanese call *oshizame,* the dumb shark. Aside from their rarity and size (they grow to a length of about ten feet), the most significant distinguishing characteristic of the Pseudotriakidae is the long, low, first dorsal fin.

Catsharks with the denticles enlarged along the crest of the caudal fin are called the filetail catsharks, and are included in the genus *Galeus,* and the genus *Parmaturus*, which seems to be monotypical, consisting of the single species *P. xaniurus*. In American waters, *Galeus* is represented by *G. arae*, the marbled catshark, and *G. piperatus*, the peppered catshark. Although we do not have much information about this genus, we do know that two very similar species reproduce differently. *G. melastoma* lays eggs and *G. polli* gives birth to live young. (It is this sort of thing that makes generalizations so risky; you ought to be able to assume that members of the same genus would deliver their young in the same fashion. With sharks, however, you can take almost nothing for granted.)

Galeus arae appears to be one of the few catsharks that have been studied in some detail. Based on extensive trawling operations aboard the research vessel *Oregon* in 1962, Harvey R. Bullis wrote "Depth Segregations and Distribution of Sex-Maturity Groups in the Marbled Catshark, *Galeus arae*."[39] Capture and examination of over 300 specimens showed a definite segregation by size and age, the more mature specimens tending to inhabit the deeper waters. *G. arae* is found in the western North Atlantic from Florida to Colombia, and *G. piperatus* is found only in the Gulf of California—one of the most limited ranges for any shark. According to Bigelow and Schroeder, other species are found in the eastern Atlantic, and the waters of Australia, Japan, Iceland, and Formosa.

The swell sharks, *Cephaloscyllium*, are found in California, South Africa, and Australia. These sharks have the ability, apparently as a defense mechanism, to inflate their stomachs with air or water, in the manner of a puffer fish. Whitley quotes New Zealand fishermen as saying that the local species, *Cephaloscyllium isabella*, "barks like a dog."[253] The California species, *C. ventriosum* (formerly known as *C. uter*), is almost completely nocturnal in its habits, and is not uncommonly caught in the kelp beds of southern California. Earl Herald wrote:

> *When pulled up on deck, the swell shark swallows air, filling the stomach until the center of the body is at least twice its normal diameter. If thrown back into the water, it floats until it is able to discharge this burden. . . . It is difficult to understand the value of this particular mechanism to the swell shark. Most certainly a floating shark would become a quick victim of any large predator in the area.*[132]

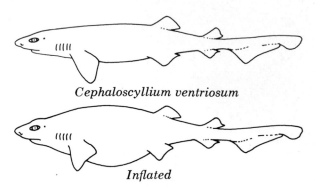

Cephaloscyllium ventriosum

Inflated

The reef whitetip, *Triaenodon obesus*, is an inshore species, found especially in the vicinity of coral formations in the Pacific and the Red Sea. It is a shark whose affiliations are not clear; some authors place it in the triakids because of its multicusped teeth, while others classify it as a carcharhinid, because of the presence of the nictitating membrane. (It is not to be confused with the oceanic whitetip, *Carcharhinus longimanus*, which is a large, deep-water species.) *Triaenodon obesus* has been studied recently by Dr. John Randall of the Bishop Museum in Honolulu, and his study (in manuscript) reports that it is a fairly sedentary animal—through tagging, Randall found that individuals remain in a fairly limited territory. Dr. Donald Nelson, who studied the same species in

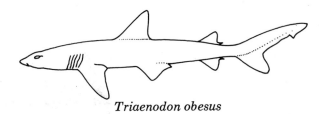

Triaenodon obesus

French Polynesia, reports that it is primarily nocturnal. *T. obesus* is easily recognized by the white-tipped first dorsal fin and upper lobe of the caudal fin, and by the small head. Four-foot specimens of this shark were used in the tests of the shark-repellent flatfish, the Moses sole, in Dr. Eugenie Clark's tests in the Red Sea laboratory. *T. obesus* would not (or could not) bite the little flatfish, *Pardachirus marmoratus*, because of a whitish substance emitted by the fish.[53]

The triakids, smoothhounds, or smooth dogfishes are the last family to be included in this confederation. They lack the nictitating membrane, the teeth of the smoothhounds are usually small and closely crowded, and they are small, harmless sharks. They are found in coastal waters all over the world, and include such common species as the leopard shark,

Triakis semifasciata, and the smoothhound or smooth dogfish, *Mustelus canis*.

Triakis semifasciata is a strongly marked species, commonly seen in West Coast aquariums, and since it travels well, it has become popular in shark tanks all over the United States. (Earl Herald, the director of the Steinhart Aquarium in San Francisco, wrote: "Since San Francisco Bay is a nursery ground for young leopard sharks, this species has become the 'stock in trade' of Steinhart Aquarium, and consequently has been shipped in sealed bags filled with water and oxygen to many different aquaria."[132]) A species similar in configuration, but without the strong markings that give the leopard shark its vernacular name, is *Triakis barbouri*, found off the coast of Cuba. Whereas *T. fasciata* can get to be about five feet long, its Atlantic relative is said to be one of the smallest of sharks; mature females just a little over a foot in length have been found.

Another genus that seems to do well in captivity is *Mustelus*. In fact, these small sharks seem to do well just about anywhere. They are extremely common sharks (second in abundance only to the profligate *Squalus acanthias* in the western North Atlantic), and their relatives are present in equal abundance in practically all the coastal waters of the Atlantic. There are two species in the western Atlantic, *M. canis* (one of the only sharks that are able to change color) and *M. norrisi*. In the eastern Atlantic, two European versions are found in abundance: *Mustelus mustelus*, and *M. asterias*. California

also has its share of smoothhounds, including *M. californicus*, *M. lunulatus*, and *M. henlei*. *M. henlei*, known as the brown smoothhound, is by far the most abundant shark in the American Pacific. According to Herald, 42.5 percent of all sharks and rays caught in San Francisco Bay between 1948 and 1954 were of this species. The females, at an average length of 2.5 feet, were about one-third longer than the males.

All the mustelids feed on small prey, including fishes and invertebrates, and they are held in high disregard by fishermen of all persuasions: net fishermen because they ruin nets; lobster and crab fishermen because they destroy so many of their income-producing invertebrates; and anglers because of the little sharks' eagerness to take bait meant for larger, more exotic fish. Smooth dogfishes hunt in packs or schools (it is thought that this habit is responsible for the name "dogfish"). They are used extensively as laboratory specimens because they are abundant, easily caught, and they have a simple, clear anatomical system, ideal for amateur dissection. The two kinds of dogfishes differ in that *Mustelus* is a truly viviparous genus, giving birth to litters of between ten and twenty pups, about one foot in length. There is a "yolk sac placental" connection, which consists of a nutritive placenta and an umbilical cord before the young are born. Since the spiny dogfish (*Squalus acanthias*) is ovoviviparous, where the young have no connection to the uterine wall, the comparative study of the two so-called "dogfish" can provide a lesson in the different types of development in sharks.

THE CARCHARHINIDS

I have before me a handwritten note from Professor J. A. F. Garrick of New Zealand that says: "I have just begun a 9-month sabbatical leave at the National Museum in Wellington and will be spending it working on carcharhinids." This modest little note is the signal for which all shark people have been waiting; it indicates that the snarl that exists for the largest family of sharks may soon be unraveled. Unfortunately, the revision of this group will not be completed until long after this book is published, so I am going to have to push forward, knowing that much of what I say about which species is which will become obsolete when Garrick's revision is published.

What is this group of sharks that is so confusing? It is the largest of all the shark families, the Carcharhinidae, known as the gray sharks, the typical sharks, or the requiem sharks. The first name presents no problem, the second seems more or less self-explanatory, but the third has given rise to all sorts of foolishness. "Requiem" is the first word of the introit to the Roman Catholic mass for the dead. It has passed unchanged from Latin into English. To some, this has been sufficient to explain the peculiar name: requiem = mass for the dead; sharks sometimes kill people, ergo, requiem sharks. This, of course, is etymological nonsense. The French word for shark is *requin*, and though it bears a certain similarity to "requiem," the two are not related except that they have been confused since the seventeenth century. In 1666, J. Davies discussed the "requiem, otherwise called the shark-fish," and in a 1696 reference, we find the requiem called "the monster of the sea that's shaped like a sea-dog." (In Pliny we discover the earliest references to sharks as dogfish; this later appears in Anglo-Saxon as *doke-fyche*.) That the words "requiem" and "requin" are similar is obvious, that the latter stems from the former is improbable. As Paul Budker, in *The Life of Sharks*, has put it, "The explanation is a little too good to be true, and serious philologists do not accept it."[38]

In any case, most of these sharks are gray or grayish, and they certainly are typical in that they conform to everyone's idea of what a shark is supposed to look like. Many of them are so similar in appearance that they have been confused for years, and every so often a new species pops up. Garrick's main preoccupation is with synonymy, that is, the identification of those heretofore distinct species that should have been classified as the same species. At one time or another, there were thought to be over a hundred different species of carcharhinids (thus adding considerably to the total number of shark species), but Garrick has said that "the number of species that can be recognized is 28 (a reduction to almost one-fourth) and, as such, there must be considerable synonymizing and name-changing. Because [this] will involve many commonly used and established scientific names, publication at this time of a bare synonymic list without the detailed reasoning to support the actions seems unwise."[88] These remarks were published in 1967, and as I write this a decade later, Garrick is preparing to spend the next nine months producing the "detailed reasoning." As of now, however, we have a collection of sharks that look alike, are found all over the world, and have a hopelessly confused nomenclature.

A small but significant portion of the confusion can be eliminated by considering those species, nominally classified as *Carcharhinus* Blainville, that have different generic names. Two of these, the blue shark (*Prionace glauca*) and the tiger shark (*Galeocerdo cuvieri*), deserve separate sections and they have been treated accordingly, and a third, the oceanic whitetip, is different enough from the other carcharhinids to have once been given its own genus (*Pterolamiops*), but it is now recognized as *Carcharhinus longimanus*. This leaves the other related carcharhinid genera *Aprionodon, Loxodon, Rhizoprionodon, Hypoprion, Negaprion,* and *Galeorhinus*. In general, these are similar to the carcharhinids, but with some significant distinguishing characteristic that has been used to set each of them apart. *Aprionodon*, for instance, is the fine-tooth shark, identified by its smooth-edged straight teeth; *Galeorhinus* includes the tope and soupfin sharks, which have peculiarly notched teeth, and *Negaprion* is the lemon shark with two dorsal fins of almost the same size.

Negaprion brevirostris

The lemon shark, *Negaprion brevirostris*, is probably the best known of the carcharhinids because it adapts well to captivity. It has therefore been extensively observed and studied.

Dr. Eugenie Clark did much of her instrumental conditioning work with lemon sharks at the Cape Haze Marine Laboratory in Placida, Florida, and she even hand-raised a litter of pups until an adult male was placed in the shark pen and proceeded to eat the pups. Her experiments showed that a shark was capable of learning simple tasks such as striking a target with its nose in order to be rewarded with a piece of fish, and even differentiating one target from another.[50] Dr. Dugald Brown happened to visit the shark pens late one night and saw what no one had ever witnessed before, the mating of carcharhinid sharks. In *The Lady and the Sharks*, Eugenie Clark described what Dugald Brown saw:

> *The sharks were mating side by side, heads slightly apart but the posterior half of their bodies in such close contact and the swimming movements so perfectly synchronized that they gave the appearance of a single individual, a two-headed monster.*[50]

Attempts were made to catch the sharks *in flagrante delicto* again, but they would not perform for the cameras. Dr. Clark also conducted extensive tests to determine the existence and acuity of color vision in sharks (still using lemon sharks), but she was not able to come up with any definitive answers. (Later experiments by other investigators have indicated that sharks probably do not see color, but, as Perry Gilbert tells us, their "rod-rich, cone-poor retina . . . comprises an eye that has low visual acuity but high sensitivity and that can readily detect an object against a contrasting background in even the dimmest light.")

Because of their hardiness, lemon sharks have been used in all sorts of experimental situations. Dr. Donald Nelson, for his doctoral dissertation "Hearing and Acoustic Orientation in the Lemon Shark," used forty-eight sharks in his experiments. In other disciplines, the lemon shark has been used to test anesthetics, chemoreception, eye movement, the nictitating membrane, adaptation to darkness, pit organs, and cardiac responses. In almost all these experiments the specimens were alive, a testimony to their recuperative powers—they survived being poked, carried, kept out of water, and so on.[178]

It is normal for experimenters to become attached to their subjects, but it is difficult to imagine an emotional involvement with a large shark. Nevertheless, Eugenie Clark felt quite strongly about the male lemon shark that was so surprised when she switched from a white target to a yellow one that "he suddenly jammed on the brakes and did a back flip out of the water." The shark never recovered from this trauma, and died after three months without eating. "We felt terrible about his death," said Dr. Clark. "For more than a year he had been part of our daily activities. We had examined hundreds of sharks by now, but it was very difficult to put the body of this lemon shark on the dock for a routine dissection. . . . We towed the remains of this once beautiful creature some miles out into the Gulf and watched it sink."

This leaves the bulk of the carcharhinids, probably not more than fifteen species, but until Dr. Garrick completes and publishes his revision, we must depend on the vague and unreliable state of the group as it now exists in the literature. Garrick identifies nine worldwide species: *Carcharhinus altimus, C. falciformis, C. galapagensis, C. leucas, C. limbatus, C. longimanus, C. milberti, C. obscurus,* and *C. remotus*. After these it becomes a mare's nest of synonyms, cognates, and confusion. There are a number of Pacific species of carcharhinids, but I am not sure which they are. There are blacktips, silvertips, bronze whalers, black whalers, spinner sharks, and bignose sharks. These of course are vernacular names, but this is one case where the scientific nomenclature does not clarify the species, since it is now being revised. Vernacular names are no help at all in this situation, because the same name can be and is applied to almost any of the gray sharks, without even taking into account variations of location and language. One publication presents the following list of common names of one species, *Carcharhinus leucas:* Zambezi shark, shovelnose grey, slipway grey, bull shark, cub shark, ground shark, river shark, Lake Nicaragua shark, Van Rooyen's shark, square-nose shark. All of these are in English; this particular shark, known from the tidal and littoral waters of the world, would have a hundred or more names in a hundred more languages and dialects.

The carcharhinids are rather large sharks, ranging from three to twelve feet in length. The second dorsal fin is much smaller than the first (except in the lemon shark); there are usually no spiracles, and the cusps of the upper teeth are serrated (except in the fine-tooth shark). They are usually grayish or mustardy brown above (except for the blue shark), fading to white or whitish below. They have a nictitating membrane (lower eyelid), and the upper lobe of the tail is considerably longer than the lower. The problem is not that the carcharhinids are not distinctive, but that we just don't know which of the Pacific species are the same as the Atlantic ones, or if some of the identifying characteristics are not so much species differentiation as a function of the growth process. Carcharhinids that look alike are not necessarily the same species. Two important variables sometimes enable the scientist to differentiate one similar species from another: the number of teeth, and the number of vertebrae. Although no *Carcharhinus* species is recognizable by its vertebral number alone, the count of precaudal vertebrae (those occurring anterior to the precaudal pit at the base of the tail) is a good species determinant when combined with external characteristics. (This system is explained in detail in Springer and Garrick's 1964 paper "A Survey of the Vertebral Numbers in Sharks."[233]) The degree of variation exists because a shark of a given species does not have a set number of vertebrae, but it has a range that is fairly consistent. Thus, a Galapagos shark (*C. galapagensis*), can be told from a dusky shark (*C. obscurus*), because *galapagensis* has 103 to 109 precaudal vertebrae, while *obscurus* has 86 to 94.

The number of teeth is more constant, but also not absolute. Each species of shark has a "dental formula," which consists of a count of the teeth in the upper and lower jaws. The teeth are counted on the left side, at the symphysis (center of a shark's jaw; teeth are usually smaller here), and on the right side, for both jaws. Here are the counts for the species discussed above:

galapagensis: $\dfrac{14\text{–}1\text{–}14}{14\text{–}1\text{–}14}$

obscurus: $\dfrac{(14\text{ or }15)\text{–}2\text{–}(14\text{ or }15)}{(13\text{ to }15)\text{–}1\text{–}(13\text{ to }15)}$

While this may seem arcane, in instances where knowledge of a species is important and guesswork will not do, a dental formula may provide the answer. Such a case is the shark that attacked and killed a swimmer in the Virgin Islands in 1963; it was a species completely unknown in the western Atlantic: *C. galapagensis*.[194]

The carcharhinids are common, often aggressive, and they comprise the largest family of sharks in the world. I will briefly discuss the species that are better known and later generalize on those that have not been so carefully studied.

Carcharhinus longimanus

OCEANIC WHITETIP. In 1970, in *The Shark: Splendid Savage of the Sea*, Jacques Cousteau gave us this description of the oceanic whitetip:

While the brute strength of other sharks is tempered by their beauty and their elegance of form and movement, this species is absolutely hideous. His yellow-brown color is not uniform, but streaked with irregular markings like a bad job of military camouflage. His body is rounder than that of other sharks and the extremities of his enormous pectoral fins and his rounded dorsal fin look as if they had been dyed a dirty gray. He swims in a jerky, irregular manner, swinging his shortened, broad snout from side to side. His tiny eyes are hard and cruel-looking.[59]

Cousteau calls them "lords of the long hands" and "the most dangerous of all sharks." In the same book, he refers to the great white shark, *Carcharodon carcharias*, as the most fearsome-looking, but accords the distinction of most dangerous to the oceanic whitetip, *Carcharhinus longimanus*. (See Plate 18.)

Although it is one of the most abundant of the offshore sharks, very little is known of its habits. Because of the rapidity with which large numbers of these sharks congregate at the scene of a mid-ocean disaster, the population of these sharks has been estimated to be extremely high. Lineaweaver and Backus indicate that it is "extraordinarily abundant, perhaps the most abundant large animal, large being over 100 pounds, on the face of the earth." It is an easily recognized member of the family Carcharhinidae, and one of the few members of this large family that can be easily differentiated from the others. (Two other genera nominally classified as carcharhinids are the tiger shark, *Galeocerdo cuvieri*, and the blue shark, *Prionace glauca*, but these have different generic names in addition to their distinctive appearance.) *C. longimanus* has a laterally flattened snout, broadly rounded in outline, with

The oceanic whitetip, Carcharhinus longimanus, *photographed from the safety of the shark cage in the waters of the Durban whaling grounds.*

the nostrils relatively far forward. The teeth of the whitetip, like those of many other carcharhinids, differ in the upper and lower jaws. The upper teeth are triangular and serrate, resembling those of the great white; the lower teeth are broad-based but narrow in the spire. Details of the snout and teeth are inconsequential compared to the characteristics that give the shark its common and scientific names—the coloration of its fins, and the length of its pectorals. The broadly rounded first dorsal fin, the second dorsal fin, and the upper lobe of the tail fin are tipped with white, and the other fins, such as the pectorals, often show this same coloration in mature whitetips. (Often in younger specimens, the pelvic and pectoral fins are tipped with black, and occasionally there are dark saddle-shaped marks on the back between the dorsal fins.)

Longimanus means "long hands," and refers to the length of the pectoral fins, the other identification giveaway. These extremely long fins are broad at the base, and not as gracefully curved as those of the blue shark. They are often lighter at the tips, but not really white.

The behavior of the whitetip has been variously described as indifferent, stubborn, lackadaisical, and lethargic. It has also been described as aggressive and dangerous. Its size and abundance would make it extremely dangerous to humans, if only they swam where *C. longimanus* swims. However, this shark is definitely an inhabitant of the open ocean; it almost never comes close to shore. Bigelow and Schroeder did not find "a single report of [a shark] caught from the beach or taken in a pound net anywhere along the coast of the United States that could be referred with certainty to this particular species." We are probably safe, then, from being attacked while swimming or diving, but shipwrecks and airplane crashes in the ocean present a different picture altogether. In its home territory, *C. longimanus* has been shown to be aggressive, determined, and anything but lackadaisical. The Cousteau expeditions sought out sharks in the Red Sea, far from shore, and found the whitetip to be the most aggressive and powerful shark they encountered. (Stewart Springer has observed that whitetips are dominant over other species of sharks, even when they are the same size.) In

The Silent World, which was published in 1953, and was therefore one of the first popular books to deal with men and sharks in the water together, Cousteau tells of an incident with a harpooned pilot whale, *Globicephalus*. They were diving off the Cape Verde Islands in the African Atlantic, and saw a shark

> *of a species we had never before seen. He was impressively neat, light gray, sleek, a real collector's item. . . . I [Cousteau] tried to identify the species. The tail was quite asymmetrical, with an unusually long top, or heterocercal caudal fin. He had huge pectorals, and the dorsal fin was rounded with a white patch on it. In outline and marking he resembled no shark we had seen or studied.*[60]

From the accompanying photographs as well as the accurate description, it is obvious that this was indeed *C. longimanus*, the shark Cousteau later described as "the most dangerous of all sharks." (It is interesting to note that over the years Cousteau's opinion of this species changed from "neat" and "sleek" to "hideous," and his description of its color went from "light gray" to "yellow-brown . . . a bad job of military camouflage.") For the sake of the camera, the divers toyed with this "collector's item" and pulled its tail, not knowing what sort it was, or how dangerous it might be. It should be pointed out, however, that Cousteau was one of the inventors of the aqua-lung, and one of the first men to use artificial breathing apparatus in the open ocean. Much useful information has been gathered from his adventures, including data on sharks. In the 1970 publication from which the first quotation is taken, Philippe Cousteau realizes that the shark they had come upon years earlier was "the great *longimanus*, well known to my father and all of us," and Jacques Cousteau himself calls that experience "a misadventure which I would judge very severely today."

There is no question that *C. longimanus* is a potential man-killer. In its open-water domain it is abundant, fairly large (estimates of its maximum length go as high as 13 feet, but the largest measured specimens have been no more than 10.5 feet), and it is almost never frightened. Stewart Springer (quoted in Lineaweaver and Backus) has described the dogged persistence of this shark: "I do not know of anything except a beaker of formalin poured down the gullet that elicits a very strong reaction. They

continue a slow and persistent attack in spite of nonmortal bullet holes."* Springer also described an incident aboard the research vessel *Oregon* in which cherry bombs thrown into the water in the presence of feeding whitetips had no effect on them except when one was swallowed by one of the sharks and it exploded in its mouth. With smoke and bits of flesh streaming from its gills, the sharks moved off rapidly.

One of the most unusual observations of whitetips in action took place in 1969 off the coast of South Africa. During the filming of *Blue Water, White Death*, Peter Gimbel, Stan Waterman, and Ron and Valerie Taylor were suspended in cages, filming a host of sharks feeding on the carcass of a dead sperm whale. The sharks in attendance were blues, duskies, whitetips, and occasionally a tiger. On one day of the filming, despite the reputation of the various sharks, Peter Gimbel left the cage (see "Peter Gimbel: Out of the Cage"). He was followed by the Taylors and by Waterman, and they filmed the feeding sharks. They all knew that an attack on any of them would be disastrous. Gimbel later said that he felt the danger to the divers was limited by the presence of the whale carcass, since the sharks seemed to be concentrating on that. Even so, Perry Gilbert, after seeing the film, said that it was an extremely dangerous and foolish thing to do. The reputation of the oceanic whitetip as being *the* open-ocean aggressor is hard to prove, but the *Blue Water* film crew seemed to be hellbent on documenting it.

Carcharhinus longimanus inhabits almost all the world's oceans in the temperate zone. As mentioned earlier, it is one of the few carcharhinids that is easy to distinguish from the others, and therefore, some authors would have it placed in a different genus. *Pterolamiops* has been suggested, and in some quarters accepted, but the issue remains undecided.

---

* The circumstances under which a beaker of formalin was poured down the whitetip's gullet were explained to me in a letter from Stewart Springer: "We had some sharks hanging on the rail of the *Oregon*. They had been there for a long time, perhaps an hour. Their mouths were open and one looked as though it might have stomach contents. Dumping shark stuff on deck is often smelly and always messy. So I got a beaker of formalin and poured it down the shark's gullet. The 'dead' shark went straight up, just missing me and either tore the hook out or broke the line, I do not remember which. It left for parts unknown."

Plate 14. **Tiger shark** (*Galeocerdo cuvieri*)

(*Overleaf*) *Plate 15.* **Blue shark** (*Prionace glauca*)

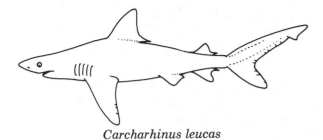

Carcharhinus leucas

BULL SHARK. This species alone has caused almost as much controversy as all the others combined. We are about to see an example of just how confusing the carcharhinids can be. The bull shark, *Carcharhinus leucas*, inhabits fresh and brackish waters as well as saltwater, and is never far from land except by accident. It is a regular inhabitant of lakes and rivers, particularly Lake Nicaragua, the Amazon, Zambezi, Ganges, and Tigris and Euphrates rivers. Naturally enough, in each of the areas in which it has been found, it was thought to be a different animal, thus *C. nicaraguensis*, *C. zambezensis*, *C. van rooyeni*, *C. gangeticus*, and so on. All of these have now been synonymized as *C. leucas*, a shark whose freshwater wanderings in North America have taken it as far as 160 miles up the Atchafalaya River in Louisiana. (Its affinity for fresh water automatically makes it a suspect in the 1916 New Jersey shark attacks in Matawan Creek; the great white shark, usually held responsible for these attacks, hardly ever enters fresh water.)

When their classic work on the sharks of the western North Atlantic was published in 1948, authors Bigelow and Schroeder classified *C. nicaraguensis* as "a landlocked representative" of *C. leucas;* they felt it was a different species because it had taken up permanent residence in a freshwater lake. The characteristics that differentiated it from *leucas* were minimal, having to do with "somewhat longer" gill openings and the relative length of the free tip of the second dorsal fin. The aspect that seemed to set it apart from *leucas*—and every other shark, for that matter—was its completely landlocked habitat. Considerable thought was given to the problem of how it became landlocked, and occasionally someone wondered if it really was—it bore a striking resemblance to Caribbean specimens of *C. leucas*. A number of guesses were made, and in 1961 Bigelow and Schroeder published a paper synonymizing *nicaraguensis* and *leucas*, although neither Bigelow nor Schroeder had ever visited Lake Nicaragua or seen a fresh specimen of *nicaraguensis*. In 1963, the results

of a full investigative study were published; Thomas Thorson, Donald Watson, and Michael Cowan, all of the University of Nebraska, had gone to Nicaragua to see for themselves. Earlier theories held that the sharks had come up the Rio San Juan, about 110 miles from the Caribbean, before the rapids had formed, or had gotten trapped in the lake from the Pacific side because of some geological catastrophe.

Thorson, the senior scientist on the expedition, found that the river was navigable by barges and small vessels for its entire length, including the eight rapids, and noted that "it seems completely indefensible to assume that the rapids present a barrier to the movements of such strong swimmers as sharks." [244] While traveling the length of the river in an outboard-powered dugout canoe, they saw "sharks immediately above and below the rapids and two actually in the uppermost part of the main rapids." They saw that the river could be traversed from the Caribbean to Lake Nicaragua by a shark, but they had not proven that it had been done. A program was instituted in which sharks were tagged at the mouth of the river and at the lake. What had been suspected by Thorson turned out to be true: the sharks were not landlocked at all; they could and *did* swim the length of the river. [241]

C. leucas has been shown to be a resident of other inland bodies of water, including Lake Jamoer in New Guinea, the Lake Izbal–Rio Dulce system in Guatemala, and numerous rivers in Africa, Asia, the Philippines, and Australia (where, among other designations, it is known as the whaler shark). In many of these locations, especially in Lake Nicaragua, the shark is recorded as having instigated attacks on people. But nowhere does this species have such a bad reputation as in South Africa. In the early 1960s, Dr. David Davies, director of the Oceanographic Research Institute at Durban, produced a series of Investigational Reports on shark attacks on the Natal coast. Davies was a recognized authority on sharks and shark attack (his major book on the subject is titled *About Sharks and Shark Attack*), and his findings were highly respected.

The most infamous of these Natal attacks took place on December 24, 1960, at Margate. Petrus Sithole was swimming some 200 feet from shore when he was attacked, thrust vertically out of the water, and then pulled down into the surf. When he was dragged to shore, it was seen that

Plate 16. **Sandbar sharks** (*Carcharhinus milberti*)

139

both legs had been severed, one just below the hip and the other at the knee. Sithole had bled to death by the time he reached the beach. In subsequent X-rays, two tooth fragments were found embedded in the right femur. Davies and D'Aubrey described the fragments:

One tooth fragment corresponded almost exactly with the antero-lateral teeth of the upper jaw and the other fragment with the antero-lateral teeth of the lower jaw of specimens of a carcharhinid species. Both tooth fragments belonged to teeth larger than those of the largest specimen which weighed 903 lbs. and was 9 feet 5 inches (2,835 mm.) in total length and presumably belonged to a shark of larger size.[73]

The shark was "provisionally" identified as *Carcharhinus zambezensis.* Other attacks followed, as did other Investigational Reports. Now that the attacker had been identified in one case, comparisons could be made in others: "The flesh wounds had clean-cut edges similar to those of Petrus Sithole, who was fatally attacked by a Zambezi River shark," and so on. It appeared that *C. zambezensis* (which is of course our old friend *C. leucas*) was the terror of the Natal coast. Certainly the conditions were appropriate—there are numerous rivers flowing down to the sea, and the bull shark is known to favor turbid waters. There seems to be no question that the species is aggressive (one was kept in the Aquarium at Durban until it began to threaten the divers, at which time it was destroyed), large, and abundant.

The chances are that *C. zambezensis* has been responsible for many of the South African attacks, although the present director of the Natal Anti-Shark Measures Board (NASMB) told me that she feels that other species might have been responsible for some of the attacks that Davies attributed to *zambezensis.* The NASMB was established in 1964 to protect the beaches with a system of nets. Except for occasional incidents, which usually occur outside the meshed areas, shark attacks in Natal have come to a halt. Recent data from the NASMB show that the dusky shark, *Carcharhinus obscurus,* is by far the most plentiful carcharhinid in the waters of Natal, so it is possible that this species, also known to be dangerous, may have contributed to the bad reputation of *C. zambezensis (leucas).**

In interior freshwater lakes and rivers, the bull shark has been known to attack young hippos.

Many of the atrocities previously ascribed to crocodiles are now thought to be the work of bull sharks. In Africa, they have been found upriver as far as 300 miles from the sea. In fact, the type locality where the specimen was collected—the spot that was first described and named—is Tette, on the Zambezi River in Mozambique, 230 miles from the ocean. (The recorded distance inland is questionable, but there is an authoritative reference to a specimen 1,000 miles up the Amazon River.)

One attack that did *not* take place is as interesting as many of those that did. Stewart Springer tells a story of his innocent encounter with this dangerous species: "Before I really accepted the possibility that bull sharks could be dangerous, I encountered some while wading in waist-deep water at Cat Island in Mississippi Sound, and I found them so docile that I was able to give a couple of them a shove. Now that I have had more experience with the power of these sharks, I realize that I was lucky not to get my ribs cracked or at least a severe abrasion from the meeting." Bull sharks are almost as omnivorous as tiger sharks, and show a strange affinity for shark meat. It is thought that the brackish waters near the Mississippi Delta are a spawning ground for the bull shark, and that the females do not feed during the time they are giving birth. If they did, they would probably eat their own young, and sharks have not survived as long as they have by actively reducing the population of their own species. This accounts for the interspecific breeding grounds, and probably for Springer's not being bitten when he pushed and shoved them.

People may not be able to recognize a bull shark, but a porpoise can. In experiments conducted at the Mote Marine Laboratory, Perry Gilbert trained a bottlenose dolphin (*Tursiops truncatus*) to ward off a shark on command. The dolphin learned to butt a sandbar shark (*C. milberti*), but when a bull shark of the same

---

* The latest word on this ongoing controversy is contained in the Oceanographic Research Institute Investigational Report No. 33, *Carcharhinids.* According to Bass, D'Aubrey, and Kistnasamy, "Re-examination of these tooth fragments in the light of knowledge gained since that date [the 1961 attack on Petrus Sithole] shows that they might have come from some other local species, notably *C. amboinensis* and *C. obscurus,* and the identification of *C. leucas* as the perpetrator of this particular attack is no longer considered definite."[20]

size was introduced into the tank, the dolphin "refused to approach and harass it."

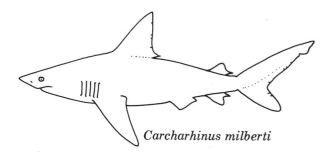

Carcharhinus milberti

SANDBAR SHARK. It is very rare that there is only one reference work for a given species, but that is virtually the case with the sandbar or brown shark, *Carcharhinus milberti*. It is mentioned in various works, since it is quite a common shark throughout its geographical range, but until 1960, it was just another carcharhinid; smaller and stockier than the others perhaps, with a high dorsal fin placed relatively far forward. (See Plate 16.) Then Stewart Springer singled it out and wrote his classic paper "Natural History of the Sandbar Shark, *Eulamia milberti*."[219] (This shark has since rejoined the ranks of the carcharhinids, in keeping with the vicissitudes of carcharhinid nomenclature. Springer wrote in this paper, "A most extraordinary snarl has developed over the years in the determination of the scientific name to be applied to the sandbar shark.") Springer's paper has been called "the best of its kind ever written." In preparation, Springer assembled data for over twenty-five years, and examined "several thousand" individual specimens, as well as the commercial fishery records of over 100,000 sandbar sharks.

The sandbar is a migratory shark, and its distribution varies with the seasons. In the western North Atlantic it is found in the summer from Cape Cod, Massachusetts, to West Palm Beach, Florida, and in the winter from the Carolinas around the tip of Florida, and into the warmer waters of the Gulf of Mexico. In addition to this seasonal variation, sandbar sharks also segregate by age and sex. The nursery grounds of the North Atlantic population are in the shallow waters of the East Coast of the United States, on the continental shelf from Cape Cod to Cape Kennedy. No young *milberti* has ever been taken further south, around the tip of Florida, or in the eastern Gulf. This seems to be related to the presence of *C. leucas*, which not only shows a fondness for shark meat, but has a

special preference for young sandbar sharks. They do pup in the same areas as the female *leucas* (the Mississippi Delta), but, as mentioned earlier, female carcharhinids do not feed during the time they are giving birth.

The males are segregated from the females during the regular migratory movement, to the degree that Springer discusses them as separate populations. Females tend to frequent inshore waters, while the males are found in the cooler, deeper waters. *Milberti* is a "ground shark" (one of its many common names), and is not often seen on the surface. Sometimes spotters in airplanes see them in large schools, usually on their southward migrations. The distribution of *milberti* is interconnected with that of *leucas* to the extent that a female carcharhinid shark taken close to shore in the summer will almost always be *milberti*, while a male taken in the same place at the same time is almost certain to be *leucas*.

The sandbar shark is not classified as a game fish—at least not by the International Game Fish Association—but since it is plentiful and it is, after all, a shark, it is often caught by sport fishermen who are seeking some excitement. In *Sportfishing for Sharks*, Frank Mundus calls the sandbar or brown shark "a lightweight but a toughie."[175]

One peculiarity of sandbar sharks that Springer was unable to explain is the apparent inequality of the sexes. On the average, five females are caught for every male, even though examination of gravid females shows an equal number of males and females in the litters. According to Springer, "The evidence that there are substantially more females than males in the adult population is very strong, if our information adequately covers the geographical range of the species." Numerous theories have been advanced to explain this discrepancy, including one that suggests that mating is so dangerous to the males that fatal accidents may occur during the process. Another theory suggests that females have a genetic tendency toward longevity, and a third postulates that males occupy a greater geographical range, and are therefore more susceptible to predation. "Whatever the explanation for the unequal sex ratio," Springer says, "the smaller number of males is not a sufficient handicap to prevent *E. milberti* from being one of the commoner sharks."

Milberti, like the other carcharhinids, is ovoviviparous, which means that the eggs hatch

Richard Ellis

Tagging a sandbar shark, Carcharhinus milberti, *in Rhode Island sound. The tape on the rails is used to estimate the length of the shark (in meters) before it is released.*

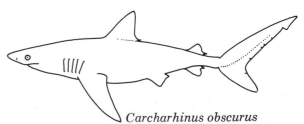

Carcharhinus obscurus

within the uterus of the female, and the young are born alive, usually averaging ten per litter and from twenty to twenty-four inches long. They reach sexual maturity at about six feet in length, but we do not know how old they have to be before they can reproduce. It was thought that sharks grew to maturity rather quickly, but through the data collected by taggers, especially from Jack Casey's program at the National Marine Fisheries Service lab at Narragansett, Rhode Island, we are discovering that they grow slowly and, barring accident, probably live for a long time. One specimen of *milberti* was recaptured after being at liberty for ten years, and it had grown only twenty inches. Casey now feels that the sandbar shark can take as long as thirteen years to reach maturity, and that it can live for twenty years.

Someone has revised the nomenclature of *C. milberti* again, and in a 1973 UNESCO publication, the specific name *plumbeus* was used.[57] It was Springer himself who recommended this in 1960, stating that "if it is finally proved that the Mediterranean form is identical with the American, the name *plumbeus* Nardo 1827 must be used for the combined species in place of *milberti*."

DUSKY SHARK. Perhaps the dusky, *Carcharhinus obscurus*, is best known for being confused with other species. It has no obvious distinguishing characteristics, and therefore people are constantly ascribing to it the characteristics of other similar species. It is a fairly common shark in the temperate waters of the world, and grows to a length of twelve feet. The dusky can be differentiated from the bull shark by the presence of a ridge between its two dorsal fins. (In South Africa it is commonly known as the "ridge-backed grey.") In New England waters, so many fishermen wanted to catch a dusky instead of a regular old sandbar, but were unable to tell them apart, that Jack Casey had to issue a flyer explaining the difference between the two. The flyer is also used by shark taggers, but fishermen usually have more time to examine their catch. According to the flyer, "The sandbar is more robust, the pectoral fins are broader, the first dorsal larger and further forward. . . . One feature . . . will conclusively separate the sandbar from the dusky (and from all similar sharks that sportsmen are likely to catch). That is—on the sandbar shark the scales (denticles) do not overlap."

Carcharhinus obscurus is the shark caught most frequently in the nets off the South African coast. No evidence exists that it was responsible for any Natal coast attack, but equally important, no evidence exists to prove that *obscurus* was *not* responsible. Only one attack has been positively attributed to a dusky (in Bermuda), but duskies are large enough, abundant enough, and aggressive enough to be considered dangerous.

Carcharhinus falciformis

SILKY SHARK. In Bigelow and Schroeder's *Fishes of the Western North Atlantic*, and in practically every other related work published before 1964, there were supposed to be two separate and distinct carcharhinid species, *C. falciformis*, the sickle shark, and *C. floridianus*, the silky shark. Dr. Garrick synonymized the two, and now there is only one species, which has the earlier name, *falciformis*, as first applied by Müller and Henle in 1841. The characteristic that distinguishes both species (now synonymized) is the long free end of the second dorsal and anal fins. Apparently, *floridianus* was called "silky" because of the small size of its dermal denticles, and therefore the relative smoothness of its skin, but in Bigelow and Schroeder we read that the denticles in *falciformis* are small as well. Most of the popular references mention the silky, so for the sake of consistency, I shall use that name. Silkies are an abundant species (Springer thinks that they are the most abundant large animal in the world), and they have figured in almost as many open-ocean experiments as the lemon shark has in laboratory experiments.

In the Atlantic, especially around the Bahamas' Tongue of the Ocean, researchers have conducted numerous experiments on the sensory reactions of silky sharks, particularly their reactions to underwater sounds. Arthur Myr-

berg and Don Nelson, scientists from the University of Miami, have had considerable experience with silkies, and Nelson has the dubious distinction of having been attacked by a silky, an event that was photographed and subsequently published in the *National Geographic*.[148] The photograph, by Jerry Greenberg, shows Nelson pushing off the shark in a flurry of bubbles, and on the next charge, he killed it with a bangstick. As we shall see (in a later section), Nelson chose to pursue shark research in the area of attacks, and in the Marshall Islands he deliberately tried to get sharks to attack him.

Nelson, Myrberg, and many other investigators, mostly from the University of Miami, conducted numerous experiments on the effects of underwater sounds on sharks. Most of the sharks were silkies. According to Myrberg, *falciformis* must "be considered a potentially dangerous shark, because of its size [about seven feet long], lack of shyness and preference for the upper layers of the epipelagic region in both the Atlantic and Pacific."[177] In other words, watch out for the silky.

GALAPAGOS SHARK. Conrad Limbaugh, shark expert and diver, described his experience with Galapagos sharks near Clipperton Island, in the Pacific, 600 miles southwest of Mexico: "Juvenile Galapagos sharks, *Carcharhinus galapagensis*, are extremely abundant and aggressive. On a visit to this island in October 1956, our SCUBA-diving operations were kept to a minimum and finally terminated because of the aggressive nature of the sharks."[153]

The Galapagos shark is a solidly built, typical carcharhinid, grayish above and lighter below. It is found worldwide, but seems to show a preference for island waters as a habitat. Its presence has been recorded from many locations in the eastern Pacific, including Revillagigedo, Cocos, Clipperton, and, naturally, the Galapagos. It is also found in the Hawaiian Islands, and offshore Colombia, Guatemala, Ecuador, and Peru.

In 1963, the range of the Galapagos shark was dramatically extended. Lt. John Gibson was swimming at Magen's Bay, St. Thomas, Virgin Islands. Magen's Bay is a beautiful, horseshoe-shaped beach, one of the most attractive and popular on St. Thomas. Gibson began to swim from the beach at one end of the rocky shore to the east. He was observed to be swimming easily, but then he seemed to change from a crawl to a sidestroke. He was seen to be in trouble, and would-be rescuers rushed to save him. According to Dr. John Randall, when he was dragged ashore, one hand was missing, "enormous bites were taken from the left shoulder and the right thigh and hip . . . the huge bite in his thigh severed the femoral artery, and as indicated later by a doctor, the man could not have lived more than about 15 seconds after this wound was inflicted." The following day, shark hooks were set in the bay, and a large shark was caught. When examined, it had the "right hand of a man plus other human remains," so there was no doubt that it was the shark that had killed Gibson. Upon hearing of the incident, Randall, then conducting a survey of reef fishes in St. John, flew to St. Thomas. He identified the shark as a carcharhinid, possibly *C. springeri*, but he was not sure, so he sent the jaws to Dr. Garrick, who was working at the National Museum (on his revision of the carcharhinids). Garrick identified the shark as *galapagensis*, a species that had not been known from the western Atlantic, although it had been found in St. Helena, Ascension, and Bermuda. The identification was made on the basis of the dental formula.

BLACKTIP REEF SHARK. One of the few carcharhinids that are easy to identify, the blacktip reef shark, *Carcharhinus melanopterus*, is a shallow-water inhabitant of the Pacific and Indian oceans. All the fins are tipped with black, and the first dorsal is lighter in color before it becomes black, which heightens the striking effect. (See Plate 17.) This is a smallish shark, seldom attaining a length of more than six feet, but, according to Herald, "it is encountered by humans more often than any other tropical Indo-Pacific shark,"[132] and occasionally this contact results in injury to the human. (More frequently, contacts between human and shark result in injury to the shark, especially if the shark is abundant and inquisitive, and particularly if the shark is found near the habitat of humans.)

During an extended expedition to the South Pacific, John Randall collected data on ten "incidents" involving *melanopterus*. With Gene Helfman, he wrote up these data for *Pacific Science*, and thereby produced a most interesting and useful document.[197] One fascinating observation concerned the size of the attacking *melanopterus*; they ranged in length from two to five feet, and Randall himself was menaced

The gray reef shark, Carcharhinus menisorrah, *in the agonistic, or threat, behavior. The back is arched, the pectoral fins dropped, and the swimming motions greatly exaggerated.*

(RE)

by a blacktip "not over 2 feet in length." Three of the incidents discussed resulted in wounds, six more involved contact between the man and the shark but no injuries, and in one, the man fired an explosive powerhead at the shark, but did not know if he hit it. All the attacks took place in water that was waist-deep or shallower, which is not too surprising when one realizes that shallow water is the natural habitat of this species. Randall theorizes that the shark may have mistaken the human's leg or calf for a fish in distress; he recommends as little splashing as possible when one is in an area known to be inhabited by *Carcharhinus melanopterus*.

GRAY REEF SHARK. In March 1961, Ron Church and Jim Stewart were installing a tidal wave recording device in a coral reef at Wake Island. They were approached by a shark that displayed "radical and erratic" swimming movements when they tried to frighten it away. The shark began to circle Stewart, suddenly made a darting pass at him, slipped by, and, making a tight turn, came back and bit the arm that Stewart had thrown up to protect his face. Badly injured, Stewart came ashore, and since Wake Island had no surgeon or anesthetist, he had to be flown to Tripler Army Hospital in Hawaii, 2,000 miles away. Stewart survived and recovered full use of his arm, and Church, who had photographed the shark "seconds before the attack," got a recording of the species of the attacking shark and its peculiar behavior. It was the gray reef shark, *Carcharhinus menisorrah*.

Church described the "radical and erratic" motions of the shark: "Not using just his tail but his whole body, he seemed to be glancing back at us with every movement. The whole body was being used to swim with, his head moving back and forth almost as much as his tail. . . . The shark started a small circle just opposite us and as he came around, his body started turning and twisting and rolling back and forth in the water as he swam." Al Giddings and Dewey Bergman, while making a film on sharks in the Pacific, noticed the same strange behavior in "sentinels" that broke away from a pack of reef sharks, and seemed to challenge the photographers before returning to the pack with normal swimming movements. Again the sharks were *menisorrah*.

This behavior was curious enough to warrant scientific investigation, and in 1971 Richard Johnson and Don Nelson went to Eniwetok to study the gray reef shark, and to film their experiments for science.[143] They were successful in triggering the "agonistic" display, in which the sharks dropped their pectoral fins, arched their backs, and began to swim with an exaggerated weaving and rolling motion. The degree of display, from "mild" to "intense," depended on the attitude of the diver-photographer, and the limitations placed on the shark's escape route. If the diver approached the shark rapidly, the shark would begin the display; if the shark was cornered, that is, backed up against the face of the reef, the display would be that much more pronounced. Johnson and Nelson concluded that this behavior specifically represented a threat. Up to this time, it was thought that the only way to annoy a shark was to pull its tail, shoot it with a speargun, or in some other way physically antagonize it. We are still not sure what the agonistic display means, but it is possible that the shark is threatening in defense of its territory, or perhaps even acting in response to some sexual stimulus. Whatever the meaning, the signal is clear and obvious, and further discredits the concept of the unpredictability of sharks, since there is nothing unpredictable about an animal that so precisely demonstrates its intention to attack.

WHALERS. I wish Garrick's work were available for this section, especially since the "whalers" are swimming in his own backyard, Australia. There are two or three (or perhaps even more) species, and as usual with the carcharhinids, the names are different in practically every publication. One name that is more or less constant is *C. macrurus* (sometimes spelled *macrura*), the black whaler. None of the carcharhinids are black, and the black whaler isn't either. It is sandy to dark gray above and whitish below, the same as most of its relatives. Found in the waters of eastern Australia and the Barrier Reef, it grows to a length of twelve feet. Other whalers are *C. ahenea*, the bronze whaler, and *C. stevensi*, the northern whaler. All of these are dangerous and aggressive sharks, and the descriptions of them seem to be interchangeable. They are called whalers because they are often seen in the vicinity of harpooned whales, taking great bites from the carcasses of the dead cetaceans. John Harding, who once killed a great white shark that was about to attack him, has filmed whalers (which he called *Eulamia macrura*) in the Coral Sea. His photographs show a shark with black-tipped fins and tail, which *macrurus* does not seem to possess. Whatever it was that he was filming was aggressive enough to bite the dive platform and the propellor of the boat. One shark came straight for him, and he was forced to defend himself by kicking it in the nose.

In Rangiroa, French Polynesia, Theo Brown attracted sharks by means of an underwater sound transducer that played the sounds of injured fish. Among the sharks that came to his broadcast were whalers, which he identified as *C. leucas*, and *C. ahenea*, which he calls the bronze whaler and describes as having "bright bronze coloring, lightening to a pure white underneath."[37] Sir Victor Coppleson, an Australian authority on shark attack, categorizes the whaler (which he calls *Galeolamna macrurus*) as a "proved man-killer."[58] In 1949 a shark identified as a whaler bit an arm off a girl swimming in Queensland, and in 1961 a man was killed by a ten-foot shark also identified as a whaler. Coppleson refers to this shark as the "cocktail shark." *C. ahenea* is also found in African waters, where it is known as the bronze shark.

There is another whaler shark, *C. stevensi*, but not much is known about it except that it is a large, blunt-nosed shark, occurring inshore in eastern Australia, and that it is "possibly" bronze when alive and gray when dead. Three unauthoritative identifications are recorded in the Shark Attack File (at the Mote Marine Laboratory, Florida) for *C. stevensi*.

Most of the carcharhinids mentioned so far have either performed some noteworthy act (such as eating a hippopotamus), or have had something noteworthy done to them (such as having their eyes tested or having music played for them). The remainder of the sharks in this large family are just ordinary or typical sharks, devoid of peculiar markings, and, for the most part, lacking peculiar habits. They are grayish brown above and whitish below; some have black spots on some of their fins and some have larger

noses than others. Fortunately, the problems of the taxonomist are not the problems of the shark, and we can safely assume that the sharks know the difference. Some of the sharks that are "good species," that is, that are probably going to retain their identities through the revision, are *C. altimus, C. limbatus, C. remotus, C. oxyrhinus, C. porosus, C. springeri, C. albimarginatus*, and *C. brevipinna*.

Since the carcharhinids are the most abundant sharks, it stands to reason that they are the species most often caught by shark fishermen. The species caught most frequently is the sandbar shark, *Carcharhinus milberti*, with the blacktip, *C. limbatus*, second. In the Gulf of California (Sea of Cortez), there is an island called *Isla Tiburón*, shark island. Here the natives fish for shark with nets; the meat is dried and sold in Mexican markets as *bacalao* (dried fish), the fins are used by Orientals for soup, the jaws and teeth are sold for souvenirs, and the skins are shipped to Newark, New Jersey, home of the Ocean Leather Corporation, the only tannery in the United States that processes shark leather.

Here, then, are the carcharhinids, inhabiting practically all the temperate and tropical oceans of the world, and a good deal of fresh water as well. There are some, such as the bull shark, that are never found far from shore, and others, such as the oceanic whitetip, whose "rather strict oceanic habitat . . . makes it largely unavailable to the seaside naturalist." Opinions vary as to the most numerous large shark, but all the guesses favor a species of carcharhinid. It may be the oceanic whitetip, the blue shark, or the silky that has this distinction, but there would seem to be no question that in their worldwide distribution the carcharhinids together outnumber any other large vertebrates. The carcharhinids are unquestionably the rulers of the seas, because of their abundance, their strength and speed, and their unchallenged position as the number one predators in the marine ecosystem.

Tiger shark.

TIGER SHARK

On Thursday, April 18, 1935, a 14.5-foot tiger shark was caught off Maroubra Point, New South Wales, Australia. It had gotten tangled in the set lines of commercial fishermen while it was feeding on a smaller shark that had been hooked. The animal was taken to the Coogee Aquarium in Sydney, where it was placed on exhibit. The huge shark, estimated to weigh 1,600 pounds, did not eat for a week, but swam incessantly around the pool. On April 25, it began to swim more actively, it flayed the water with its tail, and vomited up several objects. According to the Sydney *Morning Herald* for April 26, the disgorged objects included "pieces of flesh from another shark, a partly digested mutton-bird, a number of bones, and a human arm."

The arm, which had "a piece of kellick rope tied around the wrist" and a tattoo of two boxers on the shoulder, was taken to the Coroner's Office for examination. Australia's leading shark authorities were called in, including Victor Coppleson, a surgeon with a particular interest in shark attack; David G. Stead, an authority on sharks (whose extraordinary account of a "great, pale shark" appears in the section "The Great White Shark"), and Gilbert P. Whitley, Curator of Fishes at the Australian National Museum. They all agreed that the arm had been severed with a knife and not bitten off by the shark. Even though the shark was declared innocent of any crime, it was killed and butchered. No other human remains were found.

From the fingerprints and the tattoo, the arm was identified as belonging to one James Smith, a "billiard marker" from Gladesville, near Sydney. An extremely complicated investigation followed, with hints of multiple murders, drug traffic, dismembered bodies in trunks, and other sensational implications. The case, known as the "Shark Arm Murder," was never solved. The Australian Supreme Court, citing an English case of the year 1276, ruled that a single limb could not be considered a murder victim, and without a *corpus delicti*, there was no murder. As far as the law was concerned, James Smith was still alive, even though his left arm had been swallowed by a shark.

Among the items that have been removed at one time or another from the stomachs of tiger sharks are boat cushions, rats, tin cans, turtles, the head of a crocodile, driftwood, seals, the hind leg of a sheep, conch shells, a tom-tom, horseshoe crabs, an unopened can of salmon, a wallet, a two-pound coil of copper wire, small sharks and other fish, nuts and bolts, lobsters, and lumps of coal. From this extensive catalog, it seems reasonable to assume that a tiger shark will eat virtually anything it finds in its waters, including people. In certain parts of the world, especially the islands of the Caribbean, the tiger is the most feared of all sharks. The Shark Attack File shows twenty-seven attacks definitely attributable to *Galeocerdo cuvieri*, and they have occurred all over the world, from Australia to Florida.

On October 12, 1937, Norman Girvan was attacked 100 yards from shore at Kirra Beach, Coolangatta, Australia. He was killed, and his would-be rescuer, Jack Brinkley, died at Coolangatta Hospital after attempts to save him had failed. The next day, an 850-pound female tiger shark was caught, and its stomach contained "portions of arms and legs," including Girvan's right hand, identifiable from a scar.

Clyde Ormond, Jr., was shipwrecked off the Florida coast on October 20, 1943. A fourteen-foot tiger shark, caught at Baker's Haulover, near Miami Beach, contained his forearm, leg, and pelvis.

Eight-year-old Douglas Lawton lost his left leg to a five- to six-foot shark while swimming in shallow water off Longboat Key, Sarasota, Florida. From the bite pattern Eugenie Clark was able to identify the shark as a small tiger.

On December 13, 1958, Billy Weaver, the son of a prominent Honolulu restaurant-owner, was attacked and killed while surfing on an air mattress off Lanikai, on the east coast of Oahu. Even after the attack, the shark "was still cruising in plain sight nearby," and within the next few days, two tiger sharks, eleven and twelve feet in length, were caught in the immediate area. A great public outcry followed this gruesome incident, and in April 1959 the "Billy Weaver Shark Control Program" was started. Using three units of 24-hook longline gear, 595 sharks were caught in inshore Oahu waters during the remainder of 1959, of which 71 (12 percent) were tigers. (For comparison, in the years 1964 to 1972, only 2 percent of the thousands of sharks caught in the nets used to mesh South African beaches were tigers.)

One of the most celebrated of the known tiger shark attacks is that of Robert Pamperin, who was supposedly attacked off La Jolla in June 1959. I say "supposedly," bcause this attack, which is extremely well documented (and was, in fact, originally attributed to a great white shark), and includes a description of the victim "waist-deep in the mouth of the shark," might very well be an elaborate hoax. I have it on reputable authority that Pamperin has been seen alive and well in Mexico. Like the shark arm murder, there was never a *corpus delicti*, the only evidence of this attack being the description by Pamperin's diving companion and one of his swim-fins that was found floating nearby.

In Jurien Bay, Western Australia, Bob Bartle and Lee Warner were spearfishing in fairly cold water in August 1967, in preparation for a spearfishing tournament that was to take place the next day. As they swam over the sandy bottom, a huge shark shot under Warner and grabbed Bartle around the waist, shaking him like a terrier with a rat in its mouth. Warner (quoted in Theo Brown's *Sharks: The Silent Savages*) described the events that followed: "I went straight down and put a spear in the top of the shark's head right where I figured the brain should be. It hit with a solid clunk. But it didn't seem to affect it, except that it attracted the brute's attention to me. It sort of shook its head, then bit Bob in half and rose up at me." Warner noticed that "the eye rolled white," indicating the presence of a nictitating membrane, which the white shark does not have. The

Eugenie Clark holding an embryo tiger shark in Mexico. Notice the very strong markings on the shark.

David Doubilet

only shark of that size ("the jaw must have been a metre wide at least"), with this protective membrane in the eye, is the tiger shark.[37]

Dr. John Randall said in *Sharks and Survival:* "If the identity of every shark attacking man in the tropical Atlantic were known, the tiger shark might well be responsible for more of them than any other species."[193]

The tiger shark is a member of the family carcharhinidae, which includes most of the "typical" sharks, such as the brown, dusky, bull, lemon, and blue. The tiger is properly known as *Galeocerdo cuvieri; Galeocerdo* means "cunning" or "weasel," and *cuvieri* comes from the last name of the great nineteenth-century French naturalist, Baron Georges Léopold Cuvier, the founder of comparative anatomy and vertebrate paleontology. The "tiger" part of the shark's common name does not come from the ferocity of the shark, although as we have seen, this would be quite reasonable, but, rather, from the fact that younger specimens have a pattern of stripes and blotches on their backs. These usually fade with maturity, leaving the adult animal a dusky ocher above and lighter below. Even without stripes, this shark is particularly easy to identify. It has a very broad head that is almost square when viewed from above. Its nostrils, located near the front of the short snout, are quite pronounced, and its teeth, should you get close enough to examine them, are unique. They are sharp-pointed and serrated like those of many other species, but they are sharply notched on the side that faces away from the median line of the head, giving them an unmistakable cockscomb shape. As a further means of identification, the tiger shark has an upper tail lobe that is unusually long and pointed. (See Plate 14.)

Like many of the oceanic or pelagic sharks, the tiger has no particular range, but it is found in all tropical and semitropical seas. The largest specimen on record weighed over a ton, and was taken off Cuba. The current rod-and-reel record is a specimen that weighed 1,780 pounds, and was caught from the pier at Cherry Grove, South Carolina, in 1964. This is the largest game fish caught on rod and reel in the Western Hemisphere.

Rhett McNair, an accomplished diver and shark watcher, was diving at Eniwetok with John Randall, when a shadow passed over McNair and he looked up to see a fish so huge that he thought at first it was a whale shark. McNair knows sharks, and he quickly realized that it was a tiger shark, "considerably longer" than the 21-foot Boston Whaler from which they were diving. When I wrote to Randall, I asked him about this, and although Randall was at 150 feet and did not see the shark, he told me, "I don't think Rhett is guilty of much exaggeration in this sighting."

Tiger sharks are ovoviviparous, which means that they give birth to their pups after the eggs have hatched in the uterus. When a tiger shark is born, it is a two-foot replica of its parents, but it is much more strongly marked. Sometimes as many as eighty pups are born, but usually the number is smaller, closer to thirty or forty. Other than the information obtained from the examination of gravid females that have been caught, almost nothing is known of the breeding or reproductive habits of tiger sharks.

As a matter of fact, very little is known of any of the habits of this animal. Most of the information we have comes from the dissection of specimens that have been caught or that have died in captivity. There have been numerous attempts to keep tiger sharks alive in tanks or pens, but despite their seemingly ravenous appetites and omnivorousness, they usually do poorly. One was kept alive at Puerto Rico's Instituto de Biología Marina for over a year, but most captive tiger sharks do not eat, and expire within a few weeks.

Many scientific studies are being conducted on various species of sharks, but to date, the best— or, at least, the most noteworthy—information we have on tiger sharks concerns their eating habits. An animal so indiscriminate in its eating habits that it eats coal, boat cushions, and tom-toms, would be only too eager to taste a swimmer or a diver—which *must* look more edible than an unopened can of salmon. Perhaps the label was still on the can; maybe tiger sharks can read.

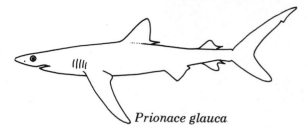

Prionace glauca

BLUE SHARK

In *Moby Dick*, sharks are feeding on the carcass of a sperm whale that is alongside the whale-ship *Pequod*. Herman Melville describes the actions of the two seamen who beat the sharks in an attempt to keep them away from the whale:

> *No small excitement was created among the sharks, for immediately upon suspending the cutting stages over the side, and suspending three lanterns so that they cast long gleams of light over the turbid sea, these two mariners, darting their long whaling-spades, kept up an incessant murdering of the sharks by striking the keen steel deep into their skulls, seemingly their only vital part. But in the foamy confusion of their mixed and struggling hosts, the marksmen could not always hit their mark; and this brought new revelations of the incredible ferocity of the foe. They viciously snapped, not only at each other's disembowelments, but like flexible bows, bent round and bit their own.*[187]

The sharks in this episode are not identified as to species, but the blue shark, *Prionace glauca*, is infamous for its ravenous feeding on harpooned whales. In fact, the Australians call this shark the "blue whaler" for just this reason, and blues were the predominant species that were feeding on the whale carcass when Peter Gimbel, Stan Waterman, and Ron and Valerie Taylor made their night dives off the whaling grounds of Durban, during the filming of *Blue Water, White Death*.

The passage from Melville is also significant because it so well describes the "feeding frenzy" that sharks will fall into in the presence of large amounts of food, such as a whale, plentiful fish, or offal, and a large enough number of competing sharks. As individuals, blues are no more susceptible to this mob feeding than any other species of shark, but blues are unusually plentiful and found in higher concentrations than most other species, so the possibilities of mass feedings are correspondingly higher.

At the Bayshore Mako Tournament, held every summer on Long Island, blues are caught almost ten times more often than all other species combined. (In 1965, a total of 918 sharks were caught, and only 7 were *not* blues.) If you are fishing or diving off Long Island, and you see a shark, the chances are it is a blue. In Peter Gimbel's first shark film, *In the World of Sharks*, the only other sharks he saw while making the film (which was shot off Montauk, using Frank Mundus' *Cricket II*, and a prototype shark cage, which Gimbel stayed out of for much of the filming) were one mako and one small tiger shark. In California, Scott Johnson and Don Nelson do most of their work with blue sharks as their subjects. (Interestingly enough, the blue shark in the Pacific, although it is the same species as the Atlantic version, never gets much over six feet in length.)

Jack Casey's shark tagging program, based at the Narragansett Laboratory of the National Marine Fisheries Service (NMFS) in Rhode Island, although nominally involved with all species, is primarily based on data gathered from blue sharks. The distance record for this program is held by a blue; originally tagged off Montauk, it was recovered two years later by a Korean longliner off Colombia, having traveled a distance of 2,070 miles. Casey's program is designed to study the population dynamics of sharks, but a side result has been to make more people aware of the abundance of the blue. Although they are not as dramatic or as exciting as makos or whites, it is blues that Casey worries about when the subject of "commercial utilization" comes up. If and when someone figures out a way to catch and process sharks so as to make them a "product," blues, which are among the most abundant of all temperate water species, will be high on the list of raw materials.

As a result of the information gathered at the Bayshore Tournament and from other autopsies, H. L. Pratt, a biologist at the NMFS Laboratory at Narragansett, has assembled considerable data on the reproductive biology of the blue shark. He has produced one of the most complete documents ever written on the sexual maturity, egg development, and parturition of any species of large shark. Physiological and histological examinations have produced no new or startling information, but we now have a much better understanding of the habits of this viviparous species. Blue sharks are born at a little over a foot in length, and the largest num-

(Overleaf) Plate 17. **Blacktip reef shark** *(Carcharhinus melanopterus)*

RICHARD ELLIS-1976

ber of embryos found in a gravid female was eighty-two. (This is the same number reported for the largest litter of tiger sharks, as quoted by Howell-Rivero in Bigelow and Schroeder.[30])

The bluedog or great blue shark, to use some of its other vernacular names, is a lithe, graceful animal, proportionally slimmer than any other carcharhinid. Although there have been reports of blues reaching 20 feet, the longest on record is 12 feet 7 inches, and the International Game Fish Association all-tackle record is for a shark 11 feet 6 inches long. This fish, caught off Rockport, Massachusetts, in 1960, weighed 410 pounds. (Just for comparison, an 11-foot 8-inch mako weighed 854 pounds, and the mako is not regarded as a particularly heavy-bodied shark.) Fishing for blue sharks is not the most exciting sport in the world—one tends to chum them up to the boat and then "hand-feed" them the bait—but it is hard work. They are not showy fighters, but they are usually determined not to be brought in, and the power of a large blue shark is quickly felt in the angler's back and shoulders.

The blue shark is long in almost all respects; long snout, long tail, long body, and especially long, curved pectoral fins. These thin, flexible fins contribute to the blue shark's extraordinary maneuverability in the water. Only the blue's teeth cannot be considered long by shark-teeth standards, but they are particularly sharp and numerous. Blues can take a 20-pound bite out of the carcass of a whale; a bite that looks as if it were made with a giant ice-cream scoop.

Not surprisingly, the blue shark is named for its color, but the color itself is surprising—it is a rich ultramarine (a fine name for the color of a shark, I think) that changes to a silvery white beneath. As with many other fishes, the color fades quickly with death, and blue sharks brought to the dock appear a drab slate or smoky gray. (See Plate 15.)

The blue shark is not considered dangerous, but it has the size and the equipment to be taken seriously. There are a number of people who have dived with blues with trepidation but no accidents, but the Shark Attack File lists eight unprovoked attacks on people, and three attacks on boats. Of course, the attacks where the species was not identified are not listed in the blue shark's column—so it may in fact have more attacks to its credit.

None of the records or files kept on shark attacks have indicated the species of sharks attracted to the scene of major shipwrecks or air disasters, where it is possible to attribute many of the deaths and injuries to the "feeding frenzy." For example, in 1942, the troop-carrier *Nova Scotia* was torpedoed off the coast of South Africa. There were over a thousand persons aboard, many of whom were injured in the initial explosions, and many more of whom were maimed or killed by the sharks that were attracted to the scene of the disaster. When rescue vessels arrived the next morning, they found many of the victims with limbs bitten off, clinging to bits of the wreckage. Many of the sharks in those waters were blues.

Even though it looks like a shark peering out of a porthole, this is the head of a blue shark in a bucket on the deck of Frank Mundus's Cricket II.

John Ebel

154

Sphyrna blochii.

HAMMERHEADS

The hammerheads (there are nine nominal species) are probably the strangest-looking of all the sharks. There are species of sharks with spots, ridges, spines, stripes, and occasionally a long nose or tail, but nothing in the shark world can match the hammerheads for weirdness. All nine species have greatly elongated and flattened lobes on the head, on which the eyes and nostrils are located. One of the criteria used to differentiate the nine species is the shape and size of these lobes, which are responsible for the vernacular name "hammerhead." The Roman poet Oppian called them "balance fish," and others have called them shovelhead, scoophead, bonnethead, and *cornuda* (which means "horned" in Spanish). (See Plate 19.)

Hammerhead species can be told apart by detailed measurements of the fin length, size, and teeth. The smallest of the hammerheads, *Sphyrna tiburo*, rarely exceeds five feet in length. It does not have a proper "hammer," but a flattened, rounded head, shaped rather like a shovel. For some reason, this shape has entered the language as bonnethead. Bonnetheads are harmless, gregarious sharks, often found in small schools of eight to fifteen individuals. They inhabit the shallow waters of the bays, estuaries, and flats of the Western Hemisphere, ranging from New England to Brazil.

The bonnethead, very common in Florida waters, was chosen as the subject of an experiment that required substantial numbers of small, easily maintained sharks. In 1970, Drs. Arthur Myrberg and Samuel Gruber of the University of Miami were looking for information on "the behavior of selected species under a variety of situations." The bonnethead was chosen "because it attains sexual maturity at a relatively small size, is easily captured, lives well in captivity and finally, its natural habitat fitted well with the semi-natural habitat available to us."[176] Ten individuals were observed during a seven-month period, and some most interesting observations were made, especially concerning the social behavior of sharks. An order of dominance was shown to exist based on size and gender, and numerous behavior patterns were consistent and regular over the entire period. (The experiment ended abruptly when "all bonnetheads suddenly perished after an unknown chemical was added to the pool.") This experiment demonstrated once again that sharks are not unpredictable, but rather that their behavior can be understood (and to a certain extent, predicted), if enough time is taken to study it properly. The difficulty of working with large, aggressive animals that do poorly in captivity has certainly been an obvious factor in assigning the concept of unpredictability to sharks. As more controlled experiments are performed, however, it becomes increasingly apparent that the behavior of sharks can be observed and understood—and at least some species have been shown to be socially organized, *predictable* animals.

Hammerheads are brownish to grayish above, and lighter below, like the carcharhinids, which they closely resemble in general body shape. *S. mokarran* is the largest of the genus, reported to reach a length of twenty feet. Studying the larger hammerheads has proven to be far more difficult than studying the smaller ones. The larger hammerheads are renowned for their fragility, and so are almost never seen in captivity. I have participated in several collecting expeditions out of the Mote Marine Laboratory in Sarasota, and the feeling on board always was that a hooked hammerhead was a dead hammerhead. Eugenie Clark, in her study of sharks in captivity, says "Large hammerheads have been exhibited in aquariums in various parts of the world, but seldom survive more than a few days."[52]

In 1974 a large female (11 feet; 417 pounds) survived long enough in Marineland, Florida, to give birth to four live pups in an exhibition tank, but the female died within an hour (probably as a result of the struggle to bring her in), and the pups lasted only a couple of days. When the female was autopsied, she was found to contain another twenty-four pups. In the observation of the four pups that were born in the tank, it was noticed that the "hammer" and fins are quite flexible at birth to permit passage through the cloaca of the female. (Gravid female hammerheads are caught rather frequently, and the inclusion of a macabre picture of a mother lying dead beside her thirty or forty babies is not uncommon in books about sharks, or books about fishing.) The ill-fated sharks in the Miami aquarium were identified as *Sphyrna mokarran*, the great hammerhead.

The larger hammerheads are easily confused by the layperson, since minor variations in the shape of the head, or in the comparative height of certain fins, are the distinguishing features.

Any specific identification, therefore, has to be tentative, so with some exceptions I am going to treat the genus in a general manner.

Because of their obvious difference from other large sharks, the hammerheads that have been authoritatively implicated in shark attacks have not been confused with any other sharks. One of the most celebrated cases of an interaction between a hammerhead and a man took place in 1805, when three large hammerheads were netted by Joshua Turry, of Riverhead, Long Island. The largest specimen was shown to contain "many detached parts of a man," as well as some articles of clothing, but it was not known if the man had been dead before being ingested. There are a number of cases in the Shark Attack File of unprovoked attacks by hammerheads on boats and swimmers.

Ernest Hemingway, also without concern for species (but probably *mokarran*, judging from the size), wrote what is perhaps the most dramatic description of a hammerhead I have ever read. In *Islands in the Stream*, one of Thomas Hudson's sons is spearfishing in the waters off Bimini, and spears a yellowtail snapper. As a hammerhead approaches the swimming boy, Hudson shoots at the shark with a rifle, and the mate shoots at it with a submachine gun:

> Then [the machine gun] clattered in a short burst and the water jumped in a tighter patch right at the base of the fin. As [the mate] shot, the clatter came again, short and tight, and the fin went under and there was a boil in the water and the biggest hammerhead he had ever seen rose white-bellied out of the sea and began to plane off over the water crazily, on his back, throwing water like an aquaplane. His belly was shining an obscene white, his yard-wide mouth like a turned-up grin, the great horns of his head with the eyes on the end, spread out wide as he bounced and slid over the water.[130]

The great hammerhead is found throughout the tropical and subtropical waters of the world, but some records are obviously of the two similar species, *S. zygaena* and *S. lewini*, which are both fairly large. *Mokarran* is best recognized by the almost flat leading edge of the "T"-shaped head; in this species the head is most nearly rectangular. *Sphyrna lewini*, sometimes known as the scalloped hammerhead, has a more rounded head, and *zygaena* (from the Greek *zygon* for "yoke"), has pronounced indentations on the front of the head at the location of the nostrils. In all the Sphrynidae the nostrils are located on the front edge of the "hammer," which presumably gives the genus an olfactory advantage over other sharks, whose nostrils are closer together and located under the overhanging snout.

Lesser known members of the genus are *Sphyrna couardi*, a large West African species, and the small bonnetheads, including *S. tiburo* (which consists of two geographical races, *S. tiburo tiburo* from the western Atlantic, and *S. tiburo vespertina* from the eastern Pacific), *S. media*, *S. corona*, and *S. tudes*.

One of the most bizarre of the hammerheads— and therefore one of the most bizarre fishes in the world—is the remaining member of this peculiar-looking group: *Sphyrna blochii*. From the Indo-Pacific region, this species has the longest head lobes of any of the hammerheads. In this shark, the maximum width of the head can be as much as 50 percent of the body length. A shark six feet long could therefore have a head three feet wide! The lobes are also backswept and narrow, so the overall impression is of a fish with wings on its head. This species is so different from the others that it has been placed in a separate subgenus, *Eusphyra*. Up to 1967, the hammerheads were, according to Bigelow and Schroeder, "a very monotonous genus, including some four or five species at most the world over."[30] Carter R. Gilbert of the University of Florida at Gainesville revised the genus, cleared up most of the confusion, and eliminated the monotony—especially for taxonomists.[94]

Ever since people have been writing about hammerheads, there has been speculation on the "purpose" of the strange lobes of the head. Among the theories that have been suggested are the following: they give the shark added lift or help in diving, like a hydroplane; they increase the maneuverability of the shark, possibly by decreasing the turning radius; they enable the shark to "triangulate" and better locate prey, by separating the eyes and nostrils; and even that the grotesque shape of the head serves to frighten rival predators away. Only one author, Paul Budker, has suggested that the lobes might also be a detriment: "In a tussle with a Tiger Shark or a White Shark, the adversary could easily inflict great damage with its jaws on these vulnerable parts."[38] The hammer-

heads are the most recently evolved sharks, and we might be seeing an evolutionary experiment at this moment. It is rather difficult to assign the concept of "detrimental development" to an animal that we have always thought of as so perfectly evolved, but overspecialization is thought to be one of the major causes of extinction.

All of the theories about the function of the lobes may be true to a certain extent; such complex and unique structures probably serve more than one purpose. There is a fairly new theory that takes into account not only the hydrodynamic properties of the lobes, but their physical and electrical capabilities as well. All sharks have a series of subcutaneous pit organs called the ampullae of Lorenzini, which are sensitive to chemical, physical, and thermal changes in the water. (One of the criteria that Carter Gilbert used to clarify the systematics of the hammerheads was the arrangement of these pores on each of the nine species.)

Early experiments showed that certain selachians were sensitive to weak electrical fields. It was concluded that in addition to their other functions, the almost miraculous ampullae of Lorenzini were electroreceptors. In fact, it was discovered that the sharks and rays possessed the greatest degree of electrical sensitivity in the animal kingdom. In tests with rays and scyliorhinid sharks, it was shown that these species are able to detect prey that is buried in the sand, by virtue of this electrical sensitivity. From this information, we have to make some small assumptions in order to return to the lobes of the hammerheads, but these seem so obvious and logical, that I am surprised no one has mentioned them before. (Of course, I realize the danger in making such an assertion; fifteen people are bound to write me and say, "Haven't you read Spoonfork's paper on "Electroreception in Hammerhead Sharks" in the latest issue of *Hammerhead Biological Journal?*") In any event, the head of a sphyrnid is ideally designed to present the largest possible number of ampullae of Lorenzini to the floor of the ocean, since the head is very much flattened and has a very large surface area. The shark swims close to the bottom, swinging its head in a "minesweeper" action, covering much more territory than a shark with an ordinary head would. It therefore stands a much better chance of detecting the presence of prey buried in the sand. (The pectoral fins of the hammerheads are proportionally small, and this seems to support the idea of the sharks' needing to get as close to the bottom as possible.) Although hammerheads are known to be almost omnivorous, they seem to favor stingrays as a dietary staple. It is a rare hammerhead that does not have at least one stingray spine embedded in its jaw, and Perry Gilbert (no relation to Carter Gilbert) reported one large specimen that was found to have ninety-six barbs in its jaw, mouth, and head.

We don't know if hammerheads can dive deeper, see better, or turn faster than other sharks. (Stewart Springer has said that "hammerheads seem to be avoided by other sharks,"[226] but there are no further data on this.) I suggest that the "hammer" serves a sensory function by increasing the exposure of the ampullae of Lorenzini to the electrical fields of prey species, thus increasing its feeding efficiency, while contributing to the development of its peculiar shape.

Perry Gilbert examines a dead hammerhead in the waters of British Honduras. Notice the proportionate size of the lobes of the head.

Mote Marine Laboratory

DOGFISHES

Homeward that night I walked barefooted in the surf, watching the convulsive, twinkling dance, now and then feeling the squirm of a fish across my toes. Presently something occurred which made me keep to the thinnest edge of the foam. Some ten feet ahead, an enormous dogfish was suddenly borne up the beach in the rim of a slide of foam; he moved with it unresisting while it carried him; the slide withdrawing and drying up, it rolled him twice over seaward; he then twisted heavily, and another minor slide carried him back again to shore. The fish was about three feet long, a real junior shark, purplish black in the increasing light—for the moon was moving west across the long axis of the breakers—and his dark, important bulk seemed strange in the bright dance of the smaller fish about him.

It was then that I began to look carefully at the width of gathering seas. Here were the greater fish, the mouths, the eaters who had driven the "eels" ashore to the edge of their world and into ours. The surf was alive with dogfish, aswarm with them, with the rush, the cold bellies, the twist and tear of their wolfish violence of life. Yet there was but little sign of it in the waters—a rare fin slicing past, and once the odd and instant glimpse of a fish embedded like a fly in amber in the bright, overturning volute of a wave.

Henry Beston
The Outermost House,
1928 [29]

If you have ever studied comparative anatomy, you are probably familiar with the spiny dogfish, *Squalus acanthias*. If you have done any offshore fishing in New England waters, you are probably familiar with the spiny dogfish. And if you have done commercial fishing in the northeastern United States, you are probably so familiar with the spiny dogfish that you would be happy if you never saw one again.

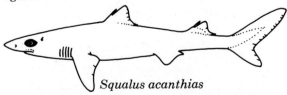

Squalus acanthias

Squalus acanthias is used in basic zoology lab courses to introduce students to the verte-

brates. J. Frank Daniel, the author of the definitive work on the anatomy of sharks, has said of *S. acanthias* that it has "system upon system so generalized as to approximate a ground plan on which nature has built up its masterpieces of vertebrate life."[64] This small shark, which reaches a maximum length of four feet, is abundant and easily caught, and therefore serves well as a laboratory specimen. *S. acanthias* is also one of the most frequently utilized animals for scientific experimentation. Its anatomy lends itself to detailed examination in many areas, and if the lemon shark, *Negaprion brevirostris*, is the most commonly used large shark in the laboratory, the spiny dogfish is surely the most commonly used small shark. Much of what we know of the biology, neurology, and anatomy of sharks has been learned from the study of the spiny dogfish. The spiny dogfish has been the subject in many behavioral tests, but it has been even more useful for its parts than for its wholeness. Scientists have examined in meticulous detail its eyes, kidneys, pharynx, brain, gills, liver, stomach, heart, blood, gall bladder, uterus, teeth, skin, and sense organs.

This biological celebrity is a nondescript little shark, slate gray or brownish above, lighter below. (In the family Squalidae we will encounter for the first time some sharks that are *not* dark above and lighter below.) Young specimens sometimes have an irregular row of small white spots, but these tend to disappear with maturity. As in almost all species of sharks, the females are larger than the males, averaging 3 to 3.5 feet in length, while the males rarely exceed 3 feet in length. As is characteristic of all the squaloids, the spiny dogfish lacks an anal fin. The average spiny dogfish weighs between 7 and 10 pounds. They have extremely effective teeth, which point sharply back from the symphysis in each jaw. Each tooth has a broad cutting edge which creates an almost continuous sharp band in the mouth. Spurdogs, as they are called in England, are efficient feeders thanks to this dental arrangement, and they take clean, round bites from whales, living or dead. When U.S. fishermen catch a spiny dogfish (or a piked dogfish, a skittledog, thorndog, or codshark, as it is also commonly known), they *carefully* remove the hook and throw the shark back, because it has little or no value as a food fish in the United States. (Experiments are currently being conducted here on the possible use of the dogfish as a cheap source of protein—it has to be elaborately processed, however; there is not much that you can do with a couple of dogfish in your own kitchen.) The hook must be removed with care because the characteristic spines that give the shark its common name can inflict a nasty wound. The shark can thrash about and stab the offending hand with its poisonous dorsal spines. I have not found any records of anyone being killed by the venom thus injected, but there are numerous accounts of fishermen being sick and bedridden for days. The venom is transmitted through a tract of white tissue from the base to the point of the spine, activated by the damaging of the venom gland when the spine comes into contact with the victim.

In commercial fishing areas of the United States the spiny dogfish has earned a totally unwholesome reputation. Spiny dogfish are often encountered in schools of thousands, following schools of fish, on which they feed ravenously. (It is this characteristic of pack feeding that is thought to be responsible for the name "dogfish.") They are virtually omnivorous, eating all kinds of fish, squid, worms, lobsters, jellyfish, and even red, brown, and green algae. Bigelow and Schroeder characterize the spiny dogfish as being "as voracious as any fish of its size." In the course of their hunting, spiny dogfish often converge on the nets of commercial fishermen, and if the nets are full of a prey species such as cod or herring, the dogfish destroy the nets as well as the catch. They are therefore despised by fishermen in the United States. Attempts to eliminate the problem have been unsuccessful. Dynamite and poison have been used, and bells have even been hung on the nets in an attempt to keep the destructive sharks away from the food fishes, but nothing seems to work.

In America we try to keep the spiny dogfish out of the nets, whereas in European waters fishermen try to keep them in. Americans have never been great consumers of shark meat, but in England and northern Europe, spiny dogfish are harvested from the sea in tremendous quantities, and served as "flake," "sea eel," or "rock salmon." Most of the "fish" in fish-and-chips is spiny dogfish. A plaintive note creeps into the prose of the otherwise unemotional Bigelow and Schroeder, when they say, "And fresh, this is a better food fish than is generally appreciated. On the coasts of the eastern United States and Canada, however, these attempts [to market shark flesh] have been short-lived." The food potential of this resource can be seen in the quantities that have been harvested in the past: in 1913, in Massachusetts, 27 million pounds of spiny dogfish were caught; in 1923, Britain landed over 9 million pounds; and in 1931, Germany harvested over 14 million pounds.

Spiny dogfish are migratory sharks. In North American waters they appear off the East Coast of the United States in the spring, and move north when the water gets too warm. By summer they have moved to the coastal waters of Newfoundland and Labrador, returning to New England by fall. They spend the colder · winter months in the cold waters of the offshore banks of Newfoundland and Labrador. The young are born in the autumn or winter in the offshore hunting grounds. Spiny dogfish are ovoviviparous (eggs hatch within the female and the young are born alive), and a young dogfish is between seven and eleven inches long. The gestation period for *Squalus acanthias* is twenty-two to twenty-four months, the longest of any vertebrate, including such behemoths as whales and elephants. Unlike most other sharks, the age of the spiny dogfish can be fairly accurately determined. The second dorsal spine shows darker and lighter rings, corresponding to annual periods of slow and fast growth. From this evidence, it has been shown that the spiny dogfish lives to the age of thirty; males reach maturity at the age of eleven, and females reach maturity at the age of nineteen or twenty. In their lifetimes, spiny dogfish have been known to do some extensive traveling in addition to their seasonal migrations. From tagging evidence, we know that one specimen traveled over 1,000 miles in one year, from Newfoundland to Cape Ann, Massachusetts, and another specimen, tagged off Washington in 1944, was recovered eight years later off Honshu Island, Japan, a straight-line distance of almost 5,000 miles.

For such active feeders, spiny dogfish do poorly in captivity. They either starve to death slowly, or batter their noses on the glass walls of the enclosing tank. They are usually kept long enough for the specific experiment at hand, and then they die of experimental or natural causes. They have been kept alive for short periods (three or four months) at various aquariums and laboratories, including the Mt. Desert Biological Lab in Maine, the New England Aquarium in Boston, and the Steinhart Aquarium in San Francisco. The species maintained in the Steinhart Aquarium was *Squalus acan-*

thias, but it was thought to be *S. suckleyi*, a different species. Bigelow and Schroeder said in 1948 that the two were synonymous, but it was not until 1957 that they published the necessary correction.[31]

There are other members of the genus *Squalus*, including *S. cubensis*, a deep-water variety from Cuban waters, and *S. blainvillei*, a dogfish of tropical and subtropical waters. These show minor anatomical variations from *S. acanthias*, but they are primarily differentiated by their range.

The genus *Squalus* includes a number of small sharks, usually characterized by the presence of fin spines, but differing in size, coloration, teeth, range, and habits. The black dogfish, *Centroscyllium fabricii*, is a little-known, deep-water shark, found off Iceland, Greenland, and the Faeroe Islands. Bigelow and Schroeder (1948) describe it as "deep chocolate brown, darkest (almost black) below and on fins generally. . . . Adults average about 2 to 2½ feet. . . . Their skins are provided with minute, deeply pigmented papillae, resembling the luminous organs of the brightly luminescent *Isistius brasiliensis*." Other members of the genus *Centroscyllium* are found in Japanese waters, the tropical Pacific, and the Bay of Bengal.

Several species of squaloids have light-emitting organs, but none can glow as brightly as the monotypical *Isistius brasiliensis*. This small shark (6 to 14.5 inches) is brownish on top, lighter below, with whitish tips on the fins and a dark collar around the neck. The entire ventral surface of the shark is covered with photophores (light-emitting organs). These decrease in density toward the dorsal surface, and there are almost none on the back. *I. brasiliensis* gives off a vivid greenish light. The light-emitting capability seems to vary from individual to individual; some specimens of *I. brasiliensis* have no photophores at all, while in others, they are quite numerous. Although very few people have seen the extraordinary sight of a glowing green shark, one nineteenth-century observer, F. D. Bennett, gave this careful description:

> When the larger specimen, taken at night, was removed into a dark apartment, it afforded a very extraordinary spectacle. The entire inferior surface of the body and head emitted a vivid and greenish phosphorescent gleam, imparting to the crea-
> ture, by its own light, a truly ghastly and terrible appearance. The luminous effect was constant, and not perceptibly increased by agitation or friction. . . . When the shark expired (which was not until it had been out of the water more than three hours), the luminous appearance faded entirely from the abdomen, and more gradually from other parts, lingering longest around the jaws and on the fins.[27]

The teeth of this luminous shark are most peculiar, differing entirely in the upper and the lower jaws. The upper teeth are narrow, slightly curved spikes that resemble in miniature the teeth of the sand tiger *(Odontaspis)*; the lower teeth are much larger, looking much like fountain-pen nibs standing in a row. Both sets of teeth are used effectively: this shark often chews or tears its way out of nets before it can be brought to the surface. On the Russian research vessel *Vitiaz*, in the central Pacific in the late 1950s and early 1960s, many more specimens were lost through damaged nets than were successfully brought aboard. Only five specimens were taken, but from the damage to the nets and the number of *I. brasiliensis* that were seen escaping from them, it was concluded that this was a schooling shark. In one of the few studies devoted to this rare and exotic species, it was discovered that all of the teeth in a row are replaced at the same time, rather than individually, as with most other species.

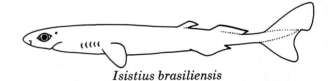

Isistius brasiliensis

This luminous shark feeds almost entirely on squid, as evidenced by the examination of the stomach contents. The function of the luminosity is not known, although it has been suggested that individuals are able to communicate with one another, either for feeding or mating purposes, through the use of this bioluminescence. *Isistius brasiliensis* is epipelagic, that is, it is found in all oceans, mainly in tropical waters, and it is usually collected at a depth of less than 2,000 feet.

There is a genus of squaloids characterized by a spine on each dorsal fin, large eyes, small size, the presence of photophores, and dark coloration. This is the genus *Etmopterus* Rafinesque

1810. Again, the teeth in the upper and lower jaws are radically different from each other; the upper teeth are multicusped and downward-pointing, and the lower teeth have a single cusp that, according to Bigelow and Schroeder (1957), is "so oblique that the inner margins are approximately parallel with the jaw."[31] It has been suggested that the different teeth serve different functions, the upper pointed ones for holding the prey, the sharp-edged saw of the lower jaw for removing a neat bite. *Etmopterus* species range in size from 7.5 to 24 inches, although most specimens are found in the lower end of this range. The species are differentiated by variations in teeth, dermal denticles, coloration, range, and luminescence.

It is not certain how many species of *Etmopterus* are recognized at this time. They are mostly deep-water inhabitants, and are not often collected. (I have seen one specimen, new to science, that was still to be described, so there is at least one species that is not mentioned in the literature.) In 1953 Bigelow, Schroeder, and Springer named the following species: *Etmopterus schultzi, E. hillianus, E. virens, E. pusillus, E. polli, E. princeps, E. lucifer, E. granulosis, E. brachyurus,* and *E. villosus.* By now there are undoubtedly synonyms or invalid species on this list.[32]

Almost all the information we have on *Etmopterus* comes from the examination of scientific specimens. It appears that no member of this genus has been maintained in captivity, so any comments on behavior must rest on speculation. And who is better qualified to speculate than Stewart Springer? Here is what he has to say about the species *Etmopterus virens:*

> *Possibly similar dog-pack feeding is carried out by . . . the green dogfish [Etmopterus virens]. This species occurs abundantly on the northern coast of the Gulf of Mexico—most commonly in depths of 350–400 m. The adults are about 25 cm long. Like some other members of the genus, this species has an elaborate and distinctive pattern of photophores. Repeated drags of trawls in the same depth and habitat usually catch many or none, suggesting that the species occurs in rather dense aggregations. Contents of hundreds of stomachs showed that more than half their food is squid or octopus. The cephalopod beaks and eyes commonly found in their stomachs were often so large that the shark's jaws and gullet must have been stretched greatly when the parts were swallowed. I deduce that green dogfish hunt in packs and may literally swarm over squid or octopus much larger than they are, biting off chunks with the razor-sharp band of lower-jaw teeth and perhaps maintaining the integrity of their school visually through their distinctive lighting system.*[226]

A school of green dogfish, Etmopterus virens, *attacking a squid. It is assumed that the sharks' photophores (light organs) enable them to maintain visual contact in the depths.*

(RE)

In the large and diverse family of squaloids, there are also "spineless" dogfishes, one of which is *Centroscymnus coelolepis*, the Portuguese shark. This sluggish, deep-water inhabitant is dark brown and gets to be about 3.5 feet long. One specimen was captured in a net that was on the bottom at 8,922 feet, which is the record depth at which any shark has been taken. In general appearance, the Portuguese shark, so named because it is the object of a longline fishery in Portugal, resembles two other squaloids—*Somniosus* and *Scymnorhinus*.

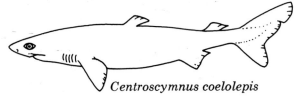

Centroscymnus coelolepis

Scymnorhinus, which used to be known as *Dalatias*, is another dark brown shark, larger (maximum length is six feet) than the Portuguese shark, with pen-nib teeth in both jaws, and found worldwide in fairly deep water.

Somniosus microcephalus, the sleeper shark, Greenland shark, or gurry shark, is a large version of *Scymnorhinus* and *Centroscymnus*. It has been reported at twenty-five feet, but the largest authoritatively measured specimen was twenty-one feet long. (Only the whale shark, basking shark, and great white shark are known to reach a greater length.) When examined, the stomach contents of this shark show an amazing variety of food, from fish of its native polar waters to seals, carrion, whale blubber (presumed to be from a dead whale), and in one instance an entire reindeer, without horns. Its varied diet, which includes salmon and other fast-swimming fishes, seems to belie its lethargic behavior; Bigelow and Schroeder (1948) have described it as "one of the most sluggish of sharks, offering no resistance whatever when hooked or even when drawn out of the water." Animals react differently to different situations, of course, and a shark that is sluggish when hooked might still be an efficient feeder. (See Plate 20.)

Until fairly recently, no female *Somniosus* had been observed to be carrying embryos, so it was assumed that this was an oviparous species. In 1954, a sixteen-foot female was caught near the Faeroe Islands, and was found to contain ten young, thereby establishing this shark as viviparous.

There may be as many as five or as few as one species in the genus *Somniosus*. The best-known is *S. microcephalus* from the North Atlantic, but there is also a North Pacific species known as *S. pacificus*, an Antarctic representative, *S. antarcticus*, one from the Mediterranean, *S. rostratus*, and a Japanese version, *S. longus*, which is thought to be the same as *S. rostratus*. As is so often the case in shark taxonomy, these may or may not be valid species.

From one of the largest sharks, *Somniosus microcephalus*, we come in the same family to the smallest of the sharks. The title of "world's smallest shark" probably goes to *Squaliolus laticaudus*, which is fully mature at about five inches. (It is somewhat more difficult to describe the world's smallest shark than to describe the largest. Obviously, all sharks are fairly small at one time in their lives, so the criterion of sexual maturity is applied. Male sharks, almost always smaller than the females, are considered mature if their claspers have become modified for reproduction, and females are considered mature if the ovaries are fully developed. Thus a mature or full-grown shark is one that is capable of

Proof positive that the Greenland shark does not lay eggs.

Norwegian Fishery and Marine Investigations

The foetus.

The foetus of the *Acanthorhinus carcharias* Gunner is exactly like a small specimen of this species. The shape and proportions of the fish are not at all different from the adult, but its small size makes it convenient for an examination (figs. 1 & 2).

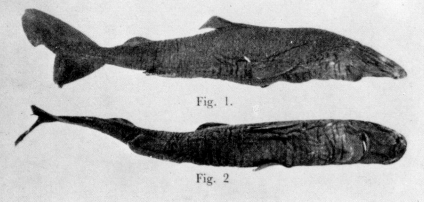

Fig. 1.

Fig. 2

A living shark of the genus Somniosus, *photographed by a robot camera at a depth of 6,300 feet, off the coast of Oahu, Hawaii. The diameter of the bait can is 13 inches.*

Marine Life Research Group, Scripps Institution of Oceanography

reproduction, although it is possible that it will grow larger with time.) *Squaliolus laticaudus* was originally discovered in Japanese waters, and it was given the vernacular name *tsuranagakobitozame*, which can be loosely translated as "dwarf shark with a long face." There is also an Atlantic species, somewhat larger, known as *Squaliolus sarmenti*.

Another tiny shark is the monotypical *Euprotomicrus bispinatus*. Six-inch specimens have been collected, and the largest known specimen was 10.5 inches long. *E. bispinatus* (which, despite its name, has no dorsal spines) is luminescent like many of the other small squaloids, and N. V. Parin, a scientist aboard the *Vitiaz*, has described their luminescence:

> *The entire ventral surface and the lower borders of the sides radiated an even, pale greenish light, which flared up at the sudden movements of the shark, and faded when the fish became quiet again.*[188]

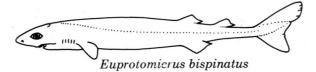
Euprotomicrus bispinatus

Another Russian scientist. Y. G. Aleev, considers the luminescence to be a means of camouflage. He wrote (quoted by Parin), "A liquidation (or diminishing) of the treacherous shadow is in these cases achieved by a special 'lightening up' of the ventral side of the body." This is an interesting theory, but it presupposes that the shark can control the intensity of the luminescence relative to its depth so that the greenish glow always eliminates the shadow, and does not shine as a signal beacon. Countershading, in which the ventral surface of a fish or shark is lighter than the upper surface, would seem to eliminate the "treacherous shadow" far more economically, and I much prefer Springer's idea that the glow serves as a means of "maintaining the visual integrity of the school" of the small dogfishes.

Euprotomicrus is ovoviviparous, and Parin describes one occasion on which the birth of young was observed "in a bathtub with seawater." A 9.25-inch female gave birth to "six little sharks, with still unabsorbed yolk sacs."[188]

Many families of sharks are homeless, in that they do not fit easily into any known larger group. One such family is the Oxynotidae. In 1948 Bigelow and Schroeder listed them under the family Squalidae, but by 1957, they had recognized them as a distinct family. They included them in their paper "A Study of the Sharks of the Suborder Squaloidea." There are two families in this suborder: the Oxynotidae and the Squalidae. In other words, since the oxynotids have to go somewhere, this is as good a place as any.

The teeth of oxynotids are different from those of any of the other squaloid sharks—and from any other sharks, for that matter. The front row is small, and the six successive functional rows get larger toward the rear of the mouth. The lower jaw has only one row of functional, blade-like teeth, pointed rearward. The oxynotids are also characterized by the presence of longitudinal ridges, down low on the flanks, and a rough skin made up of large, prominent dermal denticles. According to Bigelow and Schroeder's 1957 paper, there are three nominal species: *Oxynotus paradoxus*, from the eastern North Atlantic, *O. centrina*, from the eastern North Atlantic and the Mediterranean, and *O. bruniensis*, from Australia, Tasmania, and New Zealand.[31]

Whitley says that "they are . . . among the unloveliest of sharks,"[253] and one is inclined to agree with this description after seeing the few published photographs. Bigelow and Schroeder (1957) describe the mouth as having "thick, spongy lips with a complex series of cross-folds," and the back is extremely high, which suggested to Whitley the common name "spritsail shark." Because of the spines in each dorsal fin (which may point either backward or forward, and whose presence suggests an alliance with the squaloids), the Australian species, *O. bruniensis*, has been given the common name prickly dogfish.

Oxynotus bruniensis

(*Overleaf*) *Plate 18.* **Oceanic whitetips** (*Carcharhinus longimanus*)

The "Blue Water, White Death" film team: (left to right) *Peter Gimbel,
Valerie Taylor, Ron Taylor, Stan Waterman.*

MEN AND SHARKS

THE FATAL FASCINATION

Contrary to popular belief, the vast majority of encounters between man and shark end badly for the shark. In most situations where the two predatory animals come into contact, it is the shark that is at a disadvantage while the man is in his own element. Think on this. Man fishes for sharks, at little personal danger to himself, and the shark is invariably the loser. That man even sees the shark is a function of rod-and-reel angling; when nets or longlines are used, men only see the sharks when they are dead. The only situation in which man meets the shark on the shark's terms is when the man is swimming or diving. Even then, the man is likely to equip himself with protective or offensive weapons, ranging from spears and billy clubs to explosive powerheads and CO_2 cartridges that literally blow up the shark. Man is the most aggressive animal in the sea (and on the land as well), and all the "man-eater" stories in history will not change this designation. If sharks were as threatening as they have been made out to be, it would be unsafe to set foot in any ocean in the world. As it is, there are hundreds of millions of man-hours logged in the oceans annually, and the number of shark attacks is so small as to be statistically insignificant. It is the nature of the attacks, not their number, that fascinates and terrifies people. An investigation of man-shark interaction will not necessarily exonerate the shark, but it will surely implicate man in one of the most one-sided natural wars ever fought. For centuries, man has carried on a full-scale vendetta against sharks, killing them whenever possible, with rod and gun, with net, longline, and explosives. On the rare occasion when a shark kills a man, it is never out of malice (an emotional state probably reserved for man alone), but probably out of fear, self-defense, infrequently a desire to feed (it is not known if sharks actually experience the drive known as hunger), or perhaps some drive unknown to us at this time.

Man has certainly killed sharks to feed himself, the desire known as hunger in *Homo sapiens* proving to be a major determinant in human behavior. In many parts of the world, shark meat is an acceptable and desirable form of protein. The Italians consume millions of pounds of shark meat every year—especially of the smooth dogfish, which is known as *palumbo*, and the porbeagle, called *smeriglio*. The Japanese, always on the prowl for something else to take out of the sea, have been longlining sharks for years, and eating them in a variety of ways. In Australia and England, the fish in "fish and chips" is frequently shark, although it may be called "grayfish" or "steakfish." Shark fishing for human consumption is big business in Argentina, Peru, Mexico, and certain Central American countries. Wherever sharks are caught, there is a market for the fins; the Chinese make the exotic shark fin soup out of the pectorals and dorsal fins. As a food source, sharks seem to be well established, but this is a long way from explaining our fear and hatred of them.

It is something more that has made man react the way he does, and as with almost all questions about sharks, this one does not have an easy answer. Sharks are probably the only human source of food that has shown an inclination to turn the tables; even though the occurrence is rare, there is no question that some sharks have eaten some parts of some people. In addition, man fears what he does not understand, and of all the large creatures with which he shares this planet, man probably knows the least about the sharks. Finally there is the ongoing attempt to prove our superiority over "nature, red in tooth and claw." The shark qualifies for Tennyson's description as well as any animal alive (except for the claws), and those who see our existence as a battle with the natural world could not imagine a more redoubtable opponent.

There is no doubt that a shark attack is a fearsome and terrifying thing. The specter is of a supposedly mindless animal, armed with razor-sharp teeth, cruising off your swimming beach just out of sight, awaiting the right moment to dash in, bite your legs off and eat them. From this fantasy spring the novels, nightmares, and clichés of the shark terror. One of the most frightening aspects of shark behavior is this so-called mindlessness. It was long accepted that a shark was a "swimming nose," with almost no other functions to determine its behavior, and once it smelled its prey (or blood in the water), it homed in like a surface-to-air missile, unable to be stopped because it could not react to anything but the scent of its potential prey. Although sharks do have a pretty good sense of smell, this is by no means their dominant sense, and in addition to eyesight that is better than we thought it was, a phenomenal sense of hearing, and the ability to sense vibrations in the water, sharks have chemical and electrical receptors that are unequaled in the animal kingdom.

The discovery of the shark's sensitivities has not cleared up too many of the mysteries that surround its behavior and natural history. When we realize that we are dealing with one of the most numerous animals on earth (there are disputes about which species is the title holder, but there is a good chance that the most plentiful of all large vertebrates is a shark); that some of the sharks are gigantic, reaching a length of fifty feet and a weight of fifteen tons; that millions of sharks are caught every year for food; and that sharks often inhabit the same waters as people, it is truly a humbling thought that we know so little about them. For instance, we really have no idea how many species of sharks there are. The figure usually quoted is around 250, but the figure keeps fluctuating. Taxonomic revision keeps lowering it by demonstrating that species thought to be different are really the same, while the discovery of new species, with unsettling regularity, keeps raising it. Many of the new species are small, caught in the nets of fishermen or oceangoing scientists, but there have been new species of large sharks found recently, too. In 1966, a Cuban ichthyologist named Guitart Manday published a paper describing a new species of mako—the longfin.[121] And J. A. F. Garrick has been working on the revision of the largest genus of sharks, the Carcharhinidae, and upon completion of this monumental project, the total number of known species of sharks may be reduced by as many as seventy-five.

With nearly every species of shark there is a blank space in our knowledge. It may be the breeding habits, the maximum size, the correct scientific name, its range, or its feeding habits. To my knowledge, the mating of only one species of large shark (the lemon, *Negaprion brevirostris*) has been observed, so most of the information that we do have is based on the behavior of smaller species in captivity, and there is every reason to assume that whale sharks forty feet long mate differently than spiny dogfish three feet long.

So far, we have been discussing our ignorance of the natural history of sharks. In many instances, we are not sure of what they do, but when it comes to the question of *why* they do certain things, we are almost completely in the dark. We do not know why sharks do anything except that they breathe and eat and reproduce, for obvious reasons. Sometimes they bite people; more often they don't. Sharks have been known to feed when they're full, and starve to death when they should be hungry. Some sharks migrate thousands of miles, while others seem to stay in one place all their lives, however long that may be. We know almost nothing about the longevity of sharks, except that our earlier guesses were wrong. They seem to live for a long time, and grow very slowly. The same species of shark in different parts of the world behaves completely differently. In the Atlantic, the blue shark, *Prionace glauca*, is a large, migratory species, reaching a length of twelve feet. In the Pacific, the same shark never gets longer than six feet, and makes only daily movements from deep to shallow water. The white shark, so often implicated in attacks on people, remains one of the least-known large animals in the world. We have no idea where it breeds, whether it is common or rare, how big it is at birth, how big it has to be before it is sexually mature, or why it has the nasty habit of biting people so that they die.

As sharks represent a great void for the scientist, they also have become the last frontier of the adventurer. Not only can you fish for them, subdue them, and have the head mounted for a trophy, but you can do it almost in your own backyard. There is no society for the prevention of cruelty to sharks; even to write it is to seem ludicrous. Sharks are supposed to be the cruelest killers of all, "passionless" and "insane," swallowing seals, attacking boats, feeding in a wild frenzy on the hapless victims of shipwrecks and air disasters. If anything, one might conclude that cruelty to sharks is a good thing, a necessary thing.... Isn't it?

Not exactly. Just as ignorance breeds fear, knowledge dispels it. Those who know sharks best have developed a respect and admiration for them that belies their fearsome reputation. Beulah Davis, director of the Natal Anti-Shark Measures Board in South Africa, has told me that she would like to see the sharks protected, that she admires them and wants to figure out a way to protect the beaches of the Natal coast without killing the sharks. This comes from a person whose entire livelihood consists of killing sharks. Jack Casey, the shark-tagging biologist from Narragansett, Rhode Island, feels so strongly about sharks that he would like to be one, preferably a mako. On one occasion, while standing on the observation platform of the shark tank at the Mote Marine Laboratory in Sarasota, Perry Gilbert told me that he thought sharks were "among the most graceful and beautiful of all the vertebrates." Those who know the shark, however minimally, respect and admire this efficient predator. Those whose knowledge is based on rumor, sensational novel, or fear are certain to despise an animal that is, in fact, one of the most interesting creatures on earth.

It is obvious that the more dramatic sharks receive a disproportionate share of publicity. Man-eaters are more newsworthy than three-foot-long harmless sharks with tiny teeth. The bigger sharks tend to bring on hysterical reactions—a rumor of a shark sighting can clear the beaches for miles; it can even result in people changing their vacation plans.

Because people are so out of place in the ocean, it is not surprising that they fear the animals there. They are in an alien environment, truly "another world." It is not only beautiful and different down there; it is also populated by a lot of creatures that we don't know very much about: fire coral, stinging jellyfish, barracudas, poisonous stonefish, sharks. Even with the latest in scuba gear, people are at best observers in this watery world.

Most sharks that share their habitat with people have developed the reputation of being somewhat less than harmless. This is a function of the habits of the people, rather than the habits of the sharks. After all, the sharks have been swimming around for a long time; people have only been doing it—for recreation, at least --for a little over a hundred years. It therefore amounts to one animal (man), invading the domain of another animal (the shark), where the former still has a lot to learn about the latter, and the latter doesn't give a damn. One of the most frequently quoted observations about sharks is, "The only thing you can predict about sharks is their unpredictability." Sharks are not unpredictable; for the most part, they do exactly what an apex predator is expected to do. It is unlikely that any animal is really unpredictable, for the concept of random or haphazard behavior would be inconsistent with most natural laws and the behavior of most animals. We are calling our own inability to understand the actions of sharks their "unpredictability," while the very success of the sharks should tell us that they react regularly (for the shark, at least), in a variety of ways to a variety of stimuli. We do not know what these stimuli consist of, or how they affect the shark, but this does not mean that the shark is guilty of some sort of aberrant behavior.

We are often at a loss to explain the behavior of sharks under given conditions because of the lack of cumulative data; many more data have been assembled on the behavior of man. For the moment, let us avoid the question of the behavior of man and shark when in the water simultaneously. We will attempt to examine the attitude of man to shark (the converse being, understandably, beyond our abilities). There are a number of areas in which man interacts with sharks: for science, for art, for literature, for food, and for sport.

Science is a world unto itself, and sharks figure in it in a highly specialized way. There are scientists who study sharks because they want to learn about the behavior and physiology of sharks; there are scientists who study sharks because they want to learn about the behavior and physiology of people. Almost every aspect of the shark has been studied, from the tip of the nose to the notch at the end of the tail fin. Scientists have examined sharks' eyes, nostrils, teeth, sensory organs, brains, gills, skin, fins, muscles, blood vessels, reproductive and other internal organs. The behavior of sharks has been studied and documented, with research on their sense of smell, vision, hearing, their intelligence, their reactions to fish (living and dead), other sharks (living and dead), porpoises (living and dead), mammals, (living and dead), and people (living and dead). Sharks have been made to react to ringing bells, colored targets, lights, mazes, sounds of low and high frequencies, and changes in temperature. The evolutionary history of sharks is a study in itself, from the earliest progenitors of today's species, through the great *Carcharodon megalodon*, a monster some fifty or sixty feet long, with teeth as big as a human hand, to the present species, many of whose ancestors are still to be found. Much work has been done in the search for a satisfactory shark repellent; the range of suggested solutions seems limited only by the imaginations of the searchers. Hundreds of chemical substances have been tried, as well as bubble screens, electric fields, nets, enclosures, and the underwater broadcast of sounds. The search still goes on.

And yet, for all this research, most of which has been divided between those who would learn about sharks and those who would learn how to protect people from them, the amount of our knowledge is little indeed. People have been aware of sharks for thousands of years; for most of this time they have feared them. It might even be said that the information we have on the shark is better defined by what we do *not* know than by what we do know. To start at the very root of the problem, we do not even know what a shark is: Here is the *American Heritage Dictionary*'s definition:

> Shark. *n. Any of numerous chiefly marine fishes of the order Squaliiformes (order Selachii) having a cartilaginous skeleton and tough skin covered with small, tooth-like scales and sometimes large and voracious. (Origin obscure.)*

Not much help there, if you don't know about Squaliiformes or Selachii. The shorter *Oxford English Dictionary* gives us Selachii and Squaliiformes again, putting them both in the order Plagistomi: "In popular language chiefly applied to the large voracious fishes of this suborder, as the genera *Carcharodon*, *Carcharias*, etc." (Also, "Origin obscure.") Dictionary definitions seem to be concerned primarily with taxonomic information, and with the terms "large" and "voracious." Of course, the classification of sharks is important; it would be extremely difficult for us to talk about sharks if we didn't give them names, but the "large" and "voracious" designations are misleading. Most sharks are not large, and they're probably not voracious, either. (Voracious: "1. consuming or eager to consume great amounts of food; ravenous. 2. Having an insatiable appetite for some activity or pursuit.") Almost all sharks are carnivores (or, more precisely, piscivores), but they don't eat more than they need. Like other predators, sharks eat enough to maintain their biological equilibrium, and also like other predators, they don't expend any more energy than they have to in the process. If more energy must be put out to catch something than the something will provide when consumed, catching it would be a poor demonstration of feeding efficiency. Sharks have to be efficient feeders; they've been doing it well for so long. In fact, sharks do not even seem to be moderately voracious feeders, if our observations of them in captivity are any indication. They eat moderately, sometimes going for weeks or months without eating at all, and frequently starving to death in the presence of food. Of course, animals that have been captured and brought into pens or cages do not necessarily exhibit the same traits as those in the wild, but we have seen very little of the feeding habits of sharks in the wild, so most of what we know is based on observation of captive specimens. (One grey nurse shark in the Taronga Park Aquarium in Sydney ate only 170 to 200 pounds of fish a year. She weighed 336 pounds, and was kept in an apparently healthy state for six years.)

Of the some 250 species of sharks, perhaps 80 are large—over six feet in length. This leaves about 170 species under that length, and many of these don't even get as long as three feet. Some are mature at a length of less than twelve inches. So sharks are not only not necessarily voracious, they are not necessarily large, either. But still the image persists.

Sharks have not figured prominently in Western art, perhaps because of the ambivalent attitude that people have toward them. They are ugly and graceful at the same time; beautiful in their own watery world, but awkward and obscene on land. Before the invention of scuba gear and underwater photography equipment, people had very little idea of what sharks looked like when they were alive. They were often seen from boats, but a dorsal view of a shark, showing the broad, flattened head tapering to a narrow tail, is not necessarily the best view. The most famous painting involving sharks is Winslow Homer's *The Gulf Stream*. The picture shows a disconsolate-looking chap lying on the deck of a dismasted fishing boat; in the background one can see a tornado and a full-rigged ship. In the foreground there are at least three large sharks and some red matter in the water suggesting that the man's crewmates might not have been as lucky as he. We do not know what will happen next, but from the hopeless attitude of the man and the aggressive swirling of the sharks, we can assume the worst. Although this painting has been called "one of the greatest pictures ever painted in America," the public response to the grisly events depicted was one of horror. In order to mollify those whose sensibilities were offended by the gruesome death that seemed to await the lone survivor, Homer is reputed to have said, "Tell them it is all right; the tornado does not hit him and he is picked up by the ship."

John Singleton Copley, another of America's great painters, gave us *Watson and the Shark*, now in the Museum of Fine Arts in Boston. Rendered in 1778, this painting shows Brook Watson (later to become Lord Mayor of London), in the waters of Havana harbor, with his boatmates trying to fend off a huge and fearsome shark, mouth wide and yellow eye gleaming. This shark (species unknown) bit off Watson's leg, and it was Watson himself who described the incident to Copley and commissioned the painting.

The shark was thought to represent nature at its most cruel, and only a few painters and writers felt the need to tackle such a powerful subject. Some major American writers dealt with the shark, including Melville in *Moby Dick*. During the voyage of the *Pequod*, sharks are swirling around the carcasses of the dead whales, and Queequeg, the harpooner, demonstrates the attitude of the whalemen to sharks:

Queequeg no care what god made him shark . . . wedder Feejee god or Nantucket god, but de god what make de shark must be one dam Ingin.[167]

Ernest Hemingway was a big game fisherman, and in that context, he came into contact with many kinds of sharks. In *The Old Man and the Sea*, the sharks destroy the old man's great fish, and therefore represent the forces of nature triumphant over man.[131] As I have discussed elsewhere in this book, Hemingway has given us dramatic descriptions of the mako and the hammerhead in others of his novels.

One other novel should be mentioned in this discussion of sharks in literature. Although no one, not even its author, would put *Jaws* in the same class as the writings of Melville and Hemingway, Peter Benchley's novel has done more to make people shark-conscious than anything since the 1916 attacks on the New Jersey beaches.[26] In Melville and Hemingway, the sharks are secondary figures, but in *Jaws*, a recent best-seller and the basis for the highest-grossing movie in Hollywood history, the main character is a white shark.

Frequently while fishing for big game fish such as marlin, tuna, or swordfish, anglers find a shark on their line. Most sharks will not put up a fight in the way that a sailfish or a tuna will when caught; sharks usually stay deep and pull hard on the line. When an angler gets a shark close to the boat, the shark tends to roll in the line and cut it neatly with its sandpaper-like skin. Until quite recently, sharks were regarded as a nuisance, and if boated, they were usually thrown back. Often the catching of a shark was the occasion for an uncontrolled slaughter of the animal, which included bashing it on the head, stabbing it, kicking it, and eviscerating it before throwing the remains back into the sea.

Sharks as game fish have reached an unprecedented height of respectability and desirability. There are shark-fishing clubs all over the world, in such diverse places as Jacksonville, Florida; Durban, South Africa; Looe, England; and Palm Beach, Florida. There are charter fishing boat captains who represent themselves specifically as shark fishermen, and not a few of them fish only for sharks. One man in particular, Frank Mundus of Montauk, Long Island, has been "monster fishing" for years, and for many of those years he was the only charter captain whose clients regularly brought in blues, browns, makos, threshers, porbeagles, and whites. On one occasion, Mundus harpooned a great white that was 17.5 feet long and weighed 4,500 pounds. Its massive head is mounted and hung on the wall of a saloon near the dock at Montauk, a grim reminder of what can be found off the Long Island coast. Now Mundus's boat, the *Cricket II*, is chartered every day of the season, and shark fishermen have to sign up as much as a year in advance to obtain the benefit of his experience and expertise. (See "Frank Mundus: Monster Fisherman.")

There are now shark-fishing tournaments too, where dozens, or even hundreds, of boats set out at a certain time for the sole purpose of catching as many sharks as they can within a stated period. Sometimes it is a particular species they seek, such as the high-flying mako, and sometimes it is any shark at all. I recently saw a sign that offered $5,000 for the largest shark ("any species") caught in a Montauk tournament. With hundreds of boats participating in these tournaments, hundreds of sharks are caught. The 1975 Bayshore (Long Island) Tournament recorded 26,000 pounds of sharks caught on the first day.

Is there any point to all this, other than the fisherman's satisfaction in catching a big fish? What do you do with 26,000 pounds of sharks? Most of it is discarded, but people are becoming more and more aware of the value of the shark in a commercial, if not in a humanitarian, sense. Americans seem to have a reluctance to eat shark, but this reluctance seems to be abating. Most of the makos caught in the Bayshore Tournament were taken home to be turned into steaks, which are comparable to swordfish in taste and texture. At a recent conference in Florida, shark meat was served as a snack. Since everyone there was interested in sharks for one reason or another (they represented such organizations as the Daytona Chamber of Com-

A rare, mid-nineteenth century genre painting by Junius Brutus Stearns (1810–1885), showing a Long Island fishing club with a shark that one of the members has hooked.

merce, the Natal Anti-Shark Measures Board, the Office of Naval Research, and the Mote Marine Laboratory), they were all eager to taste the subject of the conference, and I can report that the fried shark meat with tartar sauce was a resounding success.

Other parts of the shark that are used commercially include the skin, which can be turned into an extremely durable leather; the fins, which are used in shark fin soup; and the teeth, which make interesting souvenirs, if properly cleaned. (If not properly cleaned, they begin to smell, and have to be thrown out.)

Even though the shark has certain commercial possibilities, they do not begin to explain the magnitude of human interest in sharks. The odds are pretty much against a shark attack, but the thought of being bitten in half or eaten alive is so terrifying that people overlook the odds. It's horrible enough just to know that this *could* happen. Our attitudes toward sharks are contradictory. We fear them and yet we seek them out. We fish for them, dive with them, collect and test them for science. It does not take a psychiatrist to identify the relationship between these two conflicting attitudes: if something is a potential threat, it becomes an act of personal heroism to face the threat directly. In the case of sharks, an unusual number of people have encountered sharks in the water, and gone on to do it again. During the filming of *Blue Water, White Death*, Peter Gimbel, who admits to a total fear of sharks ("These animals are as well armed as anything alive.... They have a quality that's particularly dreadful ... an insane, passionless killer..."), left the pro-

tection of a shark cage to swim in the midst of hundreds of large, dangerous sharks—oceanic whitetips, blues and duskies, all of which are considered potential man-killers—that were feeding on the bloody carcass of a sperm whale. Then he did it again, at night.

An amateur diver named Henri Bource was diving off Lady Julia Percy Island, South Australia. His leg was bitten off by a white shark. He is now a professional diver and film maker: "I've seen quite a few white sharks since that day ... and far from being a marine horror, they are really very beautiful. I admire them."[82]

Rodney Fox, the Australian national spearfishing champion in 1962, was savagely attacked by a shark in the waters of Aldinga Beach, South Australia, in 1963. He lived to describe the experience:

> *Something huge hit me on the left side with enormous force and surged me through the water.... There was a queer sensation as though all my insides were squeezed over to one side. I reached out behind and groped for the shark's eyes.... On the surface there was red everywhere. My own blood. And through it the head of the shark appeared, conical snout, great rolling body like a rust-coloured tree trunk.*[200]

His arm was ripped to the bone where he had stuck his hand down the throat of the shark. His lungs were punctured, his ribs and stomach were exposed. By the grace of God, the wetsuit that held him together, and brilliantly executed rescue procedures, Rodney Fox was saved. He now runs a motel in South Australia, and dives professionally for white sharks: it is Fox who supplies the accommodations, cages, boats, bait, and other necessary equipment for those who want to see the great white shark. (See "Brian Rodger, Rodney Fox, Henri Bource: The Survivors.")

These individuals, of course, are unique. Most people who narrowly escape death do not make a career out of risking their lives again, and then again. As with race car drivers and bullfighters, these people have a strong desire to challenge and beat the odds, and, more important, to look closely at their own death, and survive.

Ernest Hemingway probably exemplified this idea as well as anyone. His often-expressed ideal of "grace under pressure" led him to participate in all sorts of dangerous activities, from boxing to big game hunting, from bullfighting to shark fishing. (Of course, the most dangerous game is the one in which an individual pits himself against the most cunning and powerful of all the earth's creatures, *Homo sapiens*, in a little exercise known as war.) There are those who believe that the proper test of an individual is a match against a specific opponent, where the goal is not winning, but surviving. As mechani-

zation and anonymity engulf us to a greater and greater degree, the search for new tests increases. We cannot take on the system (except that a human can still beat a computer at chess), so we must look outside the system for the challenge that will enable us to prove our individual superiority. A person climbs a mountain, not only "because it is there," but also because it represents a fundamental and personal challenge. Beyond the scope of the individual challenge, it is possible to see our despoilment of our own planet as an extension of this strong desire to prove mankind triumphant. Is the fouling of our own nest anything more or less than a wildly misdirected urge to prove our superiority over the earth, the sea, the air, and the creatures that inhabit those regions?

So we are left with the shark. No matter how many species there are, no matter how many of them are small or inoffensive, the general attitude toward them is still one of fear and ignorance. We cannot entirely dispel this attitude, for, in truth, the shark has committed some atrocities that will ensure its reputation as a killer forever. But we can hope to show some aspects of this fascinating creature that will contribute to our understanding and, thus, to our tolerance.

One of the 50 makos caught at the Bayshore Mako Tournament, 1975.

Richard Ellis

SHARK TOURNAMENT

It is 6:30 Saturday night, June 28, 1975. Although it has not really begun to get dark, incandescent lights some thirty feet off the ground illuminate the dock at the Bayshore marina. The scene upon which these lights play is a bloody, stinking mess. Crowds of onlookers push up to temporary snow fence barricades to watch the center ring: in this enclosure sharks are being examined, weighed, dissected, aborted, decapitated, kicked. It is raucous as well as malodorous—the weigh-master is trying to get the necessary information on each shark caught; boatmates have lost each other or their catch; and above the noise of the crowd, the bellow of a bullhorn is heard: "Boat 91—will you please move out; we need room for other boats. Boat 38—any fish on board? Wait 'til the way is clear, then bring 'em in."

While the man on the bullhorn directs the docking and unloading operations, another member of the committtee announces the results of the weighing-in over a microphone: "Boat number 40, *Mary Bee:* a 160-pound blue shark . . . an 81-pound blue shark. *Wanderer*, boat 66: a 221-pound mako—that's a lot of steaks!"

The crowd cheers. A baby white shark is weighed, and the announcement is made: "A white shark, a great white shark, right here, the man-eater, the star of *Jaws!* The people push closer to get a look at this, the most feared of all sharks. It is four feet long and weighs 52 pounds. From the evidence of a preumbilical scar, a biologist estimates that it is six months old. The fisherman who caught this shark wants to have it mounted. Representatives from a taxidermy shop circulate among the fishermen, biologists, and onlookers, handing out business cards. "Head mount? Jaw mount? Whatever you want.... This your fish? Want it mounted?"

Most of the fishermen do not want their fish mounted. Some of those who caught makos want to eat them, but those who caught blues or browns do not want any part of them. In the enclosure reserved for the scientific examination of the sharks, an Oriental, wearing a white apron and wielding a machete-like implement, is removing the pectoral and dorsal fins, for shark fin soup. A rumor follows him to the effect that he is immensely rich, the owner of a number of restaurants. (In Oriental markets in this country, dried shark fins sell for as much as ten dollars a pound, so if this man is not rich now, he is well on his way to becoming so. In the course of the day he has removed perhaps two hundred fins.) Also milling about, despite the

efforts of the committee and the "security" personnel, are gate-crashers of every age, trying to look as if they belonged there. They are armed with every conceivable kind of edged weapon, from penknives and divers' knives to a World War I bayonet. Fishermen are knife-carriers, and most of the weapons visible are either razor-sharp or are being sharpened in the enclosure. There is a lot of knife-sharpening here. After the sharks are examined by the scientists and their fins have been removed by the restaurateur, those who want souvenirs of their efforts or of other people's try to remove the jaws from the sharks, most of which have already been eviscerated. (When a shark is hung from the gin pole of a fishing boat, its stomach is often everted, and protrudes from its mouth. Spectators often think that this is the shark's tongue.) Many sharks remain barely alive, despite the fact they have been hanging out of the water by the tail for a couple of hours. This causes great consternation and excitement in the milling, knife-wielding crowd, and from the committee platform the operator of the bullhorn announces: "Can we *please* have the security people clear the area.... There are live sharks here—they can still give you a nasty bite." When a shark twitches in its death throes, or in a final muscle spasm, the crowd moans.

The Bayshore Mako Tournament was first held in 1962. For three years it took place in September, but from 1965 to the present it has been held in late June. It is a popular event, sponsored by the Bayshore Tuna Club, and involving almost every civic organization in the town of Bayshore. Included are the fire, police, and sanitation departments. The firemen are there to prevent what could be a holocaust, with a dozen boats taking on fuel at once, and the fishermen often ignoring the "No Smoking" signs. The police are there to control the crowds, and to keep unauthorized personnel out of the enclosure. (This proves to be an almost impossible task, since there are not only infiltrators from the ranks of the public, but as the boats come in to unload their catch, crew members often disembark and mingle with the personnel in the enclosure.) The role of the sanitation men becomes obvious later in the day. In addition to the soft-drink and beer cans that will remain after the crowds have departed, they will also have to dispose of the corpses of hundreds of sharks.

I was invited to observe the 1975 tournament by Jack Casey, a biologist for the Narragansett

Laboratory of the National Marine Fisheries Service. Casey and his staff have been collecting data from these tournaments since 1965. They represent a rare opportunity for biologists to assemble a significant amount of data, with other people doing the actual collecting. (Obviously, biologists are not averse to doing their own collecting, but if there is someone else to collect the specimens, the scientists have more time to pursue their particular studies.) The tournament provides Casey with a variety of catch data that he could not possibly assemble on his own. The previous week, he and his staff had been aboard the research vessel *Geronimo*, longlining for sharks. They spent an entire week at sea, and tagged about a hundred blue sharks and one mako. The hundred-plus boats entered in the Bayshore Tournament head through the Fire Island Inlet, and out into the Atlantic, to fish in whatever area and at whatever depth they feel will produce the most fish. The information returned to Casey is much more of a random sample, rather than the result of a concentrated fishing expedition. Diverse information is more useful than that gathered in one-spot fishing, for it produces a larger view of a larger area. Casey is interested in learning about abundance, feeding habits, temperature preference, and population density of the various species, and he requests that the fishermen report to him the location at which they were fishing, water temperature, depth, bait, etc. (Tournament entries are usually elaborately equipped vessels; most have depth-finding instruments, and many have highly sophisticated "fish-finders," as well as numerous other gadgets that are supposed to improve the fishing.) Some of the boats are in the fifty-foot class, and probably cost upwards of $100,000.

Friday night, June 27, the night before the tournament: At 8 P.M. there is a "captain's meeting." All entrants convene to receive their final instructions, and a few words from Casey. The president of the Bayshore Tuna Club tells them how pleased he is with the turnout. There are 150 boats entered, the maximum allowed under the rules. Each captain has already received a folder containing full rules and regulations, so this is just a reminder and a social gathering. One of the things emphasized is the need for boats to check in upon returning, or to call in if they do not intend to come back to Bayshore. In the past, some fishermen, having been unsuccessful ("skunked"), have simply gone to their home ports, and the Coast Guard has searched for them for hours.

Visible at this meeting are jackets resplendent with tournament patches from other contests, other ports. The patches are totemic symbols of rank, complete with "hash marks" and other insignia. (This is the fourteenth running of the Bayshore Tournament, and there are some participants with fourteen half-inch-high badges on their sleeves.) There are patches from shark tournaments, tuna tournaments, billfish tournaments, even codfish tournaments. Jackets are covered with bright colors, silhouettes of fish, emblems of accomplishment. Even if he catches no fish, every entrant in a tournament receives a patch. Everyone who enters receives a trophy, however small. "I have been here; I have done this thing—look on my patches, O ye mighty, and despair!"

Jack Casey is introduced, and he thanks the officials and entrants for letting him participate. He introduces his associates, Wes Pratt and Chuck Stillwell, and tells the crowd again of his desires. He is particularly interested in the retrieval of tags, since his tagging program has been in operation for over ten years. The tournament is an excellent opportunity to collect information. Like bird bands, shark tags contain information that enables scientists to learn a great deal about migration, distribution, and growth. Someone has already handed Casey tag #875, and he is overjoyed. The tag is at least ten years old, and although he must check it with his records to be sure, he believes it has come from a sandbar shark that was tagged off Rhode Island. At the Narragansett laboratory, he has the information on the fish that was tagged (size, location, species, etc.), and returns are so infrequent that any one is an event. (Only 3 percent of all his tags, 384 out of 12,896, have been returned.) He tells the fishermen that he wants them to bring in everything they catch on the first day, even though not everything counts for points. All sharks over 75 pounds count one point per pound, except makos, which count two points per pound, no matter how small. In addition, there are prizes for the largest shark (any species), the most sharks caught by a single boat, and the largest blue, mako, and sandbar sharks. (Since these are the species most frequently caught, the largest earn prizes for their catchers.)

The tournament begins at 6 A.M. I have been told that the start is worth watching, so I agree to be awakened at 5:30. (We stayed up until 3 A.M. discussing sharks, of all things, so this agreement is made with a certain amount of reluctance.) We arrive at the dock at 5:45, to witness a watery maelstrom; boats are circling in the mist, revving their engines—they are not allowed across the starting line until the 6:00 cannon is fired. The captains hand in their cards indicating that they are officially entered, and they are each given two cans of frozen menhaden for chum, and two coffee cakes from Entenmann's Bakery. (Charlie Entenmann has not missed a start in fifteen years; he has been participant, director, committee member, judge.) There are perhaps a hundred spectators, wearing windbreakers and warm jackets. The forecast for the morning is for fog, and it is proving correct. The cannon sounds, and the armada roars off to the southwest. The normally placid waters of Great South Bay are roiled to a mist-green froth as the powerful boats race toward the inlet—where they will pass through in single file. One boat stalls, and is rocked perilously by the churning wakes of the other craft. She sways broadside into the path of the oncoming boats, which swing wide around her, creating even more dangerous conditions. In the past, this racing start has been the cause of more than one accident, usually to the local clammers, but this time there are no mishaps, and the floundering boat is started up again in time to join the race.

By 6:10 the first wave of entrants has gone, and those fishermen who do not feel the need to be first move out more slowly. They are all gone by 6:30, and the waters of the bay subside and again become the property of the clammers—small, narrow, square-bowed craft, with a single person, usually a teenager, at the tiller of the outboard.

We return to Charlie Entenmann's house for coffee and a seemingly endless supply of donuts, coffee cakes, apple strudel, and raspberry danish. A radio in the kitchen is tuned to the frequency of the communications boat, so that we can hear the news as it is called in. There will be no results for a couple of hours, so those that are able to do so, go back to sleep. I do not number among these fortunate ones, and I sit and talk to Casey about his shark experiences, shark tagging, sharks in general, and the philosophy of fishing tournaments.

By early afternoon there are sporadic, crackling reports: "200-pound mako . . . 150-pound blue . . . 312½-pound mako . . ." (Since none of the boats have facilities for weighing large fish, anything other than a rough estimate is either

a joke or a fisherman overly impressed with his ability to judge the weight of a fish.) "80-pound blue . . . 100-pound dusky . . ." (In fact, there will be no dusky sharks caught at all today, but the difference between the dusky, *Carcharhinus obscurus*, and the sandbar shark, *Carcharhinus milberti*, is slight, and since duskies grow to be larger and more dangerous, there is a tendency to report a dusky whenever possible.)

The fishing day officially ends at 3 P.M. At this time, the boats must stop fishing, or if they have a fish on the line, they must play that one and then no more. They are supposed to be in and registered by 6:00, so by 4:00 we have returned to the dock. The first boat to return has a large mako and two smaller blue sharks on the ginpole. She circles to show her starboard rail to the waiting crowd, which cheers at the sight of the tournament's first mako. There is confusion in getting the fish from the boat to the dock— too many "dock boys" and too few fish, a situation that will be reversed as more and more boats arrive. "Hold that rope . . . Gimme that . . . Don't let go . . . Watch it, he's still alive . . . Put another loop around him . . ." Finally, the first sharks are weighed. The mako weighs 251 pounds, the blues 83 and 65 pounds. The crowd, which has now swelled to some 250 people, cheers at the announced weights, and the dead mako is hoisted up to a crossbar with thickening blood dripping from its gaping jaws. Its hard, striated muscles show clearly through its drying indigo skin.

Other boats arrive, and less attention is paid to each one. There now begins a confusion that will not end until the last of the 294 fish of the day has been brought in and weighed. In order for a fish to qualify, it must be recorded, and the captain of the boat must stand by and identify his catch. In some cases, there are five, seven, or even ten fish, and the process takes more time than any of the captains are eager to spend. By 6:00, most of the boats have come in, but some are still standing off because there is no place for them to dock. The rules specify that the fish must be in by 6:00 in order to qualify, but obviously the rules must be bent for a boat that was in by 5:45, but could not get to the weigh station until 8:00.

I am observer and participant, and I try to keep out of the way of people who appear to know what they're doing, and to help those who don't. I identify sharks—I gratuitously corrected one man who was delivering a serious lecture on the

Harold L. Pratt, National Marine Fisheries Service

porbeagle (of which none was caught—or expected) while pointing at a sandbar shark, and I help in the most basic of all the required tasks: carrying sharks from place to place. After the weighing, the sharks are brought to a fenced-in area, where Pratt and Stillwell perform their examinations. Wes Pratt is studying the reproductive habits of the blue shark, and Chuck Stillwell is concerned with the stomach contents of all the species brought in.

In one case, Wes and I carefully lay out a white vinyl groundsheet in order to examine a gravid female blue shark. She is carefully opened, and eighteen perfectly formed pups are removed. Each is carefully measured (they average about fifteen inches in length), and its sex noted. I lay each one aside after calling out the measurements, and then we are called away to see a shark that "looks terrible." It is a five-foot tiger shark, with an infestation of leeches on its anal fins; we counted eight leeches in all. When we return to the female blue, every one of the pups has been taken for a souvenir.

One tag is found; it is a cause for great jubilation for Jack Casey, but some confusion exists as to which fish it came from. If he can't find this out, the information on the tag is useless. We locate a small blue with the head of the dart still in its shoulder, and we are able to correlate the specimen with the size and weight data.

Soon the numbers get ahead of us; we cannot possibly examine each fish as it is brought into the pen. Chuck Stillwell, who is examining the stomach contents, decides to pass up every shark with an everted stomach. This means about every other shark. One sandbar shark has the remains of a dogfish (a smaller species of shark) in its stomach, further proof that shark-eat-shark is one of the rules of the sea. Most of the others have been feeding on mackerel and bluefish, and occasionally squid. Of all the sharks examined, the only item discovered that is not ordinary shark food is a beef bone, probably from a garbage scow. No raincoats, tin cans, license plates, tar paper, or human remains, much to the disappointment of the spectators.

I came to this event with an open mind, with no predispositions to like or dislike it. I felt it was an important part of my research, and I wanted to see what it was like and to see the sharks. Up to this time I had never seen a great white or a thresher, and I was hoping to see either or both. We got no threshers, but we did get a six-month-old, four-foot-long white shark. (Somehow the word "great" is inapplicable to a four-foot shark. It was not white either, but a bronze-gray above and only whitish below.) It was certainly *Carcharodon carcharias*, whose common name is great white shark. Its eye was as black as it was supposed to be, but it was glazed and dusty and the size of a nickel. This was not the "eye of God" of Peter Matthiessen's *Blue Meridian*;[164] it was the eye of a dead baby shark. A 13-pound mako was also caught, probably the youngest mako ever seen in these waters. The man who caught the white shark wanted to have it mounted as a memento of the tournament. A 48-inch specimen fits neatly over the mantel, while a full-grown great white

at fourteen or fifteen feet makes an awkward trophy. (Still, I couldn't help thinking that the man's desire was a little heartless, like having a mount made of a lion cub.) Three small tiger sharks and two hammerheads are brought in. The head of the hammerhead is quickly removed. The bloody carcass lies on the asphalt, and people have to step over it to go about their business. Finally, someone kicks it out of the way.

There are dense crowds on both sides of the fence now. "Hey, mister, can you get me a tooth?" "Blue shark, 241 pounds (applause)..." "Whose fish is this... a 115-pound brown shark?" "An 80-pound bluefish..." (Throughout the tournament, the committee member who has been calling out the weights has been saying bluefish when he wanted to say blue shark. Every time he makes the mistake, the crowd laughs and comments, "That's a hell of a bluefish.") There is also a bloodthirstiness here, perhaps a desire to see someone hurt, or to see a human arm fall out of the stomach of a shark. Would there be these crowds, this avid interest, if we were cutting open tuna? swordfish? whales? Probably not. The shark is a primitive terror, uncontrollable, and fearsome. It is a primeval marine death force that needs to be conquered, even vicariously, so that man can realize his superiority over the beasts of the field and of the sea. (Besides, this is the summer of the movie *Jaws*, and it is playing at the Bayshore theater just down the street. Everyone wants to see the real thing, now that they've seen the movie or read the book.) The once-graceful sharks are dragged by the tail or by a meat hook slammed into their gills, over the rough gravel. Even here, man shows that the skin of the shark, famous for its abrasive powers, is inferior to his own devices. The sharks are worn ragged and bloody from being dragged from place to place.

An old man asks if this is "an eradication program." We tell him no, it is a fishing tournament, and the scientists are examining the fish. He looks at the blood, the corpses, the parents and children crowding in to see the "maneaters." The man does not understand, and walks away. I'm not sure I understand either. I have seen 294 sharks slaughtered. I do not return for the second day's activities.

SHARK ATTACK

There is a generation, whose teeth are as swords, and their jaw teeth as knives to devour the poor from off the earth, and the needy from among men.

Proverbs 30:14

Shark attacks are the most publicized and the least understood of all aspects of the sharks' behavior. Sharks do many other things, and most sharks never attack anybody, but the infrequent contact between human and shark when both are in the water is perhaps the most celebrated aspect of the sharks' existence.

The actual number of shark attacks around the world per year is unknown. (By "shark attack," I mean contact between a person and a shark in which the person is injured.) David Baldridge, in his comprehensive study "Shark Attack: A Program of Data Reduction and Analysis," gives the annual number at "around 30."[17] In some parts of the world, South Africa and Australia, for example, shark attack is a big enough problem for the government to be involved on a continuing basis, for both economic and humanitarian reasons. In other parts of the world, the repression of the news of shark attacks has become a government concern—at least on the municipal level. (I recently attended a symposium in Florida where one of the main topics of discussion was "Shark Attack and Its Effect on Tourism." The consensus was that not enough people were attacked to warrant the publicity. It might keep the tourists away.)

Because of the intense focus on this one aspect of shark behavior, the study of this subject has overshadowed almost all other areas of study. But other areas are critical to our understanding of shark attack, for without knowledge of the habitat, biology, abundance—or any of a dozen other facets of shark behavior—we would be unable to understand the shark at all, and we would be forced to depend on the old watchword of sharks being "unpredictable."

I propose to review the subject of shark attack from some of these different viewpoints. I have before me the statistical analyses, the gory details of maulings, mutilations, and death, the sensational novels, the lists of "dangerous species," and the accounts of practically all the methods used to combat this infrequent "enemy." It is abundantly clear that this is not a serious problem statistically. The Shark Attack File (SAF), maintained for the years 1958 to 1969, contains a total of 1,652 cases. An attempt was made to gather data on incidents that took place before 1958, from newspaper reports, medical records, and personal experiences, but most of the information concerns events that took place during the period of active data collecting. Certainly, the file is far from complete. Many attacks occurred in parts of the world where people never heard of the Shark Attack File. (In many of these areas, Pacific atolls, for example, it would have been impossible to record a shark attack—no mails, no forms, no English language. Not surprisingly, since it was primarily an American-supported project, the SAF contains a remarkable preponderance of attacks in countries where English is spoken. This does not mean that sharks have a preference for English-speaking victims, but it would be quite possible to interpret the data in that way. As we will see, the interpretation of data plays a highly significant part in the discussion of shark attacks.)

The earliest reports of shark attacks were based on the prevailing assumption that the shark was trying to eat the victim. Almost all attacks were attributed to this predisposition of the shark—any shark—to eat any person with whom it came into contact. Early seafarers feared the sharks that followed their ships, assuming (correctly, in rare instances) that the sharks would gobble up any sailor unfortunate enough to fall overboard. In truth, this ship-following was not a result of the sharks' lust for human flesh; a much more mundane form of comestible attracted the sharks to these early sailing ships: garbage. If indeed a sailor did end up in the drink, the fact that he was surrounded by scraps of food and other enticing tidbits certainly increased the possibility that he would be attacked.

Even the concept of shark "attack" as distinguished from "man-eating" is a recent one. Of the two books with the name *Shark Attack*, one of them, written by Victor Coppleson and published in 1958, deals with the supposed intentions of sharks to eat people;[58] while the second, written by David Baldridge in 1974, is an attempt to determine how, when, and where (and, to a certain extent, why) sharks attack people.[17] There is a great deal of difference in these two approaches. Coppleson illustrates the "man-eater" theories which have been handed down through time, while Baldridge makes use of contemporary science to deal with the subject, emphasizing such diverse disciplines as computer technology, ethology, operant conditioning, demography, and hydrodynamics.

(A third book, David Davies' *About Sharks and Shark Attack*, a transitional work published in 1964, bridges the gap and shows how far and how fast the pendulum has swung between these approaches.[70])

This is not to say that Baldridge (or modern science, for that matter) has *solved* the problem of shark attack. There is still as much danger as there ever was of being attacked by a shark, and perhaps even more, since there are a great many more swimmers and divers in the water than ever before. Statistically, the danger never was very high, but all the statistics in the world cannot assuage a very real, deep-rooted fear that people have of being eaten alive.

Public and private opinions about sharks vary with the times. The Polynesians always had sharks in abundance, and never lacked for real or mythical incidents that included sharks. The early Greeks, a seafaring people, knew of sharks, and perhaps the earliest known references to them are to be found in Herodotus's *Histories*, in which "sea monsters" that attacked shipwrecked sailors off the coast of Thessaly are described. From Herodotus's time onward, reports of man-eating fish circulated in countries that fronted coastal waters or sent men to sea. In most of these accounts, the shark is described as a "cruel devourer, hungry and ravenous."

It is not my intention to catalog the myriad attacks that have taken place over the centuries, nor do I plan to present an apologia for the misunderstood shark. My aim is to put the concept of shark attack into some sort of contemporary perspective, in order that we might better understand the problem and its ramifications. In summarizing the voluminous information, it will be necessary to discuss certain sanguinary incidents, but they are included only in the interests of analysis or clarification.

There is no question that sharks attack people in the water. They attack swimmers, divers, shipwrecked sailors, and any other category of people who can be in the water at a given time. They attack infrequently, it is true, but a shark attack is often a gruesome and horrible affair, with arms and legs torn off, and sometimes even the death of the victim. It may, in fact, be that the infrequency and erratic nature of shark attacks are among the most frightening aspects of the whole picture. If we knew that under a particular set of circumstances, a shark would always attack, we might be better prepared psychologically to deal with it. It is, perhaps, the unpredictability of the *attack*—not of the shark—that adds so much to our fears. In addition, our almost total ignorance of the sharks' motivation (and *all* animals are motivated, by one force or another) has led to a critical misunderstanding of the sharks' behavior, adding fuel to the fires of shark-hatred. When a shark is brought aboard ship, a frenzied orgy of destruction often takes place: the shark is kicked, chopped, eviscerated, and otherwise mauled, before being thrown unceremoniously back into the sea. This may represent an exorcising of our own fears and inner demons, for no other animal, alive or dead, is so universally feared and despised.

Tens of thousands of Americans are killed or maimed every year in automobile accidents, and yet millions of people still drive the roads in apparent unconcern for a fate that is statistically far more probable than a shark attack. One shark attack, however—or even one shark sighting—and all bathers rush from the water in fear for their lives.

I asked Peter Benchley why he thought *Jaws* had been so successful. He told me that people fear the unknown and that they like to experience fear vicariously, in the safety of their own home or in a movie theater. But it is more than that; *Jaws* struck a resonant chord in American sensitivity (disregarding for a moment the immense publicity it received, as a book and as the highest-grossing movie in Hollywood's history). People do have a fear of sharks, but much more important, they have a fear of being eaten. Moreover, we know so little about sharks; they reside in a submarine fortress we have yet to breach, and like the sea and most of its other inhabitants, they are reluctant to give up their secrets.

An appendix in Gilbert Whitley's *Fishes of Australia, Part I, Sharks, etc.* lists 226 "shark tragedies and attacks" in Australia, the earliest in 1803, and the latest in 1940, the year of the book's publication.[253] These range in severity from the scratching of a man's skin to "Boy, aged 14, Woy Woy, NSW, killed." Whitley's book was written primarily as a natural history of sharks, and the subject of shark attack, while discussed, is hardly the focus of the book.

It was Victor M. Coppleson, an Australian surgeon, who fully developed the subject of Australian shark attacks. In his book, he includes some biology, but it is obvious that his true interest lies in the predations of shark on man. He wrote: "No sphere of shark activity has been overlooked. The dangers that confront fishermen, the risks of men adrift in the open sea in boats, rafts and lifeboats, and the undersea perils of divers, spearfishermen and frogmen have all been studied and recorded." Coppleson, who died in 1963, was particularly fond of the "rogue shark" theory:

A rogue shark—if the theory is correct, and the evidence appears to prove it to the hilt —like the man-eating tiger, is a killer which, having experienced the deadly sport of killing or mauling a human, goes in search of similar game. The theory is supported by the pattern and frequency of many attacks.

Coppleson's 237-page book consists mostly of detailed descriptions of gory attacks and tables and charts to support his various theories. His "rogue sharks" cruise the beaches of Australia, New Guinea, and elsewhere, waiting—sometimes as long as three or four *years* (italics mine)—to perpetrate another attack.

In support of this theory, significant examples can be quoted. In 1922, for instance, there was a series of attacks at Coogee, near Sydney. The first attack was followed by another a month later, and two more within the next three years, the four of them within a little more than a mile off coast.

Now, four attacks in three years is more than the average for any one location, but this hardly proves that it was the work of a single shark. Many of Coppleson's examples can be used to demonstrate the opposite conclusion, that is, that there were many sharks present. And the more sharks there are, the more attacks take place.

Coppleson was a highly respected physician, and his work on the Australian shark problem led to his being knighted. He has been criticized for his less than meticulous research methods, since he relied heavily on newspaper reports, and second- and third-hand stories in most of the cases he reported. However, in his capacity as a surgeon, he examined many of the victims. (He was one of the experts brought in to examine the arm of James Smith, in the case of the "Shark Arm Murder"—see the section in this book, "Tiger Shark.") Exaggerated and even erroneous as they might have been, Copple-

son's information and publications were instrumental in creating a public awareness of the shark problem in Australia. (He said, "In 1919, when surf bathing first became popular, the shark was not regarded as a serious menace.") The first protective measures in Australia consisted of "sharkproof" enclosures, but the sharks got in, and in one instance killed someone within the enclosure. Airplane patrols were used next, but, Coppleson said, "many people, including shop owners at the beaches, complained that the patrols were making people too shark-conscious and scaring them away." In 1937, meshing was introduced to Sydney's beaches, and since that time, not one attack has taken place within a netted area. (Meshing consists of setting a series of large-mesh gill nets parallel to the shoreline, and trapping the sharks that would otherwise approach the bathers. A more detailed description of the process is given in "Beulah Davis: The Lady Who Closed the Beaches.") Australia was by no means free of shark attacks, however, and as we shall see, some spectacular events took place in Australian waters in the early 1960s. (Coppleson picked up the list of Australian shark attacks where Whitley left off in 1940, and his records show twenty-three attacks between 1940 and 1961. The second edition of Coppleson's book was published in 1961, and it is the one I am using.) Sydney beaches, by far eastern Australia's most popular, were meshed by this time, and the total is therefore much lower than before. Coppleson applied his theories to other parts of the world, and cited case after case as evidence to support the "rogue shark" theory, sometimes even modifying the theory when the shark had wandered too far afield, so that it became the "long range cruising rogue."

The attacks that took place along the New Jersey shore in July 1916 are probably the most notorious in the entire grim history of shark attacks. In a ten-day period, four people were killed by sharks, and one was seriously injured. The first victim, Charles Vansant, was attacked at Beach Haven on July 2. Charles Bruder was killed on July 6, 45 miles north of the scene of the first attack, and the last three attacks took place at Matawan Creek another 10 miles further north, on July 12. At the first attack, the Jersey coast was thrown into an uproar, and by the second incident, the whole country was aroused. (It might be pointed out that even though July 1916 was the time of the British and French counterattacks on the German positions in France, the shark attacks were front-page news.) They were the first attacks in these waters that anyone could remember, and "experts" from all walks of life were called in to try to explain what was happening. Scientists, fishermen, sailors, and even Olympic swimmers were interviewed, and they all had explanations. For example, Annette Kellerman, "America's leading woman swimmer and one of the few persons who have had actual experiences with sharks," was interviewed in the *New York American*, and made these remarks, which were obviously based on hearsay and rumor:

> First of all, the shark, no matter what species he belongs to, is at heart an arrant coward, and will flee at the slightest disturbance; that is, if he is well fed. . . . If you should find yourself in the water with a shark, watch its every move, meanwhile swimming to safety. With strong strokes lash the water if possible, for it may keep off the shark. . . . Keep your eye on the fins at all times. You can always see them. . . . Sharks always dive down, then come up with a rush, and sometimes leap clear out of the water. If when you have watched the shark disappear you wait and then dive deep down the shark will miss you, as he has to turn on his back to get you, and as he is coming at you upside down you have a chance to get away if the distance to shore or safety is not too far.

A "war" was declared on sharks after the second attack on July 6, and hundreds of people took to their boats with nets, guns, dynamite, and spears to rid the Jersey waters of sharks. Many sharks were killed, and each one was identified as the killer. Until the next attack, at any rate.

The next was not long in coming. On July 12, at Matawan Creek, despite a warning from a local fisherman that he'd seen a shark in the creek, the boys went swimming there. It was a hot, muggy day, and what better way to spend it than up the old dock, diving off the pilings. A "big black fish with a white belly" grabbed twelve-year-old Lester Stilwell, and dragged him to the bottom. Stanley Fisher, age twenty-four, led the rescue efforts. He dove into the creek, which was only waist-deep at that point, and felt around for Stilwell's body. He found it, and as he was pulling it up, the shark got him, tearing the flesh from his right leg. Both Stilwell and Fisher died.

The fifth victim in this multiple tragedy was luckier than the others. Joseph Dunn, age

USE DYNAMITE IN SEARCH FOR GIANT SHARK

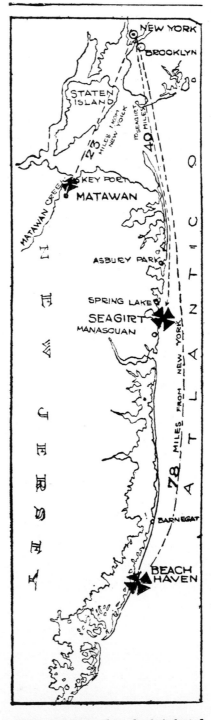

Map showing the shark-infested New Jersey coast. At Beech Haven on July 3, Charles E. Van Sant was killed. At Spring Lake on July 6, Charles Bruder was killed. In Matawan creek yesterday, Lester Stillman and Stanley Fisher were killed and Joseph Dunn seriously injured.

A 1916 map of the locations of the five attacks that took place in July of that year.

New York World, July 16, 1916

fourteen, had been swimming with friends about half a mile downstream in Matawan Creek, when someone ran up and told them of the shark attacks. Dunn was the last to leave the water, and as he climbed up the ladder, something grabbed his leg. After three months in the hospital, he was able to walk again.

Most accounts of this infamous series of attacks conclude with the capture of an 8.5-foot shark by a taxidermist named Michael Schliesser. It was identified as a white shark, *Carcharodon carcharias*, by the director of the American Museum of Natural History, Dr. Frederick A. Lucas. He also examined the stomach contents of the shark, which included "the shinbone of a boy and what appeared to be part of a human rib." The entire story is told in great detail in *Shadows in the Sea*, by McCormick, Allen, and Young, published in 1963.[158] I had the opportunity to examine the collected papers of the senior author, Harold W. McCormick, in 1975. In this collection there were an enormous number of clippings and newspaper pages from the period in question, July 2 to July 18, 1916. My examination of these sources has led me to question the long-accepted conclusion that one white shark was responsible for all five attacks.

ITEM: The first two attacks took place in the surf, 70 miles and 25 miles, respectively, from Matawan Creek.

ITEM: One species of shark that is known to frequent fresh water, especially the mouths of rivers, is the bull shark, *Carcharhinus leucas*.

ITEM: On July 14, two days after the Matawan attacks, it was reported in the *New York American* that "the man-eating shark that killed Lester Stilwell and Stanley Fisher . . . was trapped in the upper reaches of Matawan Creek. . . . Capture of the killer was expected hourly."

ITEM: New York Times, July 14, 1916— "Matawan Creek, the little stream in which two swimmers were killed by a shark and another severely bitten on Wednesday, was alive with sharks yesterday, according to the score of men who went out to hunt them with rifles, shotguns, boat hooks, harpoons, pikes and dynamite."

ITEM: New York American, July 15, 1916— "SHARK BREAKS NET, FLEES TO SEA. Bucking the line like a football halfback, a giant shark plunged through the chicken wire net that penned it in at Matawan Creek and escaped to the ocean last night."

ITEM: Six days after the attacks, a shark was caught in Matawan Creek. It was seven feet long, and weighed 230 pounds. This is a reasonable length-weight ratio for a carcharhinid shark, such as a bull shark, proving only that a species such as this was found in Matawan Creek.

There is probably no question that the shark captured by Michael Schliesser in Raritan Bay on July 14 was a white. (I say "probably," because the shark experts of the day had been making all sorts of peculiar statements up to that time, including: "A shark's jaws are not strong enough to do this sort of damage," and "White sharks are not found this far north.") There also seems to be some doubt that this shark had human bones in its stomach. The original description of the stomach contents were "the shinbone of a boy, and what appeared to be part of a human rib." In subsequent translations, this has become "Fifteen pounds of human flesh, and the leg of Vansant," the first of the victims. This white shark was caught "four miles from the mouth of Matawan Creek," which makes it circumstantially possible to connect it with the attacks. A look at a map of New Jersey shows that Raritan Bay, where Schliesser caught the shark, is not an inland body of water by any means, but an arm of the open ocean.

Carcharodon carcharias, the great white shark, is an oceanic species, and Schliesser's shark was caught in the ocean. To find it swimming in a tidal creek is, to say the least, unusual, and may even be impossible. The bull shark, however, is infamous for its freshwater meanderings, as well as for its pugnacious and aggressive nature. (In South African waters, it is thought to be the species most often responsible for attacks on swimmers.) Here is what Bigelow and Schroeder have to say on the habits of the bull shark:

> *This is a heavy, slow-swimming species, most common inshore in shoal waters, perhaps never very far from land except by accident. They are most often caught around docks, at the entrances to the passages between islands, in estuaries and in harbors. They often run up rivers for considerable distances, and it seems they do not hesitate to enter fresh water.*

Now, the bull shark is not a common species in New Jersey waters, but it does occur more frequently than the white. The events described for the Matawan Creek attacks sound much more like the attacks of a carcharhinid shark than the attack of a white. (There are two other common carcharhinid sharks in these waters, *C. milberti* and *C. obscurus*, but as with the white, neither of them shows any inclination to enter fresh water.) The repeated biting and slashing of the victims is suggestive of some of Dr. David Davies' meticulous descriptions of attacks on the Natal coast, or even Dr. John Randall's recounting of an attack on a swimmer at Magen's Bay, St. Thomas, by another carcharhinid, identified as *Carcharhinus galapagensis*.[194]

The attribution of all five attacks to one shark has always puzzled me. The evidence is long gone, and we will never really know if it was one shark or several, one species or another, that was responsible. In summary, however, I suggest that the location (of at least the three Matawan attacks) is highly unusual for a white shark, and that to try to make the facts as we know them conform to the "rogue shark" theory is stretching sensationalism and credibility beyond reasonable limits.

Sailing and flying over the world's oceans brought the shark problem into focus during World War II. Ships were regularly being torpedoed and otherwise sunk, and large numbers of men were suddenly finding themselves in mid-oceanic waters, with many dangers to contend with, not the least of which was the presence of large, aggressive sharks. A high-priority program was initiated by the Naval Research Laboratory in Washington, D.C., to find some means of protecting men in the water. In 1947, recounting the experiences of those who were required to come up with this repellent, Richard L. Tuve, a chemist who had developed the fluorescent dye marker, wrote:

One way to avoid shark attacks is to swim in a pool.

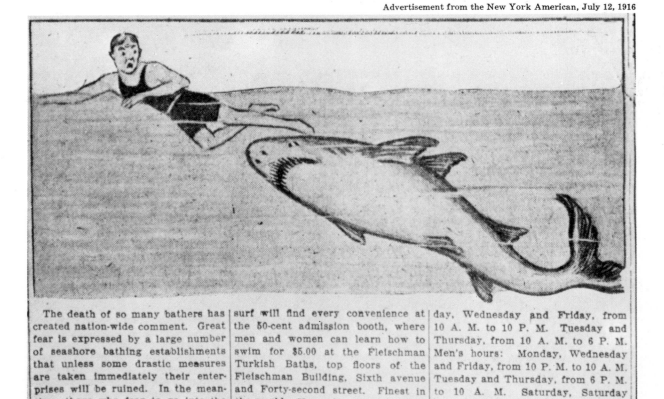

The death of so many bathers has created nation-wide comment. Great fear is expressed by a large number of seashore bathing establishments that unless some drastic measures are taken immediately their enterprises will be ruined. In the meantime, those who fear to go into the surf will find every convenience at the 50-cent admission booth, where men and women can learn how to swim for $5.00 at the Fleischman Turkish Baths, top floors of the Fleischman Building, Sixth avenue and Forty-second street. Finest in the world. Hours for women: Monday, Wednesday and Friday, from 10 A. M. to 10 P. M. Tuesday and Thursday, from 10 A. M. to 6 P. M. Men's hours: Monday, Wednesday and Friday, from 10 P. M. to 10 A. M. Tuesday and Thursday, from 6 P. M. to 10 A. M. Saturday, Saturday night, Sunday, Sunday night.

No available data or literature on the life habits of the shark revealed whether the protection of a man from this carnivorous fish would require physical methods such as light and sound waves, or whether chemical substances dissolved in the water through which the shark must pass would deter his attack. Practically all existing information on the subject could aptly be called "shark lore"—denoting its probable extent of coloration and expansion by overzealous writers and raconteurs.[248]

In other words, nobody even knew where to start. Everything that might be expected to repel sharks failed, including rotenone (a particularly potent fish poison), ink, poison gas, and sound waves. (The sharks used in the testing of these substances and devices were smooth dogfish, *Mustelus canis*, and if we couldn't repel these small, harmless sharks, how could we deter the large, dangerous ones?) Stewart Springer, then at Woods Hole, suggested that decomposing sharks on a line usually kept other sharks away from the longlines of commercial fishing operations. It would have been difficult to obtain (or package) decomposing shark meat, so its most active constituents were isolated. These were found to be ammonium acetate and acetic acid, easily attainable chemicals. Field tests were conducted using these chemicals and various dyes, to determine the effectiveness of the various combinations. (It was assumed that the chemical would keep the shark from feeding, while the cloud of dye released into the water would hide the potential victim from the approaching shark.) The tests were successful enough for the Navy to begin the distribution of packets of "Shark Chaser." Every life jacket was soon equipped with a packet of "Shark Chaser," and although it is not clear that anyone was ever actually protected, or that any sharks were chased, the psychological advantage of *thinking* you were protected was enormous. (I do not suggest for a moment that the Navy deliberately encouraged its personnel to use "Shark Chaser," knowing that it would be ineffective. At the time of its issue, it was thought to be a successful deterrent to shark attacks. Only later, and long after the war was over, were more sophisticated tests performed that demonstrated its basic shortcomings.)

No provision was made for wartime air or sea disasters, where hundreds or even thousands of men were in the water at the same time, often injured or bleeding badly. During the war, ships were damaged, bombed or torpedoed, and the troops forced to abandon ship and swim for it. Except in isolated instances, the stories of men in the water are unrecorded, but Davies quotes this story told to him by a survivor of the *Nova Scotia*, which was sunk off South Africa in 1942:

Another South African from my regiment, the Third Reconnaissance Unit, swam over and clung to the oar as well. He was wearing a life jacket.

The two of us drifted on a strong current until the next morning, by which time most of the oil had disappeared. Other survivors were visible round about on rafts, gratings, etc. When it became light, my companion said that it was better to die than to go on holding on like this. He said he was going to let go and refused to listen when I told him not to give up. So I asked him to leave me his life jacket before he let go.

As he was loosening his life-jacket, he suddenly screamed and the upper part of his body rose out of the water. He fell back and I saw that the water had become red with blood and that his foot had been bitten off. At this moment I saw the grey form of a shark swimming excitedly around and I paddled away as fast as I could. Then a number of sharks congregated round me— I estimated their lengths at between six and seven feet....

Sixty-seven hours after the ship was torpedoed we were rescued by the Portuguese sloop Alfonso do Albuquerque.[70]

The number of men in the waters of the Pacific, known to be heavily populated by sharks, at the battles of the Coral Sea or Midway is almost beyond imagining.

The atomic bomb was dropped on Hiroshima on August 6, 1945. The ship that brought the bomb from San Francisco to Tinian in the Marianas, from where it was to be flown to and dropped on Japan, was the U.S.S. *Indianapolis*. After the delivery of the bomb, the *Indianapolis* was hit by a Japanese torpedo. Only 317 of the crew of 1,000 survived. (See the last paragraph of "David Baldridge: The Shark Attack Man.")

One result of these wartime experiences was the realization that very little was known about the behavior of dangerous sharks, or, for that matter, which ones they were. Although the worst was over, at least for the moment, the question of protection of survivors in the ocean remained unanswered. During luncheon meetings at the Smithsonian Institution in the late 1950s, a number of ichthyologists would meet and casually discuss the shark problem. Out of these casual meetings, and under the eventual sponsorship of the Office of Naval Research, the American Institute of Biological Sciences (AIBS) formed the Shark Research Panel. Its original members were Leonard P. Schultz, Sidney R. Galler, John R. Olive, Stewart Springer, and Perry Gilbert, who was named chairman. Later, Albert L. Tester and H. David Baldridge were asked to join the panel. During its twelve years of operation (1958 to 1969), the Shark Research Panel was respon-

sible for much of the major research on sharks —their behavior, taxonomy, and functional anatomy. The panel held thirty-one meetings, six symposiums, and effectively catalyzed and coordinated more than 100 studies dealing with the behavior and biology of sharks around the world. In 1963, the AIBS sponsored the publication of *Sharks and Survival*, edited by Perry Gilbert, chairman of the Shark Research Panel.[98] This book, with contributions from virtually every major figure in the field of shark research, is a landmark accomplishment and, more than any single volume, it defines the problems that exist when man meets shark—in the shark's element. To demonstrate the breadth of expertise of the Shark Research Panel, I reproduce here the Table of Contents of this remarkable volume:

CONTENTS

One of the most important functions of the Shark Research Panel was the maintenance of the Shark Attack File. (Even before the formation of the Panel, Dr. Schultz, then chief of the Division of Fishes of the U.S. National Museum, had assembled a small file of data on shark attacks, including photographs.) The Shark Attack File was maintained by Dr. Schultz at the Smithsonian, with the assistance of Marilyn Malin. In 1968, upon Schultz's retirement, the task of maintaining and supervising the Shark Attack File fell to Dr. H. David Baldridge. The SAF was then shipped to Baldridge at the Mote Marine Laboratory in Sarasota, Florida. (I have actually seen and consulted this file; it is housed in four beige file cabinets, with each case in its own folder, tagged by color and numbered. The five categories used in the file are [1] Unprovoked attacks, [2] Provoked attacks, [3] Doubtful attacks, [4] Air and sea disasters, and [5] Boat attacks. The folders contain forms, newspaper clippings, medical reports, corroborating letters, and probably the goriest collection of photographs in existence.)

In 1959, the second year of its existence, the Shark Attack File received an abnormally high number of reports. Baldridge wrote, "It seems reasonable that the attendant publicity would have produced a sharp increase in efficiency in reporting attacks." Even so, 1959 was a "peak year," with fifty-six attacks reported, among them some of the worst on record.

SAF #372: May 7, 1959. Albert Kogler was swimming with Shirley O'Neill at Baker's Beach in San Francisco. Kogler was hit by a shark and began to scream. Incredibly, O'Neill swam *toward* Kogler (the shark was still visible), and hauled him out of the water. He had suffered massive lacerations of the chest, partial amputation of the left shoulder and arm, and a great loss of blood. The attack took place within 50 yards of shore and was witnessed by dozens of people. Kogler died that evening in the hospital.

SAF #376: June 14, 1959. Robert Pamperin and Gerald Lehrer were abalone diving off Alligator Rock, La Jolla, California. Lehrer saw Pamperin "erupt out of the water" some 60 feet away from him. Lehrer swam toward his companion, thinking he had suffered some sort of a cramp, but when he looked below the surface he saw that Pamperin was in the jaws of a twenty-foot shark, which was shaking its body and

lashing its tail. Pamperin's body was never recovered. (The authenticity of this report has been questioned—see "Tiger Shark," pp. 147–150.)

SAF #405: December 13, 1959. Fifteen-year-old Billy Weaver was surfing with friends off Lanikai on the east coast of Oahu, Hawaii. When his four companions caught a wave, Weaver was left behind. The boys looked back and saw that Weaver was in trouble, and when they got to his side they saw that he had lost a leg. Three of his friends tried to support him, while the fourth went for help. The shark reappeared, frightening the rescuers off, and Weaver's body was lost in the surf. The next day the body was located by helicopter, and within the next two days, two large tiger sharks were caught in the immediate area.

In 1959 there were attacks all over the world, in Africa, Japan, Venezuela, and Australia, and six air and sea disasters, in which several people were killed. The Shark Attack File shows a relatively high number of reports for 1960 and 1961, but then the figures start to level off. This can probably be attributed to the declining publicity accorded the SAF, as much as any to meteorological or behavioral phenomenon. All SAF cases were checked to the best of the investigator's ability, but there were bound to be some cases that were falsely reported or exaggerated. To further complicate matters, much of the material in the file is in the form of newspaper articles and other published accounts, as opposed to firsthand or eyewitness reports. When Baldridge summarized the data, he had this to say on the techniques of information gathering:

Now, realize exactly what this means, i.e., direct, firsthand accounts prepared by victims and/or witnesses were of prime value in determining the details of the attacks in only 10% of the cases. Perhaps it is more sobering to put it another way. In 90% of the files on human shark attack held in the SAF, accounts of the attacks were primarily based on information supplied by persons who were neither the objects of the attacks, nor were they even there at the time to actually see what happened. To be completely realistic, therefore, it must be conceded that technically the SAF is made up largely of hearsay evidence, mostly documented long after the event happened.

But, like it or not, this is all we had to work with.

By 1960, the New Jersey attacks of 1916 were but a dim memory. In fact, most people on the Jersey shore had never even heard of the Matawan Creek or Beach Haven incidents. They were soon to be jolted into a reminder of the past. It was at Sea Girt, New Jersey, that Charles Bruder was attacked and killed on July 6, 1916. (He was the second of five victims that were attacked in the period from July 1 to July 12.) On August 21, 1960, John Brodeur was swimming with his fiancée at Sea Girt, when he saw "a long blackish object about ten yards away, sticking out of the wave and being carried toward the beach." He was attacked by a shark, and his right leg, which was badly mangled, had to be amputated. Nine days later, Richard Chung was attacked by a shark at Ocean City, New Jersey, far to the south.

Now the memories of 1916 came flooding back, and under pressure to protect the beaches, the town officials adopted a recently developed Australian invention called the "bubble curtain." This consisted of a long, perforated hose attached to a compressor, which released a wall of bubbles that was said by its inventor to present a barrier "that a shark will not cross, even to get at a juicy steak." A "bubble curtain" was installed at Asbury Park in 1960, and no more attacks took place. Perry Gilbert was not convinced of the efficacy of this device, and during March and April of 1961, he tested it on twelve captive tiger sharks at the Lerner Marine Laboratory on the island of Bimini. Only one of the twelve was deterred by the bubbles; the others swam back and forth at will. If only one shark had been used in the test, the results might have been completely different. As Gilbert later wrote, "This latter observation points up the weakness of any program which employs only one or two individual sharks when testing a chemical or physical agent for its repellent properties."

The Natal coast of South Africa has always been known as an area with an abundance of dangerous sharks. Whatever the conditions are that encourage shark attacks on swimmers, they are present on the 140-mile-long Natal coast. The combination of water turbidity, temperature, salinity, prey species, and the abundance of bathers (as swimmers are called in South Africa) had made this one of the most dangerous swimming areas in the world. From 1906 to 1960, there were forty-six recorded shark attacks, half of which were fatal. Five attacks took place in 1940, all of which resulted in the death of the victim, and from 1942 to 1947 one or more attacks took place each year. In certain years (1944 and 1947), as many as six attacks per year occurred. In 1952, the beaches at Durban, South Africa's largest and most popular resort, were meshed, and no further attacks took place there. Even though the bathers at Durban were safe, the problem was far from being solved.

Michael Hely was attacked by a shark in April 1960, while swimming at Amanzimtoti, south of Durban. He was badly mauled, but survived. In October of that same year, a fishing boat was attacked by a shark in False Bay, 30 miles from Capetown. A tooth fragment left in the boat's planking was sent to Dr. David Davies at the Oceanographic Research Institute (ORI) at Durban, and he identified the shark as *Carcharodon carcharias*, the great white. (It is known as the blue pointer in South Africa.) Davies wrote a one-page report in 1961, which he innocently called Investigational Report No. 1, *Shark Attack on a Fishing Boat in South Africa.*[72]

Less than three months later, Investigational Report No. 2 was issued by the ORI. This one concerned the fatal attack on Petrus Sithole, who had been swimming at Margate on the Natal coast. Sithole's legs were bitten off, and he was dead before he could be pulled from the water. From a tooth fragment left in the man's femur, Davies identified the shark as the Zambezi or bull shark. (Davies had originally suggested that the shark that bit Michael Hely was a ragged-tooth, *Odontaspis taurus*, but he later revised this identification to the Zambezi shark.) Two weeks later (January 6, 1961), another attack took place, this one at Winkelspruit. Michael Land's right foot was bitten off, but he lived (Investigational Report No. 3). On January 22, Michael Murphy was severely bitten on the left leg while swimming at Amanzimtoti (No. 4). On February 1, 1961, Geoffrey Zimmerman was swimming at Nahoon Beach, East London, when he was attacked and killed (No. 5). By this time Davies was describing the situation as "one of national importance," and with his colleagues at the ORI, he began the process that was to result in the establishment of the Natal Anti-Shark Measures Board (see "Beulah Davis: The Lady Who Closed the Beaches"), which undertook to mesh *all* the beaches on the Natal shoreline.* The only other area in the world which uses meshing as a way to reduce shark attack is Australia. Since 1937, no attacks have occurred in a meshed area in Australia, and the only incidents that have taken place on the Natal coast have been outside the netted areas, or on persons who have been swimming after dusk. (Since over 98 percent of all the sharks caught in the nets are caught between dusk and dawn, nighttime swimming is discouraged. The official signs posted on the beaches read: "Avoid bathing at dusk and at night when shark attack is considered more likely.")

David Davies died in 1965, but his interest in sharks and his concern for his native South Africa have been carried on admirably. The ORI in Durban is probably the most important center in the world for the study of sharks, and maintains the highest level of scholarship and interest in the ongoing problems of shark research and the prevention of shark attacks.

Let us shift now from the coast of South Africa to another infamous area—the beaches of South Australia, known to be among the most perilous in the world. (The two other Australian states that form the east coast, New South Wales and Queensland, have had many of their beaches meshed for years, and the shark attack problem there is no longer a major crisis.) Southern Australia, which includes those states that face on the Great Australian Bight (Victoria, South Australia, and Western Australia), is known to be one of the primary habitats of the most feared of sharks, the great white. (In Australia, it is known as "white pointer" or "white death.") The waters of the southern coast are also the home of the Australian sea lion, *Neophoca cineria*, known locally as the "hair seal." The uncommon concentration of large white sharks here is in all likelihood due to the presence of the hair seals, on which the sharks feed. (With the exception of a 67-pound specimen that was caught on 12-pound test line off Mazatlan, Mexico, *all* the record white sharks have been caught in South Australia.)

Knowing that enormous white sharks inhabit the waters here (Alf Dean's world record shark, 16.5 feet long and weighing 2,664 pounds, was caught off Ceduna, South Australia, in 1959),

it is difficult to imagine people wanting to swim there. But because of the presence of so many other species of fish (upon which the seals feed), the Australian Spearfishing Championships used to be held annually at Aldinga Beach, south of Adelaide.

By the grace of God, no incidents had occurred at Aldinga Beach before 1961. In 1961, Brian Rodger was attacked at Aldinga Beach, while competing in a spearfishing competition. In 1962, Geoff Corner was attacked and killed at Caracalinga Head, 15 miles south of Aldinga. In 1963, Rodney Fox (see "Brian Rodger, Rodney Fox, Henri Bource: The Survivors") was attacked and nearly bitten in half at Aldinga. In 1964, Henri Bource had his leg taken off by a white shark at Lady Julia Percy Island, Victoria, while diving with seals. The *New York Times* for April 7, 1968, printed this story:

DIVER LOSES TWO LEFT LEGS

MELBOURNE, *Australia (Reuters)—A skindiver Henri Bource lost his left leg to a shark—for the second time. The first leg was a real one, lost to a white pointer shark in 1964. Recently, another white pointer took off Mr. Bource's artificial leg.*

In 1970, the Office of Naval Research cut off the funding of the Shark Attack File. By that time, David Baldridge had been maintaining it for two years, and had become thoroughly familiar with its contents. During the process of assembling and coding the material for a computer analysis of the voluminous data in the SAF, a number of interesting facts surfaced. For example, many shark attacks were suggestive of an action on the part of the shark that seemed to indicate a motive other than feeding. Many of the wounds on the victims were inflicted by only one set of teeth (the uppers), which would indicate a slashing, rather than a biting, action. Baldridge, in residence at the Mote Marine Laboratory, noticed that sharks in the pens also showed these "slash-type" wounds, which suggested that a shark's aggression, when directed toward a penmate, does not always take the form of a bite. He also noticed that there were behavior patterns in attacks where hunger did not seem to be the motivating factor, for example, the "bumping" action, and the erratic swimming movements that have been interpreted by some as threatening, or "pre-attack," postures. With this in mind, Baldridge wrote in "Shark Attack: Feeding or Fighting?":

---

* Information on the Natal Anti-Shark Measures Board was obtained from personal interviews with the director, Beulah Davis, and examination of many unpublished documents that she was kind enough to give me.

It was accordingly suggested that consideration be given to modification of the present testing procedures for repellents and repellers which rely heavily on discouraging the taking of attractive food by starved sharks. It was further suggested that studies be initiated for the purpose of identifying those behavioral activators and to attempt to produce them under laboratory conditions.[19]

It was a revolutionary assumption, one that was to change much of the thinking about shark attacks. Almost all previous preventive measures had been predicated on the assumption that the shark was trying to eat the victim. If this was not the case, then much of the "shark prevention" theory had to be discarded and new avenues of study investigated. ("Shark Chaser," for instance, was developed under the assumption that sharks did not feed in the presence of a decomposing shark and, therefore, that something suggestive of decomposing shark would keep them from feeding on humans. But now the possibility was raised that the sharks were not intending to eat the people at all. Clearly, the methods used to keep something from attacking would be very different from those used to keep it from eating.) Chemical shark repellents were found to be almost totally impracticable. Even if a substance could be found which would deter a shark that was committed to the attack, so much of the substance would have to be in the water with the diver or swimmer that the person would not be able to carry it. (Baldridge estimates that a waterborne chemical, in order to be effective in the currents and magnitude of an unlimited body of water, would have to weigh between 30 and 130 pounds.) And even if *this* problem could be overcome, the drug would have to so strong that it would be "as dangerous to the man in the water as to the shark."

Baldridge also tested some of the old clichés scientifically, and found them unsupportable. It was always assumed that blood in the water drives sharks into a frenzy, but Baldridge noticed that in the SAF there were a great many cases in which a victim, even one bleeding profusely, was not hit again by the attacking shark, and in the cases in which more than one shark was in the vicinity, the blood in the water did not draw more sharks to the scene of the attack. In one series of experiments, Baldridge put fresh rat blood in the water and, to his surprise, found that it was not a strong attractant

or excitant. (Human blood, on the other hand, strongly attracted sharks, according to experiments conducted by Albert Tester in 1963. How a shark can differentiate between the blood of a rat and the blood of a human, when it has never been exposed to either before, is a bit of a mystery.) Baldridge also showed the "one molecule of blood," usually held to be the stimulus for attracting sharks, to be another common fallacy, since a molecule of blood does not exist. A molecule is defined as "a stable configuration of atomic nuclei and electrons bound together by electrostatic and electromagnetic forces." Blood is a complex fluid, composed of many substances. Sharks can detect small quantities of various substances in the water, but a single molecule is a strain even on the shark's sophisticated sensory system. This is not to suggest that blood is distasteful to sharks, or that one should plunge into the water with profusely bleeding wounds, but a scratched knee or a cut finger does not seem to be an automatic signal for a shark to attack. In addition to sharks' highly developed olfactory sense, they see rather well, given the poor transmission of light in the medium in which they live (although they probably do not perceive color), and their hearing or "acoustic orientation" is nothing short of remarkable. Sharks are extremely sensitive to vibrations in the water, and they are much more likely to home in on low-frequency sounds (such as the thrashing of a wounded fish), than on blood in the water. Sharks are also endowed with a series of subcutaneous organs called the ampullae of Lorenzini, which are thought to be electroreceptors of extraordinary sensitivity, and we have learned that sharks can respond to the electrical field of an animal in the water in a manner heretofore unknown of members of the animal kingdom.

If it has been shown that sharks do not regularly attack out of hunger; that blood in the water does not seem to be a particularly effective attractant; that the "rogue shark" theory is a little far-fetched; that chemical repellents don't seem to have any effect—how *can* we stop shark attacks, short of keeping people out of the water altogether? Some answers have already been suggested, such as meshing, but we can't mesh all the beaches in the world, and even if we could, people would find a way to swim beyond or around the nets. In order to answer the question, we need to know a great deal more about why the sharks attack in the first place. Some of the recorded attacks appear to be based on a desire to eat the victim; there seems to be some indisputable evidence for this assumption (for example, great pieces taken from victims, human remains found in the stomachs of sharks). The concept of "hunger" does not seem to apply to sharks, however. In captivity, some species have gone for months without eating, and others literally starve themselves to death. Stewart Springer wrote in 1967:

> I find no indication . . . that the kind of internal drive that men know as hunger operates or even exists for sharks. I have no evidence to offer that a hunger drive does not exist for sharks, but suggest that it may play a minor role acting perhaps at a nearly constant but low level. My chief reason for suspecting that hunger is not very useful in describing the shark's urge to feed is that in the commercial fishery the best and largest catches I have seen were of sharks partly or nearly full of freshly eaten fish, turtles and invertebrates, not obtained from baited hooks, whereas poor catches included, for the most part, sharks with empty stomachs.[226]

A *post hoc ergo propter hoc* argument also supports the "not-to-feed-on-humans" theory. If indeed sharks were inclined to eat people, the world's oceans would be dyed crimson with the blood of millions. Given the number of swimmers, divers, and beachgoers, and the number of sharks in the oceans (the sharks have a pronounced numerical advantage), the 1,652 cases of "shark bites man" in the entire Shark Attack File are a clear indication that the occurrence is a rare one. Even if sharks do not get "hungry," they do have to eat to stay alive, and they probably would have learned by now that the beaches in summer represent an abundant and easy food source. (Sharks learn very quickly about food sources—slaughterhouses or fish processing plants that dump their wastes into the oceans always have plenty of sharks in attendance. And the way to fish for sharks is to establish a food source to which the sharks are attracted.)

Some sharks appear to be territorial, and some do not like to be threatened. At least one species of carcharhinid shark in the Pacific, the gray reef shark (*Carcharhinus menisorrah*), has demonstrated the agonistic behavior that has been interpreted as "pre-attack posturing." In June 1961, Ron Church photographed a "blacktip" shark (from the pictures, one can tell it is *menisorrah*) as it swam erratically toward him and his partner in the waters of Wake Island. It moved its head back and forth, dropped its pectoral fins, and hunched its back. Church thought the shark was sick, but his diving companion Jim Stewart later said that he had seen the same behavior in sharks at Eniwetok. After making one pass with these peculiar movements, the shark circled and returned.

> Jim sidestepped to his right. The shark, narrowly missing him, went around in a sharp V of less than a five foot radius and came back directly at Jim's face. Jim had just enough time to swing around in the opposite direction and throw out his arms in defense. The shark grabbed his elbow area, gave two quick bites, and flashed away. All this happened in less than five seconds.[48]

Don Nelson (see "Don Nelson: Sound in the Water") investigated this behavior (avoiding the actual biting part) at Eniwetok, with the same species, *Carcharhinus menisorrah*. In a series of controlled experiments, Nelson and Richard H. Johnson succeeded in eliciting the same erratic behavior from the sharks. Nelson and Johnson found that the most intense reaction occurred when the shark's escape route was reduced. If the shark could get away from the diver easily, it usually did, but if it was "backed into a corner" on the face of the reef, the display became quite pronounced, and the investigators felt that an attack would follow shortly.

On two occasions (both described to me in a letter dated March 12, 1976), Dr. John Randall observed the same behavior. While diving at Eniwetok, he was confronted by a "posturing" gray reef shark. In self-defense, he shot the shark with a Hawaiian sling, the shark shook out the spear with a few wild movements, and then, since it was facing away from Randall, it rushed the anchor line, chewed it vigorously, and then dashed away. Here is Randall's own description of the second occasion:

> I was diving with Shot Miller (who was behind me about 20 feet and about the same distance above) near the deep channel of the lagoon in 60 feet. A gray reef shark came up behind me and started its threat posturing. Shot whacked his SCUBA tank with his powerhead shaft to warn me. The shark (which was only about 4.5 feet) then veered to him and threatened him even more strongly, the head moving through an arc of nearly 180 degrees. Shot had a choice of two shells

in his hand to load the powerhead, one of which he knew was reliable; the other he had planned to use on something like a stingray. He didn't have time to look at the shells as the shark closed on him too rapidly. As luck would have it, he picked the old shell and it misfired as he struck the shark's head with it. It came right on and bit him on the head on one side (all gashes above the hair line). Cut off his face mask and he headed right for the surface. I followed with my powerhead loaded and ready to fire but the shark took off. Shot had 7 gashes that required 25 stitches to close. It was only the result of a slash with the upper jaw. An important point here. The shark's motive was not one of feeding. It was merely carrying out the threat behavior when the recipient of this posturing failed to leave the area. Or so it would seem.

This behavior has only been observed in a couple of species of Pacific carcharhinids (which may in fact be synonymous species). Given the worldwide similarities of this large family, it seems reasonable to assume that other species may display similar threat behavior. Nelson and Johnson speculate that "in diver-shark encounters, such apparently defensive attacks are elicited by violation of some type of boundary determined by the interaction of time and distance."

Another type of "threat" suggested by Baldridge is a sudden entrance into the water. Of sixty-nine recorded attacks where the entry was accomplished by a means other than wading, 84 percent were attacked upon jumping, diving, or falling into the water. Baldridge said, "A person suddenly entering the water could be taken by a nearby shark as some form of threat to which it quickly responds with violently aggressive behavior totally unrelated to feeding."

Of the always dangerous isurids, only the white shark has been observed with any degree of regularity. (A few people have seen a free-swimming mako under water. I have found no record of anyone seeing a porbeagle from any other vantage point than a boat.) White sharks have been most often observed from the safety of a shark cage, and their behavioral repertoire does not seem to include any warnings, bumpings, or pre-attack posturing. During the filming of *Blue Water, White Death*, the white sharks bit the boats, the cages, the baits—all

with the same "merciless serenity" that Peter Matthiessen described in *Blue Meridian*. He wrote:

Often they mouthed the cage metal with such violence that the teeth went spinning from their jaws. One such tooth found on the bottom had its serrated edge scraped smooth. It seemed to me that here was the explanation for the reports of white-shark attacks on boats; they do not attack boats, they attack anything.[164]

White sharks, because of their tremendous size and strength, are in a class by themselves, and their behavior is probably atypical. Almost all descriptions of white sharks comment on their stiff-bodied directness of movement. A 1952 attack off the California coast is a case in point. All during the attack, which resulted in the death of seventeen-year-old Barry Wilson, the movements of the shark were described as "deliberate and leisurely. . . . It made no abrupt charges and never appeared to be asserting itself."[16] When viewed from a cage or from the deck of a fishing boat, this shark's movements are likely to be slow and deliberate; it is being fed. Only once have I heard of a white shark at speed: Valerie Taylor was diving with seals when she heard the water go still around her. The seals disappeared, and she dove for the bottom. Like an express train, a great white shark shot over her. "It was the fastest thing I've ever seen," she said.

The Shark Attack File attributes attacks to almost every species of shark. The great white has 32 authenticated attacks. (This applies only until 1968, when the official record keeping stopped. It also includes the five entries for the 1916 New Jersey attacks, whose authenticity as to species has been questioned.) The tiger shark has 27 verified attacks. The bull shark, in all its various locations, and with all its different names, has 37. In only 267 of the total of 1,165 cases analyzed (23 percent) was any identification at all attempted. Very few people know one species from another, and if there is one chewing on your leg, you hardly have the time or the inclination to look for field marks or identifying characteristics. In his analysis, Baldridge writes, "More often than not, identifications were made on the weakest of evidence, and were evidently at times no more than snap judgements by casual observers." Even some identifications in the SAF are likely to be wrong; wherever the shark was identified, no matter how insubstantially, it was entered that way in the file.

(Overleaf) Plate 20. **Greenland shark** *(Somniosus microcephalus)*

RICHARD ELLIS-1976

One of the most recent discoveries about sharks' behavior (almost all studies of shark behavior end up being incorporated in a discussion of shark attacks) concerns their reaction to sound. Until quite recently, it was assumed that a shark was a "swimming nose, with its other sensory functions proportionally diminished. Eugenie Clark, in her experiments with lemon sharks at Cape Haze, demonstrated that sharks can see quite well, and that they can distinguish simple shapes. Arthur Myrberg and Don Nelson have experimented extensively with sharks and sound. The connection between sharks and sound is an interesting one. Since sharks hear low-frequency sounds and they are attracted by them, one obvious case of sound is to attract sharks to where you want them in order to observe them. Myrberg's studies with silky sharks *(Carcharhinus falciformis)* at Tongue of the Ocean in the Bahamas indicated that a change in sound intensities could often deter a shark from its apparent destination. One surprising observation by Myrberg was dramatically and tragically demonstrated to be true. In 1972, he wrote (with Ha, Walewski, and Banbury):

> *Based on preliminary discussions with helicopter pilots, a practical consideration again appears evident. . . . This regularly pulsed signal, emanating from the helicopter to the water surface, must contain low- as well as high-frequency noise. Thus, it is possible that helicopters of this type, when hovering for periods of more than a minute or so above a given point, may well be attracting sharks to them.*[177]

In June 1974, a family of seven, whom I will call the Baileys, set out in a 43-foot cabin cruiser, the *Lucy-Ann,* from Galveston to the Bahamas. Eighteen days out of Galveston, they were preparing to cross the Gulf of Mexico from Carabelle on the Florida panhandle southeast to Tarpon Springs, near Tampa. A violent tropical storm blew up, and the 25-year-old boat was swamped when the pumps failed, leaving the seven Baileys clinging to a single life preserver. The *Lucy-Ann* did not sink, but in the turbulent seas, they could not stay close to her, and they floated away in the night.

Their SOS had been picked up by the Coast Guard at St. Petersburg, and a cutter was dispatched to search for the *Lucy-Ann.* The Baileys bobbed in the Gulf waters all night (they had been swamped at about midnight). A fishing boat, which had also picked up their distress signal, discovered the wrecked and abandoned hull of the *Lucy-Ann* in the early morning. When a search plane flew overhead, the Baileys frantically waved their arms and shouted but the plane missed them. One of them suggested that if they weren't bunched together, they might stand a better chance of being seen. Ten-year-old David Bailey swam about six feet from the life preserver, and was hit immediately by a shark, which tore his hand off. Now the Baileys were surrounded by sharks, and they huddled together for safety. They were spotted by a Coast Guard rescue plane, which radioed for a helicopter. While waiting for the helicopter, the Baileys were harassed by a flock of sea gulls, which they drove off by splashing water at them. When the Baileys were finally pulled from the water, Mrs. Bailey had deep gouges on her legs and thighs, Mr. Bailey had a badly torn foot, three-year-old Harry, Jr., was dead from exposure, and David had died from loss of blood.

Even excluding the helicopter noise attraction, if one wanted to write a casebook about how *not* to survive in shark-infested waters, this would be a good start. After leaving the boat (mistake number one), the Baileys sang all night "to keep up their spirits." They separated at a crucial moment. And they splashed water at the sea gulls and at the plane that was passing overhead. This is a true story; I have changed only the names, since the point is not to make the "Baileys" suffer through this ordeal again, but to make some observations about shark attacks. The singing and the splashing are attractants; in fact any irregular or unfamiliar sound in the sea is likely to attract sharks. Swimmers are more likely to be attacked if they become separated from a group than if they stay together.

When Billy Weaver was attacked and killed off Oahu in 1959, his four companions had all caught a wave, leaving him behind. Coppleson's book *Shark Attack* is full of accounts of surfers who were attacked after their companions "caught a shoot." It is not so much a question of being left behind, but rather of being left alone. Coppleson summarizes the situation in this manner:

> *It is not necessarily the first bather to enter the water or the one farthest out that becomes "shark-bait." In one instance there were at least six swimmers farther out to sea than the victim. Many of the victims have been expert surfers and*

therefore more venturesome. The statement "Several were waiting for a shoot; one failed to catch it and he was attacked by a shark" is common in the description of the surf attacks. It has recurred often enough to be significant.[58]

From the assembled data, one comes to the overwhelming conclusion that most people who were attacked were swimming alone. (There have, of course, been instances in which this is not so, and even rare cases in which more than one person was attacked at one time. Examples include Lester Stilwell and Stanley Fisher, both victims of the Matawan Creek shark in 1916, and Norman Girvan and Jack Brinkley, both killed at the same time, apparently by the same shark, in October 1937. They were swimming together at Kirra Beach, New South Wales, when Girvan cried out "Quick, a shark's got me!" When Brinkley turned to help Girvan, he too was attacked. Girvan died in the water, and Brinkley on the operating table. The next day, an 850-pound tiger shark was caught, with parts of Girvan and Brinkley inside. According to Coppleson, "It is the only instance in Australia in which two lives were lost in one attack.")

Lions and cheetahs have been observed running past one gazelle or zebra in their hunting charge. It seems curious for the predator to bypass a slower animal while it continues to chase a faster one. The explanation is quite simple. Any predator that preys on animals that herd or school, has to be able to single out one individual to attack. The herd, school, or flock is, in one sense, a specific defense against this sort of hunting behavior. The predator cannot be indecisive as to which of the prey individuals it will attack, for if it is, it is likely to miss them all. It must be assumed that sharks, which feed on schooling animals, such as fishes, and herd animals, such as sea lions, are able to "lock on" to an individual, in order to capture and devour it. Random snapping at first this one, then that one, is likely to result in no meal at all. Baldridge points out that "sharks appear most often to select isolated individuals or particular persons from a collection of people and then to direct their attention primarily to them alone."

Shark attack is such a frightening sight that most victims, even when there is help nearby, are left to fend for themselves. Baldridge points this out, and says that it occurs "in spite of the fact that for some unknown reason, the hazard to rescuers seems slight." There is only one

case on record in the SAF where someone specifically attempting to effect a rescue was killed (Stanley Fisher, above). I suggest that rescuers do not rush to the aid of shark victims because they are unaware of the statistical possibility of their not being injured (Shirley O'Neill almost took the body of Albert Kogler from the jaws of the shark that killed him). This probability exists, not for "unknown reasons," but because of the shark's instinctive preference for the single victim it has selected. Henri Bource said (in Edwards' *Sharks and Shipwrecks*) that the shark that took his leg "bypassed a group of females and seal calves that were playing together over a reef, went right through the center of a group of seals near the divers, and disappeared from view only about 20 feet from the man."[82] In the case of Barry Wilson, even though four rescuers tried to float the victim to shore in a rubber tube, the shark continued to attack Wilson, who was dead by the time they got him to shore.

Shark attacks occur just about everywhere that sharks and people share the same waters. Insofar as specific locations are concerned, some areas bear mentioning because of a frequency of attacks that is considerably higher than one might expect. If the number of attacks at a given area over a certain period of time can be said to define a "dangerous area," then by far the most dangerous places to swim *used to be* New South Wales and the Natal coast of South Africa. New South Wales has had a total of 137 attacks recorded in the SAF, and Natal has had 74. Both these areas, in recognition of the problem, have installed mesh nets, and since the installation of these protective systems, the attack rate in the netted areas has been negligible. The area with the most recorded attacks that has no protective devices is the waters off Florida, with 107 attacks. Florida, which has far more coastline than any other state (except, of course, Alaska), is divided into four categories in the SAF: (1) No specifics, (2) Atlantic coast, (3) Gulf coast, and (4) Florida Keys. It should also be mentioned that compared to the premeshing statistics of Australia and South Africa, Florida's fatality rate is considerably lower. Most shark attacks in Florida waters in recent times have consisted of nips or scratches, but there have been some serious injuries, and a number of deaths as well. In 1958, eight-year-old Douglas Lawton was attacked in less than three feet of water, and he was so badly mauled by what was later identified as a young tiger shark, that his entire left leg had to be amputated. To the best of my knowledge, Florida has taken no steps to warn its visitors or inhabitants of the shark problem, nor employed any protective measures.

Of all the attacks listed in the SAF, only 1,165 are specific enough to use for data reduction and analysis. As in all cases where the SAF figures are quoted, they only apply until 1968, and there have been numerous instances all over the world that have not been "officially" recorded. Since the Shark Attack File is more or less dormant (occasionally, people send in reports or newspaper clippings), any additional analysis will have to wait until it is revived. At a recent symposium, David Baldridge was asked if he thought the file would be reactivated, and he said no. The Office of Naval Research, which originally funded the AIBS Shark Research Panel and the Shark Attack File, has as much information as it can use on the subject of statistical analysis of shark attack. Ten more years of data collecting will probably not show anything remarkably different from what is already known. The Navy, however, is still interested in the problems of shark attack, and is concentrating its efforts in other areas, such as monitoring of sharks' movements, perfection of safe flotation devices, and even protective clothing for men who might end up in the ocean.

Victor Coppleson concocted charts and maps to establish what he called "the world belt of shark attacks." Those interested in the meteorological and hydrographic details of this study are referred to his book *Shark Attack*, or to the paper he wrote for Perry Gilbert's *Sharks and Survival*. David Davies, in his book *About Sharks and Shark Attack*, also tried to find correlative factors in the shark attack statistics. Davies investigated "turbidity of the water, water temperature, salinity, depth of attack, the distance from the shore, the geomorphology of the beaches and sea-floor, condition of sky, colour of the victim's costume, colour of victim's skin, presence or absence of jewelry, season and time of attack, state of tide, the possible effects of shore-based whaling operations, the discharge of sewage and other effluent into the sea, the seasonal abundance of dangerous sharks and the extent to which the sea is used for recreational purposes."

David Baldridge, analyzing the data in 1,165 cases (which included all of Coppleson's and all of Davies' information), also produced elaborate tables, charts, and graphs. As with all statistics, it is possible to interpret them in

many different ways. For instance, I once heard someone ask if it was true that "most shark attacks take place in less than five feet of water." According to the table "Total Depth of Water at the Attack Site" in *Shark Attack: A Program of Data Reduction and Analysis* by Baldridge, this is most certainly true.[17](Of the 470 attacks in which the depth was known, 290, or 62 percent, took place in water 0 to 5 feet in depth.) One could assume from these data that it would be safer to swim in deeper water, but of course what the figures really say is since more people stay in shallow water, more attacks are likely to take place there.

Early researchers wanted to assign the attacks to some function of shark distribution or behavior, but more recent analysis places a greater burden on the distribution or behavior of the victim. Coppleson spends pages and even whole chapters developing such ideas as the "theory of a warm water law," which suggests that sharks are more likely to attack in water of above-average temperature, *but at no time does he suggest that there are more people swimming when the water is above normal temperature.* He attributes the New Jersey attacks to a "rogue shark," but he never mentions that the northeastern United States was in the grip of a massive heat wave in July 1916, and, therefore, there were many more people in the water.

Even though there are still a great many variables that we do not understand with respect to the behavior of sharks, and some that we may not even be aware of, it seems an irrefutable truth that more shark attacks take place when there are more people in the water. In other words, when conditions are favorable for recreational swimming, that is, hot weather, pleasant water temperature, and calm seas, more attacks occur—because there are more potential targets. There are very few shark attacks in winter, simply because there are very few swimmers in winter. (Keep in mind that these are statistical assumptions, and in achieving an average, the highs and lows must also be considered. Some attacks take place in cloudy weather, some on cool days—but most of them take place during the time when the most people are swimming.)

Race or color seems to have nothing to do with a shark's preference, although for years, Caucasians chose to believe that "natives," because of their coloration, were immune to shark attacks. (Writing of his trip to Samoa and Fiji, Captain Young said, "The natives, since they were dark-skinned, felt small fear of [sharks], regarding them chiefly as food.") [256] One figure that is not easily dismissed concerns sex. Of the 1,165 attacks analyzed, 1,080, or 93.1 percent, were on males. In discussing this anomaly, Baldridge suggests a number of ideas that might explain this more than 10-to-1 ratio (there are more males in the water; males are more active swimmers; males smell different; males may have more aggressive swimming movements, etc.), but he is unable to supply a definitive reason. He writes, "Clearly, there is here a need for more basic research."

Most recreational swimming takes place during the day, usually between the hours of 10 A.M. and 4 P.M. Therefore, most shark attacks take place between these same hours. While this seems obvious, it also supports an earlier point about the motivation of shark attacks. It is now believed that many species of sharks come inshore at night to feed and, therefore, that attacks made during the day are not related to the feeding process. (One more fact that would seem to add support to the nonfeeding theory is the surprising number of people that *survive* shark attacks. Of the 1,150 cases in which information was available, 64.7 percent of the human victims survived. The survival rate for fish is probably lower.) In a telemetry experiment conducted off Santa Catalina Island, California, in 1972 by T. C. Sciarotta, it was discovered that the blue sharks spent the day well away from shore, while at night, the sharks were inshore, often in relatively shallow water. In a much more spectacular demonstration of the inadvisability of night swimming where it is known that there are sharks, the Natal Anti-Shark Measures Board reports that during the years 1966 to 1972, when over 7,000 sharks were caught in the nets, over 95 percent were caught between dusk and dawn.

Almost as soon as a categorical statement is made about sharks, an exception crops up. Now that the Navy and the Air Force have discontinued their use of Shark Chaser, and chemical repellents have fallen into almost complete disfavor, along comes someone to challenge the whole concept. Dr. Eugenie Clark, during research on garden eels in the Red Sea, discovered that the Moses sole, *Pardachirus marmoratus*, emits a whitish fluid that seems to repel sharks. The research on this substance is still in its infancy, and although the sole can repel sharks, no one is quite sure how to apply this knowledge to protect man. In addition, the toxin is so complex in its molecular

structure that it is almost impossible to synthesize. The publication of Dr. Clark's cautious observations in *National Geographic* [53] led to some wild speculation in the press; *Oceans* magazine (No. 5, 1975) headlined an article: "BREAKTHROUGH! 100% EFFECTIVE SHARK REPELLENT." It is nothing of the sort—unless you happen to be a Moses sole.

The search for shark repellents and protective devices goes on. The great increase in scuba and skin diving brings many more people into the shark's realm, and Baldridge warns that there appears to be a greater danger of shark attack among divers than other potential victims. Even though divers do less splashing than surface swimmers, and they usually have face masks which permit them a much greater degree of underwater vision, these advantages seem to be outweighed by their greater distance from shore, the depths to which they can dive (the deepest attack on record took place at approximately 250 feet, off Cane Bay, St. Croix, and resulted in the death of the diver), and their different attitudes toward sharks. Divers have a tendency to provoke sharks, to take pictures of them, or even to spear them. Another factor in attracting sharks to divers is the presence of dead or dying fish which spearfishermen often spear or tow along behind them. Free divers, using just a mask, snorkel, and fins, seem to be much more attack-prone than scuba divers. (Of the 190 recorded attacks on divers, 56 percent were free divers—including all the Aldinga Beach white shark attacks—while only 11 percent were scuba divers. The remainder were pearl divers, free divers with no equipment, and hard-hat divers.) These data seem to imply that you are safer if you dive with scuba gear, but I think another reading is called for: there are so many more free divers than scuba divers that most of the attacks take place on those that form the majority.

Since there is a large market for divers' equipment, many spears, powerheads, electric repellents, and darts have been developed for the protection of divers. Cousteau's divers and Scott Johnson prefer to use a "shark billy," which consists of a wooden stick with a nail in the end, used to poke the shark away; other divers and film makers use explosive devices, spears, and underwater guns that kill the shark on contact. A man named Walter Starck invented a convict-striped wet suit, which he said resembled the pattern of the poisonous sea snakes of the Pacific. In experiments off Lord

Howe Island in the Tasman Sea, Starck "slid into the water in his zebra suit, and the armada of sharks disappeared."[81] (Other experiments with multicolored or striped wet suits produced either no discernible results or attracted sharks.)

Color does play a role in the study of shark repellents, even though no one is really sure whether or not sharks can distinguish colors. The relative brightness of an object in the water is definitely a factor in the design of life jackets or other flotation devices, according to Dr. C. Scott Johnson. Working at the Naval Undersea Center in San Diego, Johnson has experimented with various devices, including life jackets for infants and adults, and he has determined that highly reflective surfaces are more attractive to sharks than are dull, dark colors. This information was incorporated into the design of the "Shark Screen," Johnson's patented device in which a person is protected from the shark's visual and olfactory senses by a large plastic bag in which he floats. This device, which can be folded up into a packet about the size of the old Shark Chaser, is perhaps the most innovative and promising of all the new protective devices.

The Navy is also testing "sharkproof" materials, and on one occasion, I almost became an unwilling participant in an experiment. I was visiting the Mote Marine Lab in February 1975, while one of the Navy tests was in progress. The material being tested was "Kevlar," a synthetic woven material that had been shown to be able to stop a .45-caliber bullet. Now a piece of wood was wrapped in the material, and strips of fresh fish were tied around it. If the dusky sharks bit through the fish but did not tear the material, it would be shown that Kevlar could withstand the bite of a shark. (By coincidence, it was the dusky shark, *Carcharhinus obscurus*, that had been the subject of Perry Gilbert's experiments on the power of a shark's bite: duskies were shown to have a biting power of 18 tons per square inch. While this shows the enormous strength of a shark's jaws, it is a figure often quoted, and more often misunderstood. The actual measurements, using a device called the "Snodgrass Gnathodynamometer," are of the pressure exerted by the *point* of the tooth. This figure is then projected over a larger area, which produces the per-square-inch figure.)

As I walked out on the dock to watch the experiment in progress, the dock collapsed, and I found myself standing in about four feet of water in which there were three dusky sharks being encouraged to feed on legs. (The bait with the Kevlar in it had been fitted with a shoe, and during the experiments, was known as "Sam's leg.") While Sam's leg was attached by a piece of nylon line, mine were attached by bone, sinew, and muscle, materials that were already known to be extremely susceptible to the bite of a shark. Fortunately, I managed to climb out of the water before the experiment on my legs was concluded. The duskies did bite the artificial leg, and tore the Kevlar as well.

No device, repellent or powerhead or screen, is a deterrent to sharks in the throes of a so-called "frenzy." This activity, which involves large numbers of sharks feeding and fighting for food, is an uncontrolled orgy of eating. It is during these frenzies that sharks have been known to bite everything in sight, including other sharks engaged in the same activity. For the most part, frenzies are artificially stimulated, in that they are the result of some action of man, such as the dumping of trash fish or offal from a fishing boat, the underwater broadcasting of certain frequencies of sound, or the presence of a bleeding whale carcass (caught by fishermen). Theo Brown, a researcher experimenting with various species of sharks on the reefs of Rangiroa, French Polynesia, was particularly interested in this phenomenon. In one instance, after attracting the sharks with an underwater transducer, he produced this scene:

A Harpu cod of around 15 pounds swam towards the corals over the glistening white sand. Without warning, it was suddenly attacked and seized by a White-tip shark, which then attempted to flee with its struggling prey. This was the signal for the orgy to start, and the sharks exploded into a frenzy of activity. They simultaneously rushed the White-tip and converged into a circular ball of whirling, viciously snapping animals. It was an incredible sight and there was an audible roar as would be made by a distant express train as it thundered over a metal bridge. I could see open jaws furiously tearing at flesh, twisting and ripping at anything in sight. Sharks rushed from every direction to join the mêlée, and within a matter of seconds two hundred or more sharks were locked in a life-and-death struggle. They formed one solid mass of living and dying muscle and flesh, completely oblivious to pain and no longer responding to the primitive instinct of survival.[37]

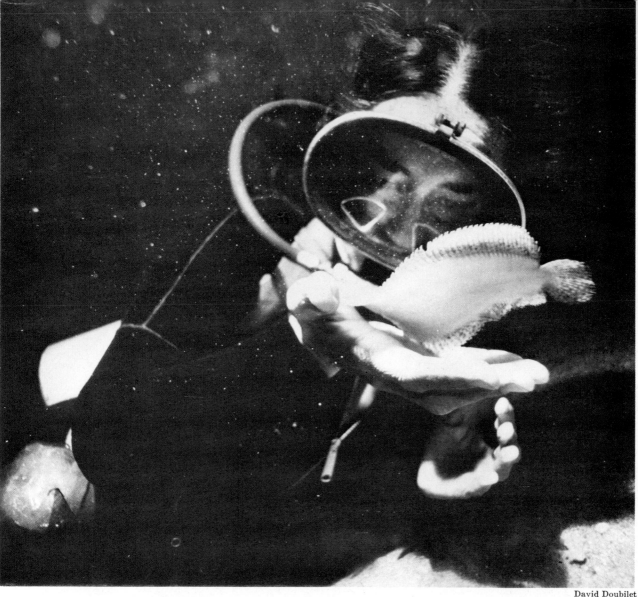

Eugenie Clark and the Moses sole, Pardachirus marmoratus; *a fish that secretes a substance that repels sharks.*

Frenzies such as this probably occur in the case of a major shipwreck or air disaster, where there are many bleeding bodies in the water. We know that, statistically, sharks are likely to attack during those periods and in those areas where there are the most people in the water, but we do not know why sharks attack on one day and not on another. Sharks still seem to prefer to attack lone swimmers, despite the statistics that show that they seem to prefer crowds. We can speculate that in many instances the sharks are not feeding on their victims, but only in a few cases can we guess what they *are* doing. One suggestion, raised in connection with some species of carcharhinids, is that they *are* feeding, but not intentionally on humans. The little blacktip reef shark, *Carcharhinus melanopterus,* has frequently attacked the legs of fishermen who are splashing through the shallows it inhabits. One suggestion is the shark mistakes the splashing feet for fish and attacks. When it discovers that the leg is not a fish (by tasting it), it lets go. This might also apply to the bull shark *C. leucas,* at least in

the rough, turbid waters of South Africa. Perhaps the visibility is so poor in these waters that the shark is attracted to any foreign object in the surf. Unlike the little reef shark, however, the bull shark is capable of inflicting fatal wounds, even in the act of rejecting its prey. (Dr. G. D. Campbell has even gone so far as to suggest "petulance" as a cause for shark attack —if the prey is not what it's supposed to be, the shark angrily bites it anyway.) Our ignorance of the motivating factors in shark attack only serves to point up the need for more behavioral and physiological studies. If we knew how the shark saw (or sensed) a human leg under water, we might have some idea as to why it reacts to it the way it does.

An area poorly understood is aggression *per se.* There are many animals—ranging in size from a mosquito to an elephant—that have been known to "attack" humans. In the case of the mosquito, the "attack" is known to be a feeding process, while in the case of the elephant, it is usually a defensive or protective action. Many other animals attack us, and we are often at a complete loss to explain their behavior. Gavin Maxwell's otters, made so famous in *Ring of Bright Water*, turned on strangers, and even on their trainers, and savagely bit them. All Maxwell has been able to suggest as an explanation for this aggressive behavior is "jealousy," an anthropomorphism that does not seem to explain very much. Domestic dogs and cats bite people, as do pet skunks, monkeys, raccoons, and almost all other animals with the necessary equipment. In very few of these instances is the animal called a "man-eater"; it is understood that it is using the only defensive or offensive weapons it possesses. The "attack," therefore, takes the form of a bite. This may also be the case with the shark, but its bite is so terrifying that it is raised to a new category, the "man-eater." (Even though I believe that sharks as a rule do not eat men, I am not going to crusade

The "Shark Screen" in action at the Lerner Marine Laboratory, Bimini. Inside the screen is its inventor, Scott Johnson; outside is a nurse shark.

Naval Undersea Center, Pasadena, California

for an etymological revision to "man-biter";
or even, given the climate of equality for women,
"person-biter.") As Gary Soucie wrote in
Audubon, "The shark, like the professional
boxer or the karate black belt, simply possesses
the means of turning a simple altercation or
misunderstanding into felonious mayhem. It
isn't the shark's fault nature gave it a full deck
when she was passing out teeth." [215]

White sharks are usually characterized as
aggressive fish, even though the term is somewhat unclear. We have no idea how many white
sharks do *not* attack people when the opportunity presents itself, so we cannot even guess
at the number of potential contact situations
in which the person is ignored or passed by.
David Baldridge summarizes the statistical
shortcomings of a system that applies only to
selected examples:

> *The questions of prime importance are
> what settings of the environmental stage
> and/or modes of shark behavior make an
> attack likely and what in the makeup or
> actions of a particular person makes him
> the likely victim. All of these considera-
> tions require not only detailed information
> on attack situations, but equally good*
> *data for the same parameters under nor-
> mal, non-attack control conditions. With-
> out the latter, it is meaningless to speak in
> terms of cause-and-effect relationships.* [17]

After all the studies, books, and data on shark
attacks, nothing has really changed. It is still
true that the best way to avoid an attack is to
stay out of the water. Only the behaviorists are
beginning to make any inroads into the understanding of the shark, and they are quick to
point out that they have a long way to go. As
we have seen, shark attack is an infrequent
occurrence, but it inspires terror in us all out of
proportion to its numerical probability. Perhaps, in our smug and scientific anthropo-
centrism, we fear the shark most because it
does not respond to our dictates. We can land
men on the moon, explore the deepest ocean
trenches, examine the most minute microorganisms and the distant stars. We can conquer malaria, split the atom, even eliminate
entire species from the face of the earth. And
yet, for all our science and technology, we have
gotten no closer to stopping a fish that wants to
bite us than did the ancient Greeks. As when we
stare up at the stars on a moonless night, this
realization makes us aware of our own helpless
insignificance.

THE SHARK PEOPLE

I am defining shark people as individuals who have spent a significant portion of their lives involved with sharks. The list includes scientists, fishermen, photographers, writers, divers, and the man who made shark leather. In addition to those I have included, there are obviously a great many other people who have caught, photographed, or written about sharks. For the obvious reasons of time and space, I have had to make a somewhat subjective selection, based on personal knowledge, familiarity with their published work, or the more general recognition of an individual as a "shark person." Many of the people whose profiles are not included in this section have been mentioned in context in earlier sections of the book, such as Dr. Victor Coppleson, an Australian surgeon with a particular interest in shark attacks; Theo W. Brown, a researcher in the area of shark repellents; and Colonel Hugh Wise, a shark fisherman who wrote a book called *Tigers of the Sea* in 1937. Henry Bigelow and William Schroeder, ichthyologists at Harvard University, are mentioned more frequently than anyone else, since they "wrote the book" on the sharks of the western North Atlantic. Without their book, certainly the most detailed ever written on the sharks of any area, much of the work that followed its publication in 1948 (including this book), could not have been written.

With very few exceptions, all the people discussed here have been involved in other pursuits, both literally and figuratively. Some are even better known for other fields of study or endeavor, but their work with sharks represents a significant contribution to the subject. For example, Gavin Maxwell is best known for his autobiographical works, such as *Ring of Bright Water*, in which the predominant animals are otters. It is not so well known that Maxwell worked for five years as a commercial shark fisherman, catching and processing basking sharks in the Hebrides. Zane Grey, America's most popular western novelist, spent a good portion of his time and money in pursuit of big game fish, among them sharks.

Many of the shark people have carefully recorded their adventures. This is particularly true of the scientists, whose experiments and research projects are regularly documented, and are therefore accessible to those who have an interest in them. Some scientists have even gone so far as to write autobiographies, thus giving us not only the results of their experiments or their bibliographies, but their motiva-

Museum of Comparative Zoology, Harvard University

Henry B. Bigelow

Museum of Comparative Zoology, Harvard University

William C. Schroeder

Some of the shark people at the Lerner Marine Laboratory, Bimini, in 1968: (left to right) *H. David Baldridge, Albert L. Tester, C. Scott Johnson, Perry W. Gilbert.*

tions, adventures, and personal histories as well. In this category, Eugenie Clark stands out, since in addition to her numerous scientific and popular publications, she has already written two volumes of her life story, *Lady with a Spear* (1953)[51] and *The Lady and the Sharks* (1969)[50]. In another category, the well-known writer-naturalist Peter Matthiessen has written about many of the shark people in one book, *Blue Meridian*.[164] This is the chronicle of the expedition that made the movie *Blue Water, White Death*, and includes Peter Gimbel, Stan Waterman, Ron and Valerie Taylor, and Rodney Fox. Peter Benchley is included as a shark person because his fictional contribution to shark lore, *Jaws*, probably did more to create an awareness of sharks in people than all the other writers, photographers, and divers combined.

Very few of the shark people operate independently of other shark people. Their interest in sharks is enough to conjoin them into a loose fraternity, and it will be seen that their interactions and overlaps are remarkable. I mentioned the *Blue Water* expedition, during which Gimbel, Waterman, Fox, and the Taylors were all aboard the same ship, looking for the white shark in order to film it in its native waters. I later discovered that Perry Gilbert was the one who suggested that they begin their search in the whaling grounds off Durban, because when he had visited Dr. David Davies in South Africa, Davies had told him of the white sharks that were often seen feeding on the whale carcasses there.

Perry W. Gilbert succeeded Eugenie Clark as director of the Mote Marine Laboratory in Sarasota, Florida. Gilbert now works with Stewart Springer and David Baldridge, two more of the shark people. (Practically everyone who has ever worked with sharks has worked at the lab in Sarasota or at its predecessor at Placida, the Cape Haze Marine Laboratory. Scott Johnson was a visiting Navy scientist at the Cape Haze lab in 1968, and it was there that I first met Beulah Davis, director of the Natal Anti-Shark Measures Board.) When I told Perry Gilbert that I was going shark fishing off

Montauk with Frank Mundus, he said, "Say hello to Frank for me. We've been friends for twenty years." Peter Gimbel's first experiences with a shark cage in the ocean took place off Montauk, from Mundus's boat, *Cricket II*. Practically all the scientists have worked together at one time or another (Gilbert, Springer, and Baldridge were members of the American Institute of Biological Sciences Shark Research Panel), and the writers and photographers are involved with one another and with the scientists as well. When I mentioned this to Stan Waterman, he told me that he had known Perry Gilbert for years, and that he and Eugenie Clark were planning an expedition to photograph the "sleeping sharks" of Japan.

There is something more than an interest in sharks that defines a shark person. At first I thought it was a function of the ego—many of the people I talked to seemed to regard the shark as a challenge to be overcome, a gauntlet thrown down that had to be picked up. It is not that simple, but I think that enters into it. Sharks represent an untamable quality that one can regard as a personal challenge. Many of the shark people seem to demonstrate a need to assert their superiority over a threatening, elemental force. This is not to say that all the shark people are roaring egomaniacs, beating their chests and slaughtering sharks whenever possible. In fact, very few of the shark people have an animosity toward sharks. (Among the shark people, only Captain Bill Young hated sharks; he tried to kill as many as he could, wherever and whenever he could.) Instead of finding a single character trait that I could identify in all the shark people, I found great diversity, but I did find one common ground: respect for the sharks. Sharks are not animals that many people feel neutral about—you either hate them or you admire them. (But there is an element of fear in this admiration. "Show me a man who isn't afraid of sharks," said Stan Waterman, "and I'll show you a damned fool.") The shark's challenge has been taken up by a handful of people who are unique in their pursuit of the shark and the knowledge thereof.

211

SHELTON P. APPLEGATE:
Shark Paleontologist

Each of the "shark people" has taken a somewhat different approach to the subject of sharks; each one by the nature of his or her special area of concentration adds something to the sum of our knowledge. Dr. Shelton P. Applegate, born in 1928 in Richmond, Virginia, has made major contributions as a result of his early interest in geology, botany, zoology, and paleontology.

Considered one of the leading authorities in the country on fossil sharks and their identification, Applegate has maintained a continuing interest in sharks from his undergraduate days at the University of Richmond, through graduate school at the University of Virginia and the University of Chicago, up to his present position as Associate Curator of Vertebrate Paleontology at the Los Angeles County Museum of Natural History. His *curriculum vitae* reads like the table of contents of a book that could be called *Fossil Sharks and Whales*. In addition to his varied activities involving extinct species, he has also been extremely active in the collection and study of modern sharks. In an L.A. County Museum publication entitled "The Mystical Fascination of the Shark,"[6] Applegate wrote: "To know fossil sharks, one must also

know Recent sharks." To learn about Recent sharks, Applegate has fished for them in practically every way known, including gill-netting, longlines, rod and reel, and the exotic, deep-set longline. In this technique, magnesium links attach the line to cinder block weights, the links corrode after eight to twelve hours, dropping the weights, and allowing the line to be buoyed to the surface by floats filled with gasoline, a liquid much lighter than water.

Shelton Applegate ready to return a spiny dogfish to the Pacific after tagging it.

When Applegate arrived at the L.A. County Museum in 1963, the number of Recent shark jaws there was exactly 2. The number of jaws of sharks, skates, and rays is now well over 500, and this valuable resource is one of the best tools in the country for identifying sharks, fossil and Recent. Applegate is quick to point out that even though sharks have been around for millions of years, there are still significant differences between the sharks of the distant past and the sharks of today. The study of each area contributes to the understanding of the other; we can learn a great deal about Recent sharks from the study of their ancestors, and much of what we know about fossil sharks is derived from comparisons with the living species. Since the only parts of the shark that are usually preserved as fossils are the teeth and the vertebrae, the material is somewhat limited in scope. It is not, however, limited in quantity, because sharks are constantly shedding and replacing teeth, and, therefore, the amount of material per shark is considerably higher than it would be for any other vertebrate. (Sharks' teeth are the most commonly found marine fossils.) Applegate successfully combines the sciences of paleontology and ichthyology with the field experience of a fisherman, and thereby gains a more complete understanding of the shark.

One of the unique fossiliferous areas in the United States is in California, not in the ocean, as one might expect, but far inland, near Bakersfield. Here we find Sharktooth Hill, "where," Applegate informs us, "the ocean bottom muds and silts have been uplifted through faulting and folding," to produce some of the richest marine vertebrate deposits found anywhere in the world. Sharks' teeth can be found on and below the surface, and other materials, such as the bones, teeth, ear bones, and whole skeletons of extinct whales, can also be found. That whale fossils and sharks' teeth should be found together is no surprise (this is also the case on the East Coast, in Calvert Cliffs, Maryland); Applegate believes that the giant shark *Carcharodon megalodon* fed on now-extinct whales, called *Cetotheres*, and the disappearance of the whales heralded the extinction of the sharks.

Shelton Applegate's professional career has been busy and varied, incorporating shark fishing, fossil hunting, writing, and teaching. He has done some of the pioneer work in determining the fossilization and calcification processes of bone and cartilage, and he has traveled around the world in search of material for his studies. Because of his special interest in *C. megalodon*, I asked him to review the manuscript for that section of this book. This he generously did, and provided me with numerous references and additional information, as well as pointing out some of my more obvious errors.

DAVID BALDRIDGE: *The Shark Attack Man*

Too often, the later endeavors of a man eclipse his earlier accomplishments, and he is known only for his most recent work. David Baldridge began his work on sharks in 1963, which ranks him as a relative newcomer to the field, but he has had such an impact on this complex and diverse subject, that his earlier career has been virtually ignored.

He was born in St. Louis and raised in Memphis, Tennessee, where he attended Southwestern University, graduating with high honors in chemistry in 1944, at the age of nineteen. He informed the Navy of his background in chemistry, and in an unusually unmilitary allocation of personnel, he was made Malaria Control Officer after his graduation from Midshipman School. By 1946, he was a 21-year-old reserve officer, and he headed for graduate school at the University of California at Berkeley. He was awarded a Ph.D. in chemistry in 1950. At this time another war was warming up, and Lt. J. G. David Baldridge was recalled to active duty and assigned to the Naval Medical Research Institute at Bethesda, Maryland, where he worked on the chemistry of drugs from plants. The Korean conflict came to an end, and so did Baldridge's second hitch in the Navy. He returned to civilian life on inactive reserve duty, and worked for private industry on various chemical and pharmacological projects, including the development of rocket fuels. In 1953, when Baldridge heard that the Navy was opening up its ranks for regular officers, he shed his reserve status and back he went. At this time the Navy was test-firing the first guided missiles, and Baldridge went to work studying the toxicological effects of the firing of missiles from ships. He was interested in the chemical aspects of naval operations, and his diverse experiences made him very valuable to the Navy. (All through his Navy career he seemed to be able to create a job where none had existed before. His unique talents and interests ensured that he "never replaced anyone"; each title was developed just for him and by him.) He had gone to sea on practically every type of Navy fighting vessel, and his combined capabilities as a deck officer and a chemist enabled him to marry his profession with his scientific interests. For several years he was liaison officer between the Medical Department of the Navy and all the Navy's rocket and missile research and development programs.

David Baldridge examines the liver lobes of an 11-foot-long tiger shark in his studies on the role of liver oil in regulating bouyancy in large sharks.

The early chemical research on effects of firing antiaircraft missiles from operational ships was done by David Baldridge.

By 1957, he was on the staff of Admiral William "Red" Rayborn, supervising identification and control of chemical and physical hazards involved in shipboard firings of Polaris missiles. At this time, missile-carrying nuclear submarines were undergoing preliminary testing, and Baldridge checked out every chemical substance aboard these ships, knowing that the crew could be "buttoned up" for as long as ninety days. In 1963, the nuclear submarine *Thresher* was lost off the New England coast. The cause of this disaster—the worst in submarine history—was never determined. Because of the questions raised about escape from submarines, the subjects of deep diving and sharks came up. Baldridge was then further assigned to the Office of Naval Research as liaison officer between ONR and the Navy's Medical Department, to investigate chemical shark repellents, and to coordinate the Navy's testing of shark repellents. Up to this time, the only repellent was Shark Chaser, made up of copper acetate and nigrosine dye, which was known to be ineffective. Just *how* ineffective was to be demonstrated by David Baldridge.

In 1968 Baldridge was asked to join the American Institute of Biological Sciences Shark Research Panel, which had been formed in 1958 to study the biology and behavior of dangerous sharks. Baldridge was particularly interested in the physical chemistry and mathematics that described responses of sharks to waterborne drugs, and he conducted extensive experiments in the field as well as in the laboratory. The major shortcoming of a chemical shark repellent now seems obvious (although it didn't seem so in the past): it disperses so quickly in the water, that even if a satisfactory concentration could be achieved, it would be diluted almost immediately to a point of ineffectiveness. According to Baldridge, any toxic drug used in such amounts as to be an effective deterrent "would be equally effective against the life of the man in the water." He is not ready to give up completely on the idea of a chemical shark repellent, but he feels that the possibility of finding such a substance is remote.

After using his chemical background to dispel some of the longstanding myths about shark repellents, Baldridge turned his analytical and inquisitive mind to some of the other shark-related problems. It had always been assumed, for instance, that a shark attacking a human being was trying to eat him. When Baldridge took over the task of analyzing case history data held in the Shark Attack File, which had been transferred from the Smithsonian Institution to the Mote Marine Laboratory (Baldridge was then stationed at the Naval Aerospace Medical Center at Pensacola, but was assigned to the Mote Marine Lab), among the things he noticed were the high survival rate of the victims and the low percentage of attacks that involved multiple strikes. Both of these factors seemed inconsistent with the idea of a "man-eating" shark. Of the 1,165 cases analyzed, 64.7 percent of the victims survived, and less than 20 percent reported multiple strikes. In many of the cases where death did result from a shark attack, shark-inflicted wounds were not the direct cause of death. Where massive loss of tissue did not occur, loss of blood and drowning were the more likely causes of the death of the victim. While this may seem like unnecessary hair-splitting, to a man such as Baldridge, the differences in cause of death are highly significant. If we can assume that the shark was not trying to eat the victim in such a high percentage of the cases, then we have to look elsewhere for the shark's motivation, and, therefore, the search for a repellent must be conducted in completely different areas.

One of the most important papers ever written on the volatile subject of shark attack appeared in *Military Medicine* in February 1969. With Joy Williams, his data analyst at the Mote Marine Laboratory, Baldridge wrote "Shark Attack: Feeding or Fighting?" in which he raised the basic question, "Why do sharks attack human beings?"[19] Although he acknowledges that there are many instances in which "wound characteristics . . . support . . . the assumption that the intent of the predator was to feed on the victim," he also raises other important questions, based on his analysis of the data and his own field observations. It was seen that there were other patterns of behavior, including "bumping" (contact with the mouth closed or with the fins), "slashing" and "raking" (open-mouth contact with only the upper teeth), and the agonistic "threat" behavior observed by Don Nelson, Ron Church, and others. Observers had realized that not all contact between human and shark was of the predator-prey variety, but

Baldridge investigated these "non-feeding" situations in a scientific manner, and eliminated many of the old wives' tales, while opening up new areas for investigation. Among the subjects he researched were "the reaction of sharks to a mammal in distress" (rats were generally ignored, unless treated with fish blood and body fluids), "the sinking factors of sharks" (demonstrating that the density factor of the shark is in such a delicate equilibrium with the ambient water that even a minor disturbance of this balance can incapacitate the shark), and, probably most important, he codified and analyzed the entire body of data in the Shark Attack File.

The Shark Attack File is discussed in greater detail in the section "Shark Attacks," but I think it is reasonable to state that much of what we know about shark attacks is derived from David Baldridge's succinct presentation in his 1973 research report to the Office of Naval Research, reprinted as "Shark Attack: A Program of Data Reduction and Analysis" by the Mote Marine Lab in 1974.[17] (Baldridge subsequently took these data and converted them into popular language for his eminently readable book *Shark Attack*.[16]) David Baldridge has taken much of the information that we have on shark attack and decoded it, giving us a much clearer picture of the relationship between sharks and humans. When he retired as a captain from the Navy in 1971 (at the age of forty-six), he accepted a full-time post at the Mote Marine Lab, where he continues his incisive and revealing studies.

An eerie footnote to the career of David Baldridge: upon his graduation as a company commander from Midshipman School at Columbia University in 1945, ceremonies were held at the New York Yacht Club. The commander of the highest-rated company would receive "good orders," and a ceremonial Navy sword. Baldridge wanted the choice posting and the sword, but his company finished second in the regiment "because of some mis-step on parade or something." Number one company commander was Thomas Brophy, who received orders to report to the U.S.S. *Indianapolis*. This ship was torpedoed and sunk on July 30, 1945, after delivering the atomic bomb from San Francisco, California to Tinian. Of the crew of over 1,000, only 317 survived the explosions and the subsequent shark attacks. Thomas Brophy, the man who beat Baldridge for the top spot, was not among the survivors.

PETER BENCHLEY: *Best-Seller*

The fish moved away. It swallowed the woman's limb without chewing. Bones and meat passed down its massive gullet in a single spasm. Now the fish turned again, homing in on the stream of blood flushing from the woman's femoral artery, a beacon as clear and true as a lighthouse on a cloudless night. This time the fish attacked from below. It hurtled up under the woman, jaws agape. The great conical head struck her like a locomotive, knocking her up out of the water. The jaws snapped shut around her torso, crushing bones and flesh into a jelly. The fish, with the woman's body in its mouth, smashed down on the water with a thunderous splash, spewing foam and blood and phosphorescence in a gaudy shower.

> Peter Benchley
> *Jaws*, 1974

There are people who have spent their lives studying about sharks, and people who have photographed them, dived with them, fished for them, and made movies about them. Until recently, these shark people operated in a narrow sphere of recognition, often known only by their peers. Occasionally a breakthrough took place, in which the public was made aware of sharks by a particularly well written passage in a novel (such as Hemingway's account of the sharks that attack the great fish in *The Old Man and the Sea*), or a documentary film about sharks (such as Peter Gimbel's *Blue Water, White Death*). Until the beginning of 1974, sharks were of interest to only a small number of people, and while others were aware of their existence, no one paid much attention to them.

In February 1974, one man changed all that. Almost single-handedly (one has to give some credit to the publicity department of Double-

day), Peter Benchley made almost the entire country shark-conscious. The reviews of his book were mostly complimentary, with occasional dissenters—there were those who felt he owed too much to Melville's great white whale. (It can hardly be considered a valid criticism that the common name of *Carcharodon carcharias* is the *great white shark*.) In the hardcover version, some 200,000 copies of *Jaws* have been sold, which is a good but not extraordinary record, and over 10 million copies of the paperback version are in print at the time of this writing, and that *is* an extraordinary number. The movie made from the book (with screenplay by Peter Benchley and Carl Gottlieb) has become the highest-grossing movie in history.

I first met Peter Benchley in 1973. A mutual friend put us in contact because I was painting sharks, and he was writing a novel that she thought had something to do with sharks. Benchley and I got together, and immediately fell to discussing our mutual and overwhelming preoccupation. Eventually, we were to work together on various aspects of our own shark interest, culminating in an ABC-TV program for the "American Sportsman" series, in which we were filmed fishing for sharks with Captain Frank Mundus out of Montauk. I found out how he wrote *Jaws*, and he found out why I painted sharks. He eventually bought the painting that was to appear with him on the cover of the *New York Times Magazine* (April 21, 1974), in conjunction with the article by Ted Morgan, "Sharks: The Making of a Best Seller." (Speaking of covers, this is probably as good a time as any to state once and for all that I did *not* do the cover illustration for either the hard-cover or the paperback version of *Jaws*. There was a time when I thought I was going to be a consultant on the mechanical shark used in the movie, but I didn't do that either.)

Peter Benchley's interest in sharks began when he was in his early teens, and his father took him swordfishing out of Nantucket, where his family spent the summers. As any angler will attest, swordfishing is a chancy business, and many fishermen go for years without even seeing a swordfish, never mind boating it. In those days blue sharks were plentiful (Benchley once counted over 150 "sunning" on the surface in one day), and they would catch the sharks when nothing else was biting. On the basis of these shark fishing experiences,

Benchley developed an interest in sharks, and began to read whatever he could find about them. By the time he had graduated from college, he had accumulated a fair knowledge of sharks, but it did not seem like the sort of information one could easily make use of.

In 1964, Frank Mundus harpooned a 17.5-foot, 4,500-pound white shark off Amagansett, and Peter, who was working at *Newsweek*, went to see the fish and the man who caught it. He went out on the *Cricket II* with Mundus twice, once as an observer and once as a participating angler. It was at this time that Benchley began to wonder what would happen if a monster shark came in to shore and began to gobble up the tourists. He went to Walter Bradbury at Doubleday in 1965 with this as an idea for a novel, but was given little encouragement and no money, so the idea was shelved—for the moment.

By 1971, Benchley was working as a free-lance magazine writer, and had completed an article for *National Geographic* on Bermuda, during which he had become interested in treasure diving. He approached Tom Congdon, a senior editor at Doubleday, with the idea of doing a book on pirates, but Congdon was not impressed. He asked Benchley if he had ever thought about doing fiction, and Peter answered, "I've been thinking about a novel about a great white shark..."

The development of *Jaws* as a novel, literary property, paperback, and movie property has been chronicled elsewhere, but a couple of additional items are of interest, given the fabulous success of *Jaws* and the attendant publicity. It is true, for example, that Doubleday offered Benchley a $1,000 advance, $500 of which was returnable if the first four chapters were deemed unsatisfactory. It took many memorandums, telephone calls, and meetings before the full $1,000—nonreturnable—was offered for the first four chapters and the outline. He began to work on the book in January 1972, and by April he had delivered the four chapters to the publisher. It is not true, on the other hand, that the novel was written by a committee of editors, agents, salespeople, and publishers. Peter Benchley, who had never before written a novel, was being guided by Tom Congdon, an experienced and capable editor, who, during the course of the writing, made editorial criticisms and suggestions. Benchley acted on these suggestions, often deferring to

Congdon's expertise, but the book was written by Peter Benchley and Peter Benchley alone.

By the summer of 1973, the book was in galleys, and I read it for the first time in that form. (It is easy to describe a book as "impossible to put down" when it is nicely bound and held together, but trying to read a book in galley form makes it almost "impossible to hold up." The sheets are about three feet long, not attached to one another, and with a nasty tendency to curl up like a snake held by the tail. It is a testimony to the carrying power and excitement of the book that anyone could read it in galleys.)

The rest is publishing history. *Jaws* was on the best-seller list for most of 1974, the paperback dominated its own class for 1975, and the movie is still drawing at theaters from California to Maine.

With Benchley's sudden jump from obscurity to fame, and his catapulting of the nation into "shark-consciousness," he became more involved with real sharks. First came the shark fishing expedition to Montauk (October 1974), during which Benchley caught a 251-pound swordfish. "At first I went swordfishing and all we saw was sharks ... Now that we go shark fishing, I catch a swordfish." In November 1974, he went to Australia, again with ABC-TV, this time to dive with sharks. The chief underwater cameraman was Stan Waterman, and their first location was the Great Barrier Reef. (It was on this occasion that Waterman found himself in the water with a great white shark, the first one anyone can remember in the warm waters of the Barrier Reef.) They were chumming with cut-up stingray for sharks, and, finally, after waiting in the water for over four hours, the sharks came—two big tigers. The larger of the two kept the other away from the proffered baits, and after about forty minutes of spectacular filming of hand-feeding a twelve-foot tiger shark, Benchley, out of air, headed for the surface. He was swimming against the current toward the dive boat, and suddenly both his legs were seized with cramps. He shouted, "I can't move!" and the unit director, Scott Ransom, jumped into the water—the two tigers were still in the vicinity—and dragged Benchley to the boat. "All I could think of was the shark that couldn't get at the baits ... He must have been really hungry by that time," Benchley said.

The next stop was South Australia, preferred location for filming the great white shark. On

Peter Benchley, identifiable by the shark billy he carries in the cage, with a real white shark off Dangerous Reef, Australia, in 1974.

their second day of diving at Dangerous Reef, two white sharks arrived. The larger of the two, a fourteen-footer weighing perhaps 1,600 pounds, was the one they were after. They entered the cages in the 50-degree water of Spencer Gulf, South Australia. In a wire mesh cage, Peter Benchley saw his first great white shark. "It was awesome . . . beyond fear. You knew that if it *wanted* to, it could demolish that flimsy cage in a minute." An often-publicized assertion is that Peter Benchley does not like to fly. In fact, he likes it so little, that there in the cage, faced by the most terrifying predator on earth, he was thinking, "I've done this, OK, but now I have to get on a goddam *airplane*."

In June 1975, Benchley and Waterman went with a film crew to the Bahamas to make a film on the ecology of the bonefish flats. They couldn't get the bonefish, but they did get some excellent footage of an oceanic whitetip (*Carcharhinus longimanus*) that circled them (they were not in cages) until Benchley poked at it with a sawed-off broom handle. The shark grabbed the stick in its teeth, shook it vigorously, and then departed.

Peter Benchley, who started out with a more-than-average interest in sharks, has created a nationwide shark-awareness. There are now perhaps millions of *Jaws* T-shirts, key rings, shark-tooth necklaces, shark posters, decals, and other characteristic examples of the "bandwagon" phenomenon. Publishers are scrambling to issue hastily written new books or to re-issue old ones. Old shark movies have been re-released. Aquariums around the country are mounting shark displays, and shark fishing has become a very popular sport, whereas in the past, most sharks were considered "trash fish" and thrown back. Scientists are besieged by questions and by requests for souvenir teeth and jaws. (This has been one of the most serious aftereffects of *Jaws*; scientists who have laboriously established their reputations as shark experts—and even some who haven't—have been deluged by this public interest—questions, requests to make public appearances, letters, unannounced visitors. All this takes up time and keeps the scientists from their work. One senior scientist told me that he spent most of the summer of 1975 on the telephone, answering questions, most of them the same. Another scientist has had to resort to a form letter that refers to "the current exceptional interest in sharks" and apologizes for not being able to write a personal letter.)

The novel *Jaws* and the movie made from it have had a significant effect on people and their attitude toward the sea. Of course, there are those who don't take it particularly seriously, but many people have been forced to think about something that they had never thought about before: sharks. I asked Peter why he thought the book had been so successful. He had no ready answers; in fact he still seems a bit surprised by all the notoriety and attention. He feels that it probably has to do with the "wanting-to-know-more" attitudes of most people, coupled with the vicarious release one gets from a terror film. After the movie, you can walk out of the theater, safe in the knowledge that you weren't the victim. Yet, certain films leave a residual memory, such as *Psycho*, and many people still feel uneasy about showering in a motel bathroom. And many people will not forget the town of Amity, Chief Brody, and Captain Quint. They will also remember, as they think about entering the ocean for a swim, his great white shark, one of the most successful and terrifying creatures in all of fiction.

Harold L. Pratt,
National Marine Fisheries Service

JACK CASEY: *The Shark Tagger*

Jack Casey works at an incredibly cluttered desk in an office at the Narragansett Laboratory of the National Marine Fisheries Service. He also works at fishing tournaments, on research vessels, on longliners, on charter fishing boats, and on ocean racers. He is probably the leading authority on the sharks of the northeastern United States. (The title of his enormously successful government publication is *Angler's Guide to Sharks of the Northeastern United States; Maine to Chesapeake Bay*.[45])

Once, while mulling over the characteristics of the various species of sharks with which he comes into contact, Casey decided that if he could be any animal, he would be a mako shark. This is not a particularly unusual desire, for the mako is indeed an admirable creature: it is probably the most graceful of all the sharks, the fastest, the best fighter, and one of the few species that has a look of intelligence about it. The large, dark eye of the mako suggests a higher sensitivity than it probably possesses; nevertheless, most other sharks have a blank, staring eye that seems to mirror only the base and primitive instincts for which sharks are renowned. The teeth of the mako are its most impressive feature—they are double-curved, knife-edged fangs, as evil-looking and dangerous as any teeth in sharkdom. Here Casey's desire to be this shark becomes uncertain; Casey's teeth are large, white, and even, and while he might envy the sleek power and speed of the mako, it is unlikely that he would trade his teeth for the snaggletoothed sneer of *Isurus oxyrinchus*.

Casey was born in 1933, in Turner's Falls, Massachusetts. He grew up with a normal kid's in-

Tagging a blue shark. After the dart is inserted, the shark will be cut loose.

terest in the outdoors, but as a youngster he had no ambition to go to college, let alone to pursue a career as a biologist. After high school and four years in the Navy, he realized the necessity of furthering his education, and began attending the University of New Hampshire, on the GI Bill. There he met John Wise, a biologist from Woods Hole Oceanographic Institute, who hired him as a summer assistant and stimulated his interest in marine biology. In his junior year, Casey transferred to the University of

Massachusetts, where he completed his undergraduate studies with a degree in Wildlife Management in 1960. Prior to that time, he had entertained thoughts of working with fish hatcheries, raising tiny fry to breeding size. He was now interested in marine fishes, and he kept turning down government offers that would have have sent him to Missouri or Idaho. Casey's repeated rejections of the Bureau of Sport Fisheries' offers made him wonder if "they would cross my name off the list," but finally an opening appeared at the Marine Laboratory at Sandy Hook, New Jersey. Jack's career was launched, in more ways than one.

August 21, 1960, Sea Girt, New Jersey. Twenty-odd miles south of the Sandy Hook station, John Brodeur, age twenty-four, was swimming in waist-deep water with his fiancée. His right leg was seized by a shark, and he thrashed and struck at the animal, which had its teeth in his leg. Brodeur was badly mauled, and after being dragged to shore, he lost consciousness. Eventually, his right leg was amputated below the knee. The next day, fourteen-year-old Clyde Trudeau was attacked at Seaside Park, New Jersey, 13 miles south of Sea Girt. It was like July 1916 all over again, when four swimmers had been killed by sharks along the Jersey shore, from Beach Haven north to Matawan Creek. Now, however, it was 1960; science reigned supreme, and we would find out about these killer sharks that were ravaging the New Jersey coast resorts. The task fell to a young fisheries biologist from the Sandy Hook Marine Laboratory—John G. Casey.

In 1961, the Smith Research and Development Company, a subsidiary of one of the major menhaden fishing companies, made one of its boats available to the Sandy Hook Laboratory. That year, Casey and his staff caught over 300 sharks during a longline fishing survey off the New York–New Jersey coast. The survey revealed that several species of large sharks were far more abundant in this area than historical records had indicated. Casey was surprised to discover how little was known about the life history of sharks in these waters. For nearly all species, fundamental information on their abundance, growth rates, reproductive cycles, food habits, and migratory patterns was lacking or extremely sparse. This lack of information was the result of many factors, as applicable in 1960 as they are today: large sharks are expensive to capture, and, in the absence of any commercial fishery for sharks, biologists could not easily obtain specimens for study. Fortunately for Casey, increasing numbers of sportsmen became interested in shark fishing, and offered their assistance to his research projects. As a result, he began a cooperative shark tagging program that is still going strong. (It was for these sportsmen that the *Angler's Guide* was originally written, when Casey discovered that most fishermen didn't know one species of shark from another.) In order for a program such as this to be successful, the creatures that

are tagged, and especially those that are recovered (since not all taggings result in the fish being brought to Casey), have to be identified. The 1964 *Angler's Guide* contains illustrations and short descriptions of thirty-three species of sharks native to New England waters, and includes an identification key that enables anglers to make at least tentative identifications of closely related species. (It is not the fault of the anglers that the dusky shark, *Carcharhinus obscurus*, and the sandbar shark, *Carcharhinus milberti*, are extremely similar in the four- to five-foot range. One diagnostic characteristic is that their dermal denticles are different, and Casey has gone so far as to supply serious fishermen with a low-power magnifier with which to examine the scales.)

In addition to his own northeastern U.S. waters, Casey has been involved in studies in such far-off locations as Cape Haze, Florida, and Durban, South Africa. Since the business of shark-tagging was highly experimental in its early years, the types of tags also presented a problem. At first, stock tags, such as those used on the ears of sheep and cattle, were used, but this involved getting the shark completely out of the water, punching a hole in the dorsal fin with an instrument like a leather punch, and then, with another pliers-like device, clamping the two elements of the tag together. It is easy to understand why very few sport fishermen were eager to use this method. The live shark had to be almost completely out of the water for the tag to be applied, and yet it had to be in good enough condition to swim away unharmed. (Contrary to popular belief, sharks out of the water are relatively fragile creatures. Scientists now believe that this is because of the tendency of the internal organs to shift and bounce around when the shark is hauled up by the mouth or by the tail. The fact that sharks take a long time to die is another matter altogether.)

A method had to be found whereby the shark could be tagged at less risk to the shark and to the angler. Eventually, Casey developed a dart-type tag which could be affixed to a long pole, and the barbed end jabbed into the shark while it was still in the water, either free-swimming or hooked. Attached to the dart is a plastic capsule containing a message in five languages, instructing the finder to return the tag to the Narragansett Laboratory, with information on where the fish was caught, how much it weighed, how long it was, etc. As of this writing, Casey and the sport fishermen have tagged

over 14,000 sharks, and have had over 400 tags returned. There have been some remarkable recoveries among sharks tagged in New England waters, including a 3,000-mile recapture from south of the Cape Verde Islands off the coast of Africa, and several from the coast of South America, over 2,000 miles from the point of tagging. The tagging program is not designed to produce long-distance records, but rather to collect information in all the areas in which Casey found it lacking in 1961: migration, abundance, longevity, growth rates, and the intriguing "population dynamics"—the rise and fall of a given population in a given time period.

In 1966, the Bureau of Sport Fisheries and Wildlife established a game fish laboratory at Narragansett, Rhode Island, and Casey, a Yankee by birth, jumped at the chance to return to his native New England. Through the complicated machinery of the federal bureaucracy, the Bureau of Commercial Fisheries Laboratory at Woods Hole, Massachusetts, and the Narragansett Laboratory were merged within the National Oceanic and Atmospheric Administration (NOAA), to form the National Marine Fisheries Service's Northeast Fisheries Center (NEFC). Casey is the chief of the Oceanic Gamefish Investigation at the NEFC. His work is almost exclusively with sharks, and his main area of concentration is still the tagging program. Many of his data are gained from fishermen, especially at the Bayshore (Long Island) Mako Tournament, which has been held annually for the past fifteen years. Although he has no advanced degrees, Casey is called "Doc" by the fishermen he has gotten to know over the years, and they feel that he lends an air of respectability and even "science" to their operation. There are enough "base-line data" on the sharks taken south of Fire Island Inlet (mostly blues, sandbars, and makos, occasional whites, tigers, and hammerheads, and very rarely a thresher) for Casey to have a good idea of the biology and possible management of these sharks as a "resource." Jack Casey now feels that it is just a matter of time before someone tries to capitalize on the commercial possibilities of a shark fishery in New England waters. He wants to have enough data to advise intelligently, and he feels that he is on the way to amassing these data.

Other people recognize Casey's enthusiasm and expertise; from Point Judith to Montauk, from Bayshore to Block Island, charter boat captains are delighted to have Casey aboard, either as an observer, a tagger, or a participating fisherman. Jack Casey is not just a laboratory biologist, he is a dedicated and accomplished fisherman as well. Once while fishing out of Montauk with John Walton, Casey caught the largest white shark ever taken on rod and reel in the Atlantic: 1,500 pounds, 13.5 feet long. The mounted head is now prominently displayed in the conference room of the Narragansett complex.

On two occasions, Casey was asked to participate in ABC-TV's "American Sportsman" program as an authority on sharks. On one show, he dove the Great Barrier Reef with Ron Taylor to test out a new antishark weapon, and on the other show, he instructed Oscar Robertson, the basketball star, in the art of shark fishing. In this episode, the shots of the mako jumping are among the most spectacular ever filmed.

How does Casey feel about the animals he works with? In Casey's own words: "The mako looks like he's poured into his skin . . . all muscle and no flab. The white shark? Sure, he's big and powerful and nasty, but did you ever notice his tail? It's . . . well . . . *fleshy*, not hard and sleek like the mako's. Actually, I'd really like to see them left alone, but I know this won't happen. Increasing world demand for marine resources makes it highly unlikely that underutilized stocks of sharks will continue to escape attention. Because of their low reproductive potential and slow growth rate, shark populations are easily depleted by intensive fisheries. My hope is that our studies will provide a better understanding of the sharks' role in the sea, and will provide some of the information needed for the wise use of sharks as a resource."

Jack Casey must be one of the most dedicated of the shark people. He is concerned primarily with living specimens, although obviously he must examine a certain number of dead ones. Casey loves being out on the open sea, seeking out, tagging, and releasing sharks. It's a good place to be if you're Jack Casey, the man who would like to be a shark.

Jack Casey, with shorter hair, and the largest white shark ever caught on rod and reel in the Atlantic: 13½ feet, 1,500 pounds.

National Marine Fisheries Service

David Doubilet © National Geographic Society

EUGENIE CLARK: *The Lady and the Sharks*

At one time or another, everyone visits the aquarium or has a tank of tropical fish. In most cases, this early enthusiasm fades, or remains restricted to the area of tropical fish tanks. In Eugenie Clark's case, her first exposure to fishes and their fascination (her mother bought her a small tank of guppies) provided the impetus for a remarkable career in ichthyology, a career that continues today with investigative diving in the Red Sea and the waters of Japan.

Eugenie Clark did her undergraduate work at Hunter College in New York City, took her master's at New York University, and wrote her Ph.D. thesis in 1951, also at NYU, on the subject of the sexual behavior of swordtails (*Xiphophorus*). In 1950 she won a Fulbright to study in Egypt, and collected and examined the fishes of the Red Sea from the biological station at Ghardaqa. Her primary interest then was poisonous fishes, and from 1951 to 1955, she collected and studied all sorts of exotic species, from such locations as Palau, Kwajelein, and Florida. On the occasion of a lecture visit to Englewood, Florida, she met Mr. and Mrs. William H. Vanderbilt, who asked her if she would

be interested in starting a marine laboratory on their property at Placida, south of Sarasota. She enthusiastically agreed, and thus was born the Cape Haze Marine Laboratory, later to become the Mote Marine Laboratory, perhaps the most important center of shark research in America.

Clark moved down to Florida in January 1955, accompanied by her husband Ilias and their two little girls, Hera and Aya. (At that time, her name was Eugenie Clark Konstantinu; she subsequently had two sons, Tak and Niki, divorced Dr. Konstantinu, married two more times, and eventually resumed her maiden name. She is half-Japanese, and both her daughters bear Japanese names, while her two sons have multisyllabic Greek names, both of which were shortened considerably.) At first, the Cape Haze Marine Laboratory consisted of a small wooden building, twelve feet by twenty feet, and a dock. The day after her arrival, she received a call from Dr. John Heller, director of the New England Institute for Medical Research. He needed a shark in order to study its liver. The following day, which was the second day of the lab's official existence, the first shark line was set, and after an impatient night, Dr. and Mrs. Heller and the entire staff of the laboratory went to check on the results. They had caught two sharks, an eleven-foot dusky weighing about 500 pounds, and a smaller sandbar shark. The examination of these two specimens, the first of the lab's official functions, lasted a little over a week, and there followed the capture of twelve more sharks. These were carefully dissected, and in one instance, a litter of shark pups was delivered. The decision was made to construct a shark pen, and soon the first of many live sharks were introduced to the environs of the Cape Haze Marine Laboratory. The first residents were a small tiger shark and a reddish nurse shark, christened Hazel and Rosy, respectively.

At Cape Haze, Clark worked on everything with enormous enthusiasm. Among her subjects were blennies, hermaphroditic groupers, and, of course, sharks. Her first series of experiments on sharks concerned the presence of a pair of abdominal pores located just behind the ventral fins. Ever since her undergraduate days at Hunter, she had been interested in the function of these pores, but despite the help of Dr. Heller and Dr. Perry Gilbert (who was then a comparative anatomist at Cornell, and later succeeded Clark as director of the laboratory), she has been unable to discover their function. She wrote, in *The Lady and the Sharks*:

Fourteen years and several thousand sharks later, after some marvelously rewarding experiences working with live captive sharks, I have yet to find the exact function of the abdominal pores. But it often happens in basic research that while trying to find the answer to one question you discover something else. We learned things about sharks that surprised and stirred us to study more.[50]

Much research on sharks was done at the laboratory, including some interesting observations on their reproductive habits. (The first observation of large sharks copulating took place there, but it was witnessed by Dr. Dugald Brown one moonlit night, and never seen again.) The most

important work was done with living sharks. One of the first such sharks to be observed was a female lemon shark that had been hooked and found to be in such bad shape that it was left for dead overnight. By the next morning, the shark had revived; it swam about in a lively fashion, and gave birth to seven pups the next day. When the pups were half grown, a male lemon was added to this family pen, but he proceeded to eat the young, one by one.

In 1958, prompted by a visit from Dr. Lester Aronson, an expert in animal behavior from the American Museum of Natural History, Clark initiated the now-classic experiments on the learning abilities of sharks. Prior to this time, it was assumed that sharks were extremely primitive creatures that operated almost on pure instinct, and were therefore incapable of any "intelligent" behavior, that is, learned responses.

Looking for "sleeping" sharks in the caves of Isla Mujeres, Mexico.

David Doubilet

Eugenie Clark examines a hooked but very much alive bull shark in Mexican waters.

The lemon sharks that remained were trained to react to a series of plywood targets in the water; as the shark pushed the correct target with its nose, an underwater bell would ring and food would be dropped into the water. All sorts of variations of the techniques were tried—no bell, no food, etc.—but it was satisfactorily demonstrated that sharks (at least these lemon sharks) are capable of being "instrumentally conditioned," and of being trained to perform simple associative actions. Sharks' vision was also tested, and again contrary to the conventional wisdom, it was discovered that sharks can differentiate colors and patterns on the targets, and although their vision is not comparable to that of an eagle, it is quite satisfactory for the job at hand. (The complex optical requirements of these experiments never really proved that sharks have true color vision, but anything that dispelled the old-fashioned image of the shark as a "swimming nose" was a great step forward.)

In 1960, the Cape Haze Marine Laboratory was moved from Placida to Siesta Key, Sarasota, and with the help of the National Science Foundation and the Vanderbilts, new quarters were built. In 1967, Clark's marriage to Dr. Konstantinu came to an end, and she decided to move north. William R. Mote, a retired transportation executive, contributed funds and property to the new facility, and since it

was no longer at Cape Haze, the laboratory was renamed the Mote Marine Laboratory. Dr. Eugenie Clark was the director from 1955 to 1967, and she regards those twelve years as "perhaps the best chapter of my life." At the conclusion of *The Lady and the Sharks*, she sums this period up:

> We found no coelacanth, no Loch Ness monster, no shark repellent. Although our sharks could tell different-colored targets apart, we could not prove they had color vision. But we had many satisfactions and fulfillments, no small part of which were the pleasures we had from the hundreds of visiting scientists and students who used the Lab as a base for collecting and studying marine life, and the teamwork which resulted. Every interested fisherman and nature lover (which I basically am, too) whom we encountered through the Lab's name contributed to the drive and stimulation to go on studying marine life.

Although Clark gave up her post as director of the lab, she is a member of its board of directors, and her enthusiasm for ichthyology remains undimmed. From 1967 to the present, she has been professor of ichthyology at the University of Maryland, where she is enormously successful in communicating her enthusiasm. In 1972, she studied the garden eels and other marine life of the Red Sea under the sponsorship of the National Geographic Society, and she returned in 1973 to pursue her studies of the remarkable Moses sole (*Pardachirus marmoratus*), which gives off a whitish substance absolutely repellent to sharks—and other predatory fishes as well. The photographs documenting this extraordinary experiment were taken by David Doubilet, one of the best underwater photographers in this difficult business. In an article in the November 1974 *National Geographic*, Clark postulated that the synthesized poison of the Moses sole might eventually lead to a shark-repellent substance that will protect divers and swimmers.[53]

In 1975, again accompanied by David Doubilet, Clark went to Isla Mujeres off the Yucatan peninsula, to investigate the mysterious "sleeping sharks" that had been discovered by local divers. Here were reef sharks, lying motionless in caves, apparently ignorant of the popular theory that sharks have to keep moving in order to stay alive. These sharks were not only immobile, but they also permitted the investigators (which included Clark and her daughter Aya) to handle them with impunity. Spotlights did not affect them, but the sudden flash of Doubilet's underwater strobe triggered them into action, and they often bolted out of the caves. Although the results of these investigations are not completely assembled, some tentative conclusions are being drawn. Clark theorizes that the sharks have sought out freshwater upwellings in certain caves, because fresh water tends to loosen the grip of parasites. The remoras that usually accompany the sharks then perform "cleaning" functions on their hosts, removing the leeches and other parasites that infest the sharks.

Thus, in one dramatic series of dives, Eugenie Clark has postulated a previously undiscovered function of remoras, dispelled the idea of perpetual motion for pelagic sharks,* and opened the door to even more exciting research: she and Stan Waterman are planning a trip to Japanese waters in 1976 to check out "sleeping sharks" there. As I write this, Clark is in Japan, on sabbatical leave from the University of Maryland, and the latest news is that she has found sharks "asleep" in Japanese caves.

---

* It has always been known that certain inshore species of sharks can and do rest on the bottom; the nurse sharks (*Ginglymostoma*) and the carpet sharks (*Orectolobidae*) spend most of their time that way.

DAVID H. DAVIES: *Scientist, Administrator, and Public Servant*

On November 3, 1965, David H. Davies was killed in an automobile accident. He was forty-three years old, and had certainly been one of the foremost "shark people" in the world. Dr. Perry Gilbert, writing in a memorial issue of the *Bulletin of the South African Association for Marine Biological Research*, had this to say: "As scientist, administrator, public servant, and good friend, the wise counsel of David Davies will be sorely missed, not only in South Africa, but in many parts of the world where problems related to the sea and its inhabitants are discussed. He has left a rich legacy of ideas, projects, and contribution, which will long serve as an inspiration to those who follow in his path."

David Herbert Davies was born in Johannesburg on March 21, 1922. He was educated in Johannesburg and Cape Town, receiving a Ph.D. from the University of Cape Town. His doctoral thesis was titled "The Biology of the South African Pilchard, *Sardinops ocellata*." (This fish, also known locally as the sardine, figures heavily in South African shark research. The annual "sardine run," during which millions of these fish come in to shore is an occasion for the congregation of all sorts of predators, including sea birds, fishermen, and sharks. During one ten-day sardine run, 1,067 sharks were caught in the nets of the Natal Anti-Shark Measures Board. During this event, the beaches are closed to swimmers.) In 1957, Davies was offered an appointment to the Scripps Institute of Oceanography at La Jolla, and he moved to California for a year, where he worked as a biologist on a research program on giant kelp, *Macrocystis*. He was highly regarded in America, and was offered many prestigious positions, but when he was asked to assume the directorship of the South African Association for Marine Biological Research, he enthusiastically accepted and returned to his homeland in 1958.

With the good humor and grace that characterized his entire career, Davies plunged into his new job, eventually creating one of the finest institutions of its kind in the world. The first building was the Centenary Aquarium, followed in 1962 by the Shark Research Tank, the only large enclosed tank in the world devoted to the display and study of large sharks. In the year of its opening, the following species were displayed alive in the tank: five Zambezi sharks, one tiger, one hammerhead, two duskies, two long-nosed greys, and numerous skates and rays. This entire collection was lost later that year due to a parasitic infection, but by the next year, an even more impressive collection was assembled, including specimens of the Zambezi or bull shark in the 250-pound class. This species was thought to be the one primarily responsible for attacks on bathers on the Natal coast. In addition, the first hammerheads ever kept in captivity anywhere in the world were kept here. The Shark Research Tank, as its name implies, was not only intended for the amusement of visitors; a great deal of significant research was conducted there under the able direction of Dr. Davies. Among the subjects investigated were the bacteriology of sharks' mouths, the hearing of sharks, the development of electrical barriers, growth rate, shark-tagging, and the rate of heartbeat of sharks. Carefully detailed records were kept on all the inhabitants of the Shark Tank. One 240-pound Zambezi shark proved so troublesome (it killed sixteen other sharks in the tank, often without eating them) that it had to be destroyed, and another member of the same species proved to be such a threat to the divers that worked in the tank that it too had to be destroyed. One of the more friendly

inhabitants of the tank was "Sally," a sixteen-foot female sawfish (*Pristis pectinatus*) who was one of the star attractions of the Shark Tank until her death in 1964. (Sawfish are more closely related to the skates and rays than to the sharks, but they are all cartilaginous fishes.)

Davies wore many hats at the Association for Marine Biological Research. He was its director, as well as the director of the Aquarium, director of the Oceanographic Research Institute, and director of the Marine Research Unit. He planned the development and expansion of the Aquarium, conducted his own research on various species of fishes and prawns, attended symposiums and meetings all over the world and he wrote meticulously researched and detailed papers on the problems of shark attack in South African waters.

South Africa, especially the Natal coast, is one of the two most notorious areas in the world for shark attacks. (The other is the east coast of Australia.) Both countries have instituted programs to protect the people from the sharks, the most recent and by far the most successful

David H. Davies.

Oceanographic Research Institute, Durban, South Africa

method being the employment of offshore gill nets. (See "Beulah Davis: The Lady Who Closed the Beaches," for details of the South African operation.) Both areas have the dubious distinction of having generated an entire book about shark attack; Australia's is *Shark Attack* by Dr. V. M. Coppleson,[58] and South Africa's is *About Sharks and Shark Attack* by Dr. David H. Davies.[70]

Davies' book is not exclusively about South African sharks or South African attacks, and it includes such chapters as "Sharks in General" and "Shark Research," but it is generally weighted toward the problems of the Natal coast. There are over twenty species of large (over six feet long) sharks that occur regularly off the east coast of South Africa. This density is probably related to water temperature, river runoff (there are a number of rivers that feed directly into the Indian Ocean on this coast), presence of normal prey, and other less clearly understood factors. Davies lists only six of these species as "considered to be dangerous to man in this area": Zambezi, blue pointer (the South African name for the white shark), ragged-tooth, tiger, mako, and hammerhead. His detailed investigations led him to conclude that the shark responsible for most attacks on the Natal coast was the Zambezi shark, otherwise known as the bull shark, *Carcharhinus leucas*.

In April 1960, a shark attacked sixteen-year-old Michael Hely at Amanzimtoti. Hely was severely bitten and mauled, his wounds including a football-sized chunk removed from his right side above the hip. Incredibly, Hely survived, and from an examination of Hely's wounds, Davies postulated that the attacking shark was *Carcharias* (now *Odontaspis*) *taurus*, the ragged-tooth shark. (In a later paper, he revised this identification, and assigned the attack to a Zambezi shark.) In December of the same year, another man was attacked in Natal waters, this time at a beach known as Margate. The victim, Petrus Sithole, was not as lucky as Hely; both his legs were bitten off, and he was dead before he could be pulled out of the water. Two tooth fragments found by Davies in the right femur of the victim led to the "provisional" identification of the attacking species as *Carcharhinus zambezensis*, the Zambezi shark. (Note that the section on carcharhinids contains the latest revisions of the fluctuating names of this species; what Davies knew as the Zambezi shark is really the bull shark, *Carcharhinus leucas*. In the interests of clarity and continuity, I have retained Davies' own identifying nomenclature, both scientific and vernacular.) Two weeks after the gory attack on Sithole, thirteen-year-old Michael Land had his right foot bitten off while he was standing in three feet of water at Winkelspruit. No specific identification was possible, but the shark was "in all probability a Grey Shark, *Carcharhinid* sp., in the nature of 7 feet in total length." On January 22, 1961, again at Amanzimtoti, Michael Murphy was attacked by a shark in six feet of water. His left leg was severely lacerated, but he survived. From his examination of Murphy's wounds, Davies concluded that it was "highly probable" that the species responsible was the Zambezi shark. On February 1, 1961, in East London, some 300 miles south of Durban, Michael Zimmerman, age fourteen, was swimming with friends at Nahoon Beach, when he was savagely attacked on the legs and arms by a shark. Zimmerman died in the ambulance on the way to the hospital.

The above information is drawn from a series of Investigational Reports written by Davies, and published by the Oceanographic Research Institute. Obviously the shark problem had reached the crisis stage, and something had to be done about it. Davies was instrumental in setting up the Natal Anti-Shark Measures Board, responsible for the meshing of all the Natal beaches. He investigated the factors of water temperature and turbidity, shark repellents, clinical treatment of shark attacks, and virtually every other element that could possibly be considered of value in understanding and thus reducing the problem.

The problem is almost gone now; since the introduction in 1964 of meshing along all the beaches of the Natal coast, there have been only six attacks, none fatal. One took place after dusk (when swimming is prohibited), three occurred outside the netted areas, and in one instance, only a surfboard was bitten.

David Davies is also gone. His brilliant career ended abruptly, and we shall never know how much more he would have contributed to our knowledge and understanding. His associates and friends at the South African Association for Marine Biological Research chose to remember him in a way that they felt he would have appreciated. The Oceanographic Research Institute purchased a 68-foot stern trawler for use as a research vessel. She was named the *David Davies*.

Perry W. Gilbert

Beulah Davis and the author at the Mote Marine Laboratory, in November 1975.

BEULAH DAVIS: *The Lady Who Closed the Beaches*

The waters of the Natal coast of South Africa are among the most shark infested in the world; that is, they contain more large and potentially aggressive sharks than almost any other waters. Not only are there plenty of sharks there, but the coast is heavily used for recreational swimming, thereby creating a situation ripe for recurrent disaster. In 1963, David Davies, director of the Oceanographic Research Institute in Durban, said this about the problem: "In South Africa, 62 shark attacks have occurred off the east coast since 1940 and the problem of devising a satisfactory means of protecting humans from being attacked has come to be regarded as one of national importance." One method used to counter the attacks involved large-mesh gill nets, set up parallel to the beaches, for the purpose of trapping sharks as they swim toward (as well as away from) the beaches. South Africa's premier seaside resort city is Durban, and it was there that the first nets were installed in 1952. The number of attacks in the Durban area was reduced to zero, but since the Natal coast has almost 150 miles of beaches, it was clear that more had to be done. A number of attacks, many of them fatal, took place at other South African beaches, and by 1963 the problem had reached crisis proportions. The government does not always step in when a couple of people are killed or mauled, but since the resort areas were suffering heavy financial losses, the Natal Anti-Shark Measures Board was formed in 1964. The NASMB is "charged with the duty of approving, controlling, and initiating measures for safeguarding bathers against shark attack." The first director was Beulah deVilliers Davis.

Davis is an energetic woman who was born in Standerton, the Transvaal, in 1930. Early in her career she was marked as a maverick (it is important to remember that South Africa is not a country known for its enlightened policies toward women). At the University of Natal she was the first woman elected president of the Student Council, the goalie on the women's international field hockey team, and the first woman in Pietermaritzburg to be issued a motorcycle license. Despite her extracurricular activities, she managed to find time to graduate with an honors degree in zoology, and a year later she received her master's degree. Beulah deVilliers began her career as a lecturer in zoology, taught for two years, and then married George Davis. They had two daughters, spent a number of years in Europe (he was with the Shell Oil Company, based in The Netherlands), returned to South Africa in 1960, and got divorced in 1965.

In August 1965, Beulah Davis had assets totaling about $300, and herself and two children to support. This high-powered zoologist with a graduate degree had to sell Tupperware to keep herself and her family going. When she heard that the newly formed NASMB was looking for a liaison officer, she applied for the job, and much to everyone's surprise (including her own), she got it. In March 1966, the NASMB consisted of Davis, a Land Rover, two borrowed cameras, and a life jacket ("because I don't swim so good"). The first nets had to be set by fishermen, who were taught the job from scratch by Davis, who was only one step ahead of them (she took an unofficial crash course in sharks from Jeannette D'Aubrey at the Oceanographic Research Institute). Originally based in the Department of Water Resources, the first home of the NASMB was a quonset hut at Umhlanga Rocks. Under Beulah Davis's dynamic leadership, the staff and equipment allocations were substantially raised (the entire operation is government-funded, partially by the municipalities and partially by the state), and in 1970 an administrative center, laboratory, cold-storage locker, and boat house were built for the Natal Anti-Shark Measures Board.

Davis, who was made director of the NASMB in 1967, now has an annual budget of R 450,000 (one Rand = $1.05). She is responsible for the meshing of forty beaches (excluding Durban, which does its own meshing). The nets are set in overlapping rows, parallel to the shoreline.

Each net is 20 feet high and 350 feet long. The nets are weighted and rest on the bottom, well beyond the surf zone. (I have seen films of the installations, and in some cases the surf is so rough that it is hard to imagine anyone even *wanting* to swim there. The sharks, however, seem to favor rough, turbid water, since it is highly oxygenated, and smaller fish are found there in large numbers.) It is not possible to catch every shark coming toward the beach, so the idea is to catch as many sharks as possible, from both directions. A great many sharks are caught in the NASMB nets; approximately as many coming as going. Since it is impossible to completely close off a beach—the roaring surf would destroy anything that purported to be even a semipermanent installation—the shark population has to be so depleted as to render the statistical danger of attack insignificant. The sharks that are trapped in the nets cannot swim and therefore cannot move the water over their gills. They drown rather quickly. Over 98 percent of the sharks are caught between dusk and dawn, suggesting that night swimming is to be assiduously avoided in South Africa. The nets are checked *every day* by Davis and her intrepid crew, in their ski-boats, which are similar to a Boston Whaler, but deeper in the hull. If the sea is too rough, or if there is some other reason that the nets cannot be checked for three consecutive days, *the beach is closed*. (Here there is none of the bureaucratic shilly-shallying that was in *Jaws;* when Beulah Davis posts a "Bathing Prohibited" sign (*Baaiery Verbied* in Afrikaans), she has the full force of the South African government behind her.) The nets have to be checked to make sure that they are functional (not tangled up and therefore useless), and the bodies of the dead sharks have to be removed.

The sharks caught in Natal waters number sixteen different species. Those most commonly caught are blackfins (*Carcharhinus brevipinna*), duskies (*Carcharhinus obscurus*), and scalloped hammerheads (*Sphyrna lewini*).

The front lawn of the headquarters building of the Natal Anti-Shark Measures Board, Umhlanga Rocks, South Africa. The catch from one net is being examined.

Beulah Davis, NASMB

From 1966 to 1972, a total of 7,155 sharks were caught. Included in this total were 579 bull sharks (*Carcharhinus leucas*, the species that David Davies believed was responsible for most of the South African attacks), 143 tiger sharks, and 143 great white sharks. Also caught in the nets are makos, lemon sharks, and the shark that the South Africans call the ragged-tooth (*Odontaspis taurus*), known in Australia as the grey nurse and in American waters as the sand tiger. The dead sharks removed from the nets are brought to the Umhlanga Rocks headquarters of the NASMB, there to be dissected, and the species, size, gender, and pertinent catch information recorded. These data are entered on computer cards, for a program that Davis hopes will enable them to understand more about the sharks of Natal.

How successful has this program been? From the time that the first nets were installed at Durban in 1952, a total of six attacks (as compared with an average of six attacks *per year* before the nets) have taken place, none of them fatal, and three of them were outside the netted areas. (In Australia, since meshing began in 1937, there have been *no* attacks inside a netted area. I asked Beulah Davis if she thought South Africa had the worst shark problem in the world, and she said emphatically, "No! Australia has!") All six of the attacks took place at Amanzimtoti, near the mouth of the Umlazi River, and one of them occurred after dusk. Beulah's record is almost perfect; under her strong leadership, the NASMB has made the beaches of the Natal coast as safe as any beach in the world. She is now investigating sonic devices that will repel the sharks without killing them. As with many people who get to know sharks, Beulah Davis doesn't hate them, even though her full-time occupation is killing them. She admires and respects them. "But," she says, "sonic and electrical instruments can fail. If we can get out there and check our nets, we stand a pretty good chance of keeping the shark problem to an absolute minimum."

"Ski-boat" going out through the surf to check the mesh nets. This surf is characteristic of the swimming conditions off the Natal coast.

Beulah Davis, NASMB

Anne Doubilet

DAVID DOUBILET: *Free Lance*

In its original usage, the term "free lance" applied to a knight errant or medieval mercenary whose services were for hire. In current parlance, it has come to mean a creative person whose abilities are in demand, but who does not bind himself to any one employer. David Doubilet describes himself as a free-lance photographer, and although he is most often associated with *National Geographic*, he is his own master, roaming the world in his search for underwater photographic excellence. He has dived and taken pictures in the Bahamas, Ceylon, the West Indies, the Jersey shore, Micronesia, Florida, the Seychelles, the Gulf of Maine, the Sargasso Sea, and the Red Sea. At the age of thirty, he is recognized as one of the best underwater photographers in the world.

For sixteen of these thirty years, Doubilet has been taking pictures under water. His first underwater cameras were 20-dollar pre-war Leicas, which were in an aluminum housing that only allowed for external control of the focus—the speed and aperture had to be pre-set.

Since his family spent their summers at Deal, on the New Jersey shore, it was there that he got his first underwater experience. When he went with his father to Small Hope Bay on Andros Island in the Bahamas, he realized that there was a lot more to diving (and underwater photography) than the murky waters of New Jersey. From the age of fifteen until his graduation from Boston University in 1970 (with a degree in film and broadcasting), he spent nearly every summer in the Bahamas, working first as a general factotum, and then, when he became more proficient as a diver, as a diving instructor. Between trips to Andros, he managed to find time to work on his photography, go to school, and continue diving in New Jersey.

For two summers he worked at the Sandy Hook Marine Lab, and it was Jack Casey, another of the "shark people," who drove him to work. Casey remembers the sixteen-year-old David as "a kid who loved the water—he was a terrific body surfer." At Sandy Hook, Doubilet was involved in research on pollutants, and participated in numerous night dives over the Hudson Canyon. The original diving was done without benefit of shark cages, but after one of the divers was nearly attacked by a blue shark, makeshift cages were used. These consisted of two ammunition crates wired together, with outdoor floodlights embedded in wax for illumination. (As David describes them, the cages, which conducted electricity and "made everyone's hair stand on end," sound far more dangerous than any blue shark.) In 1961, while spearfishing for stripers off Elberon, New Jersey, Doubilet felt a tug on his fish stringer, and turned to discover a large shark eating his 14-pound bass. He whacked the shark on the nose with his speargun, and scrambled up what he calls "a precipitous wall of rock."

By 1969, he was a professional underwater photographer, and was selling pictures to magazines all over the world. He won the prestigious Sara Prize in that year, awarded by the Italian underwater magazine *Mondo Sommerso*. He was the first American ever to win this prize.

In 1970, Doubilet went to Micronesia to photograph the reef fauna of Palau, and in 1971, he went to the Red Sea to photograph the garden eels for Eugenie Clark's *National Geographic* research project. He spent 3½ weeks setting up one photograph—a remote-camera shot of the eels, which hid in their burrows whenever they saw a diver. This became his first published

National Geographic photograph. It was also the beginning of his professional relationship with Eugenie Clark, a relationship which was to take him to the Red Sea again, to Mexico, and, perhaps in the future, to Japan.

During the garden eels investigation, one of Clark's students discovered that the Moses sole, *Pardachirus marmoratus*, emitted a whitish substance that seemed to repel sharks. In 1973, Doubilet joined Clark on an expedition to Israel to investigate this startling phenomenon. In the laboratory at Elat, an elaborate, remote-controlled camera system was constructed to record the reactions of hungry reef whitetip sharks (*Triaenodon obesus*) to the live sole. In every instance, the shark was repelled, and could not seem to close its jaws. Similar experiments were carried out in the Red Sea, again demonstrating the apparent invulnerability of this small fish to sharks.

In 1973, Doubilet and Clark went to Isla Mujeres, off the Yucatan peninsula, to investigate the curious tale of the "sleeping sharks." On their first trip, they found only one shark in a cave; other commitments forced them to leave, and they returned the following year. This time they found the sharks, identified as *Carcharhinus springeri*, motionless in the 65-foot-deep caves. It was Doubilet who suggested that the sharks had sought out the freshwater upwellings as "cleaning stations" for the remoras, since, as every aquarist knows, fresh water loosens the grip of saltwater parasites. Tiger sharks are usually riddled with parasites. However, these sharks were never seen in the caves. In order to examine the tiger sharks, the "sleeping shark expedition" went another 10 miles offshore to set a longline, using turtle meat for bait. On the twelve hooks set, eleven tigers and one bull shark were caught. David dove to a depth of eighty feet to photograph the sharks on the bottom (in April 1975, the photograph of Clark and the bull shark became his first *National Geographic* cover), when one of the tigers, supposed to be too exhausted to move, charged right for him: "I backpedaled madly; somehow my finger got stuck on the button" (it was a motorized camera), and Doubilet got the extraordinary photographs of a tiger shark attacking.

On September 15, 1974, Doubilet got married. Ten days later he took his wife, Anne, to the Red Sea, where their honeymoon was spent photographing the beautiful Red Sea reefs, fishes, and drop-offs. This resulted in Doubilet's second *National Geographic* cover, and the publication of a spectacular portfolio of photographs called *Rainbow World Beneath the Red Sea*. Included in this portfolio was a rare photo-

The shark that wouldn't bite. Triaenodon obesus *could not close its jaws on the Moses sole in the experimental tank at Elat, Israel. Note that the nictitating membrane has completely covered the eye.*

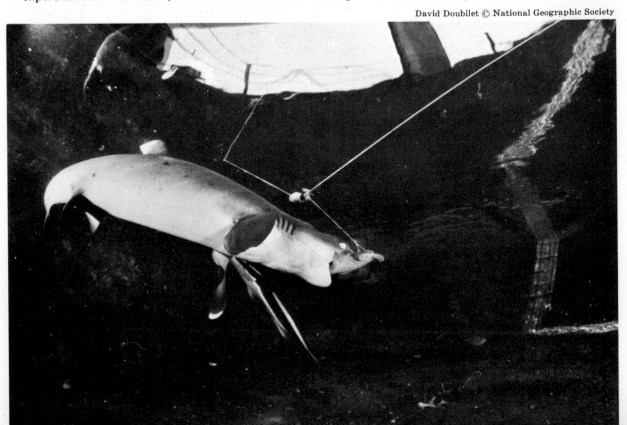

graph by Doubilet of *Carcharhinus menisorrah*, the gray reef shark, with fresh mating scars (the aggressive mating actions of these sharks were observed, but out of camera range), and two magnificent close-up photographs of soft corals—taken by Anne Doubilet. Obviously Doubilet is a good teacher as well as a good photographer.

Doubilet is fascinated by sharks, and feels that "they are the mythical beast of our age, like the unicorn in the Middle Ages. They seem to be a perfect combination of animal and machine." I interrupted him to remind him that a shark was not a machine. "I know," he said, "but they're so beautifully built, they look like they're flying. Like a jet plane with eyes." Of all the sub-

jects he has sought out, he feels that sharks are the most difficult to photograph. "You have to wait for them if you want to get natural shots ... They 'materialize,' they never just appear." When your air supply is limited, you cannot wait too long for your subjects to "materialize."

Doubilet is full of plans for future projects. He wants to dive with and photograph a whale shark; go after the Greenland shark under the polar icecap; shoot the white shark in its savage, lonely splendor, and not while it is being fed hunks of horse meat from a clanking cage. He even talks of going after the most elusive of all underwater subjects, the Loch Ness monster. If it's there, and if it can be photographed, David Doubilet will do it.

Oceanographic Research Institute, Durban, South Africa

David H. Davies, Jeannette D'Aubrey and J.A.F. Garrick at the Oceanographic Research Institute, Durban, in 1963. The unsharklike creature is Ori, a rockhopper penguin.

J. A. F. GARRICK: *Taxonomist*

John Andrew Frank Garrick, born and educated in New Zealand, is the foremost authority on the systematics of sharks and rays in the world today. The subject of elasmobranch taxonomy is so complicated that it has taken a lifetime of study to master it. Garrick has devoted his entire professional career to this intricate study, beginning with his master's thesis

at Victoria University College, titled *The Systematics and Some Aspects of the Anatomy of the Blind Electric Rays of the Genus Typhlonarke*. He received his Ph.D. in 1960; the title of his doctoral dissertation was *Sharks of the Suborder Squaloidea from New Zealand Waters*.

Upon receiving his Ph.D., Dr. Garrick was invited by the Smithsonian Institution (U.S.

National Museum) to "undertake research with and for them on the carcharhinid shark fauna of the world," undoubtedly the most complex of all the elasmobranch families. During his three-year association with the Smithsonian, Garrick visited the major museums and biological laboratories in the United States, western Europe, the Bahamas, Senegal, and South Africa. (When he visited the Oceanographic Research Institute in Durban in 1963, he was quoted as saying that he "did not know of any place in the world with facilities for shark research to compare with those of Durban.") The monumental job of revising the carcharhinids is not yet complete. Since it was begun in 1960 at the Smithsonian, Garrick has published a number of interim papers, or "progress reports." In *Sharks and Survival* (1963), Garrick and Leonard P. Schultz, also of the Smithsonian, wrote "A Guide to the Kinds of Potentially Dangerous Sharks," and since many of the "potentially dangerous sharks" are carcharhinids, a discussion of the problems of identification and a provisional key to identification are included in this important paper. The authors hope that "future study will determine the true relationships of the members of these groups, i.e., as synonyms in some cases, or as closely similar but valid species."[93] The following year, at least one species was eliminated, when Garrick (with Backus and Gibbs), identified *Carcharhinus floridianus* and *C. falciformis* as one species, *Carcharhinus falciformis*, the silky shark.[91]

Prior to Garrick's assault on the problem, there were thought to be over 100 distinct species of carcharhinids. This number was later reduced to "around 60," but by 1967, the date of his most recent published comment on carcharhinids, Garrick had reduced the number of recognized species to 28. Having reduced the working number to almost one-fourth of the earlier total, Garrick still felt that the problem was so complex that he wrote: "As a result of my own studies, I can only offer further difficulties instead of any new or easy solution to the generic problem." I have discussed the problem of the carcharhinids in some detail in the section of this book devoted to that most interest-

ing family, but no coherent discussion could have been written without the dedication and diligence of Jack Garrick. I have not met Garrick, but I have been corresponding with him for years. In November 1975 he wrote me that he had taken a nine-month sabbatical leave from his position as professor of zoology at Victoria University of Wellington, to work on the carcharhinids. Even though he has been working on the problem for sixteen years, I think we can safely assume that the final revision is in sight. In answer to another question I asked about the number of species he mentioned in 1967, he wrote: "There are no major changes in the opinions I gave in my 1967 paper. I have some alterations in distribution . . . and a great many nomenclatural changes, but overall, the picture is about the same."

Garrick's work has not been restricted to the carcharhinids. His "Studies of New Zealand Elasmobranchs," published regularly in various scientific journals, have covered almost every major family, and quite often, these papers introduce a new species to science. In 1967, he published a lengthy description of a new species of mako, the longfin, which he called "*Isurus alatus*," only to discover that a Cuban ichthyologist named Dario Guitart Manday had described the same species in 1966, naming it *Isurus paucus*. According to the rules of zoological nomenclature, the earliest published name has priority, so it is Guitart Manday's *I. paucus* that is the recognized name of this mako.

In addition to the many papers he has written, Garrick has participated in numerous expeditions, especially around the New Zealand coasts, which are particularly rich in marine life. He was largely responsible for a program of deep-water investigations in Cook Strait, and for a major field survey of Hawke Bay. J. A. F. Garrick is not only New Zealand's expert on elasmobranch fishes, he is a scholar of world renown. There is no doubt that the man who has taken on what is probably the most difficult problem in the already complex classification of sharks will resolve it with grace and clarity.

Mote Marine Laboratory

PERRY GILBERT: *Professor of Sharks*

"This makes all the paperwork worthwhile," said Perry Gilbert as we stood on the observation platform above the shark tank at the Mote Marine Laboratory. We were watching five sandbar sharks and one nurse shark as they circled gracefully in the sun-sparkled water below us. "You know," said Gilbert, "sharks are among the most graceful and beautiful of all the vertebrates."

It is rare that Perry Webster Gilbert waxes poetic about sharks, the subject of his life's work. Once, when asked by a television reporter to explain why he studied sharks, Gilbert said, "I'll have to take some time to think about that." One might expect that a man who has spent some forty years studying sharks would have had an early interest in them, or some significant experiences that would have led to his dedication to a single class of animals. In fact, upon his graduation in 1934 from Dartmouth, Gilbert began his professional career as an instructor in invertebrate zoology. He worked at Woods Hole in the summers, still concentrating on the biology of invertebrates. An increasing interest in functional anatomy took him to graduate school at Cornell, where he was awarded a Ph.D. in 1940. It was this interest that caused him to become interested in sharks. "They are beautifully suited to their environment, which means that the individuals are successful, and their methods of reproduction are extremely efficient, which means that the species will survive," he remarked. Intrigued by these animals that had evolved so successfully, Gilbert began to study them in earnest.

His first scientific paper on sharks was published in 1941, and was titled "Notes on Four Male Specimens of the Frilled Shark (*Chlamydoselachus anguineus*)." Although his interest in sharks continued, Gilbert's concerns were

wide-ranging. He studied and wrote about the structural and functional adaptations of diving birds, the origin and development of human eye muscles, and various other zoological and ecological subjects. By 1943, he was an assistant professor at Cornell, by 1946 an associate professor, and in 1952, he became a full professor in the Zoology Department, a title he still holds. (His full title is Professor, Neurobiology and Behavior.) In 1957, Gilbert received a Guggenheim Fellowship to study at the Lerner Marine Laboratory on the island of Bimini. It was there that he was able to study large sharks under almost ideal laboratory conditions, and there that his great expertise began to develop and expand.

Gilbert studied almost every aspect of the shark, using different species, and techniques that varied from working on anesthetized sharks (he and F. G. Wood developed a method of anesthetizing large sharks for as long as thirty minutes), to dissecting dead ones, to observing an induced feeding frenzy from a cage suspended in one of the shark pens. In 1958, the American Institute of Biological Sciences (AIBS) and the Office of Naval Research convened at Tulane University in New Orleans to discuss basic research on sharks and shark deterrents. Shortly after this meeting, the Shark Research Panel was formed, and Perry Gilbert was named chairman. Among the many functions of the Shark Research Panel was the establishment of the Shark Attack File, the first attempt ever made to record and tabulate worldwide attacks on humans.

It seems that virtually every investigator of shark behavior has worked with Perry Gilbert at one time or another. Gilbert himself was instrumental in testing over 200 chemical compounds to determine their effectiveness in deterring sharks. He also initiated the research on testing the visual acuity of sharks and the strength of a shark's bite, and on the mechanics of tooth replacement, the jaw dynamics, the interactions of sharks and porpoises, and various repellent devices, including the "bubble curtain" (which didn't work), and the Navy's "Shark Chaser" (ditto).

Perry Gilbert is a superb laboratory technician, and much of his work was in the area of histology and microscopy. However, as with almost every zoologist, he believes in the importance of field work, "for only then can you get an accurate picture of an animal's behavior." Given the

Perry Gilbert examines the eye of an anesthetized mako shark with an ophthalmoscope at the Lerner Marine Laboratory, Bimini. The "pit" below the nostril is a pin that was inserted to keep the shark's mouth closed.

In 1966, Perry Gilbert was asked to follow Dr. Eugenie Clark as director of the Cape Haze Marine Laboratory, at Placida. Clark had decided to move north, and Gilbert asked for and received a leave of absence from Cornell for one year. William R. Mote had donated substantial funds to the lab, which was then relocated on Siesta Key in Sarasota, and named after Mr. Mote. By July 1967, Gilbert was "hooked," and his wife Claire and five of his eight children moved to Sarasota. He retains his full professorship at Cornell, and returns four times a year to lecture there.

The Mote Marine Laboratory is dedicated to excellence in five areas: microbiology, neurobiology and behavior, estuarine ecology, the biology of sharks, and biomedical studies. It is not surprising that many of these areas are of special interest to its director, Perry Gilbert. Since the lab and Gilbert moved to Sarasota, the lab has achieved world renown for its programs. Gilbert led another expedition, this one to British Honduras, to further test the bite meter, and to record the sounds of struggling fish. En route to the Tortugas to study nurse shark behavior, Perry Gilbert had one of his "great thrills": between Naples and the Tortugas, they spotted, and observed for several hours, three whale sharks swimming together.

Perry Gilbert's office is large, neat, and comfortable. So is Perry Gilbert. He is a serious scientist, devoted to his studies, but never too busy to help a struggling student or a young biologist with a bit of advice or a kind word. Somehow, he finds time to pursue his own research while entertaining visiting firemen, raising money, and administering the 35-person staff at the Mote Marine Lab. As this is being written, he is excitedly planning another move for the lab, writing a paper on the only basking shark (*Cetorhinus maximus*) ever taken in the Gulf of Mexico, and overseeing the raising of newborn nurse sharks.

Perry W. Gilbert brings an enormous, contagious enthusiasm to his work, and he has already had a tremendous influence on the subject of elasmobranch biology. It was he who first measured the jaws of the great white shark in the British Museum in 1962, and concluded that this "36.5-foot" specimen was only (!) 16.5 feet long, thus eliminating from the literature one of its favorite myths, that of the gigantic white shark.

nature of his chosen subject, this is not easily accomplished. The Lerner Lab, with two shark pens measuring eighty feet by forty feet, provided excellent facilities for the study of captive animals, and much important work was done there. However, it had been long suspected that captive sharks behaved differently from their free-swimming brethren, no matter how large the enclosure. This realization led to Gilbert's extensive field trips. Although he has traveled widely (one lecture tour in 1962 took him to London, Durban, Bombay, Ceylon, and Sydney), he did not lead his first major expedition until 1964. This was the Tahiti-Tikihau Expedition to the Pacific. An accomplished scuba diver, Gilbert had the opportunity to observe many species of sharks in their natural environment. All aspects of the trip were successful, except for Stan Waterman's injury, which necessitated his being airlifted out. The expedition took place in the summer, and it was financed by Gilbert himself, with many participants paying their own airfare to and from Tahiti. He raised the money by mortgaging his house in Ithaca. In the contemporary scientific community, where little research is done if it is not backed by some foundation or university, it is a testimony to Gilbert's devotion and enthusiasm that he financed his own expedition.

Perry Gilbert has written over a hundred scientific papers (most of which are about some aspect of shark behavior or biology), and he has edited the two major books on sharks published in this country. Both are collections of papers presented at scientific conferences. The original AIBS meeting at Tulane led to *Sharks and Survival* in 1963;[98] and from a symposium held at the Lerner Marine Lab in 1966, the book *Sharks, Skates, and Rays* emerged in 1967.[102] (Gilbert co-edited the second book with R. F. Mathewson and David P. Rall.)

Elga Andersen

PETER GIMBEL: *Out of the Cage*

This nightmare, which also popped up occasionally as an inner vision by day, always followed the same pattern. I was swimming among the great blues in the middle ground. Abruptly, they disappeared beyond my perimeter of vision leaving only the gray-blue blankness of the open ocean. I spun round and round, trying to look in all directions at once, sensing that something enormous was just out of sight. A form appeared, huge beyond imagining. It came rapidly toward me and materialized as the great white shark, the man-eater. It bore straight in with overwhelming speed, and as the jaws opened to swallow me I would awaken and begin thinking of what desperate measures to take if the nightmare—or daymare—came true. I could never come up with more than two: feed the monster the camera, or spin at the last second to present the big double tank block on my back. In either case the rationale was that the shark would find the first course of his meal so hard on the gums that he would go after more tender prey, spitting out a cascade of two-inch teeth as he departed.

Peter Gimbel
"Shark!"
Sports Illustrated
August 29, 1966

Peter Gimbel is a superb diver and instructor. One can read of his abilities in *Blue Meridian*, in which Peter Matthiessen describes how Gimbel instructed him as a novice diver during the testing of the shark cages that Gimbel

would later use in his film-making expeditions.[164] Even during his nine-year (1952–1960) career on Wall Street, Gimbel had frequently demonstrated his courage and ability. In July 1956, he became the first diver to photograph the *Andrea Doria* (which had gone to the bottom in a collision with the *Stockholm* earlier that year). The ship went down 50 miles south of Nantucket, and in this historic dive in the cold waters of the North Atlantic, Gimbel had to pass through the ubiquitous blue sharks swimming at the surface. While diving on the *Andrea Doria* a year later, a large oceanic whitetip came right for him. He "stuck a knife right in its snoot," and the shark quickly turned and disappeared into the murky water. Gimbel was sure that the shark was going to attack, and his act was one of self-defense. Continued diving in the presence of sharks—in the Caribbean and the North Atlantic—did nothing to dispel his fear of sharks. In fact, he admits to having a "pathological fear of sharks" in those days. Before he knew much about them, Gimbel believed that all sharks were mindless killers, unpredictable in the extreme, and he maintains that one of the most frightening thoughts imaginable is that of "an insane mindless murderer, that you cannot reason with, and you cannot stop."

Peculiarly enough, it was this fear that led him to test out his first shark cage, with the idea of making a film about sharks. He believed that the fear of sharks was an inherent human characteristic, and that people would therefore be interested in seeing this fear articulated—on a movie screen. Some years earlier, he had used an old steel cage that had been left in Frank Mundus's yard at Montauk, and he realized that a good cage had to be more maneuverable than the kind that was simply hung over the side on a cable, subjected to the movement of the boat like a yo-yo. Therefore, his own cage was designed to be maneuverable in the vertical plane; it was capable of hovering at any selected depth by means of an electromechanical buoyancy system on which he holds two patents. When this cage was first tested from Mundus's boat, the *Cricket II*, in 1965, Gimbel was absolutely terrified of the sharks that swam around him. However, Gimbel is driven by a desire to overcome his fears ("to level out the peaks and valleys in your existence"), and therefore, after observing a pattern of behavior in the blues that he felt would preclude their attacking him, this man, who was pathologically afraid of sharks,

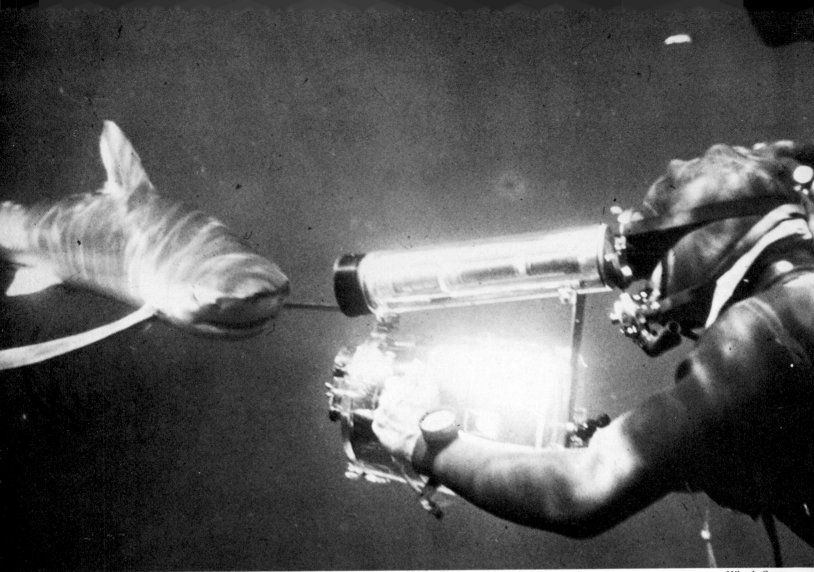

Peter Gimbel out of the cage and filming a blue shark off Montauk, in 1965.

left the cage, and swam among the sharks that were feeding on the chum that was being thrown from the boat above. First they passed the bits of fish, then they nudged the chum with their noses. Gimbel felt that the sharks would not attack a diver because they are interested in a bait that comes easily, but if the bait acts lively or reacts aggressively, the shark will look for something easier to eat. (He is quick to point out, however, that these theories apply to other than the great white: "When you're talking about whitey, all bets are off.") He was later to apply this approach to what has been called the most exciting underwater film ever made, *Blue Water, White Death*. His Montauk experiences in 1965 led to the production of the documentary film *In the World of Sharks*, which shows the sinuous grace and power of the free-swimming sharks, photographed by a free-swimming cameraman, the still-frightened Peter Gimbel.

In a discussion with Perry Gilbert, Gimbel had heard of white sharks feeding on whale carcasses on the whaling grounds off Durban, South Africa. There is no question that white sharks occur off the South African coasts, and this information, together with his desire to make a "major documentary" about sharks, induced Gimbel to make *Blue Water, White Death* as a means of breaking into the film industry where he wanted—and wants—to spend the rest of his days. He sold the idea to Cinema Center Films, a subsidiary of CBS, and they agreed to finance the project. The film was to be about the search for the great white shark, and the first stop was Durban.

In early 1969, aboard a converted South African catcher-boat, the *Terrier VIII*, the expedition began its filming of sharks. The diver-photographers were Gimbel, Stan Waterman, and Ron and Valerie Taylor. The expedition also included technicians, sound men, and additional personnel necessary for the making of a feature-length documentary. Always on the lookout for the great white, they filmed oceanic whitetips, duskies, blues, and tigers feeding on the carcasses of whales killed and left adrift until later pickup by a land-based whaling company. The first film shot from the cages was considered a great success. The oceanic white-tips, *Carcharhinus longimanus*, were by far the most numerous. Named for their exceptionally

Filming off Montauk in 1965, Peter Gimbel was attacked by a blue shark. Note that the shark's nictitating membrane has completely covered its eye.

long pectoral fins, they are heavy-bodied sharks, tawny or yellowish gray, with large white patches at the tips of the tail fin, the pectorals, and the broadly rounded dorsal. They have been described as lethargic and slow-moving, but no one doubts their aggressive inclinations. Little is known about the habits of these sharks, since they are rarely encountered close to shore, but the oceanic whitetip is the species most often implicated in air and sea disasters.

In Montauk, Gimbel had left the safety of the cage after carefully analyzing the behavior patterns of the blue sharks. In South Africa, he knew whitetips and duskies do not necessarily behave the way blues behave, and that sharks feeding on a whale are very different from sharks feeding on small pieces of menhaden. Again, he began to see certain patterns emerging—the sharks would circle before feeding, and then close in to take bites from the whale. Gimbel watched other fish swimming nearby to pick up scraps, and saw that the sharks ignored them. After observing the behavior of the sharks for a couple of days, and without a signal to his fellow divers, Peter Gimbel left the

cage. Gimbel describes himself as a cautious man, whose motto is "Check and double-check," and we must assume that he believes that he is cautious, in spite of what many would call his daredevil exploits. (He has also parachuted into the Peruvian jungles, and dived under the Antarctic ice to film the rare Wedell seal.) He calculates the risks, and acts accordingly. Although he gave no specific signal to Waterman, his action did not come as a total surprise, since they had discussed the possibility beforehand. When Gimbel and Valerie Taylor left their cage, Ron and Stan Waterman did the same. They filmed hundreds of large pelagic sharks at one time. They swam during the day, and by the eerie illumination of floodlights at night. They were bumped, nudged, brushed, and investigated, but nobody was bitten. Gimbel actually swam into the great wound in the whale carcass to get close-ups of the sharks as they convulsively tore off 20-pound chunks of whale. It was the first time *anyone* had voluntarily entered the world of feeding pelagic sharks without a protective cage. Gimbel told me that he did not want to seem arrogant or self-congratulatory, but he believes that this is the best shark footage ever

(Overleaf)
In the shadow of a sperm whale carcass, Peter Gimbel forsakes the safety of the cage to film the feeding sharks. In front of the oceanic whitetip is a pilot fish, Naucrates ductor.

Tomiko Russell

Elga Andersen helps Gimbel suit up as he prepares to dive on the
Andrea Doria, *in the summer of 1975.*

made. (Waterman feels the same way; he said that the "whale film was out in the open, adrenaline-pumping . . . thousand pound animals bumping you from behind . . . it was unbelievable.")

The film they were making was *Blue Water, White Death: The Search for the Great White Shark.* The great white had not appeared in South African waters, although Gimbel told me that its *possible* appearance was the only factor they could not calculate. "The great white is different," said Gimbel; "other sharks bump or nudge first. The white's first move is to bite. It doesn't circle, but comes straight at you, biting flotation tanks, bait, cages, propeller—whatever it sees, it bites." With no white shark footage so far, Gimbel took the existing film back to New York, and asked Cinema Center Films for another $110,000—beyond the $750,000 they had already committed—so they could try to get a proper ending for the film.

It should be borne in mind that this was a film-making enterprise and not a scientific expedition. Gimbel knew all along that they could find white sharks off the coast of South Australia. (Almost all the world-record whites had been caught there, and Ron Taylor certainly knew they were there, since he had filmed them in 1965.) But there would be no story in going straight to Australia, chumming up a white shark and taking pictures of it. Gimbel had believed that they would find whites in the Indian Ocean off Durban, and he had hoped to film them feeding on a sperm whale. The open-ocean footage, even without the great white, was tremendously powerful. It was going to be a hard act to follow.

In South Australia, in January 1970, after ten days of chumming with ground fish and whale oil, two white sharks were sighted as the *Saori* (the boat they hired in Australia) drifted in the chum slick off Cape Catastrophe, but it was too late in the day to film them. They did not return the next day, and the expedition moved south to Dangerous Reef in Spencer Gulf. They

had spent two weeks in South Australian waters, and did not have a single underwater shot of a white shark. Late in the afternoon of the fourteenth day, attracted by the combination of horse meat, whale oil, and ground tuna, two white sharks appeared. There was perhaps an hour of daylight left, and the divers hastily (but carefully) entered the cages, to film the sharks. For three days, these two sharks, plus a third, continued to feed around the boat, and they were photographed almost continuously. The Taylors, Waterman, and Gimbel were in the water for as many as six hours a day with these acknowledged man-eaters that gorged themselves on hundred-pound chunks of horse-meat and hunks of cow. They bit savagely at the boat, the cages, and anything else in the water. Gimbel's pathological fear of sharks was displaced at this time by a feeling of "sheer joy"; he had gambled and he had won. He had not only overcome his fear (in the Indian Ocean as well as in Spencer Gulf, South Australia), but he had the components of a fantastic film, including sequences that had never been shot before. This was the first time that the white shark had been filmed under water. (In 1965, Ron Taylor, leaning over the side of a fishing boat, filmed white sharks as they fed, see p. 275.) The resulting feature film, *Blue Water, White Death*, was a resounding success, and firmly established Gimbel's reputation as one of the premier adventure film makers.

It was Gimbel's idea to search for the great white shark, and Gimbel's calculated risks that produced the superb underwater footage. In these days of mechanical sharks and fictional fishermen, it is important to remember that Peter Gimbel, a real person, swam out of the cage with the dangerous whitetips, and filmed the legendary great white off South Australia as they tried to eat the cages. I asked him if he thought the sharks were just testing the cages when they bit the flotation tanks. "No, sir," he said, "they were biting so hard that their teeth were breaking off . . . Those animals were trying to eat us, no question about it."

ZANE GREY: *No Sharks on the Purple Sage*

The writer of the most popular western novels in American literary history (over 15 million copies have been sold to date and many of his books are still in print), Zane Grey at first seems a peculiar companion of the scientists, divers, and fishermen included in the category of "shark people." The son of a dentist, Zane Grey was trained as a dentist as well. (His given name was actually Pearl Zane Gray, and he wisely dropped what he considered a foolish name. At this time, to further disassociate himself from dentistry and his parents, he also changed the spelling of his last name, from Gray to Grey.) From the moment he hung out his shingle as a practicing dentist, Grey was dissatisfied with this line of work. He was interested in fishing and the outdoors, and his first published material appeared in *Recreation* magazine in 1902, on the subject of fishing the Delaware River. In that same year, Owen Wister's *The Virginian* was published, and the fledgling writer Zane Grey decided to pursue the genre of westerns as a novelist. He wrote fifty-four "frontier" novels, the best known of which is *Riders of the Purple Sage*. His books were enormously successful, and it soon became obvious that Grey had found his vocation. By 1925, he was earning an enormous amount of money, and he began to indulge himself in what was to become his lifelong passion: saltwater trophy fishing. He roamed the world in search of record fish—from Nova Scotia to Panama, from California to Australia. He fished for tuna, sailfish, and marlin, and in the waters of New Zealand, he began his romance with what he called "New Zealand's premier sporting fish," the mako shark.

In 1926, Grey made his first trip to the South Pacific. In an article in the January 1928 issue of *Natural History* magazine, Grey relates with characteristic immodesty some of the results of the expedition:

> *I took, among other fishes, one broadbill swordfish of 400 pounds—the first* Xiphias gladias *ever caught with rod and reel in New Zealand waters; one black marlin of 704 pounds; 41 striped marlin, ranging from 168 (the only specimen below 200 pounds in weight) to 450 pounds (the world's record) and averaging 268½ pounds; 17 mako ranging from 56 pounds (the next smallest being 115) to 300 and averaging 190 pounds. Among my other*

Gilbert W. Dixon

Zane Grey fishing in New Zealand waters, using a newly developed "saddle-back" harness, in 1939.

> *catches was a yellowtail of 111 pounds— another world's record.*

> *This extraordinary fishing (surely never surpassed in the angling history of the world) explains why we (Captain Mitchell, my brother R. C. Grey, my son Romer, and I) were all so desirous of making a second trip in 1927.*[109]

The article in *Natural History*, titled "Big Game Fishing in New Zealand Seas," details his second expedition, based on the success of the first, but this one was less successful, since it was marred by "forty-two days of storm." Among the fish caught on the 1927 trip was a 640-pound thresher shark, which, from the photograph in the magazine, looks to be the rare big-eye thresher, *Alopias superciliosus*. The angler was Grey's son Romer, and Grey, begrudging his son the fish, uses the event as an introduction to his favorite shark, the mako:

> *When the great fish came up so we could see him, I certainly sustained a shock—and I have seen a great many remarkable sea-creatures come out of the deeps. He was a huge, grotesque, frightful and terrible fish to gaze upon. In all my fishing years I had*

1000 lbs. White Shark
Zane Grey

longed to catch a great thresher. Here I
had struck one—a record—and had turned
the rod over to my son! The joke was on
me.

*The thresher must be classed as a game
fish. He fights deep most of the time and is
exceedingly stubborn. Comparing him
with the mako, he is pound for pound a
harder fish to whip.*

*The mako, however, is the aristocrat of all
sharks. It is really unfitting to call him a
shark at all. I seldom use the word with
regard to him. And after he attains some
weight—say over 400 pounds—he is indeed
a magnificent sporting fish. His leaps are
prodigious, inconceivably high above the
water. The ease and grace of this leap [are]
indescribable. It must be seen. He comes
out slick, glides up, turns a somersault,
and goes down head-first, like a diving gull,
almost without a splash. Then instantly
he is out again. Seldom does a mako leap
once only. I have had one go up six times—
a most thrilling sight. His third leap is
always the highest.*

In 1928, Grey visited Tahiti, there to catch a
blue marlin that weighed 1,040 pounds (the
first fish taken on rod and reel that weighed
over 1,000 pounds). Because some 200 pounds
of this huge fish had been eaten by sharks, and
because there was some question as to whether
Grey and only Grey had handled the rod, there
ensued a royal donnybrook in which Grey
credited himself with a world's record, and the
fishing and scientific communities were forced
to take sides, to no particular avail. I have
before me a handwritten letter from Grey to
Francesca LaMonte, then Assistant Curator of
Fishes at the American Museum of Natural
History in New York, in which Grey assures
Miss LaMonte that "I caught my great fish
fairly, and I can prove it." He is worried about
his reputation, and that of the Zane Grey
Corporation, "particularly because of motion
pictures, and this publicity must be corrected."
The *affaire du poisson* ended unresolved,
(Grey did not get the record), and he moved
further away, figuratively and literally, from
the American angling community.

*Outweighed but not outfought, Zane Grey poses
with a 1,000-pound white shark he caught in
Australian waters.*

Gilbert W. Dixon

In 1929, Grey went again to the "antipodes,"
on his yacht the *Fisherman II*, originally built
for Kaiser Wilhelm II. In the photographs she
looks as big and fast as a China clipper—three-
masted with sharply raked bows.

In another article in *Natural History* (May-
June 1934), Grey uses his most dramatic and
purple prose to discuss the mako. The article,
"The Great Mako," carries this introduction by
the editors of the magazine:

*The following article is especially interest-
ing because it is the first account ever published, according to E. W. Gudger, bibli-
ographer and associate of the department
of ichthyology of the American Museum,
of a shark that leaps when hooked. The
photographs, too, illustrate for the first
time this leaping fighter of the South
Seas. NATURAL HISTORY is especially
pleased, therefore, to present this account
to its readers, and regrets that lack of
space prevents the publication of all the
material submitted by Mr. Grey. The narrative will, however, amply demonstrate
that Mr. Grey's claims for the mako are
well founded.*[110]

In his article, Grey maintains that he caught
"somewhere in the neighborhood of seventy"
makos, but he also managed to lose some, since
"the mako is a fish that often gets away." The
article is accompanied by numerous photographs, presenting, as the subtitle of the article
put it, the "First Photographic Record of One
of the Most Fearless Leaping Game Fishes of
New Zealand Waters." The photographs are
quite good for the late twenties; one can be sure
that many of the camera's targets also "got
away," since leaping fish are notoriously difficult to photograph in action. The photographer
can never be sure where the fish will surface,
and therefore he has to be extremely fast (or
extremely lucky) with his camera. The mako
obliges the photographer more than most other
fish by jumping twenty or more feet out of the
water, thus presenting a far greater opportunity
for successful photographs. Grey wrote:

*The highest jump I have ever photo-
graphed up to 1932 is reproduced here-
with. This mako, weighing some 400-odd
pounds, leaped close to twenty feet higher
than Captain Mitchell's boat....*

*Mako leap every way under the sun. But
they always come up stiff as a poker. The*

energy is released under water. Swordfish, tuna, sailfish, tarpon, kingfish, dolphin—all great leapers—move their bodies, gills, fins, tails, in the air. Not so the mako.

Fishing with Grey on one of his later expeditions was "Lone Angler" Wilborn, whose failures and surprises Grey catalogs with a certain degree of poorly disguised condescension. When Wilborn indicated that he would have no trouble with the mako, Grey "laughed sardonically: Ha! Ha! Ha! Ha! Ha!" With difficulty, Wilborn finally landed a small mako, and Grey laughed: "Well, you seem to have had some trouble with a little mako. What will you do with a big one?" To Grey's smug satisfaction, Wilborn replied, "Say, I came down here to fish. Not to fight ocean monsters."

In addition to catching the fish to make records and receive trophies, Grey was also trying to catch them on motion picture film, not an easy task in the late 20s and early 30s:

He came out slick and fast, without a splash as he swept upward, stiff as a poker, gleaming blue-white, with wide pectorals spread and huge tail curled, his great savage head narrowing to a spear point, he was assuredly a spectacle to fire any angler. I yelled with the rest of them. But I was out of position and could not get my camera around in time. Emil, however, snapped him with a ringing yell. I jumped out to be ready for a second leap. It came—a long, low, grey-hound bound over the sea, ending in a furious white splash as large as my boat. That time I nailed him on the film. But it would have been better if I had waited. He shot out so close to our bow that he could have been touched, and he went up to half the height of our mast, fifteen feet above the water, and turned in the air to smack down with a resounding roar. I missed that shot because I could not lean over the gunwale far enough. Then, when he split the water just opposite the cockpit and frightfully close, I was

too excited, thrilled, and scared to remember my camera. It would have been out of focus anyway. We waited, tingling in suspense, but he did not leap again.

Zane Grey was a world-famous big-game fisherman. He roamed the seas in search of world's records and suitable opponents, and one assumes that he found a worthy adversary in the mako. Unlike many of the other "shark people," Grey was not single-minded about sharks; in fact, they represented only a small part of his overall interest. First he wrote his famous novels, and then he fished. In the fishing, he encountered the mako, the most spectacular of the sharks and the only one that can present an element of physical danger to the angler. With other big game fish, the fisherman can hurt his fingers or his back while fighting the fish, but only the mako will leap into a fishing boat (albeit accidentally), with its curved, knife-edged teeth slashing. In addition to the acrobatics of this fish, it was probably this element of personal danger that Grey found so appealing:

I have never loved sharks, but at that moment I repented of my lust to kill these death-dealing engines of the deep. If he had only leaped, I would have let him be the last mako to fall to my rod! But he would not leap. He was the ninetieth mako for me and that should be enough. He weighed 510 pounds and was the second largest I had caught. No doubt, however, he came first in exemplifying the claims I had made—that he was New Zealand's premier sporting fish, as game as he was beautiful, as ferocious as he was enduring. It could not be proved against him that, like the white shark, the tiger shark, the grey nurse, the blue pointer, and the terrible man-eaters of the Indian Ocean, he would stalk men and eat them, but I knew beyond peradventure of doubt that, when provoked or hurt, the mako would kill, and added to that, if he was hungry and tasted blood, he would become as ravenous as any other shark.

SCOTT JOHNSON: *Underwater Physicist*

Some of the most unlikely people end up working with sharks. Imagine someone trained at the Missouri School of Mines and Metallurgy, with a Ph.D. in nuclear physics, whose dissertation was called *Polarization of Cosmic-Ray Muons at Sea Level,* becoming one of the shark people. From 1959 to 1963, C. Scott Johnson worked as a research associate at the Enrico Fermi Institute for Nuclear Studies in Chicago, studying "nuclear, high energy, and elementary particle physics on the University of Chicago's synchro-cyclotron."

From 1963 to 1967, he was employed as a physicist at the U.S. Naval Ordnance Test Center at China Lake, California, where his expertise in physics led him into bio-acoustics, and he began to investigate sound transmission and reception in porpoises. In October 1969, he was named head of the Marine Bioscience Division of the Naval Undersea Center at San Diego, and as of 1976, he is still there, as Associate Department Head for Applied Sciences. Among the problems this division deals with are sharks and the repelling of them, and thus it was that the nuclear physicist from Sullivan, Missouri, came to be one of the shark people.

The Navy's concern with sharks is in one area: prevention of shark attacks on fliers and seamen in the ocean. Johnson's research has taken many forms and directions—from the analysis of shark-attracting colors to the development of antishark weapons. Before starting on this new career, however, Johnson had to thoroughly familiarize himself with the literature on shark attack and prevention. Beginning with the "Shark Chaser" of World War II, all sorts of devices had been tried, with very little success. Almost nothing was known about the behavior of sharks, the only constant being their supposed unpredictability. To a nuclear physicist, unpredictability is a weak basis from which to launch a research program. Fortunately for Johnson, at about the time he was becoming involved in shark research, a number of other investigators were beginning to ask some of the right questions. David Baldridge was preparing his paper "Feeding or Fighting," in which he questioned the hunger motivation of shark attacks; Art Myrberg discovered the reactions of sharks to underwater sounds; and Don Nelson had identified the agonistic behavior of some species. In addition, the material in the Shark Attack File was available for inspection, and a scientist such as Scott Johnson could look for correlative factors that would help him in his search for an effective shark repellent.

There were basically two situations that the Navy had to deal with in regard to sharks: "survival" circumstances, which meant human beings afloat in the sea and therefore *potential* shark victims, and "short-term operations," which had to do with repelling a shark in the process of attacking. (Of course, the two areas could overlap; if the "survival" methods failed, the "short-term" policies had to be brought to bear.) Chemical and electrical barriers had proven to be less than wholly effective, so Johnson turned his attention to developing a physical barrier. Obviously, if a shark could be kept away from a person in the water, no injury could occur. But how to provide each sailor and airman with a barrier that was light enough to carry and yet strong enough to withstand the attack of a shark? In 1968, Scott Johnson went to work at the Mote Marine Lab as a visiting Navy scientist. There he began to work on the "Shark Screen," a large bag made of thin, strong, very lightweight material, with three inflatable collars at the top. The collars are orally inflated and serve as flotation devices, while the bag, large enough to contain a person standing upright, shields the individual from the shark's senses. (Thus the name "Shark Screen." The device serves more to screen the stimuli from the shark than to physically protect the person.) The floating bag is filled with sea water, the shark cannot see or smell the person, and, in addition, blood or other body

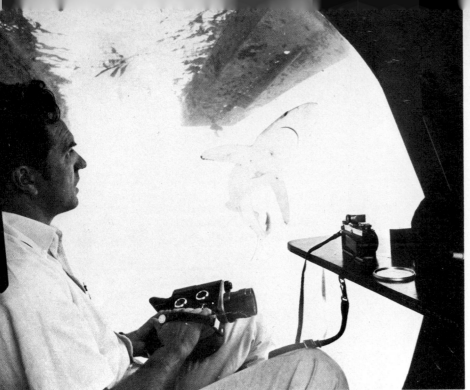

Scott Johnson in the submersible bubble of the research vessel Sea See, *10 miles west of San Diego, California, filming blue sharks.*

fluids are contained within the bag, instead of circulating in the ocean to attract sharks. Many colors and materials were tested, and it was determined that a dark, nonreflective material proved least interesting to sharks, while shiny, aluminized Mylar was the most attractive to them. (Another problem had always been the need for a bright color in any life preserver, since it had to be seen from the air by potential rescuers. The bright colors also served to attract the sharks, so Johnson's solution was especially clever: only the inflatable collars were brightly colored, and since these were out of the water, they could attract rescuers, but not sharks.) The Shark Screen can be folded up to fit in a life jacket, and in addition to its primary function, it is versatile enough to be useful in a number of other "survival" situations, not necessarily in the water. The large plastic bag can be used as a tent, a sleeping bag, a stretcher, or even a solar still, for the collection of drinking water. (See illustration, p. 208.)

In most of the tests, the human being in the Shark Screen was Johnson himself, demonstrating a remarkable faith in the thin plastic bag. There are numerous photographs of Johnson sitting in the bag, while large tiger sharks and other species known to be dangerous, swim around and ignore him. Scott Johnson holds a U.S. patent on the Shark Screen, issued February 25, 1969.

For situations in which a person is in the water, unprotected by any barrier, a different defense is required. If a shark is approaching with

intent to bite, the shark must be stopped instantly and be incapacitated in order to prevent an attack. In other words, the person has to be able to kill the shark before the shark gets to him. (Wounding a shark is not only unsatisfactory, it is probably more dangerous to be in the water with an injured shark than with an uninjured one. A shark that is not mortally wounded will thrash around and bite anything in range, including its own tail.) In direct contact with sharks, all sorts of devices have been employed, from "shark billies" (sticks with a nail in the end) to explosive devices and shotgun shells. Although many of these devices worked, they were often inaccurate, there was always the possibility of a misfire in the case of bang-sticks or powerheads (as the explosive devices are known), and some of these weapons proved to be as dangerous to the person using them as they were to the shark. In addition, there is the strong possibility that an explosion will attract other sharks to the scene, since they are so sensitive to underwater sounds. Johnson has worked on all sorts of repellent devices, including a CO_2 dart that fills the shark's body cavity with gas that is lighter than water and therefore causes the shark to float to the surface; a "drogue" dart that attaches a parachute-like device to the shark, so that it cannot swim; and an electric shark dart, developed with David Baldridge.

Scott Johnson is still working on the problems of shark and human interaction in the adversary situation. In the ocean, his lab is a unique submersible bubble, suspended between the hulls of the catamaran R/V *Sea See* (the bubble can be raised when the catamaran is in motion). From this window in the sea, Johnson observes the sharks (mostly blues) as they react to his varied experiments. Lately he has been investigating a type of "shark armor," made of overlapping plates of plastic, and testing various life preservers for adults and infants in the water. As he sees it, his role is to reduce the danger to humans in the water, not to kill sharks. The films that he has made from his submersible show the sharks in action, and it would be difficult not to admire their sleek efficiency. (A mako appears in one of his films, and in another a California sea lion is seen feeding along with the blue sharks.) Scott Johnson respects and admires the sharks, even though his job sometimes requires him to kill them. He kills the sharks, however, so that people may live.

Courtesy of James Maxwell Watt, Esq.

GAVIN MAXWELL: *Sharking in the Hebrides*

The establishment of a basking shark fishery in the Hebrides was an unusual enterprise for an unusual man. Gavin Maxwell was trained for "estate management" at Hertford College, Oxford, after a series of disastrous encounters with the British public school system. At Oxford, he had shown no interest whatsoever in estate management, and spent his three years there pursuing his childhood hobbies of natural history and painting. When the time for the final examinations arrived, Maxwell worked

hard for six weeks and passed with distinction, proving (at least to himself) that "a three-year course could be passed in six weeks' complete application."

In 1937, having come down from Oxford, he began work at an "egregious agricultural firm," but left after eighteen months to pursue natural history and painting. There followed a series of journeys to Lapland and Iceland in quest of information on breeding eiders, some journalism, and then the war, in which he served in the Scots Guards and the Special Forces, rising to the rank of major.

Gavin Maxwell's story is a truly fascinating one, and it has been told by the man who not only knew it best, but who could also write it best, Maxwell himself. He wrote his autobiography in rough blocks, and not at all in the order in which the blocks of time occurred. After *Harpoon Venture*,[165] he wrote about Sicily (*Bandit* and *The Ten Pains of Death*), Moroccans (*Lords of the Atlas*), the Iraqi marsh people (*People of the Reeds*), and the books for which he is best known, *Ring of Bright Water* and its sequels, *The Rocks Remain*, and *Raven Seek Thy Brother*. The last three are about otters and the northwest coast of Scotland, but they are mostly about a gifted and sensitive writer-naturalist, who had "an untapped wealth of creative and also of technical ability that is damped down and finally obliterated by the standard educational system." This quotation is from the only book he wrote that was intended to be autobiographical, *The House of Elrig*, published in 1965. The quote is from R. F. Mackenzie, and Maxwell uses it to describe his father, Lt. Col. Aymer Maxwell, who was killed in 1914 during the English landing at Antwerp. Gavin Maxwell was three months old at the time of his father's death.

The writing of Gavin Maxwell is clear and brilliant; he has been described as "a man of action who writes like a poet." As fascinating as his life and writings are (he died in 1969), we are concerned here with only one period in his life, the years 1945 to 1948, when he was engaged in the catching of basking sharks. We are indeed fortunate that he wrote so well and left such a complete record of his experiences. He tells the story of his failures as well as of his achievements, without pomp and without pretense.

251

*Just the gigantic tail shows above the surface as Gavin Maxwell's
crew hauls in a huge basking shark.*

The shark story began in 1940, when Maxwell was commanding an antiparachute column in London during the Battle of Britain. Amid all the noise, death, and rubble, he vowed to find a place that was quiet. Poring over a map of Scotland with a fellow officer, he arbitrarily selected some of the outermost islands in the Hebrides, the area of northwest Scotland known for its raw beauty, its closeness to the sea, and its isolation. One of the islands they circled on the map was Soay, in the Sea of the Hebrides, just south of the Isle of Skye. In 1943, while stationed in Scotland, he had an opportunity to visit this island. Maxwell bought the island from its owner, Flora MacLeod of MacLeod, but did not return until 1945. At the time of the purchase, he had no idea what he was going to do there. There was salmon fishing and lobstering, but, he said, "without the introduction of a new industry, it was difficult to see how the island could be developed or improved."

Then in 1943 he saw his first basking shark in Soay waters. (He had seen basking sharks once before but knew nothing about them at the time):

> *It was some seconds before my brain would acknowledge that these two fins must belong to the same creature. The impact of this realization was tremendous and indescribable: a muddle of excitement in which fear and a sort of exultation were uppermost, as though this were a moment for which I had been waiting for a long time.*

Maxwell was intrigued by his first adventure, and tried to find out about basking sharks. The herring fishermen knew only that they were fairly common from April to September, that they often wrecked nets, and that their local name was "muldoan." No one seemed to know where they went when they were not in Hebridean waters, what they ate, how big they got, or how they spawned. For no reason other than curiosity, Maxwell acquired two hand harpoons, which he carried aboard the *Gannet*, a lobster boat that was the first of a long line of boats to be used in the pursuit of sharks. He harpooned a shark which escaped by rolling in the line and bending the harpoon shank double, thus pulling it out.

In 1944, he was invalided out of the military and returned to his island of Soay. After making "intensive inquiries into the commercial possibilities of sharks," he took what he calls "the first false step": he bought a boat for his new fishery without examining it. Throughout the short and tumultuous history of Maxwell's shark-fishing enterprise, he was plagued by boat problems. One boat was so filled with dry rot that it had to be scrapped, another had two engines that categorically refused to work simultaneously, and one of the last boats was purchased before the estimate (which was too high) for converting it to a factory ship came in, so it was sold without being used—at a loss.

Similar crises occurred with virtually every piece of equipment involved in the basking shark fishery, from harpoons to harpoon guns, from conveyor belts to salting tanks. It was not without the best intentions that Maxwell began this enterprise; he wanted an industry for the island, and he wanted an occupation for himself. For the four years in which he fished for sharks, he was beset with malfunctioning or poorly designed machinery, unseasonably bad weather, and, most important, a dearth of information on the exigencies of the shark-fishing business. No one had ever done it on a large scale before; his was to be knowledge gained from experience, some of it beneficial, some bitter, and some not at all applicable to the solution of the problems at hand. In consultation with various people about the possible uses of these massive fish, Maxwell was told that in addition to the liver oil (which he knew was by far the most valuable product), there were also the possibilities of marketable shark meat, "either salted, fresh or as fish meal ... Manure could be made from the refuse ... Glue could probably be extracted from the membranes ... The skin should have a high market value ... There could be many more possibilities at present entirely unexplored." As he later discovered, this desire to utilize the whole fish instead of just the liver was one of the principal factors that led to the failure of the shark fishery. In order to process all these materials, a factory was needed, to which the sharks could be towed, and this took a disproportionate amount of time, that could have otherwise been spent fishing. (Later he realized that a factory ship, something along the lines of a modern whaling operation, would resolve these problems, but the cost was too high, and it was never attempted.) Because of the requirements of building the factory, refitting the boats and redesigning the harpoons and guns, most of the summer of 1945 passed before the first shark was caught. This shark was made fast, and after much experimentation, it was towed to Mallaig harbor. (Obviously, they had never towed a basking shark before—nor did they know anyone who had—and they did not realize that dragged by the tail, the fish would act as a huge sea anchor and keep their headway to a minimum.) At the harbor, two cranes were used in the attempt to raise the huge fish out of the water; after winching it some twenty feet out of the water, the tremendous weight of the fish actually caused it to tear apart, and it crashed back into the water with a "sickening, tearing sound." The tail-less body of the shark was finally drawn up on a railway slipway, and the shark fishery had its first catch—a 25-foot female:

We began by trying to skin the carcass. A South American manual, titled Guide to Shark Fishing in the Caribbean, *had been my only available instructor, and when I reached the words, "now turn the shark over" I realized we were not going to get very much help from that quarter.*

The winter of 1945–1946 was the time of the myriad preparations necessary for the next season and a major disaster in February: a cyclone had struck the half-finished factory, completely destroying it. It was rebuilt, a new catcher-boat (the *Sea Leopard*) was purchased, and by May the fishery was ready for the new season—almost a month late.

The first shark of 1946 was caught and lashed alongside the *Sea Leopard*, this time nose forward, held in place by steel hawsers. After the usual complications and misadventures, this shark was positioned on the flat-car (called a "bogie-truck"), on the rails that led down to the water level at Soay. The flat-car tipped over, dumping the five-ton carcass into the shallow water, "in a horrible position for us to cut up."

By late May of 1946, the season was on, and sharks were being caught, towed in, and processed more or less regularly. On one occasion, Maxwell and his crew encountered a shoal of sharks so abundant that they could not even estimate their number. Maxwell wrote:

Down there in the clear water they were packed as tight as sardines, each barely allowing swimming room to the next, layer upon layer of them, huge grey shapes like a herd of submerged elephants, the farthest down dim and indistinct in the sea's dusk.

In July, Maxwell harpooned the largest shark he had ever seen (later estimated to have been forty feet long), only to lose him when a manila rope with a breaking strain of seven tons snapped when the shark reached the end of it. It was this disappointment that led to the development of the technique of marking each shark with a buoy after it was shot, and coming around to pick it up later, much in the manner of the whale catchers.

During the following autumn, Maxwell traveled to Glasgow, Edinburgh, London, Manchester, and Birmingham, trying to raise money for a factory ship and additional equipment. A large company with other interests in the Hebrides finally bought the entire operation, island, boats, gear, and all. The Island of Soay Shark Fisheries Ltd. was formed, with Maxwell retained as managing director. No factory ship was forthcoming, so the 1947 season began as the 1946 season ended, "with just the same handicaps as before, the same towing difficulties and factory inadequacies, the same necessity for using the catching vessels as factory transport ships."

The season began well, however, and there was one occasion when they counted fifty-four dorsal fins at once, and felt that they were only seeing part of a much larger shoal. So many sharks were killed at this time that Maxwell decided to hire a transport ship to haul the carcasses to Soay, freeing the catcher-boats *Sea Leopard* and *Gannet* from the time-consuming drudgery of dragging each carcass in as the crew caught it. The sharks that were killed were hauled up on the beaches of the various islands, waiting for the *Moonlight*, the vessel that was to pick them up and carry them to the factory for processing.

The ISSF now seemed to be heading toward success; in one two-day period twenty sharks were caught. The first fifty-shark week was anticipated, which Maxwell felt would ensure the success of the venture. Instead, a gale came roaring out of the southwest, keeping them in port for a week, and the 1947 season ended with no more fishing. In spite of this, the season was closed on an optimistic note, with the directors voting to provide a factory ship and a spotter plane for the next year's activities.

By 1948, however, the beginning of the end was becoming visible. The salt solution for the shark flesh proved inadequate, and sixteen tons of fish rotted, with a smell "so noisome, so active and evil it is difficult to find comparison." The *Sea Leopard* was found to have dry rot throughout and had to be replaced. At this time, Maxwell finally realized that the processing of the entire shark was the reason for most of the problems. If they used only the liver and jettisoned the huge and unwieldy carcasses, there would be no need for the factory, the factory ship, and the extra equipment and personnel, and operating costs would be greatly reduced.

As an entrepreneur, Maxwell was a failure; as a natural historian and writer, he was a resounding success. His books and contributions to science bear witness to this. Much of what we know about the basking shark, *Cetorhinus maximus*, comes from Maxwell's experiences, so carefully and sensitively chronicled in *Harpoon Venture*.[165]

Ocean Leather Corporation, Newark, New Jersey

LOUIS MORESI: *The Shark Leather Man*

"Bob" Moresi is the only man I know who can make the word "shark" into a two-syllable word. When I spoke to him in 1975, he was eighty-three years old, and although he has spent most of his adult life north of the Mason-Dixon line, his speech still shows traces of his Louisiana bayou-country upbringing, when he says "shō'ark."

When he was mustered out of the Army in 1918, he came to New York to work for his uncle, Frederic C. Luthi, who represented the Swiss government in obtaining foodstuffs for that war-isolated country. It was Luthi who was originally contacted by Alfred Ehrenreich, an Austrian who had come to the United States to raise money for his new business, the commercial tanning of shark hides. Ehrenreich was highly successful at raising money, but not that good at tanning shark hides. His major asset, in addition to his "abounding confidence," was the "Bendixen Patents," which were supposed to contain the formula for turning sharkskin into usable leather. (Up to this time, it was known that the skin of the shark was extremely durable, but it could not be used as ordinary leather because it was studded with "dermal denticles"—tiny, toothlike barbs that made the skin so rough that it could be used for sandpaper. In the eighteenth and nineteenth centuries, "shagreen," as it was called, was used by furniture makers for smoothing down wood, and earlier than that, Japanese warriors used it to wrap the handles of their swords so that their hands would not slip when the handle got covered with blood.) Ehrenreich convinced a number of people that the "Bendixen Patents" would make them rich, but, unfortunately, the system did not work. Moresi's uncle, Frederic Luthi, had invested over $200,000 in the Ocean Leather Company, and after a sheriff's sale of the assets, Luthi took over the company. The Ocean Leather Company ceased to exist in

1925 (it had been doing business since 1921); a temporary holding company called Leather Finance Company was formed to reorganize it, and in 1927, Louis R. Moresi was made president of the Ocean Leather Corporation, a position he held until 1962.

The first order of business was to find a way—if indeed there was one—to make shark leather from the skin of sharks. T. H. Kohler, an industrial chemist, and Dr. Allen Rogers, a biologist from Pratt Institute in Brooklyn, New York, discovered a process, subsequently patented, which removed the denticles, and left the skin soft and pliable. (Earlier experiments had removed the denticles, but destroyed the skin in the process.) Now that they could remove the denticles, all they needed were the sharkskins to remove them from. In 1919, a "shark reduction plant" had been established near Morehead City, North Carolina, which Ehrenreich and Luthi hoped would be able to supply their tanning operations with sufficient skins. The facility included a skinning room, a shark liver oil plant, and a building for the processing of shark meat and fertilizer, which used steam cookers, tunnel dryers, and other exotic machinery for the reduction of sharks to merchandise. The company owned three boats, each with a crew of four and a "mast and derrick to haul the shark out of the nets." About twenty men were employed in this operation, and at peak periods, the Morehead City plant processed fifty to sixty sharks per day. At one time, "Captain" Bill Young was in charge of the fishing operations, but even with his single-minded dedication to the business of killing sharks, the operation resulted in a considerable loss. (It has subsequently been demonstrated that shark fishing concentrated in a given area eventually reduces the shark population to the point that it is no longer economical to remain in that spot. A shore-based shark-fishing operation which has to bring the sharks back to a specific location for processing is almost certainly destined to fail.)

The Morehead City plant was shut down in 1922, but Moresi had learned enough about the shark business by that time to take over the company with a very different concept of obtaining sharkskins. The tannery was—and still is—located in Newark, New Jersey, and so the problem seemed to be one of getting the skins to Newark, no matter where the sharks were. Moresi took it upon himself to drum up new sources of supply, and he traveled throughout the southern coastal United States, the Caribbean, and South America, getting fishermen to sell him their shark hides. From the Florida Keys to Cuba (where he went fishing with Hemingway), from Yucatan to Venezuela, Moresi told the fishermen that he would buy their shark hides, if only they were cured and packaged properly. To explain what "properly" meant, Moresi wrote a manual called *The Shark Fishing Industry*,[171] which is still as good a work as can be found on the subject of skinning, curing, and packing shark hides. The manual was reprinted several times, in Spanish as well as English, and as far as I can tell, it is still in use, especially in Mexico, where most of Ocean Leather's hides come from. (Shark fishing is a big industry on the Pacific coast of Mexico, especially in the Gulf of California, off the Baja peninsula. There is even an island in the Gulf called *Isla Tiburón*, shark island. Mexican hides are offloaded at Campeche in Yucatan, and then shipped to New York.)

Tanned properly, shark leather is a superb material for the manufacture of shoes, boots, wallets, purses, and belts. It does not scuff, because of the unique "interwoven" structure of the fibers. For a while, its primary commercial use was for the "scuffproof" tips of children's shoes. This use has ended, I assume because children now wear the eminently scuffable sneakers, and Ocean Leather's primary customers are the manufacturers of shoes, cowboy boots, and wallets. It is a fairly expensive leather, and the items made from it are sold at the high end of the price scale (a pair of sharkskin shoes sell in New York for about $65, and cowboy boots for well over $100), but the demand is steady, and business is booming. Only twice in Moresi's long tenure as president of Ocean Leather did they ever find themselves overstocked—more often, they were far behind in their ability to fill orders.

Today, Moresi serves as a consultant to the company, and goes to the plant a couple of times a week. The Ocean Leather Corporation now processes upwards of 50,000 skins per year. One of them was used to make the wallet that Bob Moresi gave me on the occasion of our last visit. I have managed to go through many wallets in my time, but I have a feeling this one will last. After all, Bob Moresi told me it would, and when he tells you something about shark leather, you'd better believe it—he wrote the book.

FRANK MUNDUS: *Monster Fisherman*

Frank Mundus wears a gold earring in his left
ear, a necklace of a gold-capped shark's tooth,
one red sock, and one green sock (when he takes
his shoes off, you see that his big toenails are
also painted red and green), and a shirt that
says "Monster Fishing" on the back. He is a
showman, a storyteller, a practical joker, and
probably the best shark fisherman on the East
Coast of the United States. His boat, the
Cricket II, a 42-foot diesel-powered charter
boat, is outfitted with all the necessary gear for
shark fishing, from spinning reels and thin rods
for light tackle enthusiasts, all the way up to
12/0 reels wound with 130-pound test line for
those after big game. There are also gaffs
(straight and flying), bait boxes, rifles, shotguns, harpoons, and Mundus's own collection of
funny hats and costumes to liven things up
when the fishing is slow. On the rail is a white
wooden box with a dragon painted on it and the
label "Monster Mash," which is used to hold
the chum that is ladled over the side as bait for
the sharks.

From his earliest days as a mate on the open
boats out of New Jersey, Frank Mundus has
had more than a passing interest in sharks. He
was born in Brooklyn, New York, in 1925, and
ten years later, his family moved to Point
Pleasant, New Jersey, since they had been told
that the seashore would be good for Mundus's
arm. He had broken it, and then it had been
operated on fourteen times before the doctors
concluded that he had a mild case of polio. This
arm prevented him from playing football in
high school ("the only reason I went in the first
place—I never was a reader"), and he quit
school when he was sixteen. Now that he was
unhindered by the requirements of school, he
began a career as a fisherman, first working in
tackle shops, then as a mate on open boats
(sometimes called "party boats"), which take
unrelated individuals or groups out together,
their only connection being the boat they're on,
and working his way up to the position of mate
on the charter boats, which small parties hire—
the boat, captain, mate and equipment—for a
day's fishing, usually for stripers, bluefish, tuna,
or swordfish.

Frank Mundus (left) *with a 1,450-pound white shark,
in July 1965.*
Lighthouse Photoshop

Mundus's first charter boat was the *Cricket*, out of Bay Head, New Jersey. He was eighteen years old, and he was now Captain Frank Mundus. Next he moved from New Jersey up to Montauk, Long Island, and bought the *Cricket II*. (She was in Virginia, and in order to pick her up, he had to drive his Model A Ford down South, put the car on the wide afterdeck, and steam north to the boat's new berth at Montauk.) He was now a charter fisherman out of Montauk, and like the other charter boats, his parties sometimes caught sharks. Unlike the other captains, he brought them in. Mundus told me,

> *Some guys would be out tuna fishing; they'd catch a whole boatload of hundred-pound tuna, and then when they saw my boat come in with a blue shark or a mako hanging from the ginpole, them guys would walk right over the piled up tuna-fish just to get a look at a shark! I knew we had something, but they all laughed at me for keeping the sharks—they all thought they were trash fish, so they kept shoving business my way—you want sharks? Go out with Mundus.*

So began the idea of "monster fishing." Mundus still took out charter parties that wanted to fish for tuna or swordfish, but gradually his reputation spread, and more and more of his customers wanted sharks. He began to chum for sharks, using whale oil and chopped whale meat. (This was before the passage of the Marine Mammal Protection Act in 1972, which makes it a federal offense to molest a whale or porpoise—let alone kill one.) Pilot whales, also known as blackfish, were fairly plentiful, and Mundus would harpoon one or two, haul them out onto the beach, and butcher them for bait. It was with this chum slick that the great whites were attracted, as they still are in Australia, where the killing of whales is still legal. (A whale oil slick and large hunks of goat, sheep, or horse meat were used in South Australia to attract the white sharks that appeared in *Blue Water, White Death*, in *Jaws*, and in other recent films of divers in cages in Australian waters, with massive white sharks lunging at them.

Frank Mundus's reputation as a monster fisherman is not undeserved. He has indeed caught monsters. In fact, he harpooned what is probably the heaviest white shark ever taken, some ten miles off Montauk. Hampered by a

defective engine, the *Cricket II* was heading into port with two porbeagles hung from the ginpole, when an enormous female white shark appeared in the chum slick. They threw her all the mackerel they had, hoping to bait her. If she would take the bait, and if by some super-human effort they could bring her to the gaff, it would surely be the largest fish ever taken on rod and reel. The shark gobbled up the mackerel "like peanuts," but spat out the baited hook.

Mundus had to have this monster, so he gave up rod-and-reel tactics, and harpooned the fish. One iron was strongly driven home, and the shark took off with a red beer keg attached to the harpoon line. Another keg was bent to the first, and *Cricket II*, defective engine and all, chased this great fish over "acres of the Atlantic Ocean." In all, five harpoons were implanted, and they towed or were towed by the shark for

The "monster fisherman" (left) and one of the monsters.

John Ebel

Peter Benchley and Captain Frank Mundus aboard the Cricket II, *in October 1974.*

over five hours. Another three hours were required to bring the fish to shore (the pump having been fixed during one of the periods when the fish was towing the boat and the power could be shut off), the fish was dragged up on the beach with a bulldozer, and dispatched with a .30 caliber rifle. The length of the fish was 17.5 feet and its girth was 13 feet (a 156-inch waist!). The weight was estimated, there being no scale available that could handle a fish of this size. The formula for calculating the weight of a shark is given in Hugh Wise's book *Tigers of the Sea*,[255] and it is as follows:

$$\frac{\text{Girth}^2 \times \text{Length}}{800} = \text{Weight}$$

Wise's formula excludes the caudal fin, so we can assume that the functional length of Mundus's fish was 82 percent* of 17.5 feet, or just over 14.3 feet (or 172.2 inches). Therefore:

$$\frac{156^2 \times 172.2}{800} = 5{,}238$$

It has subsequently been shown that Wise's formula, which was originally devised for giant tuna, is not accurate for sharks, and that a higher denominator, such as 900, 950, or even 1,000 should be used. Even if 1,000 is used as the denominator, the figure comes out to 4,191 pounds (the actual figure is 4190.6592), which is some 1,500 pounds heavier than Alf Dean's world record white shark, which weighed 2,664 pounds. Dean's is not only the largest white shark taken on rod and reel, it is the largest fish of any kind taken this way.

The mounted head of Frank Mundus's great fish now hangs in a position of honor in a restaurant in Montauk. About a year after the fish was caught (the actual date was June 5, 1964), Perry Gilbert came to Montauk to visit Mundus and examine the head. It is one thing for a charter boat captain to hang a sign on a mounted head in a restaurant, saying that his fish weighed 4,500 pounds, but it is quite another matter to tell that to Perry Webster Gilbert, one of the world's leading authorities on sharks. Mundus was understandably apprehensive about Gilbert's impending examination. As they approached the restaurant, Mundus was in a cold sweat and he "tripped over every pebble on the way." Finally, Gilbert

* From J. G. Casey, *Angler's Guide to Sharks of the Northeastern United States; Maine to Chesapeake Bay*.[45]

saw the great head. He examined it carefully (as he does everything), paused, and then passed judgment: "Yes, Frank, this is the biggest white shark I have ever seen. It could have easily weighed more than 4,000 pounds."

In the twenty years that he has been fishing out of Montauk, Frank Mundus has caught every kind of shark that swims in Long Island and adjacent waters, including makos, porbeagles, blues, browns, duskies, hammerheads, and threshers. He has had customers hunt sharks with heavy tackle, light tackle, bows and arrows, and harpoons. He has one regular customer, Harry Hoffman, who likes to fish from a small rowboat that Mundus tows along behind the *Cricket II*. (On one occasion, Hoffman boated a 528-pound giant tuna on 50-pound test line—from the rowboat.) Many record fish have been caught from *Cricket II*, including a 683-pound mako caught on 50-pound test line in 1956 (a record that was finally broken in 1970 by a New Zealand fisherman with a 690-pound fish). Fishermen—and fisherwomen—hold many of the International Game Fish Association porbeagle records from the *Cricket II*, and still standing is the amazing record of a 261-pound mako taken on 12-pound test line!

Frank Mundus is a master fisherman; he has a sixth sense about the presence of fish, as do many professionals. I have been fishing with him twice—the first time we got a swordfish and more blue sharks than we could handle, the second time we got one blue, and Frank was willing to bet (no takers) that we would not see another fish—we didn't.

Mundus's method of fishing is not unique. He just seems to do it better than other fishermen. He spreads a chum slick of ground menhaden, seasoned with fist-sized chunks of cut menhaden. He sets three baits, deep, medium, and shallow. His customers are carefully instructed in the procedures they are to follow if and when a fish takes one of the baits. There is the "fast pickup," when a fish takes the line quickly and the angler has to grab the rod, insert it into the gimbal that he has strapped around his waist, and throw the reel into gear—all before the shark has had a chance to pull all the line off the reel. The "slow pickup" is a little less like a Chinese Fire Drill, but the same steps have to be followed. If the fish seems to be a big one, a shoulder harness is strapped onto the angler, to relieve some of the pressure on his arms and shoulders. Once, during the excitement that accompanies the pickup, Mundus shouted, "Get the belt, get the belt," and as the customer picked up the rod, Frank found one of the other fishermen trying to strap a belt onto *him*.

Mundus talks his anglers to their fish, and the fish to the anglers:

> *OK . . . He's got it now . . . Let him take it . . . Don't fight him . . . Drop the rod, keep it low . . . Reel in easy when you let it down . . . If it comes easy, you're doing all right . . . Keep moving . . . He's going over this way . . . Here he comes . . . Easy . . . You want the harness now . . . Clip this on . . . He's taking off again; let him go . . . Strong, isn't he? . . . Here he comes again . . . He's going under the boat . . . Come out of there, dummy . . . Coming out . . . Whoops, back under . . . I see the wire . . . Here he comes, a big blue . . . How much? 550 pounds . . . [Whenever he's asked to estimate the weight of a fish that's being fought, he always says 550 pounds, even if it's a 75-pound blue shark.] . . . Dickie, you ready? . . . When the mate grabs the wire and we get his head out of the water, I'm going to shoot him with this carbine . . . Don't want no live shark flapping around in this boat . . . Here he is . . . Blue . . . Watch out!*

If the angler is going to take the fish in, Mundus shoots it. (Otherwise, he tags and releases it.) A tail rope is secured, and the shark is hoisted up on the ginpole. On the way back to Montauk harbor, with the mate, Dickie Bracht, driving the boat, Frank might remove the jaws of the shark. He does this with the skill of a surgeon, removing and cleaning a blue shark's jaw in twenty minutes. (The first time I tried this, it took me over three hours, and I ended up with a crooked, hacked-up mess, which I threw away.)

Even with the current shark mania, brought about in no small way by *Jaws*, Mundus is not happy with his fishing. He now receives calls from what he calls the "cuckoos," who want to go chasing all over the ocean for the great white shark so they can harpoon a man-eater, collect the teeth and jaws for souvenirs, and then take off after another one. Fortunately for Mundus (and for the white sharks), they are rare fish. Mundus can only fish seven days a week, and he is booked solid now, as he has been for years, but the fishing is not that good. He attributes this to the decline in the menhaden population ("If you was driving on the road looking for a diner and there was no diners, you'd just keep on going 'til you found one, right?"). He says that the bait fish have been fished out by foreign trawlers, particularly the Russians. Dickie Bracht told me that in "the old days [he has been working for Mundus for ten years], we would have six, eight, ten sharks hanging from the pole by noon. Then we'd turn around and go home. No more room." The fishing during the summer of 1975, the summer of *Jaws*, was particularly poor. Within the limited range of the *Cricket II* (she is a slow boat, with a maximum cruising speed of 10 knots), Mundus cannot get far enough away from shore on a one-day charter to find the sharks. Some days he will get two, some days one, often none. He "knows" that the fishing is getting poorer, but he will keep doing it, perhaps going further and further out, as long as he keeps having fun. That is the reason that he fishes for sharks; he does not hate them, he does not love them—he just has fun fishing for them.

Is Frank Mundus the model for Captain Quint in *Jaws*? There are obvious similarities. They are both shark fishermen who know their business. They both operate out of Long Island, and they have had similar experiences with monster white sharks right offshore, except that Mundus still tells his stories, while Benchley's Captain Quint got eaten. Quint was a cruel, bitter, obsessed man. Mundus is a happy, hardworking family man (with a wife and three daughters) who loves his work, and hunts sharks for fun—and profit. Mundus plays jokes on his paying customers—he dresses up in funny costumes, and he recently entered Montauk harbor with a full-dress mermaid on board, to the amazement and lusty amusement of the onlookers.

Frank Mundus may have contributed to the concept of Quint, but he is not Quint. He is unique, and no fictional characterization could do him justice. Captain Frank, the monster fisherman, is an institution.

Jaime Galindo

ART MYRBERG: *The Fish Watcher*

Arthur Myrberg always liked tropical fishes, so it seems perfectly natural that his early experiences with these brightly colored little creatures should lead to a career that he characterizes as "fish watching." Throughout his undergraduate (Ripon College, Wisconsin) and graduate school days, he watched fish, usually in tanks, and often in controlled situations. In one fairly primitive experiment in the Department of Zoology, University of Illinois, he monitored the movement of three minnows in a tank, finally noting (after staying up all night) that a social hierarchy existed. There were dominant and submissive fish, and he wanted to know how they communicated their social standing to one another. This rather simple beginning soon led him to areas of behavioral research that were to become his special fields of interest —social behavior and sensory factors involved in communication. For his master's thesis, he measured the locomotor activity of another small midwestern fish, *Notropis cornutus*, the common shiner.

He was surrounded by fishes, keeping many tanks in his home, as well as at the lab. But what to do with this piscatorial passion? He knew that he liked fishes, and he had gone to graduate school to continue this interest, with the vague idea of going into the tropical fish business. He had come into contact with many scientists and teachers, among them Charles Kendeigh, who encouraged him to work toward his doctorate. Myrberg moved from Illinois to California, where he received a teaching fellowship at the University of California at Los Angeles, and began to look for a dissertation topic. Boyd Walker, the ichthyologist at UCLA and Myrberg's chief advisor, encouraged Myrberg's interests in more than one field of study, and in addition to fish systematics, Myrberg began to study with Nicholas Collias and William Beckwith in ethology, which became his major area of concentration.

Ethology is defined as the biological study of animal behavior, and it seemed made to order for Myrberg, "the man who liked to watch fish swimming around." If fishes were actually communicating, how were they doing it? In 1961, Myrberg wrote his doctoral dissertation on the subject of preferential care of young by adult cichlid fishes. In this complicated study, which used more than sixty tanks, he was able to analyze the "imprinting" facility of adult cichlids. Such fishes, during the reproductive season, exhibit care of their eggs and their young. The question was, would they accept the young of another species, while tending the young of their own species? Myrberg demonstrated that these fishes could indeed distinguish minute differences in the young and retain this knowledge, but it was not until three years later that he discovered the *means* by which they distinguished them—it was a chemical factor.

The "father" of ethology is Konrad Lorenz, who developed the science almost single-handedly, studying the behavior of numerous animals in his native Austria—ducks, jackdaws, geese, reef fishes (in aquarium tanks), and dogs. Julian Huxley said of Lorenz that he "has done more than any single man to establish the principles and formulate the ideas behind them." Myrberg wrote to Lorenz, and eventually received a fellowship for postgraduate study with Lorenz at the Max-Planck-Institute in Seewiesen, West Germany. There he observed the curious behavior of some fishes that seemed to be "talking" to each other. Obviously what was needed was an underwater microphone, and Myrberg became the first experimenter to use this device on cichlid fishes. In the July 30, 1965, issue of *Science*, he published "Sound Production in Cichlid Fishes," in which he demonstrated that adults of three cichlid species not only produce sounds, but use them in specific social contexts. This fact was previously unknown about this group of fishes, which comprises hundreds of species ranging throughout Africa, South and Central America, and even extending into the southern portions of North America. When he returned to take a position at The Rosenstiel School of Marine and Atmospheric Sciences at the University of Miami, Myrberg became increasingly interested in underwater sounds.

An underwater television system had been developed for use off Bimini in the Bahamas, utilizing hydrophones to pick up sounds; the whole apparatus was connected by cable to an installation at the Lerner Marine Laboratory on North Bimini Island. Now, for the first time, the behavior of free-swimming fishes could be observed and monitored, without the usual problems of observer interference. By using transducers, filters, oscillators, and other sound-producing devices, Myrberg and his associates could affect, and to some extent control, by remote means, the behavior of reef fishes one and a half miles away!

So far, the word "shark" has not appeared in this essay on the activities of Dr. Arthur A. Myrberg, Jr. He is not a "shark person" in that he has an overwhelming interest in sharks —to him they are interesting subjects for etho-logical studies, efficient predators whose behavior is worth examining. Through the use of pulsed sounds, sharks were attracted to the transducers off Bimini: reef sharks, sharpnoses, and nurses. A major program of investigation was begun, to see if and how this information could be put to use. The question: Could sound be used to *control* sharks? It had already been demonstrated that sounds attracted them, and from the behaviorist's point of view, this was a major discovery. Understanding an animal involves learning what affects it, and there was no question that sound seemed to play a sig-nificant role in the reactions of sharks. It is now believed that low-frequency sounds such as those broadcast off Bimini resemble the vibra-tions given off by thrashing fishes, and that sharks often use such vibrations to locate pos-sible prey.

From Bimini, Myrberg took his studies to the deep waters of the Florida Straits and also to Tongue of the Ocean (also in the Bahamas), where his experiments involved oceanic species such as the dangerous whitetip (*Carcharhinus longimanus*) and the silky (*Carcharhinus falciformis*). These predators could also be attracted by sounds, and then made to turn away from the sound source by sudden, slight changes in the intensity of the transmitted signals. Myrberg concluded that sharks may have an internal mechanism that provides its owner with ongoing information about changes in its immediate environment relative to "go, no-go" decisions, affecting in turn important energy expenditure (most predators do not chase their prey if they would have to expend too much energy in catching it). Such a sudden change in the nature of an ongoing sound might be precisely the type of information that would result in a "no-go" decision, and this just might

deter the shark from its direct course. It was also shown that sharks learned rapidly about the value of a sound played repetitively. If no "reward," such as a piece of fish, was forth-coming, sharks soon ignored otherwise attrac-tive sounds.

Insofar as practical applications of this knowl-edge are concerned, it is obvious that the ability to attract sharks can be useful on two counts: (1) when one wants sharks in a particular area, say, for experimental purposes, and (2) when one wants sharks *away* from a particular area. (In the second case, one plays the sounds at a distance from where a given job is being per-formed; the assumption is that the sharks will head for the broadcast sound and vacate the area where the divers are working.) Another, less obvious issue presents itself, and that in-volves the sounds emitted by a hovering heli-copter. These are low-frequency, regularly pulsed sounds, very much like those used by Myrberg to attract sharks. Thus it seems pos-sible that in the process of going to the rescue of fliers or shipwreck victims, we may in fact be attracting sharks to the scene.

Another area of shark research taken up by Dr. Myrberg concerned the behavior of the bonnet-head (*Sphyrna tiburo*), a small species of hammerhead. Here, for the first time in con-trolled conditions (a "seminatural" enclosure at the Miami Seaquarium), the social behavior of a colony of sharks was observed over a fairly long period of time (six months). It was seen that they exhibited socially relevant actions, which were generally well organized, but not fully understood by the observers. The behavior observed indicated once again that sharks exhibit not random "unpredictable" behavior, but, instead, regular behavior. What we need are the time and the qualifications to under-stand what we are seeing. In the near future, Myrberg plans to carry out another behavioral study—similar to that carried out on the bonnethead—but this time it will be centered on one of the small requiem species. This is an important study since we know almost nothing about the behavior of these species, which are often involved in encounters with humans.

The man who just liked to watch fishes swim has given us new insight into the behavior of sharks. He has shown that sharks, like other animals that have been carefully observed, can be understood best by those who watch them best.

DON NELSON: *Sound in the Water*

Donald Richard Nelson was born in Plainfield, New Jersey, in 1937. He graduated from Rutgers with a degree in biological science in 1958, and has been chasing (and being chased by) sharks ever since. He is perhaps the most single-minded of the shark people, in that almost all of his professional activities have been involved with sharks. His doctoral dissertation at the University of Miami was titled *Hearing and Acoustic Orientation in the Lemon Shark.*[178] During his time at the University of Miami, he became a proficient diver, and he spent many weekends on the reefs off the Florida keys, where he became acquainted with the great diversity of fish life found there. Among this fish life were sharks. Nelson and his skin-diving companions had many encounters with bull sharks, tigers, and hammerheads, and on New Year's Day 1960, while diving off Grassy Key, Nelson met a great white shark:

> *My mind abruptly switched from identification to self-defense. As the shark neared, the large mouth with its prominent teeth became visible beneath the conical snout. I was thankful for the speargun I held but decided against firing my one spear except as a last resort. The shark came so close that I had to withdraw the gun for fear of touching its snout and possibly inciting it. Finally, with the shark at arm's length, I shouted and shook the gun in its face. The shark turned—not much—but enough to avoid hitting me and slowly passed by on my left side about a meter and a half away. For a very long minute or so the shark and I swam parallel, eye to eye, until it moved away and circled in the distance.*[179]

For his graduate research on sharks, Nelson studied under Dr. Warren Wisby. It was during this period that the sharks' ability to hear and react to low-frequency sounds was discovered. Nelson trained captive lemon sharks to respond to sound coming from underwater speakers; when they heard the sound, they would rush toward the source, where they would be rewarded with food. During this research, which was the basis of his doctoral dissertation, it was discovered that sharks have particularly sensitive hearing, especially in the very low frequencies. It was also shown that sharks possess directional hearing, which suggested one explanation for why they are able to locate their prey so quickly. Nelson postulated that this sensitivity to low-frequency sounds was the primary means by which the shark detected wounded, thrashing fish—but this was a hypothesis that had to be tested. Working with Samuel Gruber (then a graduate student; now one of the foremost shark researchers), Nelson recorded the sounds made by speared fish, and then played them back in the open ocean. These sounds attracted tiger sharks, bull sharks, hammerheads, and lemon sharks. (To determine the distances from which the sharks were being attracted, Nelson, Gruber, and Wisby took to the air, in a coordinated airplane-boat operation, and observed that the sharks approaching the sound began to do so from a distance far beyond their range of vision, sometimes as far away as 200 yards from the source of the sound.)

From the Florida reefs, Nelson took his research to Tongue of the Ocean in the Bahamas, to study the "blue-water" or pelagic sharks: oceanic whitetips, *Carcharhinus longimanus*, and silky sharks, *C. falciformis*. Diving with Jerry Greenberg, a well-known underwater photographer, Nelson observed the aggressive behavior of these sharks. On one occasion, while diving in the Gulf Stream off Florida, Nelson was actually attacked by a silky shark that had been baited to the boat. As the shark closed in on him for the second time, he managed to kill it with a powerhead.

In 1969, Don Nelson had his first taste of the tropical Pacific, while on the World Life Research Institute Expedition to Rangiroa in French Polynesia. With his student Richard Johnson, he conducted the first of a series of studies of Pacific reef sharks. In 1971, they went to Eniwetok in the Marshall Islands, to test the effect of "acoustic pulse intermittency and variability" on reef sharks. They suspended the transducer in the water about sixty feet below the observation vessel. During the broadcast of the low-frequency pulsed sounds, a total of 253 sharks appeared, while only 44 sharks were seen during the control periods, when no sounds were broadcast. (In one spectacular playback period, 35 sharks arrived within two minutes, excited to the point of rushing and biting the sound speaker.) Also during these tests, Nelson and Johnson observed the "agonistic" behavior of the gray reef shark, *Carcharhinus menisorrah*. They hypothesized that "under these circumstances, display was triggered by a conflict between one tendency to approach the source of sound (food motivated) and another tendency to withdraw from the unfamiliar apparatus (escape motivated)."

Johnson and Nelson began to investigate this behavior more carefully. Previous observers had noticed similar reactions in *C. menisorrah*, but this was the first effort made specifically to study, film, and analyze this unusual behavior. They wrote (in *Copeia*, 1973):

> *Ten test trials were conducted (no further were attempted due to the danger involved) which consisted of a diver rapidly swimming at a shark coming in on an initial approach. The diver remained stationary until the shark closed to within approximately 6.5 m at which time the charge [by the diver] was initiated.*[143]

The sharks displayed uncharacteristic swimming motions (back hunched, pectoral fins dropped, exaggerated "rolling" movements), in what the scientists describe as "approach-withdrawal conflict situations." They feel that this behavior ("agonistic" is defined as "striv-

Shark tagging in French Polynesian waters, Don Nelson takes aim at a whitetip reef shark, Triaenodon obesus.

D. J. Mosher

ing to overcome an argument; competitive; combative") is ritualized and probably also of some value in the shark's normal social encounters. The behavior—as elicited by approaching divers—probably represents a defensive action, which, if allowed to continue, could easily result in an attack (as it has in several incidents subsequent to their study). During some of the tests, the divers cornered the sharks, and found that closing off the sharks' escape route triggered the most intense agonistic responses. The concept of territoriality in sharks appears a distinct possibility, and Johnson and Nelson feel that "agonistic motivation must be considered a potentially widespread cause of shark attacks on man."

Nelson's latest endeavors involve ultrasonic telemetry, which means that he tracks and monitors sharks by attaching transmitters to free-ranging individuals. These small devices enable the investigator to study the movements of the shark (some contain sensors for speed, depth, etc.) and also to locate a specific shark at a given moment. This project, funded by the Office of Naval Research, is concerned with both instrument development and the actual monitoring of behavior. Nelson is looking forward to the time when, through the use of ultrasonic telemetry, otherwise unobtainable data can be gained on feeding, reproduction, and other little-known areas of shark behavior. Telemetry work is now being conducted with blue sharks off the California coast (Nelson is now associate professor at California State University, Long Beach), and already some surprising information has come to light. One of Nelson's students, Terry Sciarotta, using biotelemetry, discovered that "blue sharks, normally found offshore, unexpectedly moved in close to the Santa Catalina Island shoreline at night." There are several methods of transmitter application under investigation. Transmitters can be externally attached to a fin or to the back; placed in the body cavity by means of an incision; or "self-ingested," by being disguised in a bait. In a letter to me, Nelson wrote: "This telemetry technique, I believe, holds the greatest promise for really finding out what sharks do, day-in-

day-out, in the natural habitat—which is really a very concealing place for such wide-ranging, secretive, and basically nocturnal animals."

In September 1972, accompanied by his wife, Victoria, and Richard Johnson, Nelson set out on his most ambitious venture. With support from the National Geographic Society, they sailed from California aboard the forty-foot diesel ketch *Sokende Hai* (a Norwegian phrase meaning "in quest of shark") on a two-year research expedition to French Polynesia. Based in Rangiroa, the largest of the Tuamotu atolls, the expedition was concerned with an "in-the-water" study of the behavior of reef sharks, using techniques of direct underwater observation, conventional tagging, and ultrasonic telemetry. Data were gathered on day versus night patterns of activity, home ranges, grouping, agonistic display, dominance, courtship, responses to sounds, symbiosis, feeding, and reaction to humans. Major study effort was on the gray reef shark, and the reef whitetip, *Triaenodon obesus*. Both species were found to be primarily nocturnal, with limited home ranges, and were quite predictable in their day-night timetables of activity. As of this writing, the expedition is formally over, and Nelson's primary efforts are now in California, summarizing, analyzing, and writing up the data. Richard Johnson has stayed on in French Polynesia, and is continuing the shark research, especially on the subject of agonistic display in the gray reef shark.

From the success of their earlier experiments, we can assume that Don Nelson and his students will continue to add to our knowledge of shark behavior. Eventually, Nelson plans to use a unique "shark-observation submersible," which will enable him to intercept and observe sharks at greater depths (300 to 400 feet), and will also, according to a letter he wrote me, "provide protection from shark attack—a significant danger I am becoming increasingly aware of." Since Don Nelson has probably been attacked and threatened by sharks more often than anyone else, this realization about protection seems overdue.

Helen Randall

JACK RANDALL: *Diving Ichthyologist*

During his distinguished career in ichthyology, Dr. John E. Randall has managed to be where the fish are plentiful, the diving good, and the weather warm. His *curriculum vitae* reads like an advertisement for a worldwide fish watchers tour. This may not all have been done intentionally, but, on the other hand, when you find out where he's been to do his work, it's hard to imagine that it was all accidental.

Randall was born in California, went to school there, and graduated from UCLA with a B.A. in zoology in 1950. Most other people drive or take a bus or train to graduate school; Randall and three companions set out for Hawaii in a 37-foot ketch. He received his Ph.D. in marine zoology in 1955 from the University of Hawaii and then set off for Tahiti to study the biology of certain groupers and snappers. By 1957, he was back on the mainland, not in some cold, dreary, university town, but at the University of Miami, where he spent one year, and then he went to St. John to work at the Virgin Islands National Park. From the Virgin Islands, Randall moved to the University of Puerto Rico, where he was professor of zoology and director of the Institute of Marine Biology, then back to Hawaii in 1965, where he worked as director of the Oceanic Institute. In 1969, he joined the staff of the Bishop Museum in Honolulu, where he works as of this writing.

Even though it sounds as if Randall chooses his locations for their scenic beauty or their tropical climates, he is, in fact, a hard-working and dedicated ichthyologist who has published over 150 scientific papers (counting those "in press"), and whose studies in the Caribbean led to the publication of *Caribbean Reef Fishes*, one of the most comprehensive guides in existence to this varied and colorful fauna. (The book, which is far more than a simple field guide, is superbly illustrated with black-and-white and color photographs, all taken by Randall.)

In 1963, while working on St. John, Randall was notified of a fatal shark attack at Magen's

Bay, St. Thomas. It was the first shark attack within anyone's memory in the Virgin Islands, and Randall hastened to the scene. A Navy UDT diver, Lt. John Gibson, had been attacked while swimming, and he was dead by the time his companions got him out of the water. The following day, shark hooks were set in the area, and a ten-foot shark was caught. When the shark was dissected, Gibson's right hand was found in its stomach. There was no question that this was the shark that killed Gibson, but there was a question as to what kind of shark it was. Randall tentatively identified it as *Carcharhinus springeri*, the reef shark, but "there were differences . . . between the specimen and the descriptions of *springeri.*" At the time, Dr. J. A. F. Garrick was at the U.S. National Museum working on the Carcharhinidae, so Randall sent him the jaws, the measurements, and "other pieces saved from the shark." Garrick identified the shark as *Carcharhinus galapagensis*, a species previously known only from the oceanic islands of the Indo-Pacific region.

Randall was recognized as an authority on the fishes of the Caribbean, sharks included, and he was asked to contribute the chapter on the dangerous sharks of the western Atlantic to *Sharks and Survival*,[193] which was published in 1963. In his detailed and carefully documented paper, he discusses specific attacks by different species, and identifies those sharks known to be dangerous in the specified area.

As a diver, Jack Randall has more than a passing interest in sharks. He was chased by an unidentified carcharhinid in 1961, but he made "an overt movement in the direction of the shark, and it veered off." He is also concerned with the many misconceptions that exist about sharks, and he has tried to clear up many of them in his popular writings. For instance, in 1961, he wrote an article for *Sea Frontiers*, titled "Let a Sleeping Shark Lie," in which he recorded the numerous attacks on divers by the supposedly docile and harmless nurse shark, *Ginglymostoma cirratum*.[195] In almost every instance the attack was provoked by a diver grabbing the shark's tail, but the nurse shark, which can reach a length of ten feet and perhaps even more, should not be trifled with. This shark, which can lie motionless on the bottom, serves as a tempting target for a diver who would exhibit his bravery, but, as Randall says, "If the nurse shark is grabbed by the tail or speared, . . . it is very capable of putting its tormentor in the hospital."

*Jack Randall emerging from an underwater cave at Oeno, Pitcairn Island,
with two whitetip reef sharks.*

Another misconception that Randall helped to dispel was that of the "36.5-foot" white shark. I have discussed this anomaly elsewhere, but it is to Randall's credit that he was one of the few scientists who were curious enough to actually measure the jaws in question, at the British Museum. He concluded that the "Port Fairy" specimen was only about 17 feet long, based on a comparison of the tooth heights of this and other known specimens. (In the same discussion, Randall also suggests that there are white sharks as long as "25 or 26 feet," but to date, the longest specimen measured was 21 feet.)

In his travels throughout the islands of the South Pacific, Randall has come into contact with many different species of sharks. In 1957, while he was collecting fish at a depth of eighty feet outside the barrier reef at Moorea, a small blacktip reef shark (*Carcharhinus melanopterus*) approached him in an aggressive manner, "so a decision was made to terminate the collecting sooner than planned." Other information on the aggressive behavior of this small shark (it reaches a maximum length of about six feet) prompted Randall to investigate reports of attacks, and he was surprised to discover ten attacks not previously reported in the literature. Only three of these attacks had resulted in wounds, but there seemed to be no question that *melanopterus* would aggressively defend its shallow-water habitat. (Its Palauan name, *matukeyoll*, means "to dash at and turn quickly.")

Jack Randall has collected reef fishes all over the world, and has added considerably to our ichthyological knowledge. Most of his work has been with bony fishes (although he has done extensive work on marine invertebrates such as the crown-of-thorns starfish, *Acanthaster planci*), but I regard him as a shark person, and he agrees. His latest project, unpublished as of my most recent communication with him, is on the biology of the whitetip reef shark, *Triaenodon obesus*. Through the use of an extensive tagging program, he has learned that this species is nonmigratory, and that certain individuals seem to have a specific home territory; that is, they inhabit the same caves while "resting," over long periods of time. Another paper, which Randall is co-authoring and which is in press at this time, concerns the first authenticated instance of a mako attack resulting in a wound to the diver. The other author is Dr. Levy, who treated the victim.

267

BRIAN RODGER, RODNEY FOX, HENRI BOURCE: *The Survivors*

In March 1961, Brian Rodger was swimming with Rodney Fox at Aldinga Beach, south of Adelaide, in a spearfishing competition. Rodger was hit by a white shark, estimated to be about twelve feet long, and his entire lower torso was taken into the shark's mouth. As he tried to gouge the shark's eye, he plunged his arm into the shark's mouth. After ripping his hand on the shark's teeth he fired a spear into the top of the animal's head, and he "realized just how serious my condition was. Looking down at my leg, laid open to the bone in enormous rents from which the blood clouded and at my shredded and lacerated arm, I knew that unless I could stop the bleeding I wouldn't make the distant shore." He tied the rubber sling from his speargun around his upper thigh as a tourniquet, and began to swim for shore. He was picked up by a rowboat, taken to the Royal Adelaide Hospital, and after a three-hour operation, he survived to dive again.

But what of Rodney Fox, who was in the water with Rodger at the time of the attack? He never saw it happen, because he was below the surface. He did see the white shark, since it circled him after the attack, but eventually it swam off. That year, Rodney Fox won the South Australia State Spearfishing Championship. He was runner-up in 1962, the year that Geoff Corner was attacked and killed at Caracalinga Head, 15 miles south of Aldinga, where Brian Rodger had been attacked in 1961.

Aldinga Beach, August 12, 1963. The South Australia State Spearfishing Championship competition is based on the number of species caught as well as the total weight of all fish caught. One must seek out the rare species in addition to the larger, common fishes. It had been assumed that the speared fish the divers carried with them had contributed to the attacks in the previous years, so this time boats were sent periodically to pick up their catch, thus avoiding the problem of trails of dead and bleeding fish. (These are "free diving" exercises; no tanks or other breathing apparatus are used.)

"The Survivors" inspecting the wound made in one of the white sharks that was attacked by another. Left to right: Rodney Fox, Brian Rodger, Henri Bource.

Ron Taylor

Fox was swimming with Bruce Farley, when he saw a pair of dusky morwongs, which he felt would add considerably to his total. He took a breath and dove down to the coral head where he had seen the fish. He was in about fifty feet of water, over a patch of brown algae, ready to shoot the morwong, when he "sensed" a stillness in the water around him: "It was a silence. A perceptible hush. . . . Then something huge hit me on the left side with enormous force and surged me through the water. I knew at once what had happened—and was dazed with horror." His face mask was knocked off, and his speargun flew from his hand. With no mask, he was unable to see clearly, and he reached back (as Rodger had done, and with the same disastrous results) to try to gouge the shark's eyes. He pushed his hand down the shark's throat, then yanked it back out while the terrible serrated teeth tore his arm to the bone. At this moment, the shark released him and he kicked for the surface, feeling the shark under his flippers all the way. He managed to gulp one breath of air before the shark brushed by him, and he grabbed it to avoid being bitten again. With his arms and legs wrapped around this horrible steed, Fox was swooped to the bottom, where the shark tried to scrape him off on the rocks. Fox released his hold, and struggled to the top for air. In water red with his own blood, he surfaced and looked down to see "the head of the shark . . . conical snout, great rolling body like a rust-colored tree trunk."

This time the shark grabbed Fox's fish float (which was still attached to his belt), heeled over, and dragged him below again. "It seemed ridiculous to die of drowning after all I'd been through. But my fumbling fingers couldn't undo the belt." Somehow, perhaps because the shark's knife-sharp teeth cut it, the line parted, and Fox was free to float to the surface—for the third time, but the first time he was not in contact with the shark. By luck, a boat was only a few yards away when he burst to the surface yelling, "Shark!" In the boat, his injuries were seen to be terrible. His rib cage, upper stomach, and lungs were exposed; the bones of his arm were bared, his ribs were crushed, and one of his lungs was punctured. He was wearing a full black wet suit, and this was left on him in the boat. (When they had tried to remove Brian Rodger's wet suit in 1961, "his leg fell all apart.")

A series of fortuitous events (some have called them miracles) occurred with Fox's landing on the beach at Aldinga—starting with the appear-

T. Walker Lloyd/Rolex Watch Corp.

Rodney Fox.

ance of a policeman as soon as the boat had been beached. Fox was put into a car (which just happened to be close by), they headed for Adelaide, and an ambulance was dispatched to meet the car en route. Fox was at the hospital less than an hour after being picked up in the water. On duty that Sunday afternoon was a surgeon who had just returned from England, where he had taken a specialized course in chest operations.

After the four-hour operation (during which a priest was summoned within Fox's earshot, and he sat up and shouted, "But I'm a Protestant!"), Fox was declared out of danger. Four hundred sixty-two stitches were required to sew him up. He survived because he was in superb physical condition, because he never went into shock, and because as he put it, "I guess I just wasn't ready to go." (He also survived because the shark that attacked him had not been trying to eat him. If it had been, I am sure the outcome would have been very different.) The following year (1964), the Australian National Spearfishing Championship was won by the team of Bruce Farley, Brian Rodger, and Rodney Fox.

Rodney Fox still dives; in fact, he has made a career out of diving with white sharks. He owns

a motel in Port Lincoln, on Spencer Gulf, South Australia, and many of his guests want to dive with white sharks—in a cage. He has the boats, the cages, and, God knows, the experience. Practically every South Australian white shark expedition has included Rodney Fox. He was on board the *Saori* in 1970, during the filming of *Blue Water, White Death;* he went with Peter Benchley and Stan Waterman to film "The American Sportsman" in 1974; and in 1975, he went with a California travel agency's tour to Dangerous Reef, South Australia, where again, extraordinary photographs of an extraordinary animal were taken. Rodney Fox has been involved in more white shark attacks than anyone else. There is no question that he knows as much about the subject as any living man. It's a hell of a way to learn a trade.

Henri Bource used to be a two-legged recreational diver. He is now a one-legged professional diver. In Australia, on November 26, 1964, Bource was with a group of divers who had left Port Fairy for Lady Julia Percy Island, a small, rocky outcropping known for the colonies of seals that inhabit its waters. There were both scuba and skin divers on this outing, and Bource chose to enter the water without any cumbersome gear. He wanted to photograph the seals under water.

After about an hour's photography, Bource and two companions were swimming with the seals, when the seals seemed to disappear. "The water was quite empty," recalled Bource. "There was a split second of eerie silence, and our instinct as divers warned us that something was wrong." Cautiously, the divers began to make their way back to the boat. According to the information in the Shark Attack File, as recorded in David Baldridge's book *Shark Attack:* "A member of the diving party watching from the beach saw a large dorsal fin cutting the water, heading straight for the divers."[16] Henri Bource never saw the shark that hit him. He was lifted out of the water yelling "Shark!" and was then pulled under. His mask had been wrenched off by the tremendous impact of the shark's attack, and he could not see what was dragging him deeper into the water. He was being shaken "the way a dog would shake an old slipper," he later wrote. Suddenly, the shaking stopped, and Bource rose to the surface. He reached down and realized that his left leg had been bitten off, but his reaction was one of relief, not panic. If the shark had not bitten his leg off, he would have drowned.

He was lifted aboard the dive boat (which had been close by), and a tourniquet was applied to his leg. He was rushed back to Port Fairy, where an ambulance, radioed from the boat, was waiting. The wounds were closed at Warrnambool Hospital, and Bource received massive transfusions to replace the blood he had lost.

Within a month after his accident, he was diving again; he has now become a professional diver working on offshore oil rigs, and an underwater cameraman. In 1968, Bource's *artificial* leg was ripped off by a shark, and he now dives with a swim fin modified to fit his abbreviated left leg. He has made films about sharks, from both underwater and topside vantage points, including one called *Savage Shadows*, in which he reenacted (with a fake shark) the scene in which his leg was bitten off.

In 1965, a year after his attack, he joined Brian Rodger, Rodney Fox, and Alf Dean (the holder of the world's record for a white shark caught on rod and reel) aboard the *Glenmorry*, a tuna fishing boat. They were going fishing for white sharks, and Ron Taylor was aboard to film the action. It was during this expedition that Taylor hung over the side to take some of his most spectacular photographs (see p. 275). Henri Bource was reeling in a large white shark, when another one came along and attacked its hooked comrade. For the three survivors who watched the terrible power of the white shark's jaws, it was a grim reminder of their own encounters with the shark the Australians call "white death."

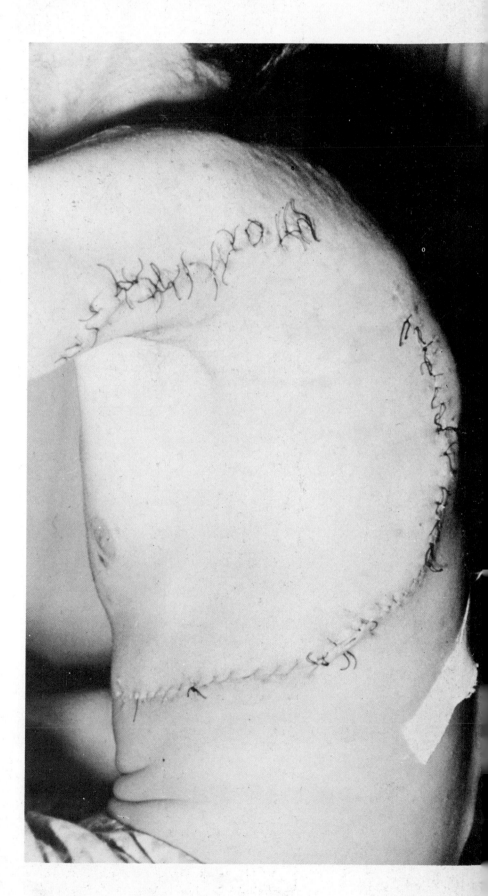

Some of the 462 stitches required to sew up Rodney Fox.
Courtesy of Rodney Fox

STEWART SPRINGER: *Adventures in the Shark Trade*

If it had not been for Al Jolson and *The Jazz Singer*, the world might have been denied the expertise of Stewart Springer. Encouraged by his father, who felt that it would build up his lungs and help prevent tuberculosis, Springer learned to play the flute. By 1929, when he was twenty-three years old, he was playing in a 35-piece orchestra in a movie house, but the advent of talkies put the young flautist out of a job. With a couple of years of college behind him (Butler College in Indianapolis), an interest in natural history, and a Model-T Ford that he'd bought for $11.00, Springer left Indianapolis for Biloxi, Mississippi, where he planned to start a biological supply business. At that time, he had no particular interest in sharks, but he had heard that one could collect spiny dogfish and sell them for laboratory purposes. When he got to Biloxi, he found no spiny dogfish, but he did find the sharpnose shark, *Rhizoprionodon terraenovae*. All he ever caught were males, and although his curiosity was piqued by this, he was not in a position to research the problem thoroughly. He had to make a living, for among other things, he had married Vergie Fayard, the local librarian, and their son Philip was born in 1934. He turned from sharks to grasshoppers and crayfish, selling hundreds of thousands to biological supply houses, but despite these figures, he was not getting rich.

In 1935, John F. Bass, Jr., contacted Springer and asked him to come to Englewood, Florida, to run the supply business of his biological laboratory on Lemon Bay. Here Springer collected cotton rats (for polio studies), and Cuban toads. After this, Springer moved around Florida for a while, from Matecumbe in the Keys to Homestead. He finally answered an advertisement that offered "hard work for low pay," and officially entered the shark business. In 1940, he became a part of the staff and management of Shark Industries, a shark-fishing operation based in Salerno, Florida.

Two years earlier, he had written a paper titled "Notes on the Sharks of Florida," which was the first legitimate paper on any shark population in North America. Prior to that, hardly anyone was interested in sharks. As Springer put it, "You couldn't put them in a tank, and when they were dead, they stank." Springer greatly influenced Henry Bigelow and William Schroeder to write their major work on sharks. In *Fishes of the Western North Atlantic, Part I, Sharks*, the introduction contains this note: "We are . . . particularly grateful to Luis Howell-Rivero and Stewart Springer for contributing much-needed specimens together with extensive notes on many species from Cuba and Florida." In addition, there are forty-two footnotes that refer to Springer by name, usually in the form of "Stewart Springer informs us . . ." or "personal communication from Stewart Springer."[30] There are many animals that scientists have named after Springer. Included in the list of animals whose specific name is *springeri* are a snipe-eel, a pipefish, a crab, a mollusk, and a stingray. According to Springer, "This was because I used to be a collector and have a good eye for inconsistencies. I sent lots of specimens to the proper experts in the group, usually at my own expense. One author named a small fish after me as *stewarti*." There is even a genus of deep-sea ray named *Springeria*, and in 1944, Bigelow and Schroeder named a shark after him, *Carcharhinus springeri*.

By 1942, with the United States in the war in the Pacific, the problem of a shark repellent had arisen. The Office of Strategic Services (OSS) "borrowed" Springer to work on this problem. He was sent to Washington, D.C., and then to Woods Hole, armed with presidential authority to requisition whatever he needed in the search for a satisfactory shark repellent. From his longline shark-fishing experiences, Springer had noticed that decomposing sharks on a line kept other sharks away. Working with John Fogelberg, Richard Tuve, and Frederick Brinnick, Springer was able to identify an acetate compound as the active agent in the decomposing shark that was keeping the other sharks from taking the baits. The group of researchers combined copper acetate with nigrosine dye, which would disperse into the water in a black cloud. This was packaged as "Shark Chaser," and by the end of the war, was included as standard equipment in every sailor's and flier's life jacket. In Springer's words, "The Shark Chaser was not wholly effective, but its morale effect was significant." (It was subsequently demonstrated that there is no known chemical substance that can deter all kinds of sharks on a regular basis, and the search for a repellent, discussed elsewhere in this volume, has been directed toward physical, electrical, and even behavioral solutions.)

During the war, Springer also worked on survival manuals, chiefly on the basis of classified "action reports," which sometimes discussed shark activity in relation to airplane crashes and shipwrecks. One of the problems then (and now) was that whatever information was available on shark behavior came from observation of inshore species, while airplane crashes and shipwrecks usually took place in the open sea, where the species were completely different. The sharks most often implicated in offshore disasters were the mako and the oceanic whitetip, and almost nothing was then known about the behavior of those pelagic sharks.

When the war ended, Springer went to work with Morris Fraser as a commercial shark fisherman. They worked for Shark Industries (later sold to the Borden Company) on the production of Vitamin A from the livers of sharks. At peak production, Shark Industries had as many as twenty boats, ranging the Atlantic from North Carolina to South America, in search of sharks. All during his government and commercial work, Stewart Springer, without so much as a college degree, had been publishing scientific papers, mostly on the subject of sharks. Now that his reputation was spreading, his experience and expertise were eagerly sought. He was asked to explore the possibilities of commercial shark fisheries in the Bahamas and Trinidad, by the governments of these islands, which were hoping to establish profitable local industries. For Shark Industries, he also fished the mouth of the Mississippi, a location where he found "more sharks than anywhere else in the world." (On one hook, he once caught four sharks: a dogfish which had been eaten by a blacktip which had been eaten by a bull shark which had been eaten by a tiger shark.)

In 1950, Springer was working for the U.S. Fish and Wildlife Service, involved in "exploratory fishing," which meant trying to locate the fish before fishing commercially for them. (It was during this time that he discovered many species new to science.) By 1955, he was chief of the Fish and Wildlife Service's Bureau of Exploratory Fishing, studying fishing methods, fish, shipping, and, of course, sharks. In 1958, he was named to the Shark Research Panel of the American Institute of Biological Services. His classic paper on the natural history of the sandbar shark was published in 1960, and shortly thereafter, he was sent by the government to complete his college education. He went to George Washington University and Duke University summer school, and received his B.A. in 1964, the same year that his son Michael graduated from George Washington University.

In 1964, Springer went to Palo Alto to work at the Branch of Fisheries Biology. He was chief scientist aboard the research vessel *Anton Bruun* on IGY (International Geophysical Year) Voyage 8 in that same year. He continued to work for the Fish and Wildlife Service (which later became the National Marine Fisheries Service) at the U.S. National Museum in Washington, D.C., where he studied the systematics of sharks. Stewart Springer officially retired in 1970, but he is now working as a research associate at the Mote Marine Laboratory in Sarasota, revising the cat sharks (Scyliorhinidae), a project he has been working on for over ten years. (He lives at Placida, the original site of the Cape Haze Marine Laboratory, so in addition to the facilities at the Mote Marine Lab in Sarasota, he also has his own lab, almost next door.)

Stewart Springer has worked his way up through the ranks—from a flautist in a moviehouse orchestra to one of America's leading experts on sharks—earning the praise and respect of his colleagues throughout the world. (At a symposium on sharks that I attended in 1975, after Springer presented his paper, he was given a special accolade by the assembled scientists, students, and fishermen, as "a man who has been an inspiration to us all.") He has been more than an inspiration to me; with all the work he has, all the papers to write and letters to answer, he found time to read major portions of the manuscript of this book, and I am confident that in those areas, I have gotten the best advice possible. In addition it was my first meeting with Stewart Springer in 1974 that prompted me to do the section on "shark people" for this book; from talking to him, I realized that the shark people could be as interesting as the sharks.

RON AND VALERIE TAYLOR:
The Hydrodynamic Duo

As a teenager, Ron Taylor was swimming in a local net pool off Sydney (the beaches there were "netted" with sharkproof steel fences), when he found a face mask on the bottom. He surfaced, put it on, and the previously hazy underwater world became clear for him—clear enough, in fact, for him to spend his professional life looking through a face mask and through the viewfinder of an underwater camera. Valerie Heighes, also born and raised in Sydney, took naturally to diving. Between them they have won almost every diving title in Australia, and they are certainly the best-known underwater diving couple in the world.

They are most frequently associated with sharks, because of their participation in the making of the film *Blue Water, White Death,* but in their native Australia, they are regarded as experts on all sorts of marine life, from moray eels to rare shells. I mentioned in "The Shark People" that I recognized a certain quality of arrogance or egotism in many of those with whom I came into personal contact. I have only met Ron and Valerie Taylor once, but even in this brief period, I could see that neither one shows a trace of arrogance. They are both soft-spoken, deferential, courteous, and one might even go so far as to say that they are shy. They do what they do because they want to, and because they enjoy working together, not, as far as I can see, out of any desire to "challenge" or "conquer" the sea or its inhabitants.

Ron Taylor is a handsome man (in one of her journal entries, Valerie, somewhat prejudiced to be sure, says, "Ron is standing at the stern. A more attractive man I have never seen"), but Valerie is even more photogenic. She has appeared on the cover of dozens of magazines, and she could qualify for that position even if she weren't holding a poisonous sea snake or feeding a barracuda. It has been said that almost everybody looks alike under water, in a wet suit, face mask, regulator, and fins, but Valerie is almost instantly recognizable, despite all this paraphernalia. With the face mask removed, she has what Peter Matthiessen called " a near-perfect face," and pale, china blue eyes. She has an almost mystical affinity for animals, fearing very few of them, and there are films of her handling and hand-feeding such notoriously bad actors as barracudas, morays, sea snakes, and even sharks.

Ron Taylor

Valerie Taylor

Ron Taylor has been filming white sharks since 1964, long before it became fashionable, or even lucrative. With Alf Dean, the Australian fisherman who holds the rod-and-reel record for the white shark (2,664 pounds), Ron first filmed the great whites as they were chummed up to the boat with a mixture of whale oil and chunks of meat. Also on board were Ron's frequent diving companions, Brian Rodger, Rodney Fox, and Henri Bource, all of whom had been attacked and seriously mauled by white sharks. (Bource had lost his leg.) Although there was a primitive cage available, Ron felt that it was "too constricting," and preferred to hang over the transom of the boat, his head, arms, and movie camera in the water, while someone held his feet. The resulting film, including some awesome footage of one white shark tearing another one apart, is probably the most dramatic and frequently reproduced of all white shark film. Since Ron was photographing without benefit of cage, there are no bars to obstruct the pictures. (The spectacular shots of the shark with its mouth stretched wide, which has appeared on book jackets, in magazines, and in almost every type of publication having to do with sharks, is from this sequence.)

Ron Taylor is undoubtedly the foremost photographer of sharks in the world. Starting with his first experiences hanging off the duckboard of a tuna boat in St. Vincent's Gulf, he has been in almost every imaginable situation with sharks, in cages and out. In 1968, Peter Gimbel asked Ron and Valerie to join his "Blue Water" expedition, to search for and make a feature film about the great white shark. (It was Ron's early footage of white sharks off Australia that Gimbel used to interest Cinema Center Films in financing the film in the first place.) Off the coast of Durban, South Africa, while hundreds of sharks were feeding on the carcass of a dead sperm whale, Gimbel, Stan Waterman, and Ron and Valerie Taylor left the cages and filmed the swarming blues, duskies, and whitetips, as they fed on the whale. No white sharks appeared in the South African waters, so in January 1970, the expedition moved to South Australia, where they knew that white sharks could be found.

On board the *Saori*, chartered for the purpose of filming the great white shark at Dangerous Reef in Spencer Gulf, South Australia, in addition to the crew and ancillary members of the Blue Water expedition, were Gimbel, Water-

One of the series of spectacular photographs taken by Ron Taylor as he hung over the transom of a fishing boat in South Australian waters. No cages or other protective devices were used.

Valerie Taylor and a whale shark. The shark's mouth is almost 6 feet across, and only the nostrils can be seen. The shark's eyes are much further back.

man, Rodney Fox, and Ron and Valerie Taylor —as experienced a group of divers and photographers as could be found anywhere. After two torturous weeks of waiting, three white sharks arrived, and Gimbel, Waterman, and the Taylors filmed them from cages for three days. The resulting film was a critical and financial success, and gave the Taylors, as well as Gimbel and Waterman, the worldwide recognition they deserved. *Blue Water, White Death* is surely the most exciting underwater documentary ever made.

In 1972, Ron and Valerie were asked to join an Italian film maker, Bruno Vailati, as he prepared to make another documentary about the great white shark. During this filming, a thirteen-foot male shark got so tangled in the lines that it was unable to move, and hung, head down, about to die if it could not be cut loose. In order to release it, someone would have to leave the safety of the cage, swim to the shark and untangle it, running the distinct possibility

that the shark, upon being released, would attack its rescuer. It was decided to tow the shark to shallow water, and release it there, even though the other members of the crew felt that the safest and easiest thing to do would be to let it hang until it died, and then cut it loose. Here is an excerpt from Valerie's journal of January 16, 1972, describing the events:

All went well until we were in about six feet of water. Then the anchor caught. To my amazement, Ron jumped in, freed the anchor and swam it to shore. (I must add that the Italians seemed to be paralyzed with astonishment at this time as none of them filmed so much as one frame of all this incredible action.) Ron then wrestled his shark into the shallows and started untangling the cable. He realised the Italians were only watching and shouted at them to film him. Bruno awoke as if from a trance and shouted also. Michel and Arlando ran for their movie cameras. My still one was working over-time. Ron hung onto the shark's lunging tail until they were positioned, then took the last twist of cable from around its tail. The great white was set free. It swam slowly in a circle before returning to Ron. Ron pushed it, shouting, "Deep water, sharky, go on, go on, deep water." The dark grey shape swung around slowly and glided away.

Two days later, Ron fell overboard at about midnight, into the midsts of three sharks feeding on half a horse. Ron swam twenty-five feet through the sharks and the chum slick, finally pulling himself aboard at the stern. A white shark passed beneath him as he pulled his legs out of the water. Valerie wrote: "Ron had spared the great white but now they are even again."

The following year, another great white got tangled in the cage lines, and again it was freed by Ron and Valerie, only this time they took its temperature and tagged its dorsal fin as it lay quiescent in the shallow water. The tag was returned six months later by a professional fisherman who had caught the shark.

Because of their skill, their awareness of ecology, and their experience, the Taylors are often in demand as still photographers and as cinematographers. The June 1973 issue of *National Geographic*, in a major article devoted to the Great Barrier Reef, contains a magnificent portfolio of their photographs.

It has not only been white sharks for Ron and Valerie; they have made films about the grey nurse shark (which they feel has an undeserved "bad press"), sea lions, leopard sharks, sea snakes, rare shells, and the whale shark. (They are among the few divers to swim with and photograph the largest fish in the world, the whale shark, *Rhincodon typus*.) In 1975, a weekly series of television films was shown in the United States, called "Ron and Valerie Taylor's Inner Space." It was one of the best series of its kind, not only because of the excellence of the photography, but because of the Taylors' sensitive and intelligent approach to their subject matter. They were not shown killing or exploiting the inhabitants of the sea; they seemed almost a part of this watery world. No man or woman can truly join the creatures of the sea, but Ron and Valerie Taylor came closer than anyone I know.

Courtesy of Stan Waterman

STAN WATERMAN: *Underwater Eye*

Until he speaks, only the sparkle in his pale blue eyes and a year-round tan give Stan Waterman away. When not working at his trade, he looks and dresses like a banker. His speech discloses him for what he really is—an adventurer below the bounding main: a combination of Anthony Trollope and Captain Bligh, he spices his conversation with obscure literary references (from Toad of Toad Hall to Shakespeare) and eighteenth-century pirate slang. His expressive eyebrows complement his personality, as he raises them in mock surprise or beetles them down to support an ominous reference to keelhauling or to walking the plank.

Born in 1923, Stanton A. Waterman graduated from Dartmouth in 1946, worked briefly for the State Department, and then moved to Maine, where he owned and operated a blueberry farm for four years. As early as 1936, he had become interested in diving (he was given a Japanese Ama mask, one of the first full masks to be used in the United States). After college, he spent four winters running a charter boat and diving service in the Bahamas. He quickly proved his competence as an underwater film maker and still photographer, and the career that he practices today was launched. In Nassau, he met Peter Gimbel, who was also an underwater photographer. From this meeting there came a lasting friendship, and during the next ten years the two met often and discussed potential subjects for films. They eventually decided that the most exciting (and salable) film they could make would be one about sharks, and the most exciting shark was unquestionably the great white. (Gimbel had already made a short film on sharks, called *In the World of Sharks*.) Waterman had been exposed to sharks during his dives in Tongue of the Ocean and the Bahamas, and he had worked with Perry Gilbert at the Lerner Marine Laboratory on Bimini in the summer of 1961. The "Blue Water" film company was formed in 1965, and because Waterman had already arranged to spend a year in Tahiti, Gimbel began to assemble the crew, material, and financing for the expedition.

Waterman and his wife and their three children went to Tahiti for a year, from the fall of 1965 to the fall of 1966. While diving off Bora Bora, northwest of Tahiti, Waterman suffered an almost fatal attack of the bends, which left him with little feeling in his left side. It has not, however, impaired his mobility, either under water or in a game of tennis, his other passion. Wherever there is a tennis court, even in the remotest of Pacific islands, Stan Waterman will look for a game. He is the champion of the Cocos-Keeling Islands Expedition, where he managed to make an exciting film, apparently between sets.

On the Blue Water expedition, Waterman served as associate producer and as underwater cinematographer, with Gimbel. As Waterman explained it to me, they fully expected to find "Old Whitey" off South Africa, and the support footage was all to be shot in and around African waters. At first, they had no intention of going to Australia, even though they were assured that white sharks could be found there. They had what they thought was good information from whale fishermen and shark experts that great whites were frequently seen in South African waters, feeding on the carcasses of sperm whales. (Even Perry Gilbert had suggested that they go to South Africa.)

They saw no great whites in South African waters, but it was in these waters that Gimbel, Waterman, and the Taylors risked their lives in the interests of underwater film making. After

watching the oceanic whitetips, some of them over twelve feet long and weighing over half a ton, the long, sinuous blues, the ten-foot duskies, and a mysterious "mustard-colored species with a curled dorsal fin" that neither they nor anyone else was able to identify, Peter Gimbel left the cage.

Waterman followed him out (as did Ron and Valerie Taylor soon after), and they filmed the feeding of these sharks, all of which are considered dangerous to humans; that is, they are usually listed as "man-eaters"—with the possible exception of the mustard-colored shark, which remains unknown. The sharks were tearing great chunks out of the dead whale, and Gimbel, Waterman, and Ron and Valerie Taylor got as close as they could to the shredded flesh of the whale, and the tearing, gaping mouths of the sharks. They were bumped, shoved, and nudged, but never bitten. "We felt real fear off Durban," Waterman told me. "We didn't know if [the sharks] would bite us as well as the whale." He also told me that he left the cage because Gimbel did, not because of any conscious desire to risk his life or to prove anything. The four divers were surrounded by as many as a hundred large sharks, all of them classified as potential man-eaters. It was the most exciting shark footage ever shot, even if you don't realize that the divers are unprotected. When you know that they were defenseless, their efforts transcend ordinary film making and become an almost surreal exercise in undersea interaction. Waterman, writing in *Sports Afield* in 1975, described the experience:

It was like standing erect in the line of fire in the middle of a pitched battle. We were jostled and bumped by two or three sharks at a time and were so busy kicking them away and shoving them off with our cameras that it was difficult to shoot steadily and focus on the action. Most nerve-wracking of all was to be struck from behind and to whirl around to find a 1000-pound animal nudging your back.

In January 1968, after almost five months of filming in African and Indian Ocean waters, the expedition headed for South Australia, to try

Dangerous Reef, South Australia, 1970. A photograph that Waterman calls "Waltzing with Whitey," made during the filming of Blue Water, White Death.

to get the necessary climax footage for the film that was still being referred to as "the search for the great white shark." After ten days of chumming with whale oil, fish, chunks of horse and cow meat, the whites finally made their appearance—three big ones, the largest estimated at fourteen feet, and weighing perhaps 1½ tons. They filmed the whites from cages only, realizing that they needed this protection against a shark known both as "man-eater" and "white death." The footage they got was awesome in the extreme, and assured the commercial success of *Blue Water, White Death.*

When I asked Waterman about the difference between filming the frenzied hordes off Durban and the whites off Dangerous Reef, South Australia, he said that at first he was frightened of the whitetips and blues, but later considered it likely that they weren't going to attack: "We became inured to their presence, and just tried to shoot the best damn film we could." He also said that he felt secure in the cage when filming the great white, since after the exhilarating and frightening experience in Africa, he felt that the whites "were just going through their act," and were not a real threat as long as divers remained in the cages.

The next time Waterman was asked to film sharks, he was the chief cameraman for an ABC-TV "American Sportsman" production, in which Peter Benchley was to dive (in a cage) with the great white shark, the redoubtable protagonist of *Jaws.* The first stop was Cairns, on the Great Barrier Reef, for smaller, less dangerous sharks, perhaps bronze whalers or even tigers. This was to be done without cages, but with divers "riding shotgun," ready to protect the cameramen and Benchley with a powerhead, if necessary. A chum was prepared of chopped-up stingray, and Waterman went in first, to test his weights, cameras, and lights. The first thing he saw upon entering the water was a large shark, accompanied by a flotilla of pilot fish, heading straight for him. He was considerably underweighted, so he kept bobbing to the surface while trying to get the approaching fish in focus. Pointed snout, triangular teeth, black eyes, massive body . . . It was indeed a great white shark, and Water-

man was the only person in the water, completely unprotected. As he continued to try to focus on it, it inexplicably (and fortunately) turned slowly and swam away. He managed to film it as it swam away from him into the blue-green mist, and thus produced a unique and remarkable document: the first footage ever taken of a free-swimming great white by an unprotected diver. Waterman says he "sensed" the great shark was not going to attack; that it just happened to be in the vicinity when the chumming began, and was simply coming up to investigate. Perhaps it was not hungry, or perhaps white sharks behave differently on the Great Barrier Reef. In thousands of hours of diving, Ron and Valerie Taylor had never even seen one there before.

A thirteen-foot tiger shark was attracted to the cut-up stingray on the bottom. Waterman filmed Benchley as he watched this man-eater eat the bait not 6 feet from where they sat, their backs to a coral wall. At one point, the tiger, trying to wrest the bait free, pivoted on the anchored stingray, and slapped Waterman's camera with its tail. Waterman kept shooting.

Then they went to Dangerous Reef. Benchley was to be in one cage, while Waterman filmed him from another. This time there was only one white shark, but according to those who saw it, it was as voracious and aggressive as any they had seen before. Waterman said that "there was no question that the shark was trying to get the 'animal' that was in the cage. He was not bumping, not just curious—he wanted that black, bubbling creature in the flimsy cage."

As people get older, they tend to become more conservative and less willing to take chances. Stan Waterman looks considerably younger than his fifty-two years, and shows no interest in curtailing his activities. He believes that if there are risks involved, that's the way you make underwater films—at least that's the way you make underwater films that people want to see. And the chances are that when the great white shark's attack is actually filmed, the cameraman will be Stan Waterman. We can only hope that the attack he films takes place on the bait and not on the cameraman.

WILLIAM YOUNG: *"Sharky Bill"*

Perhaps the first of the true "shark people," Captain William Young was a man who spent most of his life in pursuit of sharks, and was known by various nicknames, including "Sharky Bill," and *"kane mano,"* which is Hawaiian for "shark man." His autobiography, *"Shark! Shark! The Thirty-Year Odyssey of a Pioneer Shark Hunter,* was probably the first popular book to deal exclusively with sharks, and the first of many books to connect the word "shark" with an exclamation point in the title.[256]

William Young was a product of his times, and it is therefore necessary to view his book and his career from that perspective, and not apply today's ecological conscience to them. During the time he was engaged in the wholesale slaughter of sharks (roughly 1900 to 1935), sharks were considered nothing better than vermin, so Young truly believed that he was making the world safer for people by killing more and more sharks. He missed no opportunity to call sharks "rapacious monsters" or "savage killers," and his interest in his subject began with finding sharks and ended with skinning or eating them. He had virtually no understanding of the natural history of the animals he was hunting, and this shortcoming obviously does not disturb him greatly. He is at his best when discussing the methods employed in catching and killing sharks, and at his most inadequate when he tries to discuss their nature in anything but deprecatory terms. His antipathy toward sharks is either instinctive or the result of a particular experience he does not share with his readers, but from his first sighting of a shark, he wanted to kill it. The likelihood is that from 1900 to 1935, almost everyone agreed with him.

There seems to be no question that Young did the things he said he did, and no question that he felt the way he says he felt. It is when he recounts tales told to him, or when he attempts to discourse on the natural history of the shark or any other sea creature that he strays from the mark. Even some of the literary aspects of the book are open to question, such as the passage in which he quotes a Hawaiian legend, "told in the traditional manner by an old Kanaka in the soft light of a nut-oil lamp." The story is presented as if it were told to Young, who then recorded it for posterity, but, unfortunately, the same story, *word for word* (and for twelve pages) appears in Padraic Colum's *Legends of Hawaii,* published two years before Young's book, and taken from original source material in the Bishop Museum in Honolulu.

We must, perforce, deal with Young's career as a shark hunter, and not as a writer, even though I have relied on his words for most of the information in this profile. His is a fairly complete and quite readable chronicle, but I am more than a little hesitant about accepting all the material at face value. Bill Young's book ("as told to Horace S. Mazet, F.R.G.S.") is by far the best source of information about his career;* however, there is an almost total omission of names and dates.

From California, Young and his brothers headed for Hawaii, where they started in the garbage-hauling business, taking the refuse

---

* The only other record of Young's career can be found in *Shadows in the Sea,* written by Harold W. McCormick and Tom Allen, with Captain William Young. There is a chapter called "Captain Shark-Killer" which relies heavily on quotes from *Shark! Shark!* The book is dedicated to Young, and the foreword, written by McCormick, states that the original intention was to update Young's book. *Shadows in the Sea* is a comprehensive book about sharks, skates, and rays, published in 1963 by Chilton. We know that McCormick, the senior author, did exhaustive research on sharks, collecting every scientific paper, newspaper clipping, and photograph that he could find. Upon his death, his widow presented his papers to the American Museum of Natural History, and I had the privilege of examining them with Dr. James W. Atz, Associate Curator of Ichthyology.

from the city of Honolulu and dumping it far offshore. This naturally led them to sighting their first sharks. Young wrote:

There they were, the savage, armored sea tigers which had become my totem, my fetish. I thrilled to the sight. As I leaned there, staring in utter fascination, my throat contracted. Tingling shivers ran up and down my spine, to my finger tips and toes. I wished for a harpoon, a rifle, anything that would give me a chance to make my first shark kill. . . . I resolved that we would catch a shark as soon as the opportunity presented.

An example of Young's attitude toward his prey (for that is what they were to him) can be found in his description of an encounter with the chief of the Honolulu Police. He asks Chief Chillingsworth to allow his men to take target practice on the sharks that are drawn to the garbage dumping off Kalihi harbor. The chief is somewhat reluctant, hemming and hawing, until Young told him, "All you have to do is blaze away, and the more you hit, the merrier it will be."

Young obviously enjoyed his work: after a while he was running the garbage service, running a series of launches to service Honolulu harbor, and occasionally taking out fishing parties. In 1920, Young applied for and was given the post of manager of the newly built Honolulu Aquarium, at Waikiki. This was a rather peaceful period in his life, with a minimum of killing. He was interested in the colorful reef fishes that abound in the warm Hawaiian waters, but more interested in the "terrors of the sea," such as "octopi, the most repulsive of sea things." He tried to keep sharks in captivity at the aquarium, but failed with all but the smallest specimens. After about a year, he left the aquarium, entrusted his charges to the care of a young American, "and returned to the interesting and crowded life of the boathouse and the harbor."

In a conversation with a friend (hardly anyone in *Shark! Shark!* has a name; there are boatmen, Kanakas, tourists, Negroes, Arabs, etc., but with the exception of the Young brothers, Herb, Jack, and Edgar, and an occasional Caucasian, everyone else is a "scientist," "the agent," or a "friend"), Young tells of the beginning of his commercial interest in sharks:

My earlier mania to remove a menace had gradually been passing, and I found myself looking for commercial outlets for shark by-products which, up to that time, had been almost totally neglected. Shark leather would prove a tough and admirable substance once a tanning method could be evolved.

But his harbor business intervened, and the thought of sharkskin as a commercial venture was dropped for a while. By his own admission, he had "hunted the most terrible of sea creatures for almost twenty years, and at every turn had beaten him, but there was still plenty to do."

By 1921, Young Brothers had split up, and a "promising business venture" came along, causing Bill Young to leave Hawaii for New York. In this unnamed business, "conference followed conference. Promises were made and broken, prospects failed to materialize. In short, the outlook was decidedly bleak." Obviously, this was no life for the *kane mano*, so he "weighed anchor," and began to look for other, more watery, pastures. A chance encounter on lower Broadway led him to the next phase of his shark-related endeavors. He saw a sign for sharkskin shoes, and in tracking down the tanner of the leather, he began what became a full-time occupation for the rest of his very active working life: he became a commercial shark fisherman, providing hides for tanning, meat for salting, fins for "Chinamen," and advice for governments that wanted to start their own shark fisheries. In a ten-year period, roughly 1926 to 1936, he traveled all over the world in pursuit of sharks. In some instances, it is not clear whether he is employed by someone else or self-employed. (In fact, at one time he was employed by Louis Moresi of the Ocean Leather Corporation.) He started out simply, going to North Carolina and then to Florida, but then he was off to Abyssinia (where Haile Selassie asked him to join in a lion hunt, which he refused, being "so busy with sharks, we had no time for lions"), French and British Somaliland, and then to England, where he got the necessary financing for a trip to the "antipodes."

So off to Australia he went, accompanied by an Englishman and two Australians, to set up a shark fishery in Sydney. En route, Young stopped off at his old home port of Honolulu, and also at Samoa and Fiji, where he picked up more shark lore, such as this little item: "In

Suva, Fiji, the natives, since they were dark-skinned, felt small fear [of sharks], regarding them chiefly as a source of food."

In Australia it was the same as in the other places where Young plied his trade: sharks, sharks, and more sharks. A station was opened at Pindamar, on Port Stephens Bay, near Sydney. After a while, Young ran into trouble with a "director of the firm" (here again it is hard to tell for whom he is working), and soon found himself "in far-off Australia," and out of a job. For the 60-dollar passage from Sydney to Honolulu, "Sharky Bill" was headed home again. When he arrived in Honolulu, he found that his brothers had been successful in the diesel launch business, and that his children(!) had grown up without him. (Since there has been no mention of a wife up to this point in the narrative, the appearance of children comes as a bit of a surprise.)

A new station was about to open in the Virgin Islands, and counseled by his children, who said, "Go ahead, Dad, you won't be happy until you're back on the job," Young headed for New York, and then for Puerto Rico. From there he made a sweep of the Caribbean Islands in search of the best shark-fishing grounds, traveling to Tortola, Antigua, Guadeloupe, Dominica, Barbados, and Trinidad. He then returned to New York to report to "the directors," and told them that Tortola was the most promising site of all those he had visited. He returned to Fat Hog Bay, at the east end of Tortola, to establish a shark fishery there. This operation was so successful that Young was asked to open another station in the Virgin Islands, this one on the flat coral island of Anegada.

In his narrative of these later years (circa 1930), Young says that sharks are nowhere regarded as real game fish, even though he makes earlier reference to New Zealand's reluctance to have him start a shark fishery there, for fear "that the great New Zealand sport of catching 'mako' or Mackerel sharks, the only sharks that will take fast-moving bait, would speedily be brought to an untimely end!" Concerning his desire to provide "sport," he recounts a suggestion by Count Felix von

Luckner (who coincidentally wrote the foreword to *Shark! Shark!*) for adding some excitement to the sport of shark fishing:

> *He suggested the idea of attaching from one to two hundred feet of airplane rubber shock cord to an ordinary steel shark hook and chain. Imagine the surprise of a hooked shark, when he reaches the end of his tether! The back-lash of the rubber strands will snap him up into the air and right back where he started from with a splash. I can't think of any sight in fishing that would compare with it, and it would provide the sportsman with all the "playing" he wanted.*

As the Virgin Islands fisheries on Tortola and Anegada prospered, Young again became restless, and tried to interest Cuban businessmen in the idea of a shark aquarium. The idea was postponed indefinitely, and Young headed again for New York. On the trip back, he met two men, "Professors of Ichthyology at Harvard University," who, after hearing some of his adventure stories, suggested that he make an "authentic motion picture of the shark." He did this, and called the film *Tigers of the Sea*.

Young's book ends with his recollection of the movie, and his reflections on his life with the sharks:

> *Older men, I notice, like to share their wealth of experience with others, their memories and adventures are ever on the tip of their tongues, seeking a faithful listener.*
>
> *So it seems to me. And that perhaps is why I like to share my full life with others—those who have never known the supreme thrill of hunting the fierce tigers of the sea in their lair. If they can betake themselves in imagination to the scenes and events which provided such excitement, such adventure and satisfactory thrills, and relive a life with me that has known few dull moments—that, as much as anything else, makes the years of pioneering worthwhile to the kane mano.*

AFTERWORD

When I began the research that was eventually to lead to this book, I did so in a spirit of awe and admiration of sharks. I was impressed by the way they looked, by the way they swam, by the silent, savage admixture of form and function. After a while, however, I became all too familiar with sharks. I quickly learned that not all sharks were the graceful creatures that had first inspired me. Some were bottom-dwelling animals that munched on snails; others were lumpy things that lived in total darkness. Moreover, I was almost constantly in contact with one aspect of sharks or another—with the scientists, writers, photographers, or even the sharks themselves. Somewhere during the long course of the research, the magic of the shark evaporated, to be replaced by the unrelenting heaviness of the labor of a scientific project. The overwhelming pressures of keeping up with the revisions, the cataloguing, the bibliography, of talking to experts, of painting the pictures and doing the drawings—all contributed to the feelings of dull, pressured necessity. Even though many of my friends saw me as a free spirit, able to choose my subject, my hours, and my responsibilities, to me it was a job—a job from which there would be no time off until it was completed. The poetic vision had gone, leaving in its wake a cluttered pile of papers, notes, sketches, and lists, which I had to face, day after day.

As I realized that my study was reaching an end—that I would soon have to turn in all the material I had created, I experienced a rebirth of innocent fascination for my subject. It was as if by delivering the manuscript, I would be freed from the blinders of scholarly endeavor, and returned to an earlier state—of what might be called shark reverence. The book is done, my desk momentarily empty. No more checking for a reference in half a dozen books; no more searching for hours for an obscure fact or illustration. The fascination is still there; I realize that I only lost my sense of it temporarily, as I wandered about the morass of papers, books, and pictures.

In this book, if I have caught the essence of the shark, it has been only fleetingly. As in the taking of a photograph, perhaps I have stopped the shark for a millisecond, but in truth I know it swims on, unaffected by my prose or my pictures. Unlike hunters or fishermen who want to forever immobilize the animal they admire, I wanted only to hold its quicksilver essence for a moment. To draw or write about an animal is to participate in its re-creation, to kill it is to partake only of its destruction. I tried to get a grip on the shark, and I failed. But my success can be defined in terms of this failure; I never really wanted to stop the shark, I only wanted it to pause for an instant that I might get to know it better. The years I spent studying the shark are only seconds in its history. With no regard for me and no awareness of how hard I tried to hold or understand it, the shark swims on, ceaselessly, toward immortality.

That the information I have gained came so slowly and painfully shows only how reluctant the sea is to give up its secrets. Perhaps this struggle is part of the learning process, or perhaps it is nothing more dramatic than a personal shortcoming. I survived the learning, and my admiration for the shark did too. Now I have closed the circle; I know a little more about sharks than I did before I started, and while my vision was momentarily clouded, the newly acquired knowledge now strengthens my continuing admiration, the more so because it has shown me how little I really know. I know the names of the sharks—names that we have given them. I know where they live, what some of them eat, and even how some of them breed. But a shark in a book or a painting is not a real shark, no matter how detailed the description or how accurate the rendering. Only when it is in the ocean, swimming silently with measured strokes of its tail, and looking out through sleepless eyes, is it real. My initial fascination still persists, despite my efforts to desiccate and systematize it. In a way, it has been like climbing a great mountain. There is a certain measure of personal gratification, but the mountain is unchanged by man's puny attempts to "conquer" it. Like Everest, the shark will remain indomitable.

NOTES ON THE COLOR PLATES

In the dimensions of the paintings, height is given before the width.

Plate 1 (Frontispiece)
MAKO SHARK
Isurus oxyrinchus
Acrylic on board. 40″ x 30″

It is obvious that I have a particular interest in makos. The opening fictional piece, "The Predators," concerns a mako, and there are two other paintings of makos included as color plates (Plates 2 and 6).

This is one of the few "portraits" I have done of sharks—this is the complete painting, by the way, not a detail. In it, I wanted to show the salient characteristics of this shark, including the large, dark eye, the sharply pointed snout, and the unique teeth. The scars and scratches are supposed to be the results of conflicts with other sharks or prey fishes. Sharks are often seen scratched up.

Plate 2
LONGFIN MAKO and BROADBILL
SWORDFISH
Isurus paucus and *Xiphias gladias*
Acrylic on canvas. 22″ x 34″

I wanted to convey a sense of a deep-water confrontation here (something like the battle in "The Predators"), so I kept the colors subdued and tried to reduce the highlights. There are no real highlights under water, of course, and in really deep water, almost all the colors of the spectrum are invisible. That's why I kept my palette restricted to blues. This is the last color to go.

These fish are not friends, nor are they playing tag. As soon as the mako gets a little closer, she is going to have a large swordfish steak.

The mackerel sharks and the swordfish have prominent keels at the base of their tails, and the tails themselves are crescent-shaped. This is a remarkable example of what biologists call convergence, which is the development of similar anatomical modifications in completely unrelated animals.

Plate 3
GREY NURSE SHARK
Odontaspis arenarius
Acrylic on board. 28" x 36"

This is the Australian grey nurse shark (hence the exotic spelling of "grey"), but it is the same animal as the South African ragged-tooth and the North American sand tiger, seen so often in aquariums.

For some reason this is one of the most popular paintings I've ever done. I've had more requests for paintings "like the one with the shadow" than for any other one. I have no idea why, unless it has to do with the staring eye of the shark, or perhaps it's the teeth. It's one of the few paintings I've done where the bottom is lighter than the top, but I am unable to assign any significance to this at all. Whatever the reason, I could make a nice living painting this painting over and over again, with occasional minor changes for the sake of variety.

Plate 4
CARCHARODON MEGALODON,
CARCHARODON CARCHARIAS, and
HOMO SAPIENS
Acrylic on board. 20" x 30"

This painting was originally done to accompany an article I wrote for *Sports Afield* magazine. It was specifically designed to run for three pages; the tail of *C. megalodon* was on the first page (right side), and then when that page was turned, you saw the rest of the picture, and you were supposed to be surprised by the actual size of the shark whose tail was the only thing you saw at first.

White sharks are not really this white, but I wanted to achieve the highest level of contrast between the living species (*C. carcharias*) and the extinct one. The idea was to suggest *megalodon* in the background, rather like an ancestor spirit, since it has been extinct for millions of years, but I'm not sure this comes across. For scale, assume the diver is six feet tall and the white shark is fifteen feet long. *C. megalodon* is therefore forty feet long, which is about as big as they got. The diver's hands are about the same size as the big shark's teeth.

The diver in all that trouble is me.

Plate 5
WHALE SHARK
Rhincodon typus
Acrylic on canvas. 24½″ x 36″

In September 1974, Edwin Gould, his wife Sydney, Wolfgang Sterrer (the director of the Bermuda Biological Station), and several other divers were diving the Argus Tower, some 30 miles southwest of Bermuda. From out of the gloom there came an enormous creature, obviously a shark. Sydney Gould recalls her initial feeling of terror as she watched this spotted giant approach with measured strokes of its great tail, and the divers quickly surfaced. Ed Gould and Sterrer recognized it as a harmless whale shark, and Sydney descended to swim with the great fish, in the accepted fashion—hanging on to the dorsal fin, peering into its mouth—to the delight of the underwater photographers.

I have also benefited from this experience, since it is Sydney that I painted swimming with the whale shark. I worked directly from the Goulds' photographs, and I was doubly lucky: to have such good reference material for the shark, and to have such a lovely model for the swimmer. I do not ordinarily give names to my paintings, but I could not resist calling this one *Portrait of a Lady with a Large Fish.*

Plate 6
MAKO SHARK
Isurus oxyrinchus
Acrylic on canvas. 24″ x 18″

When this painting was hanging in a gallery, I overheard the following conversation as two people stood before it:

> *"Looks like a shark," said the man.*
> *"How can it be a shark?" asked his companion.*
> *"Just look at those teeth," he said.*
> *"But it's up in the air," she said. "It has to be a porpoise."*
> *"I guess you're right," he said.*

I am intrigued and fascinated by makos, and I wanted to paint one in a particularly dramatic situation. I admit that there is an element of the surreal in a picture of a flying shark, but since they do jump to extraordinary heights, I figured I could use the sky as a backdrop. You just have to imagine the horizon—just below the lower edge of the picture.

Plate 7
GREAT WHITE SHARK
Carcharodon carcharias
Acrylic on board. 36″ x 44″

Stan Waterman, who has had a great deal of firsthand experience with white sharks, had been asking me to paint a picture of a shark chasing a sea lion through the kelp of southern California waters. I'd made a couple of unsuccessful attempts at resolving this problem, but I never could get it to work. Perhaps it had something to do with the fact that I'd never seen the kelp—I could only work from photographs.

Finally, I thought I had the problem solved: I would do a close-up of the shark's head, showing the terrifying teeth, and show the sea lion attempting to escape—through the kelp. Somewhere along the line, the sea lion (and the kelp) got lost, and I ended up doing the whole shark. I figured Waterman could imagine the other elements.

The little tooth below the nostril is not an accident. In white sharks, the third tooth from the center of the upper jaw is always smaller than the ones that flank it.

Plate 8
PORBEAGLE
Lamna nasus
Acrylic on board. 36″ x 44″

As in the painting of the thresher shark, this one also has a number of fish in addition to the shark. These are mackerel, *Scomber scombrus*. Unlike the menhaden in the thresher painting, which I did freehand, I did the mackerel with a template—two templates, to be precise. I drew two mackerel (if you look closely, you'll see that there are two different sizes), and then cut them out of illustration board. I placed the cutout where I wanted a mackerel, and then traced it on in pencil. I painted each fish separately. It looks at first as if all the mackerel have their mouths open. Not so. There are two fish with closed mouths.

Note the secondary keel on the porbeagle's tail and the whitish spot at the base of the dorsal fin. It is these fieldmarks plus its overall chunkiness that distinguish it from the mako.

288

Plate 9
GREAT WHITE SHARK and SEA LION
Carcharodon carcharias and *Zalophus
californianus*
Acrylic on canvas. 24" x 36"

I have seen both animals in this picture, but not
together. In California, I saw sea lions surfing in
a wave, and on the beach at Makapuu, Hawaii,
I saw a good-sized shark in a curling breaker.
I'm pretty sure it was not a white, but we know
that white sharks feed on sea lions, so I thought
it was not unreasonable to make the substitu-
tion.

In *Life* magazine in 1960, there was a major
article about sharks. It was called "Look Out
for Sharks," and it was probably prepared in
response to the formation of the Shark Research Panel in 1958. The year 1959 was also a
pretty bad year for shark attacks. The lead
illustration was a painting of a great white
shark "poised in the upsweep of a wave," and
the shark is virtually invisible. When I saw the
shark in the wave in Hawaii, it was pretty
damned visible (I was standing on shore when
I saw it), and I decided to paint it that way.

Plate 10
BASKING SHARKS
Cetorhinus maximus
Acrylic on canvas. 20" x 24"

This started out as a sketch for a larger painting, but it seemed to be coming along so nicely
that I decided to tighten it up and use it for
the book.

Here is an instance in which a large shark has
to look large with nothing included in the painting for scale. The big fish in the foreground is
supposed to be twenty-five feet long. The next-
nearest fish is younger and therefore smaller.
Juvenile basking sharks have a longer snout,
sometimes with a hornlike protuberance on the
end. Basking sharks are plankton eaters and
have minute teeth.

Plate 11
CHAIN DOGFISH
Scyliorhinus retifer
Acrylic on canvas. 24″ x 18″

In January 1976, I walked into the office of Les Line, the editor of *Audubon*. He showed me an article in the *New York Times* titled "The Sea Yields Rare Treasures." Among the "treasures" that had been dredged up from a depth of 250 fathoms in the Gulf of Mexico were six chain dogfish, the largest of which was about fifteen inches long. I had completed most of the paintings that were to accompany Gary Soucie's *Audubon* article on sharks, but Line wanted more because the article was so long. He was especially interested in these little members of the catshark family (which for some reason are called dogfish) because they were small, rare, and, most important, different from the large pelagic sharks that I had painted for most of the other illustrations.

The sharks were on exhibit at the New York Aquarium at Coney Island, so I was sent on my first *Audubon* field trip. I went to the aquarium, saw the sharks, made color notes, and sketched them from life. It was probably the only time in *Audubon*'s history that an artist was sent *by taxi* to observe and draw a wild creature.

Plate 12
THRESHER SHARK
Alopias vulpinus
Acrylic on board. 27″ x 34″

For some reason, people seem to be interested in the number of fish in this picture. There are ninety-nine—ninety-eight menhaden (*Brevoortia gunteri*) and one thresher shark. While I was working on this painting, my daughter Elizabeth, then six years old, tried to keep track, but we both lost count regularly. Only after the painting was completed were we able to lay a piece of tracing paper over the painting and number each fish as we ticked it off.

I was fascinated by the graceful curve of the elongated tail of the thresher, and I tried to complement it with a somewhat stylized arrangement of the baitfish. I had no time-saving system for painting these fish; I just did them one at a time. When I thought the design was complete, I stopped. Besides, I was getting a little "mossbunker-happy," and I realized that another one, or even five or ten, wouldn't make a lot of difference—it would require at least twenty or thirty more fish to substantially change the design. That's when I quit.

Plate 13
BULL SHARK
Carcharinus leucas
Acrylic on canvas. 24″ x 18″

This is the shark that for so long was thought to be so many different species, depending on where it was encountered. In South Africa it was the Zambezi shark, *Carcharhinus zambezensis;* in Central America it was the Lake Nicaragua shark, *C. nicaraguensis,* and in India it was the Ganges River shark, *C. gangeticus.* It turns out to be the same species all over the world, the bull shark, *C. leucas.* I decided to paint it in a South African setting, showing the roiled and turbid water that it often inhabits. If you are familiar with South African fishes, you will recognize the white steenbras, *Lithognathus lithognathus,* a characteristic fish of the Natal coast.

Eugenie Clark saw this painting after the color proofs had been made, and she told me that *every* bull shark she had ever seen had trematode parasites between the first and second dorsal fins. By the time I learned this, it was too late to do anything about it, so you'll have to imagine some scars on the shark's back. (Even when the parasites are dislodged they leave scars, so I couldn't get away with claiming that they fell off.)

Plate 14
TIGER SHARK
Galeocerdo cuvieri
Acrylic on board. 27″ x 37¼″

Before I painted this, I had done most of my paintings with backgrounds of blue-green, in variations from dark blue-green to light blue-green. I wanted to do something different here, to suggest the warm tropical waters inhabited by the tiger shark. I had completed the painting with a funny-looking greenish ocher color, and it looked awful. I had to change the background, but since the shark was already painted in, I was forced to do the revised background *around* the fish—exactly the opposite of the way I usually work. (First I paint the background, and then I put the shark, or whale, or whatever, into its surroundings.) The new color went on rather thickly, but a lot of the original color showed through. The effect was unique, and I've never been able to duplicate it.

There's a funny optical illusion in this painting: the shark's left pectoral fin looks longer than his right one, but, in fact, measured on the leading edge, the shark's right fin is longer.

Plate 15
BLUE SHARK
Prionace glauca
Acrylic on canvas. 18" x 24"

The back of a blue shark is solid blue; it is not covered with whitish squiggles. The squiggles are light patterns on the shark, caused by the rippling surface of the ocean. I assumed that most people knew this, but I was asked about it so often that I thought I'd better explain it.

The spotty effect of light coming through the surface is the result of my carefully planned and executed spatter technique. I took a large piece of brown paper and cut out the areas I wanted to get the heaviest concentration of spots. Then I gradually moved the paper down on the painting so that the spots would be less dense further from the top. Finally, I took the paper off, and spattered the whole thing. This is a very precise exercise, and when I'm doing it, the paint spatters all over everything, including my face, the cat, and anything else that happens to be in the field of fire.

Plate 16
SANDBAR SHARKS
Carcharhinus milberti
Acrylic on canvas. 21" x 26"

No one has ever witnessed the mating of the sandbar sharks, so this painting is based on conjecture. We do know that the male (identifiable by the clasper seen projecting from the pelvic fin) grasps the upper back and dorsal fin of the female, and bites her, either before, during, or after copulation. Females are often taken with these so-called mating scars.

After I had finished this painting, I was struck by the feeling that I'd seen the male shark before. I looked through my photographic record file, and sure enough there he was: the bull shark (Plate 13). Luckily, I had managed to turn the sandbar shark around, so it didn't look as if I'd traced it from the bull shark. The sharks are closely related, and they're *supposed* to look alike, but this is too much family resemblance.

Plate 17
BLACKTIP REEF SHARK
Carcharhinus melanopterus
Acrylic on board. 17″ x 23″

Most of the carcharhinid sharks look alike; they are usually grayish above, lighter below, and "typical" in configuration (e.g., the bull shark, Plate 13, and the sandbar sharks, Plate 16, both carcharhinids). Only a few members of this large and complicated family can easily be differentiated from the others, and the blacktip reef shark is one of them.

With its strikingly marked fin tips, this small (six-foot-long) shark of the shallow waters of the Indo-Pacific Ocean is easily recognizable. It inhabits the flats of numerous Pacific islands and atolls, and for a small shark, it is surprisingly aggressive. Even at a length of two feet, it has been known to attack people, usually biting them about the legs and ankles as they splash through the shallow waters it inhabits.

Plate 18
OCEANIC WHITETIPS
Carcharhinus longimanus
Acrylic on board. 36″ x 44″

Oceanic whitetips have been called the most numerous large animals in the world. They are open-ocean sharks, almost never coming in to shore, and this is the feeling that I wanted to communicate in this picture. While filming a sequence for "The American Sportsman" off Tongue of the Ocean in the Bahamas, Stan Waterman and Peter Benchley were followed by an oceanic whitetip. They were in about 5,000 feet of water, and I suppose I was influenced by their story. I wanted to give the feeling of great depth, but I also wanted to show that the sharks were swimming near the surface.

The striped fish with the sharks are pilot fish, *Naucrates ductor*, which are usually seen in the company of pelagic sharks, especially whitetips. They are related to the jacks and pompanos, and they are about eighteen inches long.

Plate 19
HAMMERHEAD
Sphyrna mokarran
Acrylic on board. 21″ x 33″

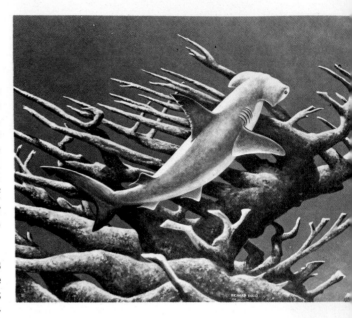

When I designed this painting, I wanted it to convey the feeling of impending doom that one associates with silent killers stalking their prey. I put in a grouper just above and beyond the elkhorn coral (*Acropora palmata*), and the idea was that the hammerhead was supposed to be rising slowly from behind the coral to surprise the grouper. Unfortunately, the sense of scale was completely lacking, and the grouper looked like a guppy. I couldn't paint it out, so I cut the top of the painting off.

As originally painted, the hammerhead was brown. When Perry Gilbert saw the painting, he said that it was all right anatomically, but that the color was wrong. He very generously provided me with photographs that showed the proper coloration. I changed it in 1975, but the painting was originally completed in 1973, so I took the date out.

Note the very high dorsal fin; this is characteristic of the hammerheads.

Plate 20
GREENLAND SHARK
Somniosus microcephalus
Acrylic on canvas. 18″ x 24″

I pride myself on my ability to recognize the source material for animal drawings, since I am constantly looking at magazines, books, and other people's work. Those who find the background of this painting familiar need look no further than page 132 of the January 1976 issue of *National Geographic*. Bill Curtsinger's spectacular photograph of a harp seal under the ice was the inspiration for this painting, and I copied the photograph as carefully as I could. I knew I would never actually see under the Greenland ice, and if I was going to paint the Greenland shark, I had to have some idea of what its habitat looked like. This is one of the most beautiful underwater photographs ever taken, and I am proud to acknowledge Mr. Curtsinger as the photographer.

Here is an example of a situation in which there is no sense of scale. This Greenland shark is fifteen feet long—you just have to take my word for it.

294

SHARKS OF AMERICAN WATERS

The following is a brief guide to the sharks that may be found in American littoral and offshore waters. I had originally wanted to prepare a complete listing of all the world's sharks, but that proved to be an example of unmitigated overreach. It was difficult enough to assemble the data on the American species; to do so for Japan or the Red Sea would have been impossible. Even assuming that this information exists (which it does not, in many cases), obtaining it and cross-referencing it for about 250 species would have been the work of a lifetime. Moreover, taxonomic research involves more than merely looking at scientific papers and cross-checking them; frequently it requires actual examination of the specimens described in the literature, not an easy task with creatures that can weigh thousands of pounds or that may be stashed away in some dusty cabinet in an obscure European museum. In some cases, the type specimen is lost completely. As a further illustration of the difficulties inherent in such an ambitious project, one taxonomist, Dr. J. A. F. Garrick of New Zealand, has been working on one family, the Carcharhinidae, for almost twenty years, and in a 1967 publication (*Sharks, Skates, and Rays*), he made this observation: "As a result of my own studies, I can only offer further difficulties instead of any new or easy solution to the generic problem."

This guide does not include all the world's shark genera, but it does include enough of them to make it a representative sample. The family Orectolobidae, for example, is poorly represented in American waters; in Australia there is a fascinating variety of nurse and carpet sharks which are striped, spotted, fringed, and tasseled. Our only delegate from this family is the drab nurse shark; *Ginglymostoma cirratum*. Japanese waters also support a rich and diverse shark fauna, including the smallest known shark, *Squaliolus laticaudus*, and the bizarre goblin shark, *Mitsukurina owstoni*. Some of the more exotic "foreign" sharks have been discussed in the text, and this list will demonstrate the amazing variety of sharks (a total of 87 species) that can be found off the shores of just one country—the United States.

Fortunately, a number of publications are available on the subject of American shark populations. These range from Bigelow and Schroeder's *Fishes of the Western North Atlantic, Part I, Sharks*, which is surely the most exhaustive and comprehensive work of its kind ever published, to small pamphlets, no less accurate but far less detailed, such as Schwartz and Burgess's *Sharks of North Carolina and Adjacent Waters*. Also used in the preparation of this guide were Jack Casey's *Angler's Guide to Sharks of the Northeastern United States; Maine to Chesapeake Bay*, Roedel and Ripley's *California Sharks and Rays*, Eugenie Clark's *Sharks of the Central West Coast of Florida*, Stewart Springer's *Notes on the Sharks of Florida*, Kato, Springer, and Wagner's *Field Guide to Eastern Pacific and Hawaiian Sharks*, and so many papers on individual genera and species that it would be impossible to list them all here. When common names have been given in the aforementioned publications, I have used them, but I have relied most heavily on the American Fisheries Society's *List of Common & Scientific Names of Fishes from the United States and Canada*. (The common names follow the scientific name, in parentheses. "NCN" after the scientific name means that there is no accepted vernacular name for that species. The letter "M" following a genus designation indicates that the genus is monotypical —it contains only one species.)

I have tried to organize the information in this list to make it comprehensible. It is intended to be a compilation from the literature, not a taxonomic revision. My desire was to assemble for the first time a fairly complete catalog of the sharks of American waters. If certain species are revised or synonymized (or if new species are discovered or described), that is a normal risk of such a catalog. If, however, there are errors of identification or natural history, they are mine, and do not reflect on the accuracy of the works I used as references.

CLASS CHONDRICHTHYES
ORDER SELACHII
SUBORDER Notidaniodea
Family Hexanchidae
Genus *Hexanchus*

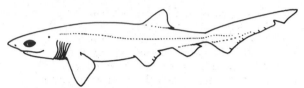

Hexanchus griseus (SIX-GILL SHARK, COW SHARK, MUD SHARK)
MAXIMUM LENGTH: 15 feet.
COLOR: Dark brown to blackish.
RANGE: Continental waters of the Atlantic, Pacific, Mediterranean, and Indian Oceans.
REMARKS: Six gill slits; single dorsal fin.

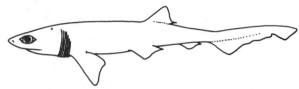

Hexanchus vitulus (LESSER SIX-GILL SHARK, CALF SHARK)
MAXIMUM LENGTH: 7 feet.
COLOR: Dark gray.
RANGE: Florida; Gulf of Maine.
REMARKS: Larger eyes than *H. griseus* (eyes have been reported as "bright green"); single dorsal fin.

Genus *Heptranchias*

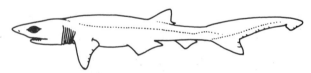

Heptranchias perlo (SEVEN-GILL SHARK)
MAXIMUM LENGTH: 3.5 feet.
COLOR: Brownish gray.
RANGE: California waters; Gulf of Mexico; worldwide.
REMARKS: Seven gill slits; rounded snout; pointed teeth in upper jaw, multicusped teeth in lower jaw.

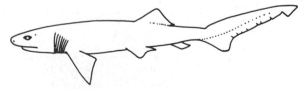

Notorhynchus maculatus (BROADHEAD SEVEN-GILL SHARK)
MAXIMUM LENGTH: 8.5 feet.
COLOR: Brownish to slate gray, usually spotted.
RANGE: Colder waters; British Columbia to Chile.
REMARKS: Seven gill slits; rounded snout.

SUBORDER Chlamydoselachoidea
Family Chlamydoselachidae
Genus *Chlamydoselachus* (M)

Chlamydoselachus anguineus (FRILLED SHARK)
MAXIMUM LENGTH: 6 feet.
COLOR: Brownish gray.
RANGE: Deep water, worldwide.
REMARKS: First gill slit completely circles underside of head; "frills" on gill slits; long, eel-like body.

SUBORDER Heterodontiodea
Family Heterodontidae
Genus *Heterodontus*

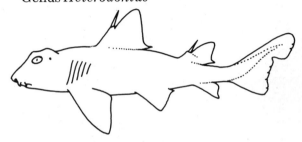

Heterodontus francisci (HORNSHARK)
MAXIMUM LENGTH: 3 feet.
COLOR: Light brown with darker spots.
RANGE: Shallow waters, central California to Baja California.
REMARKS: Large head; conspicuous labial grooves; large spine located at anterior margin of each dorsal fin.

SUBORDER Galeoidea
Family Odontaspidae
Genus *Odontaspis*

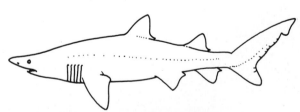

Odontaspis taurus (SAND SHARK, SAND TIGER)
MAXIMUM LENGTH: 10 feet.
COLOR: Gray-brown with irregular dark spots.
RANGE: Western Atlantic; genus represented worldwide by closely allied species.
REMARKS: Pointed snout with protruding snaggle teeth; light-colored eyes; two large dorsal fins.

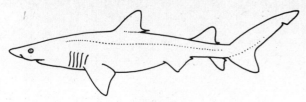

Odontaspis ferox (PACIFIC SAND SHARK, PACIFIC SAND TIGER)
MAXIMUM LENGTH: 10 feet.
COLOR: Dark grayish brown.
RANGE: Southern California to Baja California.
REMARKS: Rare; bicusped teeth; distinguished from an offshore species, *O. kamoharai*, by its size and smaller eyes.

Family Isuridae

Genus *Lamna*

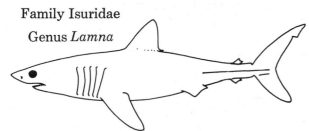

Lamna nasus (PORBEAGLE, MACKEREL SHARK)
MAXIMUM LENGTH: 10 feet.
COLOR: Blue-gray to brownish above, lighter below.
RANGE: Offshore deep waters of the Atlantic.
REMARKS: Flattened caudal peduncle with secondary keel below; distinguished from mako by white spot at base of dorsal fin and tricusped teeth.

Lamna ditropis (PACIFIC PORBEAGLE, SALMON SHARK)
MAXIMUM LENGTH: 10 feet.
COLOR: Dark above, whitish below, often with dark blotches on the underside.
RANGE: Northern Pacific, mostly in offshore waters.
REMARKS: Replaces porbeagle (*L. nasus*) in North Pacific; both have secondary caudal keels.

Genus *Isurus*

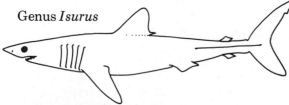

Isurus oxyrinchus (MAKO)
MAXIMUM LENGTH: 12 feet.
COLOR: Dark blue above, white below.
RANGE: Temperate waters, worldwide.
REMARKS: Sharply pointed snout; large dark eye; pronounced caudal keel; lunate tail; teeth are unserrate, slender, and proportionally large.

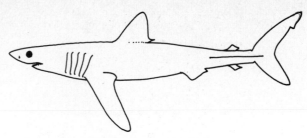

Isurus paucus (LONGFIN MAKO)
MAXIMUM LENGTH: 10 feet.
COLOR: Dark blue above, white below; undersides may be yellowish brown.
RANGE: Offshore deep waters; worldwide.
REMARKS: Distinguished from *I. oxyrinchus* by the extreme length of the pectoral fins, which may be as long as the head, and the larger eye.

Genus *Carcharodon* (M)

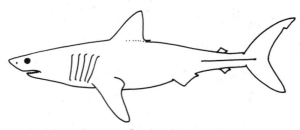

Carcharodon carcharias (GREAT WHITE SHARK, MAN-EATER)
MAXIMUM LENGTH: 21+ feet.
COLOR: Dirty brownish gray above, white below; pectoral fins are tipped with black on the undersides; there is sometimes a large black spot at the axil.
RANGE: Temperate waters, worldwide.
REMARKS: Conical snout; large black eye; pronounced caudal keel; very small second dorsal and anal fins; teeth large, triangular, serrate.

Family Cetorhinidae

Genus *Cetorhinus* (M)

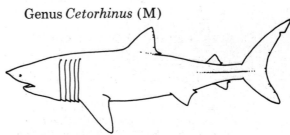

Cetorhinus maximus (BASKING SHARK)
MAXIMUM LENGTH: 33 feet.
COLOR: Dark brown.
RANGE: Temperate waters, worldwide.
REMARKS: Enormous gill slits; minute teeth; juveniles have a protuberance on end of snout.

Family Alopiidae

Genus *Alopias*

Alopias vulpinus (THRESHER SHARK, FOXTAIL, SICKLETAIL)
MAXIMUM LENGTH: 16 feet.
COLOR: Dark brown or grayish above, lighter below.
RANGE: Subtropical waters, worldwide.
REMARKS: Upper lobe of tail as long as body.

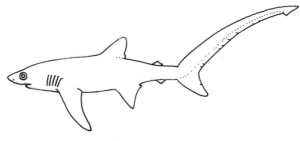

Alopias superciliosus (BIGEYE THRESHER)
MAXIMUM LENGTH: 14 feet.
COLOR: Dark brown or grayish above, lighter below.
RANGE: Deep water, tropical and subtropical water, worldwide.
REMARKS: Extremely large eyes; long pectoral fins.

Family Orectolobidae

Genus *Ginglymostoma*

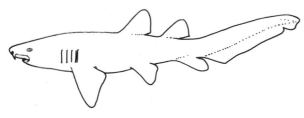

Ginglymostoma cirratum (NURSE SHARK)
MAXIMUM LENGTH: 14 feet; usually not more than 9 feet.
COLOR: Grayish to yellowish brown; younger specimens often have irregular dark spots.
RANGE: Western Atlantic, Rhode Island to Brazil.
REMARKS: Small eyes; prominent nasal barbels; fourth and fifth gill slits very close together.

Family Rhincodontidae

Genus *Rhincodon* (M)

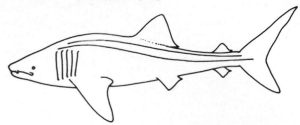

Rhincodon typus (WHALE SHARK)
MAXIMUM LENGTH: 40 feet.
COLOR: Reddish, brownish, or ochre with lighter spots and stripes.
RANGE: Tropical oceans, worldwide.
REMARKS: World's largest fish; mouth terminal rather than underslung as in most other sharks.

Family Scyliorhinidae

Genus *Apristurus*

Apristurus atlanticus (ATLANTIC CATSHARK)
MAXIMUM LENGTH: 1.5 feet (?).
COLOR: Dark sooty gray.
RANGE: Northern part of Gulf of Mexico; Canary Islands.
REMARKS: Base of anal fin nearly four times as long as base of first dorsal fin; gill filaments exposed.

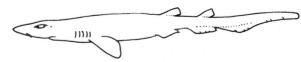

Apristurus brunneus (BROWN CATSHARK)
MAXIMUM LENGTH: 2 feet.
COLOR: Brown above and below.
RANGE: Eastern Pacific from British Columbia to Baja California.
REMARKS: Long slender body; flattened head; gill filaments exposed.

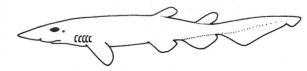

Apristurus profundorum (DEEP-WATER CATSHARK)
MAXIMUM LENGTH: 2 feet.
COLOR: Grayish brown.
RANGE: Nova Scotia to Delaware and Caribbean.
REMARKS: Base of anal fin only 2 to 2.5 times as long as base of first dorsal fin; gill filaments exposed.

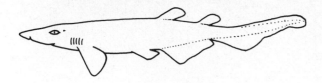

Apristurus laurussoni (NCN)
MAXIMUM LENGTH: 2 feet.
COLOR: Grayish brown to blackish.
RANGE: Deep water; Massachusetts to Delaware and Gulf of Mexico.
REMARKS: No space between second dorsal and caudal fins; gill filaments exposed.

Genus *Cephaloscyllium*

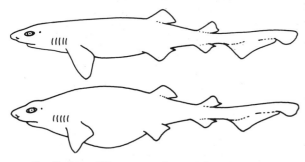

Cephaloscyllium ventriosum (SWELL SHARK)
MAXIMUM LENGTH: 3.5 feet.
COLOR: Indistinct brown saddles and blotches on brownish background.
RANGE: Monterey Bay to Southern California.
REMARKS: When caught, inflates stomach with air or water.

Genus *Galeus*

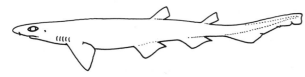

Galeus arae (MARBLED CATSHARK)
MAXIMUM LENGTH: 1.5 feet.
COLOR: Pale yellowish brown, marked with dark brown blotches and spots.
RANGE: Southern Florida; Florida Keys; Cuba.
REMARKS: Deep water; many-cusped teeth.

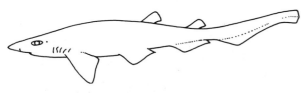

Galeus piperatus (PEPPERED SHARK)
MAXIMUM LENGTH: 1 + feet.
COLOR: Adults plain yellowish brown; juveniles have brownish mottling on dorsal surface.
RANGE: Gulf of California.
REMARKS: Tiny, pepperlike spots on lower side of head and body; lining of mouth cavity dark gray or black.

Genus *Parmaturus*

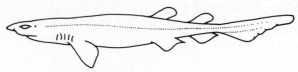

Parmaturus xaniurus (FILETAIL CATSHARK)
MAXIMUM LENGTH: 1.5 feet.
COLOR: Brownish black.
RANGE: Central California to Baja California.
REMARKS: Crest of enlarged scales on upper margin of tail fin; lining of mouth cavity white.

Genus *Cephalurus*

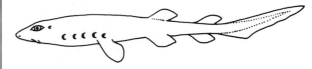

Cephalurus cephalus (HEAD SHARK)
MAXIMUM LENGTH: 10 inches.
COLOR: Brown.
RANGE: Gulf of California and eastern Pacific.
REMARKS: Gill slits and pectoral fins so far back that they give shark appearance of being mostly head.

Genus *Scyliorhinus*

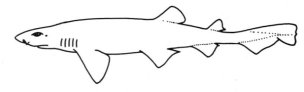

Scyliorhinus retifer (CHAIN DOGFISH)
MAXIMUM LENGTH: 1.5 feet.
COLOR: Ivory, with dark brown chainlike markings.
RANGE: Northwestern Atlantic to Gulf of Mexico.
REMARKS: Deep water; striking yellow-green eye.

(Note: Five additional subspecies of *Scyliorhinus retifer* have been identified, differentiated by color pattern. They are *S. retifer meadi*, *S. retifer boa*, *S. retifer haeckeli*, *S. retifer besnardi*, and *S. retifer retifer*.)

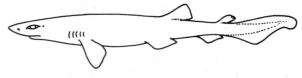

Scyliorhinus torrei (NCN)
MAXIMUM LENGTH: 11 inches.
COLOR: Pale brown, marked with indistinct dark blotches and some oval whitish spots.
RANGE: Southern Florida; Cuba.
REMARKS: Smaller at maturity than all subspecies of *S. retifer;* shorter snout; proportionally smaller fins.

Family Pseudotriakidae

Genus *Pseudotriakis*

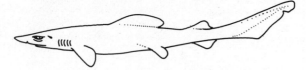

Pseudotriakis microdon (FALSE CATSHARK)
MAXIMUM LENGTH: 10 feet.
COLOR: Dark brownish gray.
RANGE: Both sides of the north Atlantic.
REMARKS: Known from very few specimens; recognizable by large size and very long dorsal fin.

Family Triakidae

Genus *Triakis*

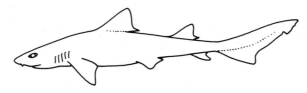

Triakis semifasciata (LEOPARD SHARK)
MAXIMUM LENGTH: 5.5 feet.
COLOR: Light brown with strong, dark saddles and spots.
RANGE: Oregon to Baja California.
REMARKS: Some individuals have stripes instead of spots.

Genus *Mustelus*

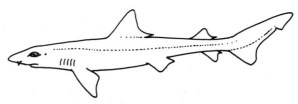

Mustelus californicus (GRAY SMOOTHHOUND)
MAXIMUM LENGTH: 3.5 feet.
COLOR: Gray.
RANGE: Inshore central California to Baja California.
REMARKS: Rounded, pavement-like teeth; prominent lateral line.

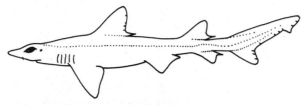

Mustelus canis (SMOOTH DOGFISH)
MAXIMUM LENGTH: 5 feet.
COLOR: Grayish to brownish above, whitish below.
RANGE: Western North Atlantic to Caribbean.
REMARKS: Migrates north in spring (as far as Cape Cod); south in winter (to North Carolina); can change color.

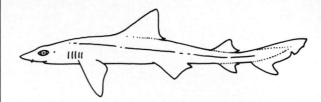

Mustelus norrisi (FLORIDA DOGFISH, FLORIDA SMOOTHHOUND)
MAXIMUM LENGTH: 3.5 feet.
COLOR: Grayish to brownish above, lighter below.
RANGE: West coast of southern Florida to Florida Keys.
REMARKS: Smaller teeth and narrower mouth than *M. canis*.

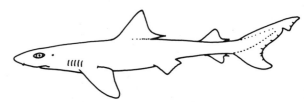

Mustelus lunulatus (SICKLEFIN SMOOTHHOUND)
MAXIMUM LENGTH: 4 feet.
COLOR: Brown or gray.
RANGE: Inshore, southern California to Baja California.
REMARKS: Sharp, concave curve in rear margin of first dorsal fin; in larger specimens, lower lobe of caudal fin is hooked.

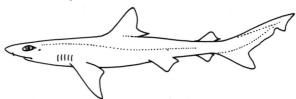

Mustelus henlei (BROWN SMOOTHHOUND)
MAXIMUM LENGTH: 2.5 feet.
COLOR: Uniformly brown.
RANGE: Central California to Gulf of California.
REMARKS: Rear margins of both dorsal fins usually frayed and worn; pointed snout; no distinct lower lobe on caudal fin.

Family Carcharhinidae

Genus *Galeocerdo* (M)

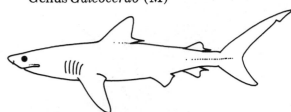

Galeocerdo cuvieri (TIGER SHARK)
MAXIMUM LENGTH: 20+ feet.
COLOR: Gray to ochre, marked with transverse bands that fade with age.
RANGE: Tropical waters, worldwide.
REMARKS: Squarish snout; pronounced labial fold on upper lip; teeth uniquely cockscomb-shaped; long upper tail lobe.

Genus *Paragaleus*

Paragaleus pectoralis (NCN)
MAXIMUM LENGTH: 5 feet.
COLOR: Grayish brown above, lighter below.
RANGE: New England waters.
REMARKS: Rare, little-known shark, carcharhinid in form, but with spiracles and an anal fin considerably smaller than second dorsal fin.

Genus *Prionace* (M)

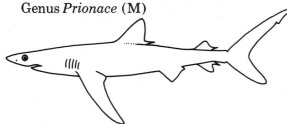

Prionace glauca (BLUE SHARK)
MAXIMUM LENGTH: 9 feet.
COLOR: Cobalt blue above, separated from the snow-white underside by a broad band of silver, color fades to gray in death.
RANGE: All temperate and tropical seas.
REMARKS: Long, pointed overhanging snout; long sickle-shaped pectoral fins; pronounced white rim on eye, Pacific specimens considerably smaller than those found in Atlantic.

Genus *Rhizoprionodon*

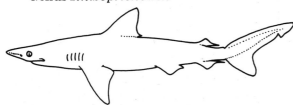

Rhizoprionodon terraenovae (ATLANTIC SHARPNOSE SHARK)
MAXIMUM LENGTH: 3.5 feet.
COLOR: Olive-gray to brownish above, lighter below.
RANGE: Western North Atlantic.
REMARKS: Inshore; never reported more than a mile offshore.

Rhizoprionodon longurio (PACIFIC SHARPNOSE SHARK)
MAXIMUM LENGTH: 3.5 feet.
COLOR: Grayish to brown above, lighter below.
RANGE: Southern California to Peru.
REMARKS: Differs from *R. terraenovae* in length of labial furrows, and range.

Genus *Aprionodon*

Aprionodon isodon (FINE-TOOTH SHARK)
MAXIMUM LENGTH: 5 feet.
COLOR: Slate blue above, shading through gray to white below.
RANGE: Tropical waters, occasionally strays to temperate Atlantic coastal waters.
REMARKS: Smooth-edged, straight teeth, similar in both jaws.

Genus *Negaprion*

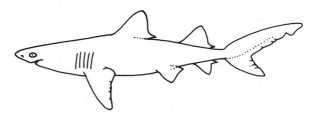

Negaprion brevirostris (LEMON SHARK)
MAXIMUM LENGTH: 11 feet.
COLOR: Yellowish brown above, lighter below.
RANGE: Inshore in the western Atlantic.
REMARKS: Short, wide snout; dorsal fins of almost equal size.

Genus *Hypoprion*

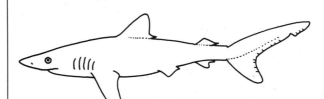

Hypoprion signatus (NIGHT SHARK)
MAXIMUM LENGTH: 10 feet; usually not more than 7 feet.
COLOR: Bluish gray above, lighter below.
RANGE: Key West to Tortugas and Cuba.
REMARKS: Long, pointed snout; smooth, cusped teeth; green eye.

Genus *Carcharhinus*

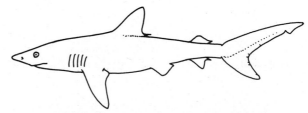

Carcharhinus acronotus (BLACK-NOSED SHARK)
MAXIMUM LENGTH: 4 feet.
COLOR: Cream to brownish, usually lighter below.
RANGE: Western and subtropical Atlantic.
REMARKS: Long snout; asymmetrical upper teeth; no ridge between dorsal fins.

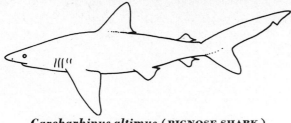

Carcharhinus altimus (BIGNOSE SHARK)
MAXIMUM LENGTH: 9 feet.
COLOR: Grayish brown above, whitish below.
RANGE: West Indies; tropical Pacific.
REMARKS: Pointed snout; lobe on nostrils;
prominent dorsal ridge.

Carcharhinus falciformis (SILKY SHARK,
SICKLE SHARK)
MAXIMUM LENGTH: 10 feet.
COLOR: Dark gray to blackish above, lighter
below.
RANGE: Warm waters of the Atlantic and
Pacific.
REMARKS: Prominent dorsal ridge; small
dermal denticles resulting in fairly smooth
skin; extremely abundant; synonymous
with *C. floridianus.*

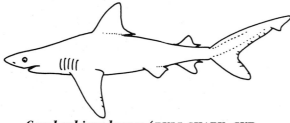

Carcharhinus leucas (BULL SHARK, CUB
SHARK)
MAXIMUM LENGTH: 10 feet.
COLOR: Grayish above, lighter below.
RANGE: Worldwide inshore waters, including
many freshwater lakes and rivers.
REMARKS: Lake Nicaragua shark, Ganges
River shark, Zambezi shark, and other
widely distributed species have all been
identified as *C. leucas;* no dorsal ridge, but
often trematode parasites or scars between
dorsal fins.

Carcharhinus limbatus (BLACKTIP SHARK)
MAXIMUM LENGTH: 7 feet.
COLOR: Dark gray, bronze, or slate blue
above, lighter below.
RANGE: New York to Brazil in the Atlantic;
Lower California to Peru in the Pacific.
REMARKS: No dorsal ridge; black-tipped fins.

Carcharhinus longimanus (OCEANIC
WHITETIP)
MAXIMUM LENGTH: 12 feet; usually not more
than 8 feet.
COLOR: Grayish brown to ochre above, lighter
below.
RANGE: Offshore waters, worldwide.
REMARKS: Broad, rounded first dorsal fin,
tipped with white, as are the other fins;
short snout; extremely long pectoral fins.

Carcharhinus brevipinna (SPINNER SHARK)
MAXIMUM LENGTH: 8 feet.
COLOR: Dark gray to bronze or bluish above,
lighter below.
RANGE: Tropical and subtropical Atlantic.
REMARKS: No dorsal ridge; smaller eyes than
C. limbatus, which it strongly resembles;
both species known to leap from water and
spin before reentering; synonymous with
C. maculipinnis.

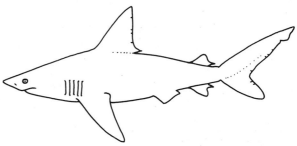

Carcharhinus milberti (SANDBAR SHARK,
BROWN SHARK)
MAXIMUM LENGTH: 7.5 feet.
COLOR: Brownish gray above, lighter below.
RANGE: Inshore and offshore waters, Cape
Cod to Florida.
REMARKS: Most common large shark in New
York–New Jersey waters; distinguished
from *C. obscurus* by its heavier "shoulders"
and higher dorsal fin, situated further
forward; has dorsal ridge; synonymous
with *C. plumbeus.*

Carcharhinus obscurus (DUSKY SHARK)
MAXIMUM LENGTH: 11 feet.
COLOR: Grayish to bluish above, lighter below.
RANGE: Inshore and offshore waters, tropical and temperate Atlantic and Pacific.
REMARKS: Ridge-backed; similar to, but generally larger and more slender than, *C. milberti.*

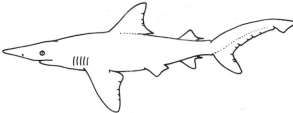

Carcharhinus oxyrhynchus (NCN)
MAXIMUM LENGTH: 4.5 feet.
COLOR: Yellowish gray above, white below.
RANGE: Western tropical Atlantic.
REMARKS: Rare; now thought to be distinct genus (*Isogomphodon*); distinguished from other carcharhinids by large number of teeth and long, narrow snout.

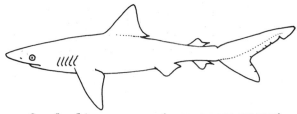

Carcharhinus porosus (SMALLTAIL SHARK)
MAXIMUM LENGTH: 3 feet.
COLOR: Leaden or bluish gray above, lighter below.
RANGE: Western tropical Atlantic; Gulf of California to Peru.
REMARKS: Distinctive upper and lower precaudal pits; rear portion of first dorsal often ragged and torn.

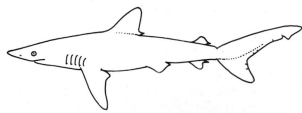

Carcharhinus remotus (NARROWTOOTH SHARK)
MAXIMUM LENGTH: 9 feet.
COLOR: Mousy gray to brownish gray above, lighter below.
RANGE: Rare in American waters; mostly tropical Atlantic and Pacific.
REMARKS: Shorter gill openings than other smooth-backed members of genus, *C. limbatus* and *C. brevipinna,* which it resembles.

Carcharhinus springeri (REEF SHARK)
MAXIMUM LENGTH: 7 feet.
COLOR: Olivaceous above, yellowish white below.
RANGE: West coast of Florida to Cozumel, Yucatan.
REMARKS: Ridge-backed; closely resembles *C. obscurus,* but with larger eye and larger dorsal fin.

Genus *Galeorhinus*

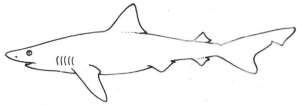

Galeorhinus zyopterus (SOUPFIN SHARK)
MAXIMUM LENGTH: 6 feet.
COLOR: Uniformly grayish.
RANGE: British Columbia to Baja California.
REMARKS: Almond-shaped eyes; fished extensively in the 1950s for vitamin A content of liver and for fins.

Family Sphyrnidae

Genus *Sphyrna*

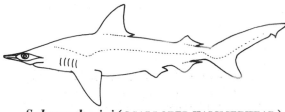

Sphyrna lewini (SCALLOPED HAMMERHEAD)
MAXIMUM LENGTH: 11 feet.
COLOR: Grayish above, paler below.
RANGE: Inshore and offshore tropical waters, Atlantic and Pacific.
REMARKS: Smooth-edged teeth; head indented at midline.

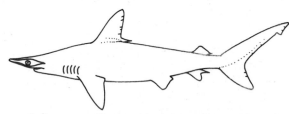

Sphyrna mokarran (GREAT HAMMERHEAD)
MAXIMUM LENGTH: 15 feet; rarely, 18 to 19 feet.
COLOR: Olive-brown above, lighter below.
RANGE: Mostly offshore; tropical and subtropical Atlantic and Pacific.
REMARKS: Head almost rectangular; largest of hammerheads.

Sphyrna zygaena (SMOOTH
  HAMMERHEAD)
MAXIMUM LENGTH: 13 feet.
COLOR: Grayish above, lighter below.
RANGE: Inshore and offshore waters, Atlantic
  and Pacific.
REMARKS: Most rounded anterior margin of
  head of all large hammerheads; high erect
  dorsal fin.

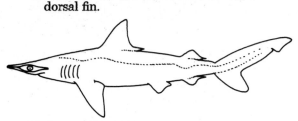

Sphyrna tiburo (BONNETHEAD,
  SHOVELHEAD)
MAXIMUM LENGTH: 3.5 feet.
COLOR: Grayish brown, lighter below.
RANGE: Tropical and subtropical shallow
  waters: flats, bays, passes, estuaries.
REMARKS: Rounded, shovel-shaped head;
  often seen in small groups of 10 to 20
  individuals.

SUBORDER Squaloidea

Family Squalidae

Genus *Squalus*

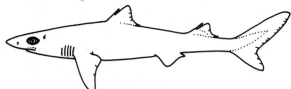

Squalus acanthias (SPINY DOGFISH,
  SPURDOG, PIKED DOGFISH)
MAXIMUM LENGTH: 3 feet.
COLOR: Brownish or grayish, with irregular
  white spots.
RANGE: Temperate waters, worldwide.
REMARKS: No anal fin; poisonous spines on
  anterior edges of both dorsal fins.

Squalus blainvillei (BLAINVILLE'S DOGFISH)
MAXIMUM LENGTH: 3 feet.
COLOR: Brownish gray, no white spots.
RANGE: Eastern Pacific.
REMARKS: No lateral grooves on dorsal fin
  spines; often confused with *S. acanthias;*
  synonymous with *S. fernandinus.*

Squalus cubensis (CUBAN DOGFISH)
MAXIMUM LENGTH: 2.5 feet.
COLOR: Brownish gray.
RANGE: North Carolina to Cuba.
REMARKS: Concave posterior edge of wide
  pectorals; otherwise very similar to
  S. acanthias and *S. blainvillei;* double flap
  on nostril.

Genus *Centroscyllium*

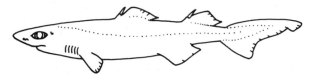

Centroscyllium fabricii (BLACK DOGFISH)
MAXIMUM LENGTH: 3.5 feet.
COLOR: Dark brown to blackish.
RANGE: Deep water, both sides of the Atlantic.
REMARKS: Multicusped teeth in upper and
  lower jaws; longer fin spines than *Squalus.*

Genus *Centrophorus*

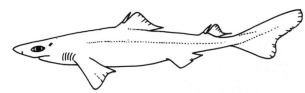

Centrophorus granulosus (GULPER)
MAXIMUM LENGTH: 6 feet.
COLOR: Dark gray above, lighter below.
RANGE: Gulf of Mexico.
REMARKS: Lining of mouth dark-spotted;
  when stroked, skin feels same front to back
  as back to front; pectoral fins have pointed
  trailing edge.

Centrophorus uyato (NCN)
MAXIMUM LENGTH: 3 feet.
COLOR: Mousy gray above, lighter below.
RANGE: Eastern Atlantic; Gulf of Mexico.
REMARKS: Lining of mouth dark gray or
  black; when stroked, skin is rougher from
  back to front than front to back; pectoral
  fins have pointed trailing edge.

Genus *Deania* (M)

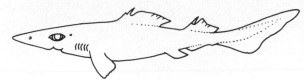

Deania profundorum (NCN)
MAXIMUM LENGTH: 3 feet.
COLOR: Black.
RANGE: Deep water, western north Atlantic.
REMARKS: Long, pointed nose; spines with
   lateral grooves on each side.

Genus *Isistius* (M)

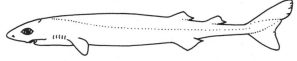

Isistius brasiliensis (LUMINOUS SHARK)
MAXIMUM LENGTH: 1.5 feet.
COLOR: Grayish with white-tipped fins, dark
   collar around neck in region of gill
   openings.
RANGE: Midwater, tropical and subtropical
   seas.
REMARKS: Schooling shark, capable of bright
   green luminescence when captured; use of
   this luminescence unknown.

Genus *Etmopterus*

Etmopterus bullisi (NCN)
MAXIMUM LENGTH: Size at maturity
   unknown; probably less than 2 feet.
COLOR: Sooty gray above, black below.
RANGE: Northeast coast of Florida.
REMARKS: Differs from other species in
   arrangement of dermal denticles; distal
   parts of fins pale gray; all members of
   genus have exposed dorsal spines.

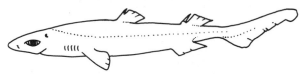

Etmopterus hillianus (NCN)
MAXIMUM LENGTH: 1 + feet.
COLOR: Grayish above, black below.
RANGE: Chesapeake Bay to Florida; probably
   Bermuda.
REMARKS: Black dots sparsely scattered on
   top of head and rearward; presumably
   these are luminous organs.

Etmopterus princeps (NCN)
MAXIMUM LENGTH: 2 feet.
COLOR: Dark blackish brown above, black
   belly.
RANGE: North Atlantic to Southern New
   England.
REMARKS: Probably not luminescent; unlike
   other species, *princeps* does not have a
   yellowish spot between eyes.

Etmopterus pusillus (NCN)
MAXIMUM LENGTH: 2 feet.
COLOR: Dark above, black belly.
RANGE: Gulf of Mexico.
REMARKS: Found in all oceans except eastern
   Pacific.

Etmopterus schultzi (NCN)
MAXIMUM LENGTH: 1 + feet.
COLOR: Dark sooty gray above, black belly.
RANGE: Northern Gulf of Mexico.
REMARKS: Long caudal fin; other fins fringed;
   probably luminescent.

Etmopterus virens (GREEN DOGFISH)
MAXIMUM LENGTH: 1 foot.
COLOR: Pronounced pattern of pale and dark
   markings, black belly.
RANGE: Northern Gulf of Mexico.
REMARKS: In life, belly shines bright
   iridescent green.

Etmopterus gracilispinis (NCN)
MAXIMUM LENGTH: 1 + feet.
COLOR: Dark gray above, black below.
RANGE: Virginia to Florida; common off
   Virginia capes.
REMARKS: Winglike marks on flanks.

Genus *Euprotomicrus* (M)

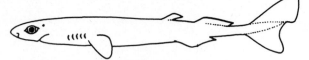

Euprotomicrus bispinatus (NCN)
MAXIMUM LENGTH: 1 foot.
COLOR: Brownish gray.
RANGE: Deep, tropical waters, worldwide.
REMARKS: Fin edges devoid of dermal
    denticles and transparent; second dorsal
    larger than first; luminescent.

Genus *Centroscymnus* (M)

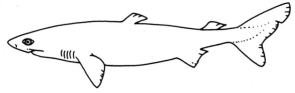

Centroscymnus coelolepis (PORTUGUESE
    SHARK)
MAXIMUM LENGTH: 4 feet.
COLOR: Uniformly dark brown.
RANGE: Deep water, both sides of the Atlantic.
REMARKS: Tiny fin spines; easily confused
    with *Somniosus* or *Scymnorhinus*, but with
    different teeth and dermal denticles.

Genus *Scymnorhinus* (M)

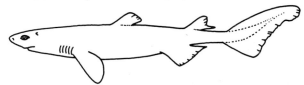

Scymnorhinus licha (KITEFIN SHARK)
MAXIMUM LENGTH: 6+ feet.
COLOR: Uniformly chocolate or cinnamon
    brown.
RANGE: Moderately deep waters, worldwide
    temperate zones.
REMARKS: Pen-nib–shaped teeth in upper and
    lower jaws; no fin spines.

Genus *Somniosus*

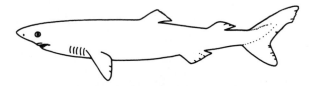

Somniosus microcephalus (GREENLAND
    SHARK, SLEEPER SHARK)
MAXIMUM LENGTH: 20+ feet.
COLOR: Coffee brown to ash gray above and
    below.
RANGE: Arctic waters; Gulf of Maine.
REMARKS: A huge squaloid shark; no anal fin;
    no fin spines; often found with copepod
    parasites in vicinity of eyes.

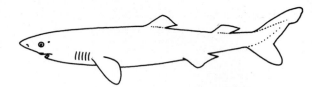

Somniosus pacificus (PACIFIC SLEEPER
    SHARK)
MAXIMUM LENGTH: 20 feet.
COLOR: Grayish to brownish overall.
RANGE: Colder waters of Alaska, western
    Canada, northwestern United States.
REMARKS: Pacific version of *S. microcephalus*;
    the two may be synonymous.

Genus *Echinorhinus*

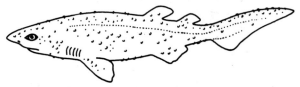

Echinorhinus brucus (SPINY SHARK,
    BRAMBLE SHARK, ALLIGATOR DOGFISH)
MAXIMUM LENGTH: 10 feet.
COLOR: Ash gray or brownish, sometimes
    mottled with white.
RANGE: Accidental in western North Atlantic.
REMARKS: No dorsal spines; large gill open-
    ings; skin covered with shieldlike
    protuberances more than ½″ wide.

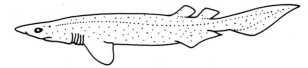

Echinorhinus cookei (PRICKLY SHARK)
MAXIMUM LENGTH: 13 feet.
COLOR: Grayish to brownish.
RANGE: Southern California to Baja
    California; Peru; Guadeloupe.
REMARKS: Smaller scale spines than
    E. brucus; both dorsal fins far back and
    close together.

SUBORDER Squatinoidea

Family Squatinidae

Genus *Squatina*

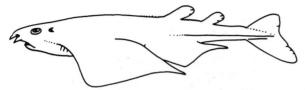

Squatina dumerili (ATLANTIC ANGEL
  SHARK)
MAXIMUM LENGTH: 5 feet.
COLOR: Surface grayish or yellowish brown
  above, white below.
RANGE: Southeastern New England to Gulf
  of Mexico.
REMARKS: Flattened and skatelike in appear-
  ance, but pectorals not attached to sides
  of head.

Squatina californica (PACIFIC ANGEL
  SHARK)
MAXIMUM LENGTH: 5 feet.
COLOR: Brownish above, white below.
RANGE: Southern Alaska to Baja California.
REMARKS: As in *S. dumerili,* dorsal fins small
  and located far back on body.

SUBORDER Pristiophoidea

Family Pristiophoridae

Genus *Pristiophorus*

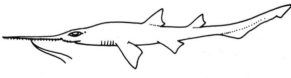

Pristiophorus schroederi (SAWSHARK)
MAXIMUM LENGTH: 3+ feet.
COLOR: Light grayish brown above, white
  below.
RANGE: Southeastern coast of Florida to
  Bahamas.
REMARKS: Long, beaklike snout, studded with
  rostral teeth; differs from sawfish (which
  is classified as a ray) in that gill slits are
  on sides, not bottom of head; two long
  barbels extend from midpoint of rostrum.

BIBLIOGRAPHY AND REFERENCES

1. AASEN, O. "Length and Growth of the Porbeagle (*Lamna nasus* Bonaterre) in the Northwest Atlantic." *Rep. Norw. Fishery Mar. Invest.,* Vol. 13, No. 6, 1963.

2. ALEXANDER, ANNE J. "Shark Feeding Behaviour." *Bulletin of the South African Association for Marine Biological Research,* No. 6, 1966.

3. ANON. "An Interesting Japanese Shark." *Ex. Japan Daily Advertiser.* March 4, 1903.

4. APPLEGATE, SHELTON P. "A Possible Record-Sized Bonito Shark, *Isurus oxyrinchus* Rafinesque, from Southern California." *Calif. Fish and Game,* Vol. 52, No. 3, 1966.

5. APPLEGATE, SHELTON P. Cover copy for *Science,* Vol. 174, No. 4005, October 8, 1971.

6. APPLEGATE, SHELTON P. "The Mystical Fascination of the Shark." *L.A. County Museum Quarterly,* Vol. 5, No. 2, Fall 1966.

7. APPLEGATE, SHELTON P. "A Survey of Shark Hard Parts." In P. W. Gilbert et al., eds., *Sharks, Skates, and Rays.* Johns Hopkins Press, Baltimore, Md., 1967.

8. ATZ, JAMES W. "Shark Attack." *Animal Kingdom,* Vol. 63, No. 1, January–February 1960.

9. BACKUS, RICHARD H. "Hearing in Elasmobranchs." In P. W. Gilbert, ed., *Sharks and Survival.* D. C. Heath, Boston, 1963.

10. BACKUS, RICHARD, SPRINGER, STEWART, and ARNOLD, EDGAR. "A Contribution to the Natural History of the Whitetip Shark, *Pterolamiops longimanus* (Poey)." *Deep Sea Research,* Vol. 3, 1956.

11. BALDRIDGE, H. DAVID, JR. "Accumulation and Function of Liver Oil in Florida Sharks." *Copeia* (2), June 8, 1972.

12. BALDRIDGE, H. DAVID. "Reactions of Sharks to a Mammal in Distress." *Military Medicine,* Vol. 131, No. 5, May 1966.

13. BALDRIDGE, H. DAVID. "Analytic Indication of the Impracticability of Incapacitating an Attacking Shark by Exposure to Waterborne Drugs." *Military Medicine,* Vol. 134, No. 12, November 1969.

14. BALDRIDGE, H. DAVID. "Kinetics of Onset of Response by Sharks to Waterborne Drugs." *Bull. Marine Science,* Vol. 19, No. 4, December 1969.

15. BALDRIDGE, H. DAVID. *Studies on Physical and Chemical Factors Influencing Shark Behavior.* Final Report, Office of Naval Research, October 25, 1971.

16. BALDRIDGE, H. DAVID. *Shark Attack.* Berkeley Medallion Books, New York, 1974.

17. BALDRIDGE, H. DAVID. *Shark Attack: A Program of Data Reduction and Analysis.* Contributions from the Mote Marine Laboratory, Vol. 1, No. 2, Sarasota, Fla., 1974.

18. BALDRIDGE, H. DAVID, JR. "Sinking Factors and Average Densities of Florida Sharks as a Function of Liver Buoyancy." *Copeia* (4), December 12, 1970.

19. BALDRIDGE, H. DAVID, and WILLIAMS, JOY. "Shark Attack: Feeding or Fighting?" *Military Medicine,* Vol. 134, No. 2, February 1969.

20. BASS, A. J., D'AUBREY, J. D., and KISTNASAMY, N. *Sharks of the East Coast of Southern Africa. I. The Genus* Carcharhinus (Carcharhinidae). Investigational Report No. 33, Oceanographic Research Institute, Durban, 1973.

21. BASS, A. J., D'AUBREY, J. D., and KISTNASAMY, N. *Sharks of the East Coast of Southern Africa. IV. The Families Odontaspididae, Scapanorhynchidae, Isuridae, Cetorhinidae, Alopiidae, Orectolobidae and Rhiniodontidae.* Oceanographic Research Institute, Investigational Report No. 39, Durban, 1975.

22. BASS, A. J., D'AUBREY, J. D., and KISTNASAMY, N. *Sharks of the East Coast of Southern Africa, V. The Families Hexanchidae, Chlamydoselachidae, Heterodontidae, Pristiophoridae and Squatinidae.* Oceanographic Research Institute, Investigational Report No. 43, Durban, 1975.

23. BAUGHMAN, J. L. "The Oviparity of the Whale Shark, *Rhineodon typus,* with Records of This and Other Fishes in Texas Waters." *Copeia* (1), 1955.

24. BEEBE, WILLIAM, AND TEE-VAN, JOHN. *Field Book of the Fishes of Bermuda and the West Indies.* Dover, New York, 1970. (Originally published in 1933.)

25. BELYAEV, G. M., and GLIKMAN, L. S. "On the Geological Age of the Teeth of the Shark *Megaselachus megalodon.*" *Trans. P. Shirskov. Inst. Oceanol.,* Vol. 88, 1970.

26. BENCHLEY, PETER, *Jaws.* Doubleday, New York, 1974.

27. BENNETT, F. D. *Narrative of a Whaling Voyage Round the Globe from the Year 1833 to 1836.* Vol. 2. Richard Bentley, London, 1840.

28. BERGMAN, DEWEY. "The Great Shark Hoax." *Skin Diver,* November 1969.

29. BESTON, HENRY. *The Outermost House.* Holt, Rinehart and Winston, New York, 1928.

30. BIGELOW, HENRY B., and SCHROEDER, WILLIAM C. *Fishes of the Western North Atlantic.* Memoir of the Sears Foundation for Marine Research, Yale University, New Haven, Part 1: *Sharks,* 1948.

31. BIGELOW, HENRY B., and SCHROEDER, WILLIAM C. "A Study of the Sharks of the Suborder Squaloidea." *Bulletin of the Museum of Comparative Zoology,* Vol. 117, No. 1, August 1957.

32. BIGELOW, HENRY B., SCHROEDER, WILLIAM C., and SPRINGER, STEWART. "New and Little Known Sharks from the Atlantic and from the Gulf of Mexico." *Bulletin of the Museum of Comparative Zoology,* Vol. 109, No. 3, July 1953.

33. BJERKAN, PAUL, and KOEFOED, EINAR. "Notes on the Greenland Shark (*Acanthorhinus carcharias*)." *Reports on Norwegian Fishery and Marine Investigations,* Vol. 11, No. 10, 1957.

34. BOYD, ELLSWORTH. "Monster Teeth of Chesapeake Bay." *Skin Diver,* Vol. 24, No. 1, 1975.

35. BREDER, CHARLES M., and ROSEN, DONN E. *Modes of Reproduction in Fishes.* TFH Publications, Jersey City, N.J., 1966.

36. BRODEUR, JOHN (as told to Si Lieberman). "I Lost My Leg to a Shark." *Saturday Evening Post,* January 7, 1961.

37. BROWN, THEO W. *Sharks: The Silent Savages.* Little, Brown, Boston, 1973. (First published under the title *Sharks: The Search for a Repellent.*)

38. BUDKER, PAUL. *The Life of Sharks (La Vie des Requins).* Columbia University Press, New York, 1971. (Revised; original French version, Paris, 1946.)

39. BULLIS, HARVEY R. "Depth Segregations and Distribution of Sex-Maturity Groups in the Marbled Catshark, *Galeus arae."* In P. W. Gilbert et al., eds., *Sharks, Skates, and Rays.* Johns Hopkins Press, Baltimore, Md., 1967.

40. BURTON, E. MILBY. "Shark Attacks Along the South Carolina Coast." *Scientific Monthly,* Vol. 40, 1935.

41. CAMPBELL, G. D. "Does a Shark Problem Now Exist in South Africa?" *Documenta Geigy Nautilus.* Geigy Pharmaceuticals, Ardsley, N.Y., June 1968.

42. CAREY, FRANCIS G., and TEAL, JOHN M. "Mako and Porbeagle: Warm-Bodied Sharks." *Comp. Biochem. Physiol.,* Vol. 24, 1968.

43. CARVALLO, ANATOLIO HERNANDEZ. "Observations on the Hammerhead Sharks (*Sphyrna*) in Waters Near Mazatlan, Sinaloa, Mexico." In P. W. Gilbert et al., eds., *Sharks, Skates, and Rays.* Johns Hopkins Press, Baltimore, Md., 1967.

44. CASE, GERARD R. *Fossil Sharks: A Pictorial Review.* Pioneer Lithography, New York, 1973.

45. CASEY, JOHN G. *Angler's Guide to Sharks of the Northeastern United States; Maine to Chesapeake Bay.* Bureau of Sport Fisheries & Wildlife Circular No. 179, Washington, D.C., 1964.

46. CASEY, JOHN G., STILLWELL, CHARLES, and PRATT, HAROLD L. *Bayshore Mako Tournament (Summary Data 1965–1973).* National Marine Fisheries Service, Narragansett Laboratory, June 24, 1974.

47. CASEY, JOHN G., STILLWELL, CHARLES, and PRATT, HAROLD L. *Cooperative Shark Tagging Program; 1974 Tagging Summary.* Supplement to *The International Marine Angler,* Vol. 37, No. 3, May–June 1975.

48. CHURCH, RON. "Shark Attack!!" *Skin Diver,* June 1961.

49. CLARK, EUGENIE. "Into the Lairs of Sleeping Sharks." *National Geographic,* Vol. 147, No. 4, April 1975.

50. CLARK, EUGENIE. *The Lady and the Sharks.* Harper & Row, New York, 1969.

51. CLARK, EUGENIE. *Lady with a Spear.* Ballantine Books, New York, 1974. (Originally published in 1951.)

52. CLARK, EUGENIE. "The Maintenance of Sharks in Captivity, with a Report on Their Instrumental Conditioning." In P. W. Gilbert, ed., *Sharks and Survival.* D. C. Heath, Boston, 1963.

53. CLARK, EUGENIE. "The Red Sea's Sharkproof Fish." *National Geographic,* Vol. 146, No. 5, November 1974.

54. CLARK, JAMES F. *Serpents, Sea Creatures and Giant Sharks.* Unpublished manuscript, Harvard University, 1968.

55. COLBERT, EDWIN H. *Evolution of the Vertebrates.* Wiley, New York, 1955.

56. COLBERT, EDWIN H. *Vanishing Lands and Animals.* Dutton, New York, 1973.

57. COMPAGNO, L. J. V. "Carcharhinidae." *Check-List of the Fishes of the North-Eastern Atlantic and of the Mediterranean,* Vol. 1, UNESCO, Paris, 1973.

58. COPPLESON, VICTOR M. *Shark Attack.* Angus & Robertson, Sydney, 1958.

59. COUSTEAU, JACQUES-YVES, and COUSTEAU, PHILIPPE. *The Shark: Splendid Savage of the Sea.* Doubleday, New York, 1970.

60. COUSTEAU, JACQUES-YVES, and DUMAS, FREDERIC. *The Silent World.* Harper & Row, New York, 1953.

61. CROPP, BEN. "Australia's Mesh of Death." *Oceans,* Vol. 2, No. 5–6, 1969.

62. CROPP, BEN. *Shark Hunters.* Macmillan, New York, 1964.

63. CURTIS, BRIAN. *The Life Story of the Fish.* Harcourt Brace, New York, 1949.

64. DANIEL, J. FRANK. *The Elasmobranch Fishes.* University of California Press, Berkeley, 1934.

65. D'AUBREY, JEANNETTE D. "A Brief History of Sharks." *Bulletin of the South African Association for Marine Research,* No. 4, 1962.

66. D'AUBREY, JEANNETTE D. "Elasmobranch Reproduction." *Bull. South Africa Association for Marine Research,* No. 4, 1963.

67. D'AUBREY, J. D., and DAVIES, D. H. *Shark Attack off the East Coast of South Africa, 1st February, 1961.* Oceanographic Research Institute, Investigational Report No. 5, Durban, 1961.

68. D'AUBREY, JEANNETTE D. "Sharks of the Family Carcharhinidae of the South West Indian Ocean." *Bull. South African Association for Marine Research,* No. 5, 1965.

69. D'AUBREY, JEANNETTE. "The Zambezi Shark." *Bull. South African Association for Marine Research,* No. 6, 1966.

70. DAVIES, DAVID H. *About Sharks and Shark Attack.* Shuter and Shooter, Pietermaritzburg, 1964.

71. DAVIES, DAVID H. *The Miocene Shark Fauna of the Southern St. Lucia Area.* Oceanographic Research Institute, Investigational Report No. 10, Durban, 1964.

72. DAVIES, DAVID H. *Shark Attack on a Fishing Boat in South Africa.* Oceanographic Research Institute, Investigational Report No. 1, Durban, 1961.

73. DAVIES, DAVID H., and D'AUBREY, J. D. *Shark Attack off the East Coast of South Africa, 24 December, 1960, with Notes on the Species of Shark Responsible for the Attack.* Oceanographic Research Institute, Investigational Report No. 2, Durban, 1961.

74. DAVIES, DAVID H. *Shark Attack off the East Coast of South Africa, 6 January, 1961*. Oceanographic Research Institute, Investigational Report No. 3, Durban, 1961.

75. DAVIES, DAVID H. *Shark Attack off the East Coast of South Africa, 22nd January, 1961*. Oceanographic Research Institute, Investigational Report No. 4, Durban, 1961.

76. DAVIS, BEULAH. "Reports of the Natal Anti-Shark Measures Board." South Africa. Unpublished (notes), 1973–5.

77. DEAN, BASHFORD. "Additional Specimens of the Japanese Shark, *Mitsukurina*." *Science*, N. S., Vol. 17, No. 433, 1903.

78. DEMPSTER, ROBERT P., and HERALD, EARL S. "Notes on the Horn Shark, *Heterodontus francisci*, with Observations on Mating Activities." *Occasional papers of the California Academy of Sciences*, San Francisco, 1961.

79. DIJKGRAAF, SVEN. "The Functioning and Significance of the Lateral Line Organs." *Biol. Rev.*, 51-105, Vol. 38, 1963.

80. DIJKGRAAF, S., and KALMIJN, A. J. "Untersuchungen über die Funktion der Lorenzinschen Ampullen an Haifischen." *Z. Vergl. Physiol.*, Vol. 47, 1963.

81. DOAK, WADE. "Revolutionary Weapon: Anti-Shark Wet Suit." *Skin Diver*, June 1974.

82. EDWARDS, HUGH. *Sharks and Shipwrecks*. Quadrangle, New York, 1975.

83. EVANS, WILLIAM E., and GILBERT, PERRY W. *The Force of Bites by the Silky Shark (Carcharhinus falciformis) Measured Under Field Conditions*. Naval Undersea Research and Development Center, San Diego, California, 1971.

84. FOLLETT, W. I. "Man-eater of the California Coast." *Pacific Discovery*, Vol. 19, No. 1, January–February 1966.

85. GALLER, SIDNEY R. *ONR's "Shark Research Program. Naval Research Reviews,"* Department of the Navy, Office of Naval Research, October 1960.

86. GARMAN, SAMUEL. *The Plagiostoma (Sharks, Skates and Rays)*. Memoir of the Museum of Comparative Zoology at Harvard College, Vol. XXXVI, Boston, 1913.

87. GARRICK, J. A. F. "Additional Information on the Morphology of an Embryo Whale Shark." *Proc. U.S. National Museum*, Vol. 15, No. 3476, 1964.

88. GARRICK, J. A. F. "A Broad View of *Carcharhinus* Species, Their Systemics and Distribution." In P. W. Gilbert et al., eds., *Sharks, Skates, and Rays*. Johns Hopkins Press, Baltimore, Md., 1967.

89. GARRICK, J. A. F. "First Record of an Odontaspid Shark in New Zealand Waters." *New Zealand Journal of Marine and Freshwater Research*, Vol. 8, No. 4, December 1974.

90. GARRICK, J. A. F. "Revision of Sharks of Genus *Isurus* with Description of a New Species (*Galeoidea Lamnidae*)." *Proceedings of the U.S. National Museum*, Vol. 118, No. 3537, 1967.

91. GARRICK, J. A. F., BACKUS, R. H., and GIBBS, R. H., JR. "*Carcharhinus floridanus*, the Silky Shark, a Synonym of *C. falciformis*." *Copeia* (2), 1964.

92. GARRICK, J. A. F., and PAUL, L. J. "*Heptranchias dakini*, a Synonym of *H. perlo*, the Sharpsnouted Sevengill or Perlon Shark with Notes on Sexual Dimorphism in this Species." *Zool. Pub. Univ. of Wellington*. New Zealand. No. 54, August 1971.

93. GARRICK, J. A. F., and SCHULTZ, LEONARD P. "A Guide to the Kinds of Potentially Dangerous Sharks." In Gilbert, ed., *Sharks and Survival*. D. C. Heath, Boston, 1963.

94. GILBERT, CARTER R. "A Taxonomic Synopsis of the Hammerhead Sharks (Family Sphyrnidae)." In P. W. Gilbert et al., *Sharks, Skates, and Rays*. Johns Hopkins Press, Baltimore, Md., 1967.

95. GILBERT, PERRY W. "The AIBS Shark Research Panel." In Gilbert, *Sharks and Survival*. D. C. Heath, Boston, 1963.

96. GILBERT, PERRY W. "The Behavior of Sharks." *Scientific American*, Vol. 207, No. 1, July 1962.

97. GILBERT, PERRY W. *Final Report: Studies on the Anatomy, Physiology, and Behavior of Sharks*. Office of Naval Research, 1970.

98. GILBERT, PERRY, ed. *Sharks and Survival*. D. C. Heath, Boston, 1963.

99. GILBERT, PERRY W. "The Visual Apparatus of Sharks." In P. W. Gilbert, ed., *Sharks and Survival*. D. C. Heath, Boston, 1963.

100. GILBERT, P. W., and GILBERT, CLAIRE. "The Shark." *Science Journal*, Vol. 3, No. 11, December 1967.

101. GILBERT, PERRY, and GILBERT, CLAIRE. "Sharks and Shark Deterrents." *Underwater Journal*, Vol. 5, No. 2, 1973.

102. GILBERT, PERRY, MATHEWSON, ROBERT F., and RALL, DAVID P., eds. *Sharks, Skates, and Rays*. Johns Hopkins Press, Baltimore, Md., 1967.

103. GILBERT, P. W., SCHULTZ, L. P., and SPRINGER, S. "Shark Attacks During 1959." *Science*, Vol. 132, No. 3423, August 5, 1960.

104. GIMBEL, PETER. "Shark!" *Sports Illustrated*, August 29, 1966.

105. GOADBY, PETER. *Big Fish and Blue Water*. Holt, Rinehart and Winston, New York, 1972.

106. GOADBY, PETER. *Sharks (Attacks—Habits—Species)*. Ure Smith, Sydney, 1975.

107. GOSLINE, WILLIAM A., and BROCK, VERNON E. *Handbook of Hawaiian Fishes*. University of Hawaii Press, Honolulu, 1960.

108. GREENBERG, JERRY. *Fish Men Fear ... Shark!* Seahawk Press, Miami, Fla., 1969.

109. GREY, ZANE. "Big Game Fishing in New Zealand Seas." *Natural History*, Vol. 28, No. 1, January–February 1928.

110. GREY, ZANE. "The Great Mako." *Natural History*, Vol. 34, No. 3, May–June 1934.

111. GUDGER, E. W. "The Alleged Pugnacity of the Swordfish and the Spearfishes as Shown by Their Attacks on Vessels." *Memoirs of the Royal Asiatic Society of Bengal*, Vol. 12, No. 2, 1940.

112. GUDGER, E. W. "A Boy Attacked by a Shark, July 25, 1936, in Buzzard's Bay." *American Midland Naturalist*, Vol. 44, No. 3, November 1950.

113. GUDGER, E. W. "The Food and Feeding Habits of the Whale Shark, *Rhineodon typus.*" *Journal Elisha Mitchell Science Society,* Vol. 57, No. 1, 1941.

114. GUDGER, E. W. "How Different Parturition in Certain Viviparous Sharks and Rays Is Overcome." *Journal of the Elisha Mitchell Scientific Society,* Vol. 67, 1951.

115. GUDGER, E. W. "Natural History of the Whale Shark." *Zoologica,* Vol. 1, No. 19, 1915.

116. GUDGER, E. W. "The Whale Shark, *Rhineodon typus,* in the Gulf of California." *Science,* Vol. 65, No. 1678, 1927.

117. GUDGER, E. W. "The Whale Shark Unafraid." *American Naturalist,* Vol. 75, 1941.

118. GUDGER, E. W. "Whale Sharks Rammed by Ocean Vessels." *New England Naturalist,* Vol. 7, 1940.

119. GUDGER, E. W. "Will Sharks Attack Human Beings?" *Natural History,* Vol. 40, No. 1, 1937.

120. GUDGER, E. W., and SMITH, BERTRAM G. "The Natural History of the Frilled Shark, *Chlamydoselachus anguineus.*" *Bashford Dean Memorial Volume Archaic Fishes,* AMNH, Article V, 1933.

121. GUITART MANDAY, DARIO. *Nuevo Nombre para una Especie de Tiburón del Género Isurus (Elasmobranchii: Isuridae) de Aguas Cubanas.* Poeyana, Instituto de Biología, Habana, Cuba, July 1966.

122. GUNTHER, A. *Catalogue of the Fishes in the British Museum.* Vol. 8. Taylor and Francis, London, 1870.

123. HALSTEAD, BRUCE W. *Dangerous Marine Animals.* Cornell Maritime Press, Cambridge, Md., 1959.

124. HARDING, JOHN H. "Filming the Whaler Shark." *Sea Frontiers,* Vol 21, No. 2, March–April 1975.

125. HARRIS, DAVID. "Vagabondos del Mar: Shark Fishermen of the Sea of Cortez." *Oceans,* No. 1, 1972.

126. HASS, HANS. *Challenging the Deep: Thirty Years of Undersea Adventures.* William Morrow, New York, 1972.

127. HASS, HANS. *Manta: Under the Red Sea with Spear and Camera.* Rand McNally, New York, 1952.

128. HASS, HANS. *We Come from the Sea.* Doubleday, New York, 1959.

129. HELM, THOMAS. *Shark! Unpredictable Killer of the Sea.* Dodd, Mead, New York, 1961.

130. HEMINGWAY, ERNEST. *Islands in the Stream.* Scribner's, New York, 1970.

131. HEMINGWAY, ERNEST. *The Old Man and the Sea.* Scribner's, New York, 1952.

132. HERALD, EARL S. *Living Fishes of the World.* Doubleday, New York, 1961.

133. HERALD, EARL S. and RIPLEY, WILLIAM E. "The Relative Abundance of Sharks and Bat Stingrays in San Francisco Bay." *Cal. Fish & Game,* Vol. 37, No. 3, 1951.

134. HEUVELMANS, BERNARD. *In the Wake of Sea-Serpents.* Hill & Wang, New York, 1965.

135. HEYERDAHL, THOR. *Kon-Tiki.* Rand McNally, New York, 1950.

136. HOBSON, EDWARD, and CHAVE, E. H. *Hawaiian Reef Animals.* University of Hawaii Press, Honolulu, 1972.

137. HODGSON, EDWARD S. "An Invasion of Sharks." *Natural History,* Vol. 80, No. 10, December 1971.

138. HOUSBY, TREVOR. *The Rubby-Dubby Trail: Shark Fishing in British Waters.* Gentry Books, London, 1972.

139. HUSSAKOF, L. "A Newly Discovered Goblin Shark of Japan." *Scientific American,* February 26, 1910.

140. INTERNATIONAL GAME FISH ASSOCIATION. *World Record Marine Fishes.* IGFA, Fort Lauderdale, Fla., 1976.

141. Interview with ANNETTE KELLERMAN, *New York American,* July 16, 1916, p. 2-LII.

142. ISAACS, JOHN P., and SCHWARTZLOSE, RICHARD A. "Active Animals of the Deep Sea Floor." *Scientific American,* Vol. 233, No. 4, October 1975.

143. JOHNSON, RICHARD H., and NELSON, DONALD R. "Agonistic Display in the Gray Reef Shark, *Carcharhinus menisorrah,* and Its Relationship to Attacks on Man." *Copeia* (1), March 5, 1973.

144. JOHNSON, C. SCOTT, "Countermeasures to Shark Attack." In *Handbook of Dangerous Animals for Field Personnel.* Naval Undersea Center, San Diego, 1974.

145. KALMIJN, ADRIANUS, J. *Bioelectric Fields in Sea Water and the Function of the Ampullae of Lorenzini in Elasmobranch Fishes.* Scripps Institute of Oceanography Reference Series 72-83. October 1972.

146. KATO, S., SPRINGER, S., and WAGNER, M. "Field Guide to Eastern Pacific and Hawaiian Sharks." *U.S. Fish and Wildlife Service,* Bureau of Commercial Fisheries, Circular 271, December 1967.

147. KELLEY, JEROME E. "Fishing the Maneaters." *Yankee,* July 1974.

148. KENNEY, NATHANIEL T. "Sharks, Wolves of the Sea." *National Geographic,* Vol. 133, No. 2, February 1968.

149. KENYON, CARL. "A Fifteen Foot Maneater from San Miguel Island, California." *California Fish & Game,* Vol. 45, No. 1, January 1959.

150. KREFT, G., and TORTONESE, E. "Squalidae." *Check-List of the Fishes of the North-Eastern Atlantic and of the Mediterranean,* Vol. 1, UNESCO, Paris, 1973.

151. LAGLER, K. F., BARDACH, J. E., and MILLER, R. R. *Ichthyology.* Wiley, New York, 1962.

152. LA MONTE, FRANCESCA. *Marine Game Fishes of the World.* Doubleday, New York, 1952.

153. LIMBAUGH, CONRAD. "Field Notes on Sharks." In Gilbert, *Sharks and Survival.* D. C. Heath, Boston, 1963.

154. LINEAWEAVER, THOMAS H., III, and BACKUS, RICHARD H. *The Natural History of Sharks.* Lippincott, Philadelphia, 1969.

155. LLANO, GEORGE A. "Open-Ocean Shark Attacks." In Gilbert, *Sharks and Survival.* D. C. Heath, Boston, 1963.

156. LLANO, GEORGE A. *Sharks: Attacks on Man.* Tempo Books, Grosset & Dunlap, New York, 1975.

157. LLANO, GEORGE A. "Sharks vs. Men." *Scientific American,* Vol. 196, No. 6, June 1957.

158. McCORMICK, H. W., ALLEN, T., and YOUNG, W. *Shadows in the Sea: The Sharks, Skates and Rays.* Chilton, Philadelphia, 1963.

159. McLAUGHLIN, R. H., and O'GOWER, A. K. "Life History and Underwater Studies of a Heterodontid Shark." *Ecol. Monographs,* Vol. 41, No. 4, 1971.

160. McNAIR, RHETT. "Sharks I Have Known." *Skin Diver,* Vol. 24, No. 1, 1975.

161. MARSHALL, TOM. *Tropical Fishes of the Great Barrier Reef.* Angus & Robertson, Sydney, 1966.

162. MATTHEWS, L. HARRISON. "Reproduction in the Basking Shark (*Cetorhinus maximus*)." *Philosophical Transactions of the Royal Society of London,* Series B, No. 612, April 5, 1950.

163. MATTHEWS, L. HARRISON. "The Shark That Hibernates." *Smithsonian Report* No. 4555, 1963.

164. MATTHIESSEN, PETER. *Blue Meridian: The Search for the Great White Shark.* Random House, New York, 1971.

165. MAXWELL, GAVIN. *Harpoon Venture.* Viking Press, New York, 1952.

166. MAXWELL, GAVIN. *Ring of Bright Water.* Ballantine, New York, 1974.

167. MELVILLE, HERMAN. *Moby Dick.* Random House, New York, 1930.

168. MERRETT, NIGEL R. Personal communication to John G. Casey. Subject: pregnant *Isurus glaucus,* and records of smallest free-swimming makos, National Institute of Oceanography, Surrey, England, 1972.

169. MILES, PHILLIP. "The Mystery of the Great White Shark." *Oceans,* Vol. 4, No. 5, September–October 1971.

170. MOONEY, MICHAEL J. "Hammerheads Born in Captivity." *Sea Frontiers,* Vol. 21, No. 6, November–December 1975.

171. MORESI. *The Shark Fishing Industry.* Ocean Leather Corp., Newark, 1935.

172. MORRIS, ROBERT F., and STOUFFER, JAMES R. "New Food Products from Sharks." *New York's Food and Life Sciences Quarterly,* Vol. 8, No. 2, April–June 1975.

173. MOSS, SANFORD A. "Tooth Replacement in the Lemon Shark, *Negaprion brevirostris.*" In P. W. Gilbert et al., eds. *Sharks, Skates, and Rays.* Johns Hopkins Press, Baltimore, Md., 1967.

174. MOTE MARINE LABORATORY. *Newsletter.* Sarasota, Fla., April 1975.

175. MUNDUS, FRANK, and WISNER, BILL. *Sportfishing for Sharks.* Macmillan, New York, 1971.

176. MYRBERG, ARTHUR A. and GRUBER, SAMUEL H. "The Behavior of the Bonnethead Shark, *Sphyrna tiburo.*" *Copeia* (2), June 13, 1974.

177. MYRBERG, A . A., HA, S. J., WALEWSKI, S., and BANBURY, J. C. "Effectiveness of Acoustic Signals in Attracting Epipelagic Sharks to an Underwater Sound Source." *Bull. Marine Science,* Vol. 22, No. 4, December 1972.

178. NELSON, D. R. *Hearing and Acoustic Orientation in the Lemon Shark,* Negaprion brevirostris *(Poey) and Other Large Sharks.* University of Miami, Ph.D., University Microfilm, Ann Arbor, Michigan, 1965.

179. NELSON, DONALD R. "The Silent Savages." *Oceans,* Vol. 1, No. 4, April 1969.

180. NELSON, DONALD R. *Ultrasonic Telemetry of Shark Behavior.* Naval Research Reviews, Department of the Navy, December 1974.

181. NELSON, D. R., and JOHNSON, R. H. "Diel Activity in the Nocturnal, Bottom-Dwelling Sharks, *Heterodontus francisci* and *Cephaloscyllium ventriosum.*" *Copeia* (4), December 1970.

182. NELSON, D. R., JOHNSON, R. H., and WALDROP, L. G. "Responses of Bahamian Sharks and Groupers to Low-Frequency Pulsed Sounds." *California Academy of Sciences Bull.,* Vol. 68, Part 3, July–September 1969.

183. *NEW YORK AMERICAN,* July 16, 1916, p. 2-LII.

184. NORMAN, J. R., and FRASER, F. C. *Giant Fishes, Whales and Dolphins.* Norton, New York, 1938.

185. NORMAN, J. R., and GREENWOOD, P. H. *A History of Fishes.* Hill & Wang, New York, 1963.

186. O'CONNOR, P. F. *Shark-O!* Secker & Warburg, London, 1953.

187. O'GOWER, A. K. "Underwater Studies on the Port Jackson Shark." *Australian Natural History,* Vol. 17, No. 1, March 15, 1971.

188. PARIN, N. V. "Data on the Biology and Distribution of the Pelagic Sharks *Euprotomicrus bispinatus* and *Isistius brasiliensis* (Squalidae, Pisces)." *Transactions of the Institute of Oceanology,* Academy of Sciences of USSR, Vol. 73, 1966. Translated from the Russian by Edith Roden; reviewed and edited by Carl L. Hubbs.

189. PHILLIPS, J. B. "Basking Shark Fishery Revived in California." *California Fish & Game,* Vol. 34, No. 1, 1948.

190. POPE, PATRICIA. *A Dictionary of Sharks.* Great Outdoors, St. Petersburg, Fla., 1973.

191. PRATT, HAROLD L. *Reproduction in the Blue Shark* (Prionace glauca). In press.

192. RANDALL, JOHN E. *Caribbean Reef Fishes.* TFH Publications, Jersey City, N.J., 1968.

193. RANDALL, JOHN E. "Dangerous Sharks of the Western Atlantic." In P. W. Gilbert, ed., *Sharks and Survival.* D. C. Heath, Boston, 1963.

194. RANDALL, JOHN E. "A Fatal Attack by the Shark *C. galapagensis* at St. Thomas, Virgin Islands." *Caribbean Journal of Sciences,* Vol. 3, No. 4, December 1963.

195. RANDALL, JOHN E. "Let a Sleeping Shark Lie." *Sea Frontiers,* Vol. 7, No. 3, 1961.

196. RANDALL, JOHN E. "Size of the Great White Shark (*Carcharodon*)." *Science,* Vol. 181, No. 4095, Washington, D.C., July 13, 1973.

197. RANDALL, JOHN E., and HELFMAN, GENE S. "Attacks on Humans by the Blacktip Reef Shark, *Carcharhinus melanopterus.*" *Pac. Sci.,* Vol. 27, No. 3, 1973.

198. RIPLEY, WILLIAM E. "The Biology of the Soupfin (*Galeorhinus zyopterus*) and Biochemical Studies of the Liver." *Bull. Marine Fisheries,* California Division of Fish and Game, 1946.

199. ROMER, ALFRED SHERWOOD. *Vertebrate Paleontology.* 3rd ed. University of Chicago Press, Chicago, 1966.

200. RUHEN, OLAF. *Shark: Attacks and Adventures with Rodney Fox.* O'Neill Wetsuits, Adelaide, 1975.

201. SANFORD, S. N. F. "Fossils of Colorful Gay Head." *Bull. Boston Society of Natural History,* No. 71, April 1934.

202. SCHAEFFER, BOBB. "Comments on Elasmobranch Evolution." In P. W. Gilbert et al., eds., *Sharks, Skates, and Rays.* Johns Hopkins Press, Baltimore, Md., 1967.

203. "Shark Kills a Man." *Life,* June 16, 1968.

204. SCHARP, HAL. *Shark Safari.* A. S. Barnes, New York, 1975.

205. SCHNEIDER, K. M. *Haie werden im Leipziger Zoo geboren.* Der Zoologische Garten, Leipzig, 1961.

206. SCHWARTZ, F. J., and BURGESS, G. H. *Sharks of North Carolina and Adjacent Waters.* North Carolina Department of Natural and Economic Resources, Division of Marine Fisheries, Morehead City, N.C., 1975.

207. SEILOFF, HORST. "Breeding the Cat Shark: Who Said It Couldn't Be Done?" *Tropical Fish Hobbyist,* Vol. 11, No. 9, 1963.

208. SHAFER, THAYER C. *Population Structure and Range of the Spiny Dogfish,* Squalus acanthias, *in the Western North Atlantic During the Fall of 1967, and the Spring and Fall of 1968.* University of Rhode Island Graduate School of Oceanography. Unpublished manuscript.

209. SMITH, BERTRAM G. "The Heterodontid Sharks: Their Natural History, and the External Development of *H. japonicus,* Based on Notes and Drawings by Bashford Dean. *Bashford Dean Memorial Volume Archaic Fishes,* AMNH, Article VIII, 1942.

210. SMITH, HOMER W. "The Absorption and Excretion of Water and Salts by Elasmobranch Fishes. II. Marine Elasmobranchs." *Am. Jour. Physiol.,* Vol. 98, 1931.

211. SMITH, HOMER W. *From Fish to Philosopher.* Anchor Books, American Museum of Natural History, New York, 1961. (Originally published in 1953.)

212. SMITH, J. L. B. *The Sea Fishes of Southern Africa.* Central News Agency Ltd., South Africa, 1949, revised 1961.

213. SMITH, J. L. B. "Shark Attacks in South African Seas." In Gilbert, *Sharks and Survival.* D. C. Heath, Boston, 1963.

214. SNODGRASS, JAMES M., and GILBERT, PERRY W. "A Shark-Bite Meter." In Gilbert et al., *Sharks, Skates, and Rays.* Johns Hopkins Press, Baltimore, Md., 1967.

215. SOUCIE, GARY. "Consider the Shark." *Audubon,* September 1976.

216. SPRINGER, STEWART. *The Ecology of the Top Predators of the Littoral Zone.* Abstract of a paper given at "Sharks and Man—A Perspective." Sea Grant Conference, Orlando, Florida, November 28, 1975.

217. SPRINGER, STEWART. "The Feeding Habits of Whale Sharks." *Ecology,* January 1957.

218. SPRINGER, STEWART. "Field Observations on Large Sharks of the Florida-Caribbean Region." In P. W. Gilbert, ed., *Sharks and Survival.* D. C. Heath, Boston, 1963.

219. SPRINGER, STEWART. "Natural History of the Sandbar Shark (*Eulamia milberti*)." *Bull. U.S. Fish and Wildlife Service,* Vol. 61, No. 178, 1960.

220. SPRINGER, STEWART. "A New Cat Shark (Scyliorhinidae) from New Zealand." *Records of the Dominion Museum,* Wellington, N.Z., Vol. 7, No. 18, November 22, 1971.

221. SPRINGER, STEWART. "Odontaspidae." In *Check List of the Fishes of the North-Eastern Atlantic and of the Mediterranean.* UNESCO, Paris, 1973.

222. SPRINGER, STEWART. "The Oregon's Fishery Explorations in the Gulf of Mexico." *Commercial Fisheries Review,* Vol. 13, No. 4, 1950.

223. SPRINGER, STEWART. "Oviphagous Embryos of the Sand Shark, *Carcharias taurus.*" *Copeia* (3), 1948.

224. SPRINGER, STEWART. "A Revision of North American Sharks Allied to the Genus *Carcharhinus.*" *American Museum of Natural History Novitates,* No. 1451, 1950.

225. SPRINGER, STEWART. "Scyliorhinidae and Pseudotriakidae." *Check-List of the Fishes of the North-Eastern Atlantic and of the Mediterranean,* UNESCO, Paris, 1973.

226. SPRINGER, STEWART. "Social Organization of Shark Populations." In Gilbert et al., *Sharks, Skates, and Rays.* Johns Hopkins Press, Baltimore, Md., 1967.

227. SPRINGER, STEWART. "*Triakis fehlmanni,* A New Shark from the Coast of Somalia." *Proceedings of the Biological Society of Washington,* Vol. 81, December 30, 1968.

228. SPRINGER, STEWART, and GILBERT, PERRY W. "Anti-Shark Measures." In Gilbert, *Sharks and Survival.* D. C. Heath, Boston, 1963.

229. SPRINGER, STEWART, and SADOWSKY, VICTOR. "Subspecies of the Western Atlantic Cat Shark, *Scyliorhinus retifer.*" *Proceedings of the Biological Society of Washington,* Vol. 83, No. 7, May 27, 1970.

230. SPRINGER, STEWART, and WAGNER, MARY H. "*Galeus piperatus,* a New Shark of the Family Scyliorhinidae, from the Gulf of California." *L.A. County Museum Contributions in Science,* No. 110, 1966.

231. SPRINGER, STEWART, and WALLER, ROBERT A. "*Hexanchus vitulus,* a New Sixgill Shark from the Bahamas." *Bull. Marine Science,* Vol. 19, No. 1, 1969.

232. SPRINGER, VICTOR G. "A Revision of the Carcharhinid Shark Genera *Sciolodon, Loxodon,* and *Rhizoprionodon.*" *Proceedings U. S. National Museum,* Vol. 115, No. 3493, 1964.

233. SPRINGER, VICTOR G., and GARRICK, J. A. F. "A Survey of the Vertebral Numbers in Sharks." *Proceedings U. S. National Museum,* Vol. 115, No. 3493, 1964.

234. STEAD, D. G. *Sharks and Rays of Australian Seas.* Angus & Robertson, Sydney, 1963.

235. STEVENS, J. D. "The Occurrence and Significance of Tooth Cuts on the Blue Shark *(Prionace glauca)* from British Waters." *Jour. Marine Biol. Assoc. U.K.,* Vol. 54, No. 2, 1974.

236. SULLIVAN, WALTER. *Continents in Motion: The New Earth Debate.* McGraw-Hill, New York, 1974.

237. TESTER, ALBERT L. "Fatal Shark Attack in Oahu, Hawaii, Dec. 13, 1958." *Pacific Science,* Vol. 14, No. 2, April 1960.

238. TESTER, ALBERT L. "Olfaction, Gustatation and the Common Chemical Sense in Sharks." In Gilbert, *Sharks and Survival.* D. C. Heath, Boston, 1963.

239. TESTER, A. L., NELSON, G., and DANIELS, C. I. *Final Report: Test of NOTS Shark Attack Deterrent Device.* U.S. Naval Ordinance Test Station, Honolulu, Hawaii, 1966.

240. TESTER, ALBERT L., and NELSON, G. J. "Free Neuromasts (Pit Organs) in Sharks." In Gilbert et al., *Sharks, Skates, and Rays.* Johns Hopkins Press, Baltimore, Md., 1967.

241. THORSON, THOMAS B. "Movement of Bull Sharks, *Carcharhinus leucas,* between Caribbean Sea and Lake Nicaragua Demonstrated by Tagging." *Copeia* (2), 1971.

242. THORSON, THOMAS B. "Osmoregulation in Freshwater Elasmobranchs." In Gilbert et al., *Sharks, Skates, and Rays.* Johns Hopkins Press, Baltimore, Md., 1967.

243. THORSON, T. B., WATSON, D. E., and COWAN, C. M. "Sharks and Sawfish in the Lake Izbal-Rio Dulce System, Guatemala." In *Copeia* (3), 1966.

244. THORSON, T. B., WATSON, D. E., and COWAN, C. M. "The Status of the Freshwater Shark of Lake Nicaragua." *Copeia* (3), 1966.

245. TINKER, SPENCER W., and DeLUCA, CHARLES J. *Sharks and Rays: A Handbook of the Sharks and Rays of Hawaii and the Central Pacific Ocean.* Charles E. Tuttle, Rutland, Vt., and Tokyo, Japan, 1973.

246. TRAVIS, WILLIAM. *Shark for Sale.* Rand McNally, New York, 1961.

247. TSCHERNEZKY, W. "Age of *Carcharodon megalodon?*" *Nature,* October 24, 1959.

248. TUVE, RICHARD L. "The Technology of the U.S. Navy 'Shark Chaser.'" *U.S. Naval Inst. Proc.,* Vol. 73, No. 5, May 1947.

249. WATERMAN, STAN. "Bermuda Behemoth: The Shark That Wouldn't Bite." *Skin Diver,* April 1975.

250. WEBSTER, DAVID K. *Myth and Maneater.* Norton, New York, 1962.

251. WHITE, E. G. "A Classification and Phylogeny of the Elasmobranch Fishes." *AMNH Novitates,* No. 837, April 3, 1936.

252. WHITE, E. G. "Some Transitional Elasmobranchs Connecting the Catuloida with the Carcharhinidae." *AMNH Novitates,* No. 879, October 6, 1936.

253. WHITLEY, GILBERT P. *The Fishes of Australia, Part I, Sharks, etc.* Royal Zoological Society of New South Wales. Australian Zoological Handbook. Sydney, 1940.

254. WHITLEY, GILBERT P. "Shark Attacks in Australia." In Gilbert, *Sharks and Survival.* D. C. Heath, Boston, 1963.

255. WISE, HUGH D. *Tigers of the Sea.* Derrydale Press, New York, 1937.

256. YOUNG, WILLIAM E., and MAZET, HORACE F. *Shark! Shark!* Gotham House, New York, 1934.

257. ZAHURANEC, B., ed. *Shark Research: Present Status and Future Direction.* Office of Naval Research Report ACR-208. Arlington, Va., April 1975.

flask cells, 35
Florida waters, 53, 59, 101, 111, 123, 141, 148, 156, 204
Florida Straits, 262
Fogelberg, John, 272
food chain, oceanic, 19, 70
food-getting. See filter feeders, parasites; predators; scavengers
food pyramid, oceanic, 7
Formosa waters, 128
fossil sharks, 15–16, 17, 22–23, 26–27, 29, 38, 40–41, 64, 66, 67, 79, 87, 98–102, 98, 99, 118, 174, 212, 213, 286
Fox, Rodney, 95, 97, 177–78, 196, 211, 269–70, 268, 270, 271, 271, 274, 276
foxtail shark (Alopias), 110, 298
fox shark (Alopias), 110
Fraser, F. C., 68, 82
Fraser, Morris, 273
French, Leroy, 97
freshwater sharks, 46, 139
frilled shark (Chlamydoselache), 20, 26, 35, 48, 50, 54, 237, 296
Furgaleus shark, 51

Galapagos shark (Carcharhinus galapagensis), 132, 143–44
Galapagos waters, 55, 143
Galeocerdo (tiger shark), 26, 43, 51; G. cuvieri, 61, 130, 132, 135, 148, 150, 291, 300
Galeolamna macrurus (black whaler shark), 146
Galeorhinus (tope, soupfin, school shark), 51, 130; G. galeus (tope), 42; G. zyopterus (soupfin), 45, 90, 303
Galeus (cat sharks), 51, 125, 127; G. arae (marbled), 128, 299; G. melastoma, 43, 128; G. piperatus (peppered), 128, 299; G. polli, 43, 128
Galler, Sidney R., 193
Ganges River, 46, 139
Ganges river shark (Carcharhinus gangeticus), 93, 291
Garcia, Carlos, 44
Garrick, John Andrew Frank, 53, 60, 61, 62, 78, 79, 80, 125, 130, 132, 143, 144, 145, 173, 193, 235–36, 235, 266, 295
gestation period, length of, 43, 161
Gibson, Lt. John, 143–44, 266
Giddings, Al, 145
gigantism, 101
Gilbert, Carter R., 158, 159
Gilbert, Perry Webster, 32, 33, 39, 77, 79, 85, 90, 98, 123, 131, 134, 140, 159, 159, 173, 193, 195, 204, 206, 211, 211, 224, 237–38, 238, 259, 278, 294
gill rakers, 103, 123
gill slits, multiple, 17, 28, 31, 36, 44, 49, 52, 54, 55, 103
Gimbel, Peter, 16, 90, 95, 112, 134, 151, 170–171, 177, 211, 216, 239–44, 239, 240, 241, 242, 257, 275, 276, 278
Ginglymostoma sharks, 26, 42, 43, 50, 227; G. brevicaudatum, 112; G. cirratum

(nurse), 61, 111, 111, 112, 266, 295, 298
Girvan, Norman, 148, 203
gnathodynamometer (shark bite measurer), 39, 206
Goadby, Peter, 87
goblin shark (Mitsukurina owstoni), 26, 48, 64, 65, 295
Goodrichthys (fossil shark), 23
Gottlieb, Carl, 216
Gould, Mr. & Mrs. Edwin, 124, 287
Gray, Pearl Zane. See Grey, Zane
gray reef shark (Carcharhinus menisorrah), 144, 145, 198, 235, 264, 265
gray sharks (Carcharhinus), 26, 34, 51, 130, 228, 229
gray smoothhounds (Mustelus californicus), 90, 300
Great Australian Bight, 196
Great Barrier Reef, Australia, 33, 91, 145, 217, 223, 277, 280
great hammerhead (Sphyrna mokarran), 157, 184–185, 303
Great South Bay, L. I., 181
great white shark (Carcharodon carcharias), 18, 21, 26, 32, 37–38, 46, 49, 50, 66, 66, 69, 70, 72–73, 75, 76, 78, 79, 81–97, 81, 84, 86, 88–89, 92, 173, 176, 179, 183, 191, 195, 196, 199, 216, 218, 218, 222, 223, 229, 238, 240, 246, 256, 257, 259, 263, 274–75, 277, 278, 280, 288, 289, 297
Greeks, 187
Greenberg, Jerry, 16, 143, 263
green dogfish shark (Etmopterus virens), 20, 32, 163, 163, 305
Geenland shark (Somniosus microcephalus), 44, 49, 51, 164, 164, 200–201, 294, 306
Gregor, Manfred, 97
Grey, Zane, 78, 79, 110, 210, 245–48, 245, 247
grey nurse shark (Odontaspis arenarius), 24–25, 50, 61, 111, 175, 277, 286
ground shark (Carcharhinus), 131, 141
groupers, 224
growth rates, shark, 221–23
Gruber, Samuel H., 33, 156, 263
Guatemala waters, 143
Gudger, E. W., 78, 118, 247
Guitart Manday, Dario, 20, 50, 80, 173, 236
Gulf of California, 127, 128, 146, 255
Gulf of Mexico, 46, 47, 103, 123, 125, 141, 202, 238
Gulf of Siam, 118
Gulf Stream, 263
gulper shark (Centrophorus granulosus), 304
Günther, A., 85
gurry shark (Somniosus microcephalus), 164

Ha. S. J., 202
habitats: freshwater, See lakes, rivers; oceanic, See bottom, deep water, niches, ocean, open, shoreline, surface

hagfishes, 23
Halaelurus (catsharks), 51, 126–27; H. bivius, 126; H. canescens, 126; H. chilensis, 126; H. dawsoni, 127; H. natalensis, 126
Halstead, Bruce W., 193
hammerhead sharks (Sphyrna), 27, 29, 33, 36, 43, 48, 51, 78, 156–59, 156, 159, 176, 183, 184–185, 228, 229, 232, 259, 262, 263, 294, 303–304
Haploblepharus (catsharks), 51, 126
Harding, John, 97, 145
Hass, Hans, 16, 34, 124
hatching. See eggs; oviparity; ovoviviparity
Hawke Bay, New Zealand, 236
Hay, James, 97
head shark (Cephalurus), 51, 127, 299
hearing, sense of, 34–35, 143, 172, 197, 202, 262–65
Helfman, Gene, 144
Heller, John, 224
Helm, Thomas, 15, 17
Hely, Michael, 195, 229
Hemigaleus shark, 51
Hemingway, Ernest, 76–77, 157, 176, 178, 216, 255
Hemiscyllium (epaulette sharks), 51, 54, 113
Hemitriakis shark, 51
Heptranchias (seven-gill sharks), 26, 50, 53–54; H. dakini, 53; H. perlo (sharpnose), 32, 53, 53, 296
Herald, Earl, 42, 55, 87, 128, 129, 144
Herodotus, 16, 187
herring, 110, 161
Heterodontidae sharks, 26, 50, 54, 296
heterodontid sharks, 43, 54
Heterodontus: francisci (horn shark), 26, 50, 54, 55, 296; H. portusjacksoni (Port Jackson shark), 26, 54, 55; H. quoyi, 54; H. ramalheira, 55
Heteroscyllium colcloughi (Colclough's shark), 51, 54, 113
Heteroscymnoides shark, 51
Heuvelmans, Bernard, 54, 107, 118
hexanchid sharks, 37, 50, 52, 296
Hexanchiformes suborder, 50
Hexanchus (six-gill sharks), 26, 32, 50, 296; H. griseus (bluntnose), 52–53, 58, 296; H. vitulus (bigeye), 32, 52, 53, 296
Heyerdahl, Thor, 115–18
hibernation, 106
Hodgson, Edward S., 111
Holohaelurus (catshark), 126
Homer, Winslow, 175–76
horn shark (Heterodontus francisci), 26, 42, 43, 50, 54, 55, 296
Housby, Trevor, 67, 70, 78
Howell-Rivero, Luis, 43, 85–86, 154, 272
Hudson Canyon, 233
hunting behavior, 203
Hussakof, L., 65
Huxley, Julian, 261

Hybodont sharks, 23
Hybodus (fossil shark), 23
"hymen" membrane, 42
Hypogaleus shark, 51
Hypoprion (night shark), 51, 130; H. signatus, 32, 301

Iago shark, 51
Iceland waters, 127, 128
Indian coast, 54, 61
Indian Ocean, 46, 65, 80, 113, 124, 125, 144, 229, 244, 278
internal organs, shark, 45, 45, 221
intestine, 45, 45
In the World of Sharks (film), 95, 151, 240, 278
invertebrates, 30, 129
Isistius (luminous shark), 51; I. brasiliensis, 38, 162, 305
Isla de Mujeres, Mexico, 44, 227, 234
Isla Tiburon (shark island), 146, 255
Isogomphodon shark, 51
Isurid sharks, 50, 66, 67, 70, 79, 102, 199, 297
Isuropsis dekayi (mako), 79
Isurus (mako sharks), 50, 66; I. alatus, 80, 236; I. desorii, 79; I. glaucus, 79; I. hastelis, 79; I. mako, 79; I. mantelli, 79; I. oxyrinchus (shortfin), 20, 66, 71, 79–80, 285, 287, 297; I. paucus (longfin), 8–9, 20, 66, 80, 236, 285, 297; I. retioflexa, 79; I. tigris, 79; I. willsoni, 79
Izbal, Lake, Guatemala, 46, 139

Jacobs, James, 97
Jaffee, L. S., 193
Jamoer Lake, New Guinea, 46, 139
Japanese waters, 26, 52, 54, 59, 61, 64–65, 127, 128, 162, 164, 166, 194, 224, 295
Java shark (Carcharhinus leucas), 93
Jaws (film), 81, 96, 183, 216, 219, 257, 260
jaws, shark, 17, 38–39, 77, 98–100, 99, 212; protusible, 12, 23, 38; size, 17; strength, 39, 206
jellyfish, 161
Johnson, Richard, 145, 198, 199, 263, 264, 265
Johnson, C. Scott, 80, 96, 151, 205, 211, 211, 249–50, 249, 250
Jordan, David Starr, 64, 65
Juncrus (catshark), 126
Jurassic Period, 22
Jurien Bay, Australia, 97, 148
juvenile sharks, 49, 81–82, 106, 107, 112, 113, 150

Kalmijn, Adrianus, 35–36
Kato, S., 60, 126
Kellerman, Annette, 38, 189
Kelley, Jerome, E., 77, 90
Kendeigh, Charles, 261
Kenya waters, 53
Kermadec-Tonga Trench, 7
killer whales, 96
Kistnasamy, N., 50, 110, 112
kitefin shark (Scymnorhinus licha), 306
Kiwa Canyon, 7